Jesus of Nazareth

The Man Approved by God

Alexander Frias

Copyright © 2024

All Rights Reserved

Acknowledgment

I would like to take this time to show my most sincere gratitude in this work to a large number of very special people in my life, people to whom I owe all my love and respect, who in one way or another have been part of our lives. People that have offered us unconditional support before and during the process of this work, others that have been part of our life, development, and growth. Firstly, I give infinite thanks to my God and Lord Jesus Christ who is deserving of all the glory and honor. Thanks to my beloved wife Olga Frías, without whom none of this would be possible, who has supported me and has always remained by my side, thank you for all your patience with me during all the long hours in the office writing while you took care of all like a superhero that you have always been, I love you. Thanks to my children, Krystal Frias, Caleb Frias, and Gabriela Frias, they are my driving force and my strength to continue. Thanks to my very special parents Irma L Frías, my hero, the one who introduced me and made the Lord known in my life, the woman to whom I owe my entire life, I love you mommy, thank you always, my father Victor Renan Frias, I love you daddy. My brothers Neftaly, Yahaira, and Victor Frias for their always support. My mother-in-law Olga Lantigua always for her prayers which I have always needed, Very special thanks to the Ebenezer M. I Christian Church of Lawrence Ma, for all her love and prayers always, we love you very much. To my pastors and spiritual father Dr. Victor and Ana Jarvis for always giving us all their help, support, advice and lovingly guiding me on the right path, Pastor, words would not have enough to show my gratitude and the many thanks I give to God for honoring me with a most excellent friend, counselor, and pastor, thank you for being a mirror and an example for my life. Thanks to the pastor and Dr. Gabriel Elias Paulino, to Dr. Hiddekel N. Paulino, a teacher of teachers, who I admire very much in my life, thank you for all the advice, the teachings, and above all for putting in my life that desire and that awakening to the serious study and investigation of good knowledge in our Lord Jesus Christ. to BCC Adonai Elohim, Christian University, to all its staff, and the teachers for helping me in my theological career, and granting me thanks to God honorably with magna cum laude the bachelor's degree and with summa cum laude the master's degree which through the process and time have helped me a lot in the entire process and development of knowledge and this work. Thanks to all the pastors, churches and friends who have always helped and supported us, there are so many that time does not give me. Hugs for all with love from your brother Alexander Frias.

Contents

Acknowledgment iii
Preface vii
A perspective on the life of Jesus between the Bible and the Apocryphal Gospels of the New Testament x
Introduction xii
THE PROPHETIC BIRTH OF JESUS 1
PROPHECIES ABOUT THE LIFE OF JESUS BEFORE HE ARRIVED 8
THE CHILDHOOD AND INFANCY OF JESUS OF NAZARETH 27
THE CHILDHOOD OF JESUS IN THE APOCRYPHAL GOSPELS 42
REASONS FOR WRITING THE NEW TESTAMENT APOCRYPHA 45
THE BIRTH, CHILDHOOD, AND INFANCY OF JESUS IN THE HISTORY OF THE INFANCY OF JESUS ACCORDING TO THOMAS 53
THE BIRTH, CHILDHOOD, AND INFANCY OF JESUS IN THE PROTOEVANGELIUM OF JAMES, OR THE GOSPEL OF JAMES: 65
THE BIRTH AND CHILDHOOD IN THE ARAB GOSPEL OF THE INFANCY OF JESUS 79
THE BIRTH AND CHILDHOOD IN THE PSEUDO MATTHEW GOSPEL OF THE INFANCY OF JESUS: 95
THE BIRTH AND CHILDHOOD IN THE ARMENIAN GOSPEL OF THE INFANCY OF JESUS: 111
THE BAPTISM OF JESUS AND HIS PUBLIC LIFE 121
JESUS OF NAZARETH, THE RABBI Part 1 166
JESUS AS A PROPHET 181

v

JESUS OF NAZARETH THE SHEPHERD Part 3	187
JESUS OF NAZARETH THE KING	196
JESUS THE PRIEST AND HIGH PRIEST	211
WHO DID JESUS SAY HE WAS	229
TITLES AND NAMES USED BY JESUS HIMSELF:	233
THE SON OF MAN:	233
THE TESTIMONY OF EYEWITNESSES OF JESUS Part 2	245
THE TESTIMONY OF THE CHURCH FATHERS ABOUT JESUS Part 3	276
JESUS AND FAITH	287
JESUS AND TEMPTATION	294
JESUS AND HIS MESSAGE	301
JESUS AND PRAYER	309
JESUS HIS MIRACLES AND WONDERS	314
JESUS AND FORGIVENESS	319
JESUS AND HIS PROMISES	325
JESUS AND SALVATION	332
JESUS AND DEATH	342
JESUS AND HELL	346
JESUS AND THE CHURCH	355
JESUS AND THE RESURRECTION	358
JESUS AND THE HOLY SPIRIT	368
Bibliography	381

Preface

In my almost 25 years as a believer in Jesus of Nazareth, serving Him in every way we could, by His grace in different areas, currently serving as director and teacher of the theological educational institution the Biblical Institute El Mizpa in the city of Lawrence, MA, founder and director, Lic/Ma: Evangelist of the ministry of the Word of God Divine Restoration. Throughout all these years, I thought I had known the entire story of the greatest example to follow in my life, Jesus, but it turns out that one day in one of my classes, I heard the term "Apocryphal" mentioned. For me, it was a hidden world, as from the beginning, I had always heard that Christians could not read or investigate that part of history. Personally, I always thought that everything that existed about this Jesus could only be found in the four Gospels, until I came to understand that since the 2nd century, there were already many books that in some way contained similar stories and some slightly exaggerated ones about the life of Jesus.

As a believer in Jesus, my greatest interest is to know Him in all aspects of His life, and also in all the ancient literature that in some way spoke of Him. It is true that not all sources were historical, and perhaps not all were plausible, but this does not detract from the reality of knowing how all the ancient Christian communities saw Jesus and preserved the traditions that surrounded them. I believe that today, more than ever, there is such a need to write down the history or the life of the man Jesus of Nazareth, both in the biblical texts and in the texts that have remained hidden and unknown for so many centuries among thousands, if not millions, of Christians.

In this work, we will learn about some of the most important parts of Jesus in the Bible, and also the most important parts of Jesus in the apocryphal Gospels. Due to confessional tradition and its general purpose in churches, we hear about the Jesus who was divinely resurrected and is now seated at the right hand of the Father. In the most famous christian week, which we know as Holy Week, a short time is taken to commemorate all the suffering, including the death of Jesus, but after this, very little is usually said about the Jesus who had to live his whole life from childhood with his mother without a biological father, and who knows if on some occasions he saw his stepfather Joseph during his adolescence as his true biological father when theologically he was not.

All these stories and more will be known in this work. We are aware and in full agreement with what Saint Paul himself tells us in 2 Corinthians 5:16, So from now on we regard no one from a worldly point of view. Though we once regarded Christ in this way, we do so no longer. Paul, as a good preacher, most likely in his life, even though we do not have texts that show us that he saw or knew Jesus while he was present on earth, it is most likely that he did not, but we see that his greatest interest was for everyone to know the same Jesus resurrected who appeared to him on the road to Damascus. Certainly, this Jesus who was crucified and raised on the third day from among the dead, the Son of God, was and is constituted as the only way to the Father and the savior of the world whom the world must receive.

Now, in the same way that Saint Paul preached about the resurrected Jesus, he also showed us by writing to those in Galatia in Asia Minor in his letter to the Galatians 4:4, But when the set time had fully come, God sent his Son, born of a woman, born under the law. Paul also made it quite clear that this Jesus, before receiving His glory in the resurrection, was born and lived like any human being. Also in the book of Hebrews, we see the writer telling us the following in Hebrews 4:15, For we do not have a high priest who is unable to empathize with our weaknesses, but we have one who has been tempted in every way, just as we are—yet he did not sin. Jesus, to become the great high priest of all men, first had to suffer as a man in every way so that he could be a priest for all. This Jesus is the center of this work; I believe it will be very important to know the man Jesus.

I will dare to say the following: knowing and confessing the resurrected Jesus will give you eternal life after death, but knowing the man Jesus of Nazareth who walked on earth with his living example will bring you success and the best image a human being can achieve on this earth. It is in the character and life of this humble Jesus of Nazareth that we learn how to live on earth. Many people today go through situations where they need to know and meet this Jesus of Nazareth; it will be the best school in life, the best way to learn how to face the worst situations or circumstances in life and ultimately become a victorious conqueror. Jesus, as a man, had to learn to depend on his Father, his God, in order to overcome in life, just as you and I must also do. In our Christianity, our sermons, and our testimonies, we have ignored and hidden this Jesus who was all a man.

This Jesus suffered and also learned in life step by step until he became the perfect teacher, brother, friend, and son; this is the Jesus whom we all must and can imitate. We cannot fully identify Jesus with the great religious phenomenon called Christianity, although it is the largest religion at the moment, and although the person of Jesus is the foundation of Christianity, Jesus is much more than Christianity. Christianity and no religion can claim ownership of Jesus as if He belonged solely and exclusively to it because Jesus is and belongs to all humanity.

And in this work, we invite you to know both in the biblical text and also the part of history in some of the apocryphal Gospels of the New Testament. In this work, we will try to present how Jesus, being all man, behaved and acted in every circumstance of his life; we will walk through many biblical portions and experiences, extracting, teaching, and explaining how this extraordinary humble man managed to sell himself to the world, Jesus of Nazareth.

A perspective on the life of Jesus between the Bible and the Apocryphal Gospels of the New Testament

Jesus of Nazareth won over the hearts of people without revealing His True Essence. Before each person, He revealed Himself to the extent that person could comprehend. He did so in the following manner: before the great ones, He presented Himself as great, before the small ones as small, before the angels as an angel, and before humans, as a human. At the same time, His divinity was hidden from all. Some, seeing Him, thought they were simply seeing a person like themselves. But when He revealed Himself to His disciples in all His glory on the mountain, at that moment He was not small, but truly great. However, before this, He had made His disciples great enough so that they could see His glory and greatness. (Evag, according to Philip v26 apocryphal)

Commentary:

This book you hold in your hand has a great purpose; its overall goal is for the reader to comprehensively understand the most extraordinary man who has ever lived on the face of the earth: Jesus of Nazareth. We will share the most important events of Jesus' life between the biblical text and many of the apocryphal texts of the New Testament. We will learn many stories of Jesus' life that, among the various early Christianities that existed from the 2nd century onwards, are not well known in our current Christianity. We will see how the Son of God, Jesus of Nazareth, being fully human, became the best example for all humanity. A second purpose for the reader of this work: as soon as you begin reading, do so with an open mind ready to learn something new, which you may not have known before. Just as Jesus, having been perfected according to the writer of the book of Hebrews and becoming the author of eternal salvation for all, this same Jesus also grew in wisdom towards God and towards men. We should know how possible it is for us also to grow, to perfect our lives until we reach the measure of Jesus of Nazareth, and my prayer is that by reading this work, God may continue perfecting the field of knowledge in your life. The glorified Jesus, while we are alive in flesh, will not be possible to equal, much less to imitate.

He is and was the first fruits of the resurrection, the first to rise and never see death again; this is the true resurrection. But the example of the human Jesus, the one who was born, lived, and died, left us with the best example for our lives. This book will deal with all the humanity of 'Jesus of Nazareth' as an example to follow. We will try to maintain a balance between the 'high and low Christology' of Jesus, both in His humanity and His divinity, in all the canonical gospels and the same apocryphal ones in their final redaction as they were written in their theological intention and purpose. We will show the divine aspects of Jesus, and also the human ones, as we seek to become imitators of this extraordinary Jesus of Nazareth.

Introduction

Welcome to "Jesus of Nazareth" The most extraordinary man who ever existed, in this compelling and provocative book, where we captively embark on a journey back to the 1st and 2nd centuries onwards to explore the life, teachings, and great impact on the entire history of the most influential and famous man who has ever lived, "Jesus of Nazareth." For many centuries, Jesus has been the central figure of the Christian religion, worshipped and revered by millions around the world.

However, amidst theological interpretations, religious dogmas, and legendary narratives created over time about Jesus of Nazareth, we have increasingly seen the importance of delving deeply into the historical context to authentically understand who the man Jesus of Nazareth was, who lived and walked among us two millennia ago. This book aims to bridge the gap between religious fervor around Jesus and the historical evidence of the earthly and cultural life that existed in the land of Israel where Jesus was born, grew up, and died. In this book, we will unravel the layers of time, examining the ways Jesus spoke, saw, acted, and worked not only theologically but also in all his historical and cultural senses.

For this work, we have researched and used a fairly extensive bibliography and have originated our idea from the collection of many thoughts or sayings of great and serious scholars and teachers who will help us better understand and comprehend with their experiences in the fields of scholarship and investigative study, which will help us better understand the life of Jesus of Nazareth according to the biblical texts and also the apocryphal gospels that we have used.

Meticulously, we will explore and analyze the events provided by the different gospels, especially that of Mark, as it is considered the most historical; we will scrutinize the works of historians and scholarly writers who have shared the dynamic cultural and political life of the 1st century in Palestine, which is the name later given by the Emperor Hadrian in (129-135) to the land where Jesus of Nazareth was born. By doing this, we hope to remove once and for all the perceptions, prejudices, and misconceptions that have clouded and blinded our understanding of Jesus; we will have a broader knowledge of the life of Jesus of Nazareth, and we will also reveal a deeper, authentic, and appreciated knowledge of the life and teachings of this great man.

It is important to note that this book does not seek to diminish in any way the significance of Jesus as a religious figure, but rather to provide a fresh, notable perspective and a lively experience of the real life of Jesus of Nazareth. We will gain a better and richer understanding of Jesus, the interest in true and serious research about Jesus to such an extent that there will be no way for our life to remain the same; it will change for the better and for good. We hope to shine light into your life, light for you to impact as Jesus has impacted the world. Therefore, as I embark, join me on this profound journey where we will navigate to know Jesus of Nazareth, the man approved by God.

Prepare to challenge your preconceptions, to awaken curiosity, and be inspired by the life, character, work, and teachings of Jesus the Nazarene, not only as that religious example, but rather as the historical man Jesus of Nazareth, the man whose example and history continue to captivate and influence not only religious people but also scientists, skeptics, agnostics, atheists, the list will continue endlessly because there is no doubt among anyone that Jesus of Nazareth was the man who left the greatest example of how a human being should live on earth. Let's journey together as we unveil the life of Jesus of Nazareth.

THE PROPHETIC BIRTH OF JESUS
Part 1
Luke 1:28-33

The angel went to where Mary was, greeted her, and said, "God has blessed you in a special way! The Lord is with you." Mary was very surprised to hear such a strange greeting and wondered what it meant. Then the angel said to her, "Do not be afraid, Mary, for God has given you a great privilege. You will become pregnant and give birth to a son, and you are to name him Jesus. He will be very important and will be called the Son of the Highest God. The Lord God will make him a king, as his ancestor David was, and he will rule the people of Israel forever; his kingdom will never end."

The most anticipated day in all of human history is found precisely between 4 BCE and 6 BCE; the exact day is still uncertain, but there is no doubt about the verifiable and historical birth of Jesus. Matthew and Luke tell us that he was born in Bethlehem of Judea, fulfilling the prophecy. Historians believe that Jesus may have actually been born and raised in Nazareth of Galilee; they think that Matthew may have theologized and taken a prophetic place for Jesus's birth, placing him in the same location where his ancestor David was born. Matthew is the writer who will present Jesus as the new Moses or the new Messiah, the new hope for Israel. Nevertheless, Christian tradition has maintained its position in agreement with Matthew and Luke regarding the birthplace in Bethlehem of Judea.

All the life and events that occurred in Jesus's life had been prophesied hundreds of years before his arrival. The birth of Jesus, the anointed and awaited Messiah in Israel, is the most prophesied event, both directly and indirectly, found in the Hebrew Bible. The word "Messiah" is a Greek word, which is why we do not see it in the Old Testament, but it is also not found directly in the Bible. It is the word used in Hebrew for what in the Greek language means "anointed," which we do find in the Bible. Being anointed in the Hebrew Bible, or Tanakh, also known as the Old Testament, is similar and equal to being a Messiah in the Hebrew language. In Israel, the Messianism or the figure of the awaited Messiah originated with the prophet Isaiah, although theologically, Isaiah was not the first according to the canonical order or traditional historical time; historically, he is believed to be the first to prophesy the coming Messiah. We see some prophecies in the early books of Genesis and Deuteronomy, to which traditionally, Moses is credited with authorship.

For example, *in Deuteronomy 18:15:*

"A prophet will the LORD your God raise up for you from among your brothers, like me. You shall listen to him."

Moses tells them that God will raise up a prophet among them, from their brothers, like himself, for them to listen to. It would be quite difficult to recognize a prophet on par with Moses among the people of Israel and the Jews; the only one who, more than any other, compared to Moses, was Jesus of Nazareth. It is true that we do not see Jesus directly say something like this because he always kept and honored the law that God gave to Moses for his people, but we do see him reforming some of the things that only Moses had imposed on them, and also saying that Moses himself had written about him.

As for the Messiah or the anointed one who will be born from the womb of a woman in Genesis 3, who will crush the head of the serpent, the symbol of spiritual evil or Satan, this type of Messiah or anointed one who was to be born to crush the head of the serpent is a direct and theological reference to the arrival of Jesus Christ himself as the expected Messiah. We see some prophecies that directly allude not so much to a theological Jesus who will confront the serpent, symbol of spiritual evil or Satan as seen in Christianity, but rather to a human Jesus who will be born from a woman's womb as a sign to bring peace, love, salvation, and joy to Israel and all nations.

The scholar J. Barton Payne was able to find around 574 verses in the Old Testament that in some way refer or point to the coming of

Jesus of Nazareth

an expected anointed Messiah; Alfred Edersheim found some 456 verses concerning the Messiah, but conservatively Jesus fulfilled about 300 prophecies from the Old Testament in his ministry. It is true that in academic circles, some scholars have preferred to ignore the historical prophecies fulfilled in Jesus of Nazareth to attribute them to a certain historical event correlated to a specific moment in history when the prophet spoke.

For example, *in the case of the suffering servant that we see in Isaiah 53, since the 1st century, we see Jesus's followers seeing the prophecy of the suffering servant fulfilled better in Jesus than in anyone else in all its description. The Rabbis from the 2nd century onwards, having not seen Jesus as the Messiah, decided to reinterpret Isaiah 53 and see the suffering servant as the people of Israel themselves, something that has caused controversy among themselves because Israel is by no means the suffering servant of Isaiah 53.*

This idea that some scholars and scholars have believed for various reasons, first because for them, it would have no reason or sense for a prophet to prophesy something that would come to fulfillment 700 years later, second, it would be considered a post-event, an event that without anything to do with Jesus, Christians decided to take to put the name of Jesus on the servant mentioned in Isaiah 53. In any case, we see that it was not the Christians directly who saw Jesus as the suffering servant; it was the same Jewish apostles starting with John the Baptist, who was not an apostle but announced that Jesus would take away the sin of the world, and this is exactly what the suffering servant does in Isaiah, as a sacrifice, he is wounded and killed to forgive sin. The problem arises when historically they have no conclusive explanation to show how the chapter refers to exact events to the people of Israel. Some have even gone so far as to say that this chapter is a song or a poem.

Cesar Vidal, the author of the book "More than a Rabbi," says that the Rabbis of the Middle Ages went so far as to prohibit Jews from using chapter 53 of Isaiah because of the strong reference it makes to the only person of Jesus. Nevertheless, they continued to believe and develop a reinterpretation regarding the suffering servant as the people of Israel. Nonetheless, we remain knowing that Isaiah 53 is a very old chapter, probably written in Babylon while the Jews were preparing to leave and return to Jerusalem.

There is no doubt that this chapter fits perfectly with the passion and suffering that Jesus faced; throughout the centuries, it has had the most effect on the lives of the thousands and thousands converted to Jesus. Later, we will clarify this point; for now, let us continue showing some of the prophecies where we clearly see Jesus of Nazareth prophesied before his arrival. The prophet Micah, for the 8th century BCE, in prophecy tells us the following:

Micah 5:2:

"But you, Bethlehem Ephrathah, though you are small among the clans of Judah, out of you will come for me one who will be ruler over Israel, whose origins are from of old, from ancient times." (NIV)

It must be said that since the 8th century BCE, no one has arisen from the family of Judah or from the same tribe other than Jesus, who has been called or recognized as the Lord of Israel. It is true that historically we can see this prophecy deeply involved with the high Christology of Jesus, where he is shown from the beginning, and from ancient times, as a reference to what the Evangelist John will use in his first chapter to describe Jesus as the Word from the beginning, being with God, and being God himself, pre-existent through whom all things were created and exist, all things were created by him, and without him nothing would exist. John, with a quite high theology, seems to have used the last phrase of this prophecy in Micah, where it tells us that he was from the beginning, and from ancient times.

The book of John, despite containing a quite high Christology, we cannot deny that John is the one who emphasizes the importance of not overlooking the Jesus of Nazareth who came in the flesh, lived in the flesh, died in the flesh, and rose in a palpable spiritual body. By the time of John, there was a Christian branch known as the

Jesus of Nazareth

"Gnostics," who were quite mystical Christians. They came to believe and teach what to this day many ignore or reject, which is the historical existence of Jesus of Nazareth as a man in the flesh. The Gnostics said that Jesus was a mere image or a spiritual being but was never a man in whom divinity dwelled in one body. This thought is still seen today in some academic scholars and some mystical liberal theologians. Furthermore, the historical and biblical sources are both much older and accepted than those who reject or deny the historical existence of Jesus of Nazareth.

Some respected philologists and historians, such as Dr. Antonio Piñero, in a large number of public debates and books such as "Approaching the Historical Jesus," have dared to say that denying the existence of Jesus of Nazareth is the most ridiculous thing anyone can say. He has also supported the idea that the vast majority of scholars cannot deny the historical truth of so much tradition compiled from the 1st century when Jesus of Nazareth lived. Saying that everything was a simple invention of the information acquired at a time so close or in the same century as the existence of Jesus himself would be almost impossible to credibly sustain that Jesus never existed.

We see the fulfillment of the prophetic birth of Micah about Jesus in the Gospels of Matthew and Luke. Both writers, with few distinctions, tell us that Jesus's birth was fulfilled in Bethlehem, as prophesied by Micah. This small town, with a population most likely of fewer than 200 people, but the ancestral place of Joseph and Mary, the place where the greatest of all kings of the tribe of Judah, King David, was born. The great question we ask ourselves in the magnificence of the specific fulfillment of the prophecy is as follows: from Nazareth to Bethlehem, it is about 150 km. How could this young pregnant woman, almost ready to give birth, most likely a month early or a few weeks, traveling possibly on a donkey for her better comfort, or very possibly walking, how could this young woman after passing so many cities, experience birth pains precisely in the same city that Micah had prophesied about some 8 centuries before Jesus was born?

Some academics have no choice but to create hypotheses and put in the hands of both Matthew and Luke the idea of having invented the story of Jesus's birth to make him king. There are many hypotheses that academic scholars or liberal theologians have thought about Jesus's birth, without doubting his human existence, but with very little plausible credibility because they are hypotheses without sufficient evidence. In the book of Isaiah 9:6, we have a prophecy that also shows the birth of the Messiah, and it says the following:

"For to us a child is born, to us a son is given, and the government will be on his shoulders. And he will be called Wonderful Counselor, Mighty God, Everlasting Father, Prince of Peace." (NIV)

This child who was to be born would play a very important role in the history and life of the Lord's people. This prophecy has been heavily questioned by many academic scholars. Some say that this child prophesied by the prophet Isaiah is the same one announced in his chapter 7:14, where it says the following:

"Therefore the Lord himself will give you a sign: The virgin will conceive and give birth to a son, and will call him Immanuel." (NIV)

Some academic scholars tell us that this child would be none other than one of Isaiah's own sons who would be born as a sign to strengthen the king of Judah and as a new king for Israel before King Ahaz. The people of Ephraim (Israel) had joined the Syrians and others to go against the tribe of Judah, but God had spoken to the prophet Isaiah asking Ahaz not to fear his enemies, and with this consolation, he asks Ahaz to ask God for confirmation. Ahaz refused to ask God not to tempt him, but it is when Isaiah prophesied what the sign would be as evidence of God's plan for the house of David. The first thing is that Isaiah asks the whole house of David to hear the prophecy.

It seems that the prophecy and the importance would be primarily for the house of David, the same tribe, and the same lineage from which our Lord and Messiah Jesus would come. Never in history have we seen any son of Isaiah born of a virgin, born as a special sign in Israel, become a prophet although many inherited the office, become a king, announce any peace, and least represent God with his people. The only one from the tribe of Judah, who came by descent from David, who can be compared with every word predicted by Isaiah in both chapters 7:14 and 9:6, is none other than Jesus of Nazareth. As Isaiah says, the virgin will give birth to a son, and she will call him Emmanuel, which means God with us. In Israel, it was customary for parents to name their children. The matter was so special that even when John received his name through the angel, when Zachariah came out of the temple, when asked about the child's name, he said that his name would be John, even though Elizabeth already knew the name, it was not her responsibility to name him because it was not the custom. But in the case of Jesus, the prophecy was so specific about Him that when the angel Gabriel told Joseph what the child's name would be, Joseph had nothing to do with the name of the child who was born from Mary's womb. She named him exactly as Isaiah had said she would, God with us.

Who else among the sons of David or among the 14 generations between David and Jesus of his own descent was so admirable, a counselor, strong, prince of peace, compared to Jesus? Not even Solomon with all his glory and wisdom could have been the fulfillment of this prophecy as Jesus of Nazareth was, since Bathsheba, Solomon's mother, was not a virgin, and above all, Solomon was not the messianic sign of the best example and the presence of God among his people predicted by Isaiah, who came much later than Solomon, which is why he could not have been the prophesied child. This child prophesied by Isaiah was none other than Jesus of Nazareth, the most awaited Messiah in all of Israel.

Alexander Frias

PROPHECIES ABOUT THE LIFE OF JESUS BEFORE HE ARRIVED

Part 2

We have many prophetic passages that point to Jesus of Nazareth himself, not to his birth as we have shown, but to prophecies that refer only to the life of Jesus of Nazareth. We begin with Psalm 41:9, which says the following:

Psalm 41:9:

"Even my close friend, someone I trusted, one who shared my bread, has turned against me." (NIV)

We have many prophetic passages that point to Jesus of Nazareth himself, not to his birth as we have shown, but to the life of Jesus of Nazareth. We start with Psalm 41:9, which tells us the following:

There are many different opinions and thoughts regarding Psalm 41. Many theologians who seek to harmonize this Psalm at some historical point in Israel do so in the life of King David during his reign and the rebellion of his eldest son, Absalom, against him. C.F Keil and F.J Delitzsch in their Commentary *"The Psalms,"* in chapter 41, allude to this psalm of David being dedicated to his son Absalom for his rebellion against his father, trying to usurp his kingdom. Absalom takes a large number of soldiers and goes in search of his father David, who, rising, flees to avoid facing his own son. It is true that this portion of Psalm 41:9 can apply to the situation between David and Absalom, but we know that David also had many other sons, and David, addressing someone who is not his son, speaks as if to a friendship or a friend of trust or someone quite close to him.

We do not see any friend as special in David's life or someone to whom this verse could strongly refer in its sense as to Mephibosheth when David himself says that this comet from the portion of the king every day. Some say that Ahithophel may have been David's advisor during his reign, who would later turn his back on him, joining Absalom and ending up hanging himself. This could be the historical character of Psalm 41.9 but not the prophetic character, since this psalm is not only a historical event, Jewish tradition gives the authorship and composition of the psalm to King David himself. We see in the book of Acts of the Apostles in chapter 2 Peter referring to Psalm 110:1 where we see David himself prophetically say that the Lord (Yahweh) told his Lord (Christ) to sit at his right hand. In short words, this portion is the entire life of Jesus before and after prophesied by David himself, this is what we see Peter confirm before everyone in Jerusalem. theologically this shows that David did speak prophetically about the Christ who would be the same incarnate Word Jesus, but in this specific case with this verse of Psalm 41.9 a large number of scholars and historians tell us that there is a possibility that this psalm for being quite messianic was written or re-interpreted by some wise men or scribe of the same line or prophetic era of the deutero or post-Isaiah. This thought arises for the reason that with the prophet Isaiah the historical beginning of prophetic hope in Israel called or known as the messianic era aroused, it is during this entire era where we will see the greatest number of prophetic portions and prophecies about Jesus the messiah in both prophetic books and psalms. We must reiterate and clarify well as we have shown from the beginning of this work, it must be clear that the life of Jesus was announced and prophesied theologically in the biblical text from the beginning of creation as we see it from Genesis 3, all the prophets From Moses to Isaiah theologically spoke something with typological and prophetic reference about Jesus, but it must be clear that it is not until the emergence of the prophet Isaiah that we are able to see the broader prophetic panorama of the entire predicted life of our Jesus the messiah. This is the fundamental reason why scholars and historians grant the verse or portion to some scribe full of messianic hope. This verse is completely messianic and prophetic, for this reason it is also worth saying that it could have been composed by a disciple of the third generation of Isaiah upon leaving the babylonian captivity since in the Jews this hope was maintained until the arrival of Jesus as we see in the gospels. There is also the great possibility of a prophetic act of double reference, in any case it would be a shadow of Judas for the prophetic fulfillment in Jesus. Since for me personally the prophecy, its fulfillment and its interpretation are more important and more edifying for my life and faith, this last reference to Judas the Iscariot is my favorite in all complete sense. In Christian theology and Christological prophecy this character points directly and only to Judas, a close friend of Jesus who ate his bread. At first Mephibosheth, Jonathan's son, and the house of Saul were considered David's enemy, then he arrives at the king's palace and becomes an intimate servant of David. However, we never see Mephibosheth betray David in the texts, although for a moment David thought that if by a momentary cunning of Ziba who had been placed by David to serve Mephibosheth, this doubt in David became clear and resolved once Mephibosheth reappeared before him. For this reason, not everyone compares the character in the verse with Mephibosheth even though he was among those who did eat with the king from his own plate and from his same portion according to the texts. It is worth adding that when David fled from Saul the only one who gave him peace and hope was his friend Jonathan, therefore who else could give him that same peace in his reign as the same son of Jonathan Mephibosheth the same representation of Jonathan with whom He made a perpetual covenant and never forgot.

The verse tells us that this man who ate with him was his man of peace. We never see Absalom as a man of peace for David. We see that Ahithophel was David's advisor and his words were like the words of God, this could be a reference to the peace that David felt, some commentators say that Ahithophel, being Bathshebe's grandfather, always had something against David for having killed Uriah. Every time Absalom appears in the story, he is mentioned directly by name and not as an anonymous person or as a man of peace. It is assumed that the parents trust their children, but here we see that the writer tells us that the person in question, if it was David, trusted Absalom and Absalom betrayed him.

It is true that Absalom betrayed his father David, and for those who believe that this verse is historically directed from David to his son Absalom or to his advisor Ahithophel, the reason is plausible, but it is not accepted or believed generally as strongly as the prophetic fulfillment in the union between Jesus and his great friend Judas Iscariot. The verse tells us that this man who ate with him was the man of his peace; Judas, being of Iscariot, was one of those called and chosen by Jesus to be with him, receive power, and go with the others to preach what Jesus taught. We see that on the night of the Lord's supper, Jesus, knowing that one among them would betray him, in the Gospels of Matthew and John, says the following.

Matthew 26:23-25:

"Jesus replied, 'The one who has dipped his hand into the bowl with me will betray me. The Son of Man will go just as it is written about him. But woe to that man who betrays the Son of Man! It would be better for him if he had not been born.' Then Judas, the one who would betray him, said, 'Surely you don't mean me, Rabbi?' Jesus answered, 'You have said so.'"

Mark 14:17:

"When evening came, Jesus arrived with the Twelve. While they were reclining at the table eating, he said, 'Truly I tell you, one of you will betray me—one who is eating with me.'"

John 13:26:

"Jesus answered, 'It is the one to whom I will give this piece of bread when I have dipped it in the dish.' Then, dipping the piece of bread, he gave it to Judas, the son of Simon Iscariot."

The disciples of Jesus were his family, according to what he had previously said; those who do the will of God he referred to as his family. Obviously, we must understand the theology of the spiritual family to which Jesus is referring, because according to the Gospels, he had some brothers and sisters in his family. However, the closest friends that Jesus had were also considered his family, since in his ministry he spent more time with them in the last years of his life than with other people. We see that Jesus sat down at the table to eat with his friends, and sitting together in the first century was a gesture of composure and importance. Sitting down to eat with people showed intimacy and communion with them; not just anyone would sit with anyone else to eat. We see this issue with the Pharisees when Jesus himself sat down to eat with sinners and tax collectors. For a teacher or a Jew to sit and eat with a sinful, pagan, or impure individual was seen as participating in union with them. This was greatly frowned upon by the traditionalist religious practitioners of the time, including some Pharisees.

In their traditions, they believed they had to live separated from the world and from others who were not in the same spiritual or cultural position as them. For these religious individuals, anyone who did not live according to their traditions, known as the traditions of the elders (now recognized as the 603/613 Mitzvot), was viewed as outside their community. These traditions began centuries before Jesus during, and after with the arrival and presence of strict orthodox jews and pharisees, who were legal scholars progressively reinterpreting the Torah and altering its meaning based on contemporary circumstances. Alongside the written laws, they claimed to have received oral laws from Moses at Sinai during his 40 days there. They provided explanations for the laws so that people could understand and observe them.

However, part of the problem was that each teacher or Pharisaic sect offered different interpretations depending on the teacher's perspective. It is reported that these traditions eventually numbered in the thousands as they continued to add to them over time. Traditionally, it is believed that the climax of this tradition manifested shortly before and during the first century of our era. There were two Jewish schools led by the most prominent rabbis of the time, Bet Shammai and Hillel. These rabbis held different viewpoints on Jewish traditions. To learn more about them, I invite you to research the lives of both rabbis. In simple terms, Shammai represented a strict orthodox Pharisaic line, while Hillel followed a less orthodox or strict approach. Shammai mostly interpreted the Torah literally as it was written, whereas Hillel gave it a more spiritual or allegorical meaning without excluding the possibility of a literal interpretation based on the scriptures. The kind of Jewish religious leaders we predominantly see in the Gospels during Jesus' lifetime, who often clashed with the Pharisees, were clearly aligned against the school of thought and disciples of Shammai.

The strict and exclusive nature of these religious individuals, seen in the school of Shammai, led them to enforce a literal separation from anyone who did not share their beliefs or adhere to their traditions as they saw fit. Jesus, as a devoted Jew completely dedicated to God's service, understood that he had come to demonstrate a significant difference. Jesus had come to bring forth his light and the purity of a heart truly surrendered to God. He came to proclaim good news to the poor and to his people, to heal the brokenhearted, to preach freedom to the captives, to give sight to the blind, to free oppressed hearts, and to announce the favorable year of the Lord. This arrival by Jesus was entirely distinct from all who had come before him. Jesus had come to show that neither sin nor impurity could defile or make impure a heart liberated by God.

In this regard, Jesus had no fear of compromising his holiness or becoming contaminated by approaching the most despised and sick individuals as the religious adherents believed in their traditions. Jesus descended to the lowest depths of the earth to give hope and courage; he taught us that true love does not contaminate the heart of man but rather dispels all indifference and impurities. Jesus showed that the light in the hearts of God's children should shine in and among the darkness. *"Let your light shine before men, that they may see your good deeds and glorify your Father in heaven."*

There is a famous saying that goes, *"Tell me who your friends are, and I'll tell you who you are."* Parents often use this phrase when advising their children to stay away from bad influences. To some extent, this saying makes sense and serves its purpose. However, when it comes to reaching out to friends and those in need, we must be cautious about using this saying to isolate ourselves from society entirely.

Jesus never cared much about what the world or religious leaders thought of him negatively. He once asked, "Who do men say that I am?"

But it was never a cause for concern who was pointing fingers or speaking ill of Him; He even said, "Woe to you when all men speak well of you, for so did their fathers to the false prophets." Jesus knew that even among the religious, He wouldn't be well-received because of the way He associated with and approached sinners. This doesn't mean Jesus was sinning alongside them or participating in their sins; on the contrary, His light prompted sinners to repent. This is the example we should take from Jesus regardless of what the world or religion thinks of us. We should approach sinners, share with them, make them part of us, and love them just as they are, allowing the light of Jesus within us to illuminate them, because the contamination of the world cannot make impure those who have Jesus in their hearts. Like Jesus, we should share, assist the needy no matter the cost, leaving behind whatever we must and disregarding any criticism we may receive.

I believe that this proverb would be quite difficult for Jesus to fully accept. We cannot deny the good advice of our parents; this same advice can be seen in other verses like 1 Corinthians 15:33 *"Do not be deceived: 'Bad company corrupts good morals'"* and Proverbs 13:20 *"He who walks with wise men will be wise, but the companion of fools will suffer harm."* The written advice is quite clear, understandable, and good. However, what we want to emphasize is the other side of this proverb, which is that as Christians or followers of Jesus, we have sometimes been taught that our friendships should only be with other Christians or those of similar religious beliefs. This has been and remains a significant mistake that I personally, as a Christian, acknowledge among the vast number of Christians I have seen over many years.

For a long time, it was thought that getting close to, sharing with, or even having friendly communion with non-Christian people was completely wrong. Many have left behind close friendships of many years, family, and individuals simply because they did not share the same beliefs and were thought incapable of being friends or having mutual friendship. In my personal case, my conversion came at the age of 14. I loved breakdancing and was among the most well-known and prominent dancers in the city where I grew up, Lawrence, which is a well-known city in the state of Massachusetts. The problem arose once I converted. My ignorance was so vast that I thought I had to slightly distance myself absolutely from all the thousands I had come to know and dedicate myself solely to new Christian friends. I ignored all the friendships I once had when they called. It took me a long time to mature and recognize the great mistake I had made in my ignorance.

While many traditionalist Christians viewed me favorably, I thought I was pleasing God in this way. Once baptized at nearly 15 years old, I began studying to prepare myself because I had a burning desire to preach Jesus to the whole world. From then on, I stood out in all the following years, traveling to numerous nations and spreading the gospel of Jesus wherever and whenever possible. It was only a few years ago that I began to truly think about how I had reached so many people for Jesus outside my own environment and in other countries, but where was my own light among those who were once my friends and acquaintances, whom I had abandoned due to my conversion to Jesus?

My heart felt a restlessness at a voice inside me saying, "why, instead of preaching for Jesus and being a light among them, reaching them and act for Jesus, did you decide to distance yourself and abandon them?" I had never felt such a huge mistake in my life. I felt that I had chosen to please the Christian circle I was in rather than return to those who had once grown up with me and were with me before I knew Jesus. I felt I needed to make a change. Even today, many Christian friendships did not see it well, but just as we were called to major Christian events hoping to meet all my friends again to introduce them to the most extraordinary man in my life, Jesus, it happened that one of my closest companions with whom I once danced had died from drugs.

I felt so guilty hearing the news that I had no choice but to return to my old friends to preach Jesus to them. It happened that to raise some money, all those who danced in the city had decided to hold a large event in favor of the friend who had died to support his family. I received a phone call; it turned out that a young pastor from our city, looking to gather all the youth, had organized the event. When I received the call, the pastor, who had known me for a long time and knew the influence I had previously had in that world, asked me two things: one, to help invite as many people as I could, and two, to be the one to pray and bring the preaching of the occasion.

The moment I had been waiting for had arrived. I felt it was the biggest door that God had ever opened in my life for preaching. Our events and gatherings usually filled with only Christians, and our celebrations, though done primarily for worshiping God, were very different this night. The entire hall was filled with what, according to the Bible, would be considered sinners and pagans. The only Christians present were our family and the congregation's pastor; everyone else there was unconverted. I saw a great opportunity to introduce everyone present to this great friend and man of humanity, Jesus of Nazareth. Immediately, many of the old friends I hadn't seen in so long were embracing and crying with love. While many congratulated me for accepting Jesus into my life, inside I felt, "This is where I should be, where I should have started." It felt like I was starting anew in my walk with Jesus. That night, many young people accepted and confessed Jesus as their Savior. I don't remember ever experiencing such a special night with Jesus like that.

I share this testimony so we understand the concept and importance of being a light in the darkness. Being a Christian does not mean we have to distance ourselves from people, separate from them, or even ignore them as we have often done. Being a Christian in the image of Jesus is to eat and give to eat to everyone, to participate amiably and help everyone without condition or expectation of anything in return. If possible, we should even sit down to eat with our neighbor without any prejudice. It is time for us as Christians to mend the damage, heal the wounds, and correct the mistakes we have made. As Jesus did, so should we. Jesus loved the world, ate with them, drank with them, shared with them, showed them love, and among many, He never forbade them from walking with Him. He said, "Whoever comes to me, I will never drive away." We cannot exclude or drive away anyone either.

The needy world longs for and seeks people who resemble and are like Jesus of Nazareth. The world does not need religious Christians who believe they have earned heaven or are so good that they are not contaminated by anyone or anything, Christians who only shine in temples and congregational walls. The world needs human beings who love more and aspire to resemble this Jesus of Nazareth, whom we will delve into more in the coming chapters. This type of Christianity, though not all, but the most legalistic ones projecting themselves as the holiest I have known and seen, resembles nothing of who Jesus of Nazareth truly was and is.

We must imitate every step Jesus left us, and we see that Jesus often felt and saw the need to sit down and even enter the homes of sinners and eat with them. We see this Jesus sitting with sinners to eat; this gesture by Jesus changed and transformed the lives and families for the better of each sinner, with the exception of His friend Judas Iscariot, who betrayed Him. Returning to the meaning of sitting to eat with someone in Jewish culture of the 1st century, it meant having significant intimacy or being close friends with that person. Between Jesus and Judas, we know they were good friends. Judas, scholars say, could have been a Jew considered a zealot.

The zealots were a political-nationalist movement. They were the most violent faction of Judaism of their time, frequently clashing with other factions like the Pharisees or Sadducees. The term zealot has become synonymous in several languages with intransigence, fanaticism, or militant radicalism. Some historians consider them one of the first terrorist groups in history because they used the murder of civilians they believed were collaborating with the Roman government to dissuade others from doing the same. Within the zealot movement, a radicalized faction known as the Sicarii stood out for their particular virulence and sectarianism. Their goal was an independent Judea free from the Roman Empire through armed struggle, as happened in the First Jewish-Roman War (66-73 AD), during which they controlled Jerusalem until it was taken by the Romans, who destroyed the Temple, and three years later occupied the fortress of Masada, the last zealot refuge, after the defenders' suicide.

It is of utmost importance to understand that among Jesus' friends and disciples, everyone expected a Messiah who would deliver them from Roman rule, destroying the Roman Empire. They believed they could achieve this by provoking the present Messiah and turning Him against the Roman Empire.

It is true that in Christian theology, we understand and recognize that the entire plan for the salvation of the world through Jesus' sacrifice on the cross was orchestrated by His Father, as foreseen before the foundation of the world, as we see in the first letter of Peter 1:20. However, when we try to understand historically and from a human perspective why Judas had to betray his friend, who had never done him any harm, we can only delve into the heart of a religious zealot Jew who sought to provoke Jesus once and for all to lead a rebellion against their enemies.

What we are trying to explain is the following: Judas had thought that if he betrayed Jesus into the hands of Jewish leaders, they would then hand Him over to the Romans. Once in the hands of the Romans, Jesus would defend Himself by rising up against the Romans, initiating and leading a war similar to the one seen in the Maccabean revolts led by Judah Maccabee "The Hammer" against Antiochus IV Epiphanes and the Hellenistic Seleucid dynasty in the 2nd century BC. The Jews had managed to gain and retain independence for a time until the arrival of the Romans under Pompey, when they once again lost the independence they had gained.

Flavius Josephus, the great Jewish Christian historian, shares another similar revolt that took place around the time of Jesus' arrival, led by a political-religious leader named Judas the Galilean, who resisted the census decreed for fiscal purposes in the Roman province of Judea by the Roman legate in Syria, Quirinius, in the year 6 AD. This occurred shortly after Judea, with the exile of Herod Archelaus, came under direct Roman administration. His revolt was harshly suppressed by the Romans. These events are recounted by Flavius Josephus in "The Jewish War" (Book II, Chapter 8) and in "Jewish Antiquities" (Book XVIII). Judas is also mentioned by Gamaliel, a member of the Sanhedrin, in a speech attributed to him in the Acts of the Apostles (Acts 5:37). Gamaliel uses him as an example of a failed Messiah. In "Jewish Antiquities," Josephus asserts that Judas, along with the Pharisee Zadok, founded the Zealot movement, which he considers the fourth sect of Judaism in the 1st century (alongside the Sadducees, Pharisees, and Essenes). Josephus blames the Zealots for the First Jewish-Roman War and the destruction of the Second Temple in Jerusalem. The zealots preached that only God was the true ruler of Israel and refused to pay taxes to the romans.

Judas Iscariot, like the other Judases who had previously organized revolts against their oppressors, sought a way for Jesus to become the Messiah and leader of such a rebellion. Judas probably never thought that his betrayal of Jesus would end the way it did. Judas came face to face with a Jesus who, knowing He would be betrayed by His close friend, remained near him until the end. That last night, Jesus, seeing Judas' attitude, asked him to do quickly what he had already planned to do against Him. Jesus, refusing to defend Himself and forbidding His friends to defend Him, asked them not to use their swords but to put them away. What kind of man sees his enemies coming against him, yet instead of defending himself, allows himself to be taken without speaking a single word? This is the kind of person who also once said, "*Do not be overcome by evil, but overcome evil with good.*" These words came from the apostle Paul in his letter to the christians in rome, knowing that just as Jesus had overcome the oppressive Roman world with good. This victory is seen on two occasions: the first in Matthew 27:54, where the centurion and those with him guarding Jesus, upon seeing the earthquake and the events that occurred, were greatly frightened and declared, "Truly, this was the Son of God."

All these romans at the foot of the cross, seeing a righteous man punished without having done anything wrong, giving and sacrificing His life solely for the good that dwelt within Him, could do nothing but accept and acknowledge that Jesus was indeed the Son of God. The second time we see the greatest victory is in the 4th century, when the entire Roman Empire converted to Christianity, the same Christianity it had once persecuted, fulfilling Jesus' words in the parable of the mustard seed—smaller than all others but growing to become greater and larger than all. The movement that started as small as a mustard seed with Jesus, in just a few centuries compared to the Roman Empire, which had hundreds and hundreds of years to grow to its climax, was now bowing down, accepting Jesus, and joining the empire of Christ and His Church. The entire world had been conquered by this Jesus whom the nations accepted. This is why we say today that the largest religion in the world is christianity, making a clear distinction that although not everyone thinks or believes the same, they all share the two main foundations—the Bible as the word of God for all and Jesus as the universal savior, the only path to salvation provided by God the Father.

Judas, upon realizing that his plan had resulted in the death of his friend, knowing that in the law it was established that anyone who shed innocent blood would be guilty of death, felt a deep sense of guilt and anguish. Seeing that the Sanhedrin of Sadducees and some pharisees among the priests had ignored and rejected him, he likely believed that by betraying his friend, he too would be handed over to the Romans to die according to the established law. With all his anxiety, restlessness, and soul-crushing bitterness for having betrayed his friend, he decided that the only resolution was to take his own life to fulfill what was written in the law—that anyone who shed innocent blood would be guilty of death.

We cannot be certain of what went through Judas' mind or why he chose to end his life in the manner he did. However, it is reasonable to conclude that this would likely be the decision made by a religious Jewish zealot upon betraying his friend.

To conclude with the prophetic portion, we have in Psalm 41:9, we can say that there is no clearer vision that makes more sense than the theological fulfillment in the life of Jesus as the Messiah being delivered and betrayed by that trusted friend and treasurer who ate of His own bread, as the psalmist described.

Returning to the passage from Isaiah 53, which we previously did not conclude, let us now show how strong the fulfillment in the life of Jesus is compared to the words of the prophet Isaiah in chapter 53:

Isaiah 53:

"Who has believed our message? And to whom has the arm of the Lord been revealed?" He grew up before him like a tender shoot, and like a root out of dry ground. He had no beauty or majesty to attract us to him, nothing in his appearance that we should desire him. He was despised and rejected by mankind, a man of suffering, and familiar with pain. Like one from whom people hide their faces he was despised, and we held him in low esteem. Surely he took up our pain and bore our suffering, yet we considered him punished by God, stricken by him, and afflicted. But he was pierced for our transgressions, he was crushed for our iniquities; the punishment that brought us peace was on him, and by his wounds we are healed. We all, like sheep, have gone astray, each of us has turned to our own way; and the Lord has laid on him the iniquity of us all. He was oppressed and afflicted, yet he did not open his mouth; he was led like a lamb to the slaughter, and as a sheep before its shearers is silent, so he did not open his mouth. By oppression and judgment, he was taken away. Yet who of his generation protested? For he was cut off from the land of the living; for the transgression of my people he was punished. He was assigned a grave with the wicked, and with the rich in his death, though he had done no violence, nor was any deceit in his mouth. Yet it was the Lord's will to crush him and cause him to suffer, and though the Lord makes his life an offering for sin, he will see his offspring and prolong his days, and the will of the Lord will prosper in his hand. After he has suffered, he will see the light of life and be satisfied; by his knowledge my righteous servant

will justify many, and he will bear their iniquities. Therefore, I will give him a portion among the great, and he will divide the spoils with the strong, because he poured out his life unto death, and was numbered with the transgressors. For he bore the sin of many, and made intercession for the transgressors."

This passage from Isaiah vividly portrays the suffering and sacrifice of Jesus, who fulfilled these prophecies through His life, death, and resurrection, becoming the ultimate sacrifice for the sins of humanity and bringing redemption and salvation to all who believe in Him.

This arm of Jehovah was never seen so manifested upon another person as upon Jesus himself, when it tells us that there was no appearance in him, nor beauty, we will see him more unattractive for us to desire him, it is so obvious that because of the mistreatment he had received from his oppressors, he had lost all the human beauty that God had given him, Jesus had been despised by many Jews, and by all the religious people of his era, he was considered the man of sorrows because he endured the abuse of his own and the Romans who beat him without compassion, the Jews and the Romans hid their faces from him without anyone defending him or helping him throughout his process to death, there was no one to fight or assist him on his behalf, he remained silent until the last moment of his death, he was taken like a lamb to the altar to be sacrificed and slaughtered, bound by the Romans, taken by force, Jesus was cut off from the earth, the rebellion of the Jews silent streets cried out for him to be crucified led to his death on the Cross, placed in the midst of clean thief criminals, never doing evil, nor deceiving anyone, it was clear that the whole plan of his sacrifice had to have come from his Father to forgive, reconcile, and regenerate the whole world through this unique perfect sacrifice. Jesus laid down his life, could have fled far away but instead offered himself to fulfill all that the prophets had said and written about him, Jesus had chosen to obey what was written for the righteousness of all. Today Jesus sees the fruit of those of us who are his church, Jesus has received the power to justify whomever He wishes, and

John tells us that Jesus is faithful to forgive all our sins if we ask him sincerely to forgive us, He is both the Judge and the advocate who fights and pays our debts before God, forgiving all our sins solely through his sacrifice given on the Cross to God the Father. Finally, shortly before his death nailed to the cross, he asked his Father, crying out, "Father, forgive them, for they do not know what they are doing." Jesus could have asked God to bring justice and avenge all those who had treated him so badly, but instead chose to pray for forgiveness for all those who had done him such wrong. This living example of love that overcomes evil with good is seen only in the most extraordinary man who has ever lived, Jesus of Nazareth. Some of the ancient prophets prophesied that the anointed "Messiah" would be physically pierced, both the portion that Isaiah 53 grants us and also Zechariah 12:10 which tells us the following.

Zechariah 12:10;

And I will pour out on the house of David and the inhabitants of Jerusalem a spirit of grace and supplication. They will look on me, the one they have pierced, and they will mourn for him as one mourns for an only child, and grieve bitterly for him as one grieves for a firstborn son. NIV.

I find it quite impossible not to see the clear fulfillment that this portion has on the life of the Messiah Jesus of Nazareth, after Jesus' resurrection, we see that the upper room had been filled with Jews in communion where the book of Acts tells us that they had remained praying united fervently, through time they all came to see Jesus setting their eyes on Him as the one they had pierced and killed, after Peter's first preaching in Jerusalem on the day of Pentecost we see the great number of repentant Jews turning to this Jesus they had killed. from the first century onwards after Jesus' death following the preaching of the apostles and the continuity of Jesus' church we see how the world has really been afflicted in its need mourning for Jesus the only begotten, whom they put to death. The same Psalmist in his chapter 22:16-18; For dogs have surrounded me; A band of evildoers has encompassed me; They pierced my hands and my feet. I can count all my bones. They look, they stare at me; They divide my garments among them, and for my clothing they cast lots. NASB, not even to David himself did they do everything that these verses declare, the only one we can compare such verses to is Jesus of Nazareth himself, this Jesus was surrounded by religious leaders who sought to kill him at every moment, they nailed his hands and feet to a cross, they mistreated him so much that his bones could even be seen, everyone could see Jesus among the people because they forced him to walk to Calvary together with Simon whom they forced to carry his cross, the Roman soldiers once Jesus was crucified took his clothes and made four parts of them, they also took his tunic, and casting lots to see who would keep them. Finally, there is a prophetic event that many overlook, and it is what we see in Psalm 34:20 where it tells us the following;

Psalm 34:20;

He protects all his bones;not one of them will be broken.

The Passover lamb had to be without blemish, and during its sacrifice and meal "they shall not break any of its bones." When Jesus was sacrificed, John teaches that unlike the men hanging on either side of him and all the other crucified men in the crucifixion fields, not a single bone of Jesus' body was broken. The most legitimate explanation I have been able to investigate is as follows.

Then the jews, because it was the day of preparation, so that the bodies would not remain on the cross on the Sabbath (for that Sabbath was a high day), asked Pilate that their legs might be broken and that they might be taken away. So the soldiers came and broke the legs of the first, and of the other who had been crucified with him. But when they came to Jesus and saw that he was already dead, they did not break his legs. But one of the soldiers pierced his side with a spear, and at once there came out blood and water. He who saw it has borne witness—his testimony is true, and he knows that he is telling the truth—that you also may believe. For these things took place that the Scripture might be fulfilled: *"Not one of his bones will be broken." (John 19:31-36)*

Jesus of Nazareth

The text that John is quoting is the same Psalm 34:20-21 (Jewish version), where the psalmist had said a verse earlier, *"Many are the afflictions of the righteous,"* and then, a verse later, speaking of this one whom he calls righteous, says that God *"protects all his bones; not one of them will be broken."* But what does the righteousness of an individual have to do with not breaking his bones? The answer is found in the custom of the ancient shepherds of Israel in dealing with their flock. When a lamb strayed from the flock and wandered away from its shepherd, not obeying his voice, the shepherd, in pursuit, would go after the lamb. When the shepherd found the lamb that had gone astray, he would strike the lamb with his staff and break one of its legs. Then he would bind up the broken leg with a bandage so that the leg would heal and be restored. The pain suffered by this lamb in its leg prevented the lamb from walking; thus, it was impossible for the lamb to stray again, disobeying the voice of its shepherd. Since the wounded animal was unable to walk with the broken leg, the custom was for the shepherd to take the lamb in his arms and place it on his shoulders; in this way, the lamb learned that at all times its duty was to follow the steps of its shepherd, that it had to follow him wherever he went and obey his voice. All this was done so that the lamb would learn not to go astray and not to disobey the voice of its shepherd. The Hebrew word for punishment is anásh (עֲנָשׁ), which, upon analysis, is understood to mean "notice that you are falling." The first letter of this word is the letter Ayin (ע), pronounced like the word עִין, which literally means eye or also 'observe.' The work of an eye is to observe, analyze, and investigate. And the word Nash (נָשׁ) refers to the act of "falling" or "being falling," which provides us with the meaning: "notice that you are falling" (עִינָשׁ), that is, notice that you are straying from the path. This means that every punishment from God is a warning for the human being to observe that he is falling or straying from the right path so that, once warned, he begins to rectify. From here we can understand why it is written in the book of Proverbs, *"The Lord disciplines the one he loves"* (Proverbs 3:12). When a shepherd broke the leg of his lamb that had disobeyed, the punishment fell upon the lamb so that it would realize that it had disobeyed the voice of its shepherd and thus learn not to disobey again. The reason why no bone was broken in the Passover lamb is that this lamb had to give the image of a lamb that never strayed and never disobeyed the voice of its shepherd. Jesus, who is called 'the righteous' and also 'the Lamb of God,' did not have a single bone broken, just as no bone was to be broken in the Passover lamb. This was carried out in this way because Jesus fulfilled the role as the Passover lamb. Jesus qualified as the Passover lamb because he never sinned or disobeyed the voice of his Father. He never committed iniquity, and for that significant reason, Jesus did not have a single bone broken. We have concluded this first part with the birth and prophetic arrival of Jesus of Nazareth the "Messiah" using some of the prophetic portions spoken and used by some of the ancient prophets of Israel; now it is up to us to continue with the development and growth of Jesus of Nazareth to see why he truly was and is the most extraordinary man who lived in this world.

THE CHILDHOOD AND INFANCY OF JESUS OF NAZARETH

Part 3

Now that we have shown the prophecies spoken many centuries before Jesus' arrival and seen their fulfillment in the present, we are ready to focus on the entire life of Jesus from his childhood, youth, adulthood to his death, and his current state. Despite having more textual information about Jesus than any other religiously venerated figure, there is a significant portion of Jesus' life known as the lost years of Jesus, the childhood of Jesus, the late theory journey to India, or simply the unknown years of Jesus. It is named as such because although there are very ancient sources and texts that do speak of Jesus' childhood, they never entered the biblical canon. It is very important to consider the primary reason why I will use all these extra-biblical sources, pseudepigrapha or apocryphal, to talk about Jesus' childhood and infancy. I believe that both friends and christians should know the different thoughts that some early communities or writers had about Jesus at an early age. It is worth mentioning from now on that personally, I do not believe that these apocryphal or deuterocanonical sources can be authentic or completely credible as historical sources of events that occurred in Jesus' life, but neither can we completely discount all the information in these books since some books of the New Testament make use of verses found in the apocryphal or pseudepigrapha texts as authentic. Let's delve into the childhood and infancy of Jesus, but with our minds prepared to learn what may be edifying for the same. In this part we will use the Bible the gospel or story of the infancy of Jesus by Thomas the protoevangelium of James the Arabic gospel of the infancy of Jesus pseudo Matthew the Armenian gospel of the infancy of Jesus the book Essential Judaism by George Robinson and others to emphasize the cultural childhood of Jesus in the lives of the Jews.

Alexander Frias

CHILDHOOD AND INFANCY OF JESUS IN THE BIBLE:
Presentation of Jesus

In the Bible, we have some events about the childhood of Jesus. The apostle Paul, along with the Gospel writers, shows us that Jesus was born fully human, went through every process that every human being has to go through. In his letter to the Galatians, Paul tells us, *"But when the fullness of the time had come, God sent forth His Son, born of a woman, under the law of Moses..." (Galatians 4:4, NKJV).* Jesus was born and lived as every human being in Bethlehem of Judea. His parents were devout Jews, completely devoted to the law of Moses and the Jewish traditions of their time. The law of Moses established that every newborn male, if firstborn, had to be taken to the temple after eight days to be circumcised, presented, and given a name. This child was to be dedicated to God for temple service. In cases where it was not a human being, the firstborn of animals were also presented for sacrifice. According to this law (Numbers 18:15-16), "Everything that opens the womb of all flesh, which they bring to the Lord, whether man or beast, shall be yours; nevertheless, the firstborn of man you shall surely redeem, and the firstborn of unclean animals you shall redeem. And those redeemed of the devoted things you shall redeem when one month old, according to your valuation, for five shekels of silver, according to the shekel of the sanctuary, which is twenty gerahs (hebrew unit, weight and currency)." According to this law, we know that the case of Jesus was a special one, where Joseph and Mary had to pay the five shekels to redeem Jesus from being offered to God for temple service. Five shekels in our days are equivalent to about 40 dollars. We see in the Gospel of Luke that Mary and Joseph took Jesus to the Temple. This is a clear indication that they observed Jewish customs and traditions. After the days of purification, Luke tells us that there was a man named Simeon in Jerusalem. It will be quite important to know who this Simeon was. According to Jewish tradition, Simeon was a Pharisee belonging to the Jewish Sanhedrin that was in the Temple. While there were many smaller Sanhedrin with less judges in each city, the largest Sanhedrin was located in

Jesus of Nazareth

Jerusalem, precisely in the Temple. It consisted of 70 elderly judges, and sometimes 71 so that in cases of judicial matters, the votes of the judges would never be split, tied, or parallel. A very important fact is that the true schools in Israel at the beginning did not have a formal or orderly structure. The well-structured schools began in the second century with the rabbis. The education system in Israel was directed by the Sanhedrin for the rabbis and the most advanced disciples, and they were taught all kinds of law and tradition. In Jewish tradition, it is believed that this Simeon was the father of the great teacher of Paul and Pharisee Gamaliel, and it is also believed that this Simeon was the son of the Pharisee rabbi Hillel, who had one of the most famous Jewish schools of the first century. Simeon eagerly awaited the Messiah who would bring consolation to Israel. Historically, it is believed that because Simeon believed and saw Jesus as the Messiah, he had to leave his position in the Sanhedrin. This is the first event we see in Jesus' childhood in the temple after the visit by the wise men to Bethlehem where he was born. If there is something that Luke wants to teach us in this narrative part of Jesus' childhood, it is the following: if God has blessed us to be a father or mother, religious customs and traditions can be important in our lives. Jesus was instructed from childhood to serve God. We can ask the following question: what would have happened if Mary and Joseph had never instructed Jesus in the customs and service of their God? Would it have been possible for Jesus to fulfill his purpose on earth without the help and spiritual education of his parents? They were the first to set the necessary example of how to serve God, complying with everything established in the law of Moses. It will always help on the path of the child if the parents are an example to them because sometimes as parents, we want our children to walk in the ways of the Lord by themselves, and this is not the example that Luke gives us. Mary and Joseph took Jesus to the Temple to be presented before God, as many of us do by custom in our days, but Mary and Joseph were determined and committed to paying to redeem Jesus from temple service with the purpose of educating him well in their home in Nazareth until the appointed time. Luke will continue to confirm Jesus' development when in chapter 2:52 he tells us, *"And Jesus increased in wisdom and stature, and in favor with God and men" (Luke 2:52, NKJV)*. Luke is telling us three very important things:

(1) Jesus increased in wisdom (the mental aspect)

(2) Jesus increased in stature (physical aspect)

(3) Jesus increased in favor with God and men (spiritual aspect)

It is clear that for God to fulfill His purpose in Jesus' life and for Jesus to learn well who God was in his life, his parents played a very important role in his life. Even before Jesus was born, we see the kind of woman Mary was, a young woman devoted to God. When the angel spoke to her about what would be deposited in her womb, she never opposed God's purpose for her life, and we see that her last words were, *"Then Mary said, 'Behold the maidservant of the Lord! Let it be to me according to your word'" (Luke 1:38, NKJV)*. This is the kind of attitude that God expects from every mother and father towards their children in God. Mary was among the most blessed for her complete surrender to God to care for what God had placed in her. We must always be the greatest example for our children; thus, it will be much more possible for God's purpose to be fulfilled in them.

Jesus in the Temple

The second biblical scene we have of Jesus is found in the same chapter 2 of the book of Luke, where it tells us that the Passover feast in Jerusalem was ending. The Passover feast lasted about 50 days and ended with the feast of Pentecost, as we see in the book of Leviticus.

Leviticus 23:15-16:

"And you shall count for yourselves from the day after the Sabbath, from the day that you brought the sheaf of the wave offering: seven Sabbaths shall be completed. Count fifty days to the day after the seventh Sabbath; then you shall offer a new grain offering to the Lord" (Leviticus 23:15-16, NKJV).

Jesus of Nazareth

The Acts of the Apostles tells us that from all parts of the world under heaven where there were Jews, they came to Jerusalem to celebrate the Passover feast. This is the reason we see Mary and Joseph traveling to Jerusalem. At this time, Jesus is 12 years old. This is a very important number and moment in Jesus' life. It is not a coincidence that Luke decides to include this narrative of Jesus in his book. There are very ancient customs and processes through which Jewish children had to go through. These processes and new stages are known as a new birth depending on the stage. There is a very ancient ceremony in Israel and among the Jews that we see today among children aged 12 to 13, and it is as follows: According to Judaism, the Bar/Bat Mitzvah ceremony marks the transition age from childhood to adolescence. Every girl who turns 12 and boy who turns 13 are considered, from that moment on, responsible for their actions and are obligated to fulfill all the precepts of Judaism. The age, which was determined in the time of the Mishnah (second to fifth century) (the oral law), was according to the expectations that society had of people. At that time, shortly after reaching that age, between 15-18, young people would marry and start families. For this reason, the Bar/Bat Mitzvah ceremonies were the formal transition from childhood to adulthood. Over the years, the meaning of the Bar Mitzvah changed, according to the changes that modern society underwent; however, the ceremony continued to mark a significant transition stage in the person's life. Like in other societies that celebrate initiation and transition ceremonies to adulthood, it is a process that culminates with the ceremony. This includes preparations, where the young person studies his role as an adult and is supported during these preparations by his close family and the society in which he lives. The preparations for the Bar Mitzvah involve becoming aware of responsibility and developing a more independent space of action, as expressed in the blessing that the father says to his son: "Blessed are you who freed us from their sins," which means that from this moment on, the father is no longer responsible for the actions of his son. From now on, children must be accountable for their actions and build their own identity. This is the transition process from being children to becoming mature individuals. After the Bar Mitzvah ceremony, the young man or woman is considered to have the obligation to fulfill all the precepts, which until this moment were fulfilled only as learning. In addition, there are precepts in Judaism that only the young person is allowed to fulfill from this moment on, when they become an adult. Thus, for example, shortly before the Bar Mitzvah, the young person learns to put on tefillin (phylacteries), and when he reaches his Bar Mitzvah, the young man will say the blessing of the tefillin for the first time. Putting them on symbolizes the acceptance of the relationship between the Jew and his God. We must clarify that this custom as we see it today is not actually the one we see in biblical times; this kind of custom began around the fifth to fifteenth centuries of our era although if we see it mentioned in the Mishnah, it is important to know that the ceremony as such is post-biblical; the custom of transitioning into a Jewish child's life if it is practiced, the example we see in (Genesis 34:25) where Levi himself is already a soldier with a sword, it is believed that the age of this teenager was 13 years, the law established that to enter the military, one must be at least 20 years old. The Mishnah as the code of oral laws and Jewish traditions mentions that the age of transition from childhood to adult life as responsible in the commandments of God and the 613 precepts of ordinances is 13 years old. It is of utmost importance that in Luke's account, he tells us that Jesus was 12; there was an exception that allowed Jewish children to move up, enter the new birth or stage of maturity in their new life in the commandments of the Torah and its precepts, and this was only allowed to children who in some way were more advanced in their development and knowledge. Luke deliberately shows Jesus at an age that is not actually the age he should have been for his new stage, knowing that this Jesus was a special and different child on whom rested unparalleled knowledge and wisdom shows us that by his capacity and development even if he did not have the necessary age, he had everything necessary to qualify and enter a new spiritual stage in his life.

The orderly treaty of Neziqin, of the Mishnah and the Talmud tells us the following in "Pirkei Avot 5:24": at 5 years old, the study of the Torah begins, at 10 the study of the Mishnah, and at 13 the fulfillment of the precepts. According to the Talmud, the vows of a thirteen-year-old male are legally binding, which is the result of becoming a "man" as required in Numbers 6:2. The term Bar Mitzvah, as used today, comes from the 14th-century rabbinic term "gadol" (adult) or "bar 'onshin" (son of punishment). This means he can be punished if he has done something wrong. The Bar Mitzvah ceremony originated, according to most sources, only in the Middle Ages. However, there is sufficient earlier evidence regarding the obligation of fulfilling the Torah's commandments upon turning 13 years old. (https://es.wikipedia.org/wiki/Benei_Mitzvá, BeneiMitzvá).

We see that at the age of 12, Jesus, after the conclusion of the festival, had to return from Jerusalem with his parents to Nazareth in Galilee. There's quite an important issue we can't overlook for our lives at this early age of Jesus. The custom for every Jew at the end of the festival was to return home. Jesus's parents had fulfilled what was demanded of them in the tradition of going to Jerusalem for the Passover, and now it was time to go back home. The detail that Luke doesn't give us at this moment, but which Jesus later shares with us in his parables, is the following: it happened that a large number of Jews went to the festivals in Jerusalem. One could say that many of the other villages and cities were almost empty, or deserted, due to the many people traveling to Jerusalem. The Jews living farther north, in the case of Mary and Joseph, would have to walk for a day, a route known as "the pilgrim's way." This route crossed from Galilee to the other side and descended southward toward the Jordan. This was necessary because although there was a shorter route, it passed through Samaria, and the Jews did not enter Samaria, so they had to take the longer route. The problem we have is that when the Jews reached the banks on the other side of the Jordan to cross and reach Jerusalem, they all had to pass through the great city of Jericho before reaching Jerusalem. Here's where things got quite dangerous because, while crossing from the Jordan to Jerusalem, most likely already at night on the way through Jericho, there were many caves where thieves and robbers hid.

This is the road we later see Jesus announce in the parable of the Good Samaritan. This road was quite dangerous. This gives us a very important detail: Luke only mentions that Mary, Joseph, and the child were going because the story focuses on them, but in reality, they weren't alone. It happened that the Jews traveled in large groups of families to avoid being attacked by thieves between the Jordan and Jerusalem. The custom was to divide the groups: a number of men went in front, the women in the middle, and another group of men at the back. This was how they protected themselves to avoid any trouble.

After the festivals had ended, the Jews returned home. In Jesus's case, he had most likely become enamored with everything he was seeing in Jerusalem and the temple. It seemed as if that was the place where he was meant to stay. Every devout Jew who saw what Jesus was seeing in the temple during that time fell in love with being there. During that time, it's very possible that Jesus was seeing the sacrifices being offered, all the priests in their garments, the grand temple of Jerusalem and all its majesty, surrounded by teachers and rabbis of his time. Jesus was seeing a different world than what he was used to seeing in Nazareth. The only thing there was where Jesus lived to hear and learn was the synagogue once a week. For Jesus, the synagogue once a week was probably not enough. This Jesus had such a hunger for God in his life that he did everything possible to be close to knowledge.

In one of my theses, which I titled "Can Anything Good Come from Nazareth?" I had to do a very deep investigation of Nazareth. One of the things that struck me the most about this city is that it is not found anywhere in the Old Testament or in any of the lists of cities mentioned in the Talmud or Jewish literature. Nazareth gained its fame precisely because of Jesus himself, who grew up there, but it's important to know that in Nazareth at the time of Jesus, it is said that there were no more than 400 people. Above all, not a single school has been recorded where Jesus could have studied. Conservative traditionalist theologians and scholars teach us that all of Jesus's education must have come from his parents, especially his mother, since mothers were the ones who educated their children at home while fathers engaged in social work unless they were rabbis or Torah teachers. In the case of Jesus, we know that Joseph was a carpenter or artisan; therefore, he must have received his training and knowledge from his mother and the synagogue in Nazareth. Later on, in the section on Jesus's public life, this section is found in more detail and better explained.

This Jesus is the young almost-adult who feels a fire and a passion for God in his life, also the Jesus who always wants to remain in the presence of his Father and God all the time. There is a great difference between the Western world and the Middle Eastern world in terms of child-rearing and education. I personally belong to the West and grew up here, but I have traveled extensively in search of knowledge to different areas of the Middle East, such as Israel and Turkey. I have visited the Western Wall in Jerusalem numerous times, and something I have noticed there is the presence of parents with children together reading the Torah or the Tanakh. This custom of keeping children reading and studying their sacred book or text at an early age is not frequently seen in our Western world. The number of parents who instruct their children in this kind of education and spiritual formation in the West is a minority.

I believe the purpose of including this part of Jesus's life in this book is so that every teenager and young person can allow their heart to burn and be stirred just as Jesus did at his early age in the temple. Jesus loved being around that environment. The scene was so impactful that while everyone was going back home, the festival had ended, for Jesus, the festival was just beginning. For Jesus, the festival had not ended. We see the same Psalm 23:6 ("Surely goodness and mercy shall follow me all the days of my life, and I shall dwell in the house of the Lord forever") being fulfilled in the life of this teenager who is about to enter a new stage in his life before the world. Luke continues by telling us that his parents had left, thinking Jesus was with them, and when they realized Jesus had stayed in Jerusalem, they immediately returned for him.

His parents had searched everywhere possible and couldn't find him.

Three days had passed until they finally managed to find him. Here, Lucas presents clear theology; the number 3 has always represented divinity, perfection, fulfillment, resurrection, new beginning, and completion. Lucas is clearly showing us a Jesus in a new spiritual stage whom his parents found after three days. Lucas tells us that after they found him, his mother asked him why he had done such a thing, and she and his father Joseph had been anxiously looking for him. Jesus's response seems to have been quite different from what was expected. Jesus replied to his mother, after she mentioned his father Joseph, that they were looking for him, "Why were you searching for me? Didn't you know that I had to be in my Father's house?" The text concludes by telling us that his parents didn't understand what he meant. Unable to do anything more, Jesus, subject to his parents, returned to Nazareth, but his mother treasured all that Jesus said in her heart.

There's a very curious hypothesis in the book "Rabbi Jesus" by Bruce Chilton that I think is worth mentioning. It's also worth mentioning and clarifying that many historians and scholars don't find it quite credible. But apparently, when the Bible tells us that Jesus is found by his parents in Jerusalem and they return to Nazareth, it is assumed that in Nazareth, as the Gospel of Thomas tells us, Jesus grew up working alongside his father in the carpentry shop. There he would have lived until the age of marriage and lived a normal and common life like any Jew in Israel. Young people who desired to study at the feet of the rabbis until they themselves became rabbis would reach a certain age, probably around 18. Once they decided to enter the studies, they would devote themselves to their rabbis while studying. Generally, those who did not dedicate themselves to study at 18 or younger, if they were mature enough, would marry and start a family.

We don't exactly know where and how Jesus received his intelligence and great wisdom. Theologically, we know that this Jesus came full of wisdom and intelligence. Tradition tells us that he said, "I speak not of myself or by myself, but what I speak is what my Father has given me to speak." This highly skilled Jesus is also seen in the Gospel of John. For faith, there is no way or reason how Jesus managed to develop and learn all that he knew; it is simply believed that being a human being, the Word or Logos within him had equipped him to fulfill his goal and purpose to the end. This is how the religious fathers of the church, like Saint Athanasius and others, thought.

The reason I use Chilton's hypothesis, clarifying that it is not historically approved as authentic or probably true, is solely to put in critical and academic perspective what could have happened for Jesus to have had such intelligence and wisdom as a human being. We know that his authority came from God and the Torah itself, but his intelligence and wisdom, as he grew in grace with God and men, show us the possibility of where and how he could have found it. Chilton says that in reality, it is most likely that Jesus never returned to Nazareth. The part where Lucas says they "returned to Nazareth" after the festivals could have been an addition to Lucas or the thought of a tradition in the community that Lucas had received. Eastern thought is not the same as Western thought, which gives us a completely different perspective of Jesus. To the Western eye, this Jesus would be a teenage boy, while to the Eastern eye, this Jesus is almost an adult.

For the Jews of this time, the fact that Jesus wanted to stay in Jerusalem was completely normal; he could stay if he wanted to. The issue lies in the fact that this Jesus probably couldn't stay because he worked and helped both Joseph and his mother Mary, and she needed him back. But from a Western perspective, Jesus's parents would be seen as completely negligent, having left Jesus behind, as a 12-year-old child is very immature and incapable of walking alone. Let's remember that on the return to Nazareth, they weren't completely alone. What probably happened was that among the groups of men who were at the back or in the front, while the women were in the middle, Joseph could have been at the back and left Jesus, almost an adult, thinking he would catch up later. Or Joseph could have been at the front, thinking that Jesus was among those at the back, until Mary realized that Jesus wasn't with them and had stayed in Jerusalem.

Jesus, having stayed in Jerusalem to receive his spiritual capacity and formation, was where he met the most respected of teachers and prophets, John the Baptist, who most likely lived in the desert but also came to Jerusalem to fulfill the custom. It is believed that Jesus spent a large part of his life with John the Baptist, where he received his great capacity and wisdom. The hypothesis concludes by saying that it is not a coincidence that Jesus had such a strong closeness to John, being baptized by him as a disciple to his master, and that John the Baptist knew him as the Lamb of God. Obviously, the Gospels are not about John the Baptist; rather, they are about Jesus Christ as the savior of Israel and the world. Therefore, the primary and protagonist figure will not be that of John, but that of Jesus. The Bible does not coincide with this idea or hypothesis of academic Chilton. Personally, as a believing Christian, and faithful to historical confessional theological study, we also investigate and study the critical academic line along with biblical sciences to acquire the greatest possible knowledge of the general biblical text. However, without neglecting faithfulness to the faith and confession of the biblical text, we believe and choose what the Bible establishes as historical fact, even though it probably wasn't written under completely historical content. We faithfully keep the great purpose for which it was given to us.

We cannot ignore the existence of a completely consensual traditional voice of high authority and accepted for almost 20 centuries, starting from the apostolic fathers to the fathers of the modern era of the church, who from the beginning, although possibly historically confessional by faith, have helped us to a better textual comprehension than the modern and late ideas that men and studies have been able to elaborate on the Bible and a historical Jesus. Returning to the text, a characteristic of this Jesus at his early age is submission and obedience to his parents, which cannot be overlooked. It is clear that Jesus wanted to remain in the temple, but subject to his parents, he had to return with them. In Israel, the obedience of children to parents is very important and critically obligatory; obedience of children to parents is not an option, it is mandatory to the point that if a child disobeys their parents, they could be stoned by the leaders of the people. Deuteronomy 21:18-21 tells us the following: "If someone has a stubborn and rebellious son who does not obey his father and mother and will not listen to them when they discipline him, his father and mother shall take hold of him and bring him to the elders at the gate of his town. They shall say to the elders, 'This son of ours is stubborn and rebellious. He will not obey us. He is a glutton and a drunkard.' Then all the men of his town are to stone him to death. You must purge the evil from among you. All Israel will hear of it and be afraid." Some academic and liberalist scholars use this portion to show Jesus as rebellious or even disobedient to his parents; some have even gone so far as to say that his response was very harsh against his parents. Each scholar has their own opinion, but to make or come to a conclusion in this way and say that Jesus was a disobedient son because of this case is totally a very poor and erroneous opinion toward Jesus. We must put ourselves in Jesus's shoes and clearly see the strong desire he had to remain in the presence and matters of God. I would dare to say and opine that not even his parents knew how great the passion was in Jesus's heart for his Father. Another thing that every person should know is that for every Jew, Jerusalem was the Garden of Eden, the spiritual paradise, the dwelling place of God, and not everyone traveled to Jerusalem all the time. In the example of Jesus, he lived a considerable distance away to return; it was not customary for a teenage child with poor parents to travel frequently.

Lucas tells us that Jesus was found after three days, a clear representation of the Jesus who would resurrect after three days. The similarity is seen in the response of both Jesus, the teenage boy, and the resurrected one. The boy, for the first time theologically, manages to show his mother that he knows who his Father is, instead of Joseph the carpenter, and the communion bond he must have with Him in His affairs. Meanwhile, the resurrected Jesus announces to Mary and his disciples that it is necessary for him to ascend to the Father, to be and have the same union bond with the Father. Jesus, as an example, will show us that for those who desire to have God as father and master, it is obligatory to be involved in the affairs of God, that communion with the Father is obligatory. It is the only way we will know and understand the true purpose of life. It's not a decision or an option; it's the example of Jesus himself at a young age. Jesus is teaching us early on to be in communion with the Father.

This Jesus, says Luke, when his parents found him, was sitting. This gesture and posture of Jesus will also be very important. We see it later when he is already an adult ascending the mount of the Beatitudes. Matthew tells us that as he climbed with his disciples, he sat down and opened his mouth to teach them. It is on that mount where we will see the beginning of Jesus as the new Moses and messiah who has come to save Israel. Jewish teachers used to teach while sitting, unlike other cultures where many did it standing or on their feet in front of their listeners. Jesus was among the teachers of the law, listening to them and questioning them. Everyone who heard him marveled at his intelligence and his answers. This young Jesus loved the Torah, the Tanakh; he enjoyed every moment he could with the word of God. If there's one thing this world needs, it's youth passionate about the word of God. We have many young people serving God at this time, and that's beautiful, but despite having many serving God, very few are committed to deep and serious study of the sacred scriptures. Young person, as you read this book, God is calling you to a commitment to His word. Psalm 119:105 tells us, "Your word is a lamp to my feet and a light to my path." We need young men and women who make the word of God their daily lamp, whose path is illuminated by the word of God, who can shine in the midst of this dark world with the torch that is the word of God to everyone who is in darkness. Everyone marveled at Jesus for his intelligence and the way he responded. Believe me, responding to a doctor of the law was not easy, much less making these learned men marvel. They were the interpreters of the law, the Pharisees who lived separated in continuous study of the Torah and the Tanakh, men studied in the best schools of Jerusalem at the feet of the best rabbis. Later on, we will show why Jesus managed to become a true rabbi. In the meantime, let's take the example of this

Jesus of Nazareth

Jesus at his early age, a young man full of passion and love for being in his Father's business.

Alexander Frias

THE CHILDHOOD OF JESUS IN THE APOCRYPHAL GOSPELS

There are many books and documents that historians have dated from the 1st century onwards which contain many stories and information related to Jesus of Nazareth. It is widely believed that there were hundreds, even thousands of such books written about Jesus, many of which contained unknown, lost, or suppressed stories about him. The majority of these books were ordered to be burned or destroyed by the early orthodox Christian Church, which viewed them as heretical. While many of these books disappeared, others survived and have surfaced over the centuries. It appears that not all of them were destroyed or eliminated as decreed in the early ecumenical councils. It is believed that from the 4th century onwards, orthodox Christians no longer wanted to completely destroy them, for reasons that remain unclear.

Early orthodox Christianity, according to many of the early apostolic, apologetic, philosophical, and theological fathers, did not endorse these books or documents that contained stories different from the canonical Gospels of Jesus. One of the well-known early Christian bishops, Irenaeus of Lyon, author of the book "*Against Heresies*" around 180 AD, was staunchly opposed to all apocryphal or additional gospels beyond the four canonical Gospels we have in the Bible. He stated:

"The Gospels cannot be either more or fewer in number than they are. Since there are four zones of the world in which we live, and four principal winds, while the church is scattered throughout all the world, and the 'pillar and ground' of the church is the Gospel and the spirit of life; it is fitting that she should have four pillars... For the living creatures are quadriform, and the Gospel is quadriform, as is also the course followed by the Lord." – Irenaeus of Lyon, "Against Heresies"

We see that Irenaeus early on disqualified all other Gospels present in the early centuries. However, archaeological discoveries have gradually unearthed many books and documents about the

Jesus of Nazareth

childhood, life, and ministries of Jesus of Nazareth. So many of these documents and Gospels have been found and continue to be discovered that, when compared to the canonical Gospels, it is clear that many of them contain the same, or nearly identical, passages. It is uncertain whether these were written at the same time as the canonical Gospels and used as sources for them. This idea is rejected within mainstream and traditional christianity but accepted by many historians and scholars.

For the vast majority of Christians, the Bible used today in the West, such as the 1960 Reina-Valera version, contains only 66 books – 39 in the Old Testament and 27 in the New Testament. Traditional Christianity views the Bible as the infallible, inerrant word of God, meaning it contains all necessary revelation without omission or addition. This view solidified within the Church from the 4th century onwards.

It's important to note that different canons of the Bible have existed and still exist. The first canon of our era is believed to be the canon of the Hebrew Bible around 70-90 AD, by Jewish Tanaim. The second canon, proposed by Marcion around 144 AD, has been archaeologically supported by fragments such as the Muratorian Canon, composed around 170 AD – nearly 1 to almost 2 centuries before the current canon, which first appears with St. Athanasius in 367 AD.

Additionally, it is worth noting that other countries and branches of Christianity have different canons with varying numbers of books. The Christian Church rejects these apocryphal books for several reasons. Early methods were used to authenticate or examine whether a book was genuine or contained authentic stories, including: **(1)** The book had to be named after an apostle or someone closely associated with them. **(2)** The book had to have been known and used by the apostles or the Church itself. **(3)** The book had to be in agreement with apostolic doctrine, harmonious with the other Gospels, and in accordance with the Church's faith. **(4)** The books had to be approved by bishops and Church fathers.

While these apocryphal texts are valuable for reading, understanding, and gaining knowledge, especially about the diverse traditions and beliefs surrounding Jesus from the 2nd century onwards, traditional christianity established a necessary canon of books that made the most authentic sense. Some scholars believe there is a possibility that writers of the canonical Gospels were aware of early traditions found in the apocryphal texts, but this is not universally accepted.

The practice of including false books or documents under genuine titles, styles, and forms of writing was done to make them seem authentic and acceptable within the churches. Some falsely attributed books were so convincing that they were accepted and used in christian churches in the early centuries. Despite these challenges, it is important to note that just because these books are considered apocryphal – meaning hidden, false, or of doubtful authenticity regarding content or attribution – does not mean they lack true events or real stories that occurred. I believe it is important to read them to better understand the history of one's own religion or belief system. For a long time, Christian Churches forbade their members from reading apocryphal texts with the famous saying "they were not inspired, therefore we do not read them," and to this day, there are still traces of prohibition among evangelical Christians who are unaware of the existence of these apocryphal books.

I think it's time, and this is the time, the age of knowledge and information. Every christian who reads the Bible and is interested in understanding the origin of orthodox christianity, how orthodox christianity was formed, and the major wars and conflicts against other heterodox christianities from the late 1st century onwards, would find it very useful to at least analytically investigate the history of the apocrypha.

REASONS FOR WRITING THE NEW TESTAMENT APOCRYPHA

This work is not intended to present the events written in these apocryphal Gospels as historical facts. For Catholicism, these books are probably more familiar than they are for Protestant evangelical Christianity, simply because they were never accepted, received, or even mentioned very often. I would even dare to say that there are still a large number of conservative evangelical Christians who do not know what the New Testament apocrypha are. From very early on, the fathers of the orthodox Christian Church were mostly opposed to all gnostic and non-gnostic apocrypha. From Irenaeus in the 2nd century, who vehemently declared that only four are the true Gospels and all others are invented, corrupt, and false, to St. Athanasius, who provided a similar canon or list of accepted books in the New Testament that we have today. With this clarified, it doesn't mean that everything written in these books was completely untrue or devoid of any cultural or historical accuracy. According to scholars, it is clear that the Gospel of Thomas contains sayings of Jesus found in the New Testament, and some suggest that it may have been written before or during the same time as the canonical Gospels. The primary purpose of bringing this important but hidden information to light is because it is crucial to understand the thoughts that emerged from the 2nd century throughout the entire Christian Church. All these apocryphal books were appearing in various Christian communities; mystical Christian Gnosticism was growing to become a threat to traditional orthodox Christianity, alongside other Gnostic and mystical philosophical branches that persisted for almost four centuries alongside orthodox Christianity.

It's important to note that during this period from the 2nd century onwards, writing was not an everyday luxury; it was a costly art form. Writers had to buy papyrus, parchment, or whatever material they used for writing, as well as expensive ink. This implies that writers not only invested money but also dedicated considerable time to their writing. Therefore, it's unlikely that writers of this era would have spent so much money and time on writing something without a purpose or that they believed could be viewed differently. Let's take a moment to step out of our current context, where anyone can easily write anything without spending a cent or much time, even if it's false and purposeless. Today, these apocryphal texts generally lose their significance and purpose because they are viewed through a different lens, influenced by the famous saying, "History is written by the victors." But here, it's a bit different because although these apocryphal writers lost the major battles against orthodox Christian Church, many of them were likely Christian believers themselves. We will approach them with the purpose of investigating and analyzing the imaginable reasons why these authors wrote down all these stories about the life of Jesus and everyone involved with him. To do this, we will travel back to the earliest centuries and try to understand each book according to its context, environment, and worldview of its time.

There are many reasons why these apocryphal books were written and why they were accepted and used within certain Christian circles in different regions. Some of the most commonly believed reasons for writing the apocrypha include:

Jesus did many things that were not written in the Gospels.

John 21:25

And there are also many other things that Jesus did, which if they were written one by one, I suppose that even the world itself could not contain the books that would be written. Amen. (RV1960)

Clearly, the author of the Gospel of John tells us that there was no book that could contain all the things that Jesus did in his life or ministry. It's reasonable to assume that just as John himself witnessed many of the things that Jesus did, others were also present when Jesus performed his miracles or wonders, and it's likely that these events were later written down based on oral traditions by unknown individuals during or after that time. We also see in John the following:

Jesus of Nazareth

John 20:30-31

And truly Jesus did many other signs in the presence of His disciples, which are not written in this book; but these are written that you may believe that Jesus is the Christ, the Son of God, and that believing you may have life in His name. (RV1960)

John clearly indicates the main and general intention behind everything he wrote in his book. The overall purpose was for every reader to believe that Jesus is the Christ, the Son of God, and thus receive life in His name. For John, all the other things found in many apocryphal writings were not as important, and furthermore, many of them were possibly unknown to John himself.

1. The silence or unknown time of Jesus:

Mostly, the interest or start of Jesus' public life begins around his almost 30 years, as Luke says. Generally, everything we have about Jesus is when he was already an adult after his baptism. Matthew and Luke are the only two writers who share a few traditions from Jesus' early life. Luke begins his book by telling us the following:

Luke 1:1-4

In as much as many have taken in hand to set in order a narrative of those things which have been fulfilled among us, just as those who from the beginning were eyewitnesses and ministers of the word delivered them to us, it seemed good to me also, having had perfect understanding of all things from the very first, to write to you an orderly account, most excellent Theophilus, that you may know the certainty of those things in which you were instructed. (RV1960)

With this, Luke indicates that he had thoroughly investigated before writing anything incorrect or untrue. Regarding Matthew, traditionally among the early Christians, it was considered the first and most original of the Gospels. Despite this, both were the only ones to share a few verses about Jesus' birth, his presentation in Jerusalem, and his visit to the temple at the age of 12. This was all that was known about Jesus' early life, unlike prophets, kings, and other prominent figures in Israel, about whom there was almost a complete history. It would be unusual that so little was known about the great king and the most awaited Messiah, the most prophesied by the prophets, from his birth, adolescence, and youth until he began his public life at 30 years old. It's so intriguing that even today; we don't know much about Jesus' daily life outside of his ministry. Part of the intention of this work, in addition to presenting Jesus' life from both canonical and apocryphal perspectives, is to showcase this extraordinary and magnificent human being who serves as the greatest example that a teenager, young person, man, woman, father, mother, son/daughter, friend, etc., can imitate and follow, becoming the most excellent human being possible. These absent and unknown years in Jesus' life soon led many Christians to question and feel the need to create stories that could fill in and explain these unknown years of Jesus. This is why we see stories in the apocrypha of Jesus performing miracles at ages 2, 5, 6, 8, and others.

2. The time between the death and resurrection of Jesus of Nazareth.

We also have a number of apocryphal Gospels that contain stories about the curious events of Jesus descending into hell, as interpreted in Christian catechetical tradition derived from Ephesians 4:9, 1 Peter 3:19-20, and 1 Peter 4:6. These verses, which the early Church used to interpret Jesus' visit to the underworld or hell, formed a type of thinking about what Jesus was doing during the time between his death and resurrection.

Ephesians 4:9-10

(Now this, "He ascended"—what does it mean but that He also first descended into the lower parts of the earth? He who descended is also the One who ascended far above all the heavens, that He might fill all things.) (RV1960)

1 Peter 3:19-20

by whom also He went and preached to the spirits in prison, who formerly were disobedient, when once the Divine longsuffering waited in the days of Noah, while the ark was being prepared, in which a few, that is, eight souls, were saved through water. (RV1960)

1 Peter 4:6

For this reason, the gospel was preached also to those who are dead, that they might be judged according to men in the flesh, but live according to God in the spirit. (RV1960)

A number of Christians or apocryphal authors, aware of these traditions, were somewhat detailed in writing about Jesus' encounter and confrontation with Satan and death during this time. More about this tradition can be found in the apocryphal "Gospel of Nicodemus."

3. The time between Jesus' resurrection and his ascension to his Father:

The Acts of the Apostles in its first chapter and the first three verses tell us the following:

Acts 1:1-3;

"In my former book, Theophilus, I wrote about all that Jesus began to do and to teach until the day he was taken up to heaven, after giving instructions through the Holy Spirit to the apostles he had chosen. After his suffering, he presented himself to them and gave many convincing proofs that he was alive. He appeared to them over a period of forty days and spoke about the kingdom of God." (NIV)

The writer of Acts does not specify what Jesus did during these 40 days on earth after his resurrection, though it is mentioned that he spoke about the kingdom of God. This period has been of interest to various apocryphal authors, leading to traditions such as the suggestion that during these 40 days, or perhaps during the unknown years between ages 17 and 29, Jesus may have traveled to or visited India, where he preached the kingdom of God to the Indians, with many accepting the gospel. While this tradition is not widely accepted within mainstream Christianity or among historians and theological scholars, it remains of interest to some Indian Christians. It is possible that eyewitnesses of Jesus' resurrection among the living disciples contributed to the traditions found in certain apocryphal texts.

4. Jesus sometimes forbade disclosure of his deeds:

In the canonical Gospels, Jesus often instructed those he healed not to publicize the miracles, and he also directed his disciples to remain silent about certain events for a time.

Matthew 8:4;

"Then Jesus said to him, 'See that you don't tell anyone. But go, show yourself to the priest and offer the gift Moses commanded, as a testimony to them.'" (NIV)

Matthew 9:30;

"And their eyes were opened. Jesus warned them sternly, 'See that no one knows about this.'" (NIV)

Mark 5:43;

"He gave strict orders not to let anyone know about this, and told them to give her something to eat." (NIV)

These are a few examples among many instances where Jesus instructed either his disciples or those healed by him to keep silent for a certain period. While various interpretations exist regarding the reasons behind these commands, it is clear that Jesus sometimes required secrecy. It is interesting to note that certain events, like the transfiguration on the mountain with Peter, James, and John, were initially kept secret as Jesus instructed, yet details eventually surfaced in the Gospel of Matthew, authored by someone who was not present at the event, suggesting that these events were eventually disclosed by others against Jesus' instructions. Such ideas may have contributed to the development of apocryphal accounts of Jesus' life and ministry.

The emergence of apocryphal Gospels is attributed to a variety of factors, as discussed previously. In the following section, we will explore the birth and childhood narratives of Jesus along with theological interpretations, similar to what we find in the apocryphal texts.

THE APOCRYPHAL GOSPELS:

- The Gospel of Thomas; (Early 2nd century)
- The Gospel of Peter; (Early 2nd century)
- The Proto-Gospel of James; (Mid-2nd century)
- The Infancy Gospel of Thomas; (Early 2nd century)
- The Epistle of the Apostles; (2nd century)
- The Acts of Peter; (Late 2nd century)
- The Acts of Paul; (Late 2nd century)
- The Acts of Thecla; (Late 2nd century)
- The Acts of John; (Late 2nd century)
- The Acts of Thomas; (3rd century)
- The Third Letter of Paul to the Corinthians; (2nd century)
- The Correspondence between Paul and Seneca; (4th century)
- The Letter of Paul to Laodicea; (2nd century)
- The Apocalypse of Peter; (2nd century)
- The Apocalypse of Paul, etc. (4th century)
- Gospel of the Hebrews; (2nd century)
- Gospel of the Nazarenes; (2nd century)
- Gospel of Mary Magdalene; (2nd century)
- Gospel of Nicodemus; (5th century)
- Gospel of Philip; (3rd century)
- Secret Gospel of Mark, (Probable 1st century), and others.

This list is just a selection of many more existing apocryphal texts. For a more comprehensive list with complete texts accessible for reading or research on each of these and other works, I recommend two books by the scholar and historian Bart D. Ehrman: "Lost Christianities" and "After the New Testament."

THE BIRTH, CHILDHOOD, AND INFANCY OF JESUS IN THE HISTORY OF THE INFANCY OF JESUS ACCORDING TO THOMAS

In an attempt to fill in what we know as the lost or unknown years of Jesus, we will focus here on what we have from the Infancy Gospel of Thomas. I must clarify that this infancy gospel is different from the Gospel of Thomas; there are sufficient reasons why this infancy gospel did not enter the biblical canon accepted earlier by the Church in general or into the canon of the Protestant Church. The Infancy Gospel of Thomas is known as an apocryphal or deuterocanonical gospel. Although it is quite ancient, it is believed to have been composed around the middle of the 2nd century, around 150 AD. This is a very early date for a gospel containing the information it offers. This gospel promptly shows the various thoughts in different Christian communities and how quickly different gospels with different perspectives on Jesus of Nazareth were developed.

Something I will emphasize is that no credible source confirms the authenticity of this gospel attributed to Thomas; it is highly doubtful that the apostle Thomas was its author, as all the apostles died well before the timeframe associated with this gospel. Let's look at some of the experiences in the childhood and adolescence of Jesus that some Christians possibly believed based on the Gospel of Thomas.

1. The Childhood and Infancy of Jesus

Jesus in Egypt:

The Infancy Gospel of Thomas begins with Joseph and Mary fleeing after Herod's order to kill all male children. This gospel provides information not specified in the Bible; it tells us that when the angel told Joseph to take the child and his mother and flee to Egypt, Jesus was two years old—a detail not mentioned in the Bible. It also shares how, on the journey, on the journey, Jesus crossing by a sown field, reaped or picked grains, putting it in the fire then ate it. Upon reaching Egypt, they stayed with a widow for a year until Jesus turned three. Watching other children play, Jesus joined in their games. This gospel presents aspects of Jesus's childhood not found in the Bible. The overall purpose of the Bible or the synoptic Gospels, including John's, is not to narrate Jesus's story but rather to show him as the Son of God and the sole Savior.

I find it very plausible that Jesus, at three years old, would start playing with other children, as this gospel suggests. The purpose for mentioning this early, very human characteristic of Jesus is unknown, but it's common sense that a child running and playing like others at that age is natural. This gospel promptly shows Jesus beginning to perform miracles and signs at the age of three. The first recorded miracle is said to be him finding a dried fish, putting it on a plate, commanding it to move, and it started to move. He then commanded it to lose its salt and return to the water. When the widow hosting them heard this, she immediately expelled them from her home.

In this narrative, we see Jesus at three years old commanding fish, which historically is seen as constructive but possibly difficult to accept or believe. It's more likely that the author developed this theological thought to exalt Jesus as divine from birth. It's clear that Jesus possessed authority not only over humans but also over fish from the beginning. In the Bible, we see Jesus with the same authority with Peter and the temple tax collectors.

Matthew 17:27 states, *"However, so that we do not offend them, go to the sea and throw in a hook, and take the first fish that comes up; and when you open its mouth, you will find a shekel. Take that and give it to them for you and Me."*

The Jesus depicted by Matthew is one of order and authority. We also see him directing fishermen where to cast their nets when they caught nothing. The author of this infancy gospel shows that Jesus had this power from the start. Some Christians generally claim that Jesus acquired his power at his baptism around the age of 30, where

Jesus of Nazareth

the Synoptic Gospels tell us he was filled with the Holy Spirit's power. For Mark, the first sign was the liberation of a demon-possessed man. However, in John's Gospel, it says the beginning of Jesus's signs was at the wedding at Cana, where he turned water into wine. Here, Mary had asked Jesus to do something. Sometimes we question whether this was truly the start of Jesus's signs, how his mother knew he could do something about the situation. I won't go into detail because some think she was asking for something natural rather than a miracle. Jesus's response clearly indicated that he was seeking an opportunity to reveal who he truly was, but his time had not yet come. Personally, I don't believe this was the beginning of the miracles or signs Jesus performed. I might agree with John if he meant that this was the start of publicly expressed signs, but I think there was something special about Jesus from childhood. His entire scriptural process is an example we should follow.

We also see this Jesus with his mother passing through plazas where a teacher is instructing his disciples. The gospel tells us that twelve birds decided to come where the teacher was teaching, and Jesus, upon seeing the birds, started laughing. The teacher became angry with Jesus, grabbed him by the ear, and asked why he was laughing. Jesus's response is crucial for theological understanding. He said he had a handful of wheat, showed it to the birds, scattered it, and the birds hurried to eat the grain. Jesus remained there until the birds had distributed the wheat, and the uncomfortable teacher expelled him from the city. The theology and teaching in this portion are quite clear. There were many teachers and rabbis in Israel, many of whom disagreed with Jesus, but here we see Jesus with a handful of wheat—wheat representing his word, the true Torah of God. The number of birds, twelve, represents the totality of the tribes of Israel comprising the people of God. For Jesus, the teachers did not possess the true wheat for the people. Here, Jesus shows that he is the one who brings and holds the necessary wheat for all the people of God. We see Jesus laughing; the reason for this laughter, and its intention, is unknown. Previously, when the prophet Elijah confronted the false prophets at Mount Carmel, seeing them worship Baal without any response, Elijah seemed to mock them, seeing how the false prophets believed in a false god invented by men. It's possible that in the writer's view, Jesus's laughter was sarcastic, indicating that the words of many teachers will never have the true wheat needed for life. It's obvious that this writer must have read and been familiar with the synoptic Gospels. To write this portion, they must have read **Matthew 6:26,** *which says, "Look at the birds of the air, that they do not sow, nor reap, nor gather into barns, and yet your heavenly Father feeds them. Are you not worth much more than they?"* For this gospel, Jesus is clearly the one who sustains the birds and, in this portion, the people of Israel. On the other hand, the gospel tells us that the uncomfortable teacher expelled him from the city. This is already the second time Jesus is expelled from places early on. Therefore, we see that from the beginning, he was accustomed to being expelled from many places, as we will later see in the synoptic Gospels in his own hometown, Nazareth.

Jesus in Nazareth:

Thomas shows us that upon Jesus's arrival in Nazareth at the age of five, he immediately continues performing signs. Seeing a heavy rain falling, Jesus gathered it all into a cistern and commanded it to clear up, and it did. Taking the mud from that well, he fashioned it into the shape of twelve birds. He did these things on a Sabbath day, in the midst of Jewish children. From a very young age, according to the writer's thought, Jesus was criticized by the Jews for violating the Sabbath with the works he did. The theological interpretation here is clear. We know from Genesis that waters covered the earth, and God formed man from clay. The submerged earth, with the command for the waters to separate, emerged as dry land, with the waters below known as seas. Now we have the earth supporting the seas. In the same way, the water that fell, collected, and placed in the clay cistern represents humans or the twelve tribes of Israel. The water, which comprises 98% of our internal fluid, shows Jesus as the creator of both water and mud, representing humans.

In the Gospel of John, this Jesus is also closely associated with water. We see him telling the Samaritan woman, "If you knew who was asking you for a drink, you would ask him for living water." He continues, "But whoever drinks of the water that I will give him shall never thirst; but the water that I will give him will become in him a well of water springing up to eternal life." Jesus is the only one who can place and give true clarified living water within and upon the mud, which is humanity. This portion clearly demonstrates theology, presenting Jesus as the life-giving water for the twelve birds created from clay, representing the twelve tribes of Israel.

Because of this action, we see Joseph asking Jesus why he does what is not permitted on the Sabbath. Jesus opened his hands to the birds and told them to rise and fly. Once again, we see the Lord of the Sabbath granting true freedom to the birds, representing Israel, by the voice and command of Jesus. For Jesus, life's freedom did not consist of what one could or could not do on the Sabbath. In the synoptic, it's clear that man was not created for the Sabbath; rather, the Sabbath was created for man. This demonstrates that human life is much more valuable than a commandment or law given for the good and freedom of humanity, not for its harm or enslavement.

The biblical Jesus never broke the Sabbath; he always kept it and never did any work not permitted by the Law of Moses. The prohibitions against Jesus's works on the Sabbath were not from the Torah or Moses's law but rather from altered oral traditions by the rabbis and Pharisees in Israel. While the religious were slaves to tradition and the Sabbath, Jesus came to show and grant true freedom to life from sin's power over man and the traditional slavery that ruled over Israel.

An interesting point in this incident is the appearance of a Pharisee, who is not well-regarded in the canonical Gospels. We see Jesus constantly at odds with the Pharisees for their rigid ways toward people. In this case, it's said that a Pharisee approached the child (Jesus), took an olive branch, and began to destroy the fountain Jesus had made. Seeing this, Jesus became angry with the Pharisee to the point that he commanded him to dry up like a tree without leaves or fruit and to be without roots. Instantly, the Pharisee fell to the ground dry and dead. All of this occurred when Jesus was five years old, according to the Infancy Gospel of Thomas.

Alexander Frias

We are beginning to see a completely an usual Jesus. Despite the theology or allegorism contained in this gospel, the character, personality, and presentation of Jesus in his early childhood are highly improbable compared to the Jesus we see in the synoptic Gospels, even with the little we have in them. We quickly understand why these apocryphal texts were never accepted into any ecclesiastical canon. In this gospel, we have Jesus commanding death and killing a Pharisee with his word. If this were the case, how many of the nearly 6,000 Pharisees that Flavius Josephus tells us were in Israel during the 1st century would have died by Jesus's word every time these Pharisees opposed him, tempting him and accusing him of being a sinner and a child of fornication? Not a single Pharisee dies by Jesus's hand in the canonical Gospels. On the contrary, we have the righteous one laying down his life, dying by the order of the Jews and at the hands of the Romans. There is no doubt that these stories of Jesus's childhood are and were constructed inventions to fill the unknown void of Jesus's years, written for purposes that we still do not fully understand.

After the death of this Pharisee by Jesus, we see another similar event. One day, as Jesus and Joseph were walking through the city, a child ran ahead of them and intentionally stumbled into Jesus, injuring him severely in the side. Jesus said to this child, "You shall not complete the way you have started." The child immediately fell to the ground and died. Everyone who saw this asked, "Where is this child (Jesus) from?" They asked Joseph to take him far away from the city. Supposedly, they asked Joseph to teach him to be obedient and to pray, not to curse the children because they were driving them crazy, losing their minds. Now we see a disobedient Jesus who does not know how to pray, kills children, and drives them crazy. I don't know how to describe this Jesus, but I believe there is no way or human being who truly believes that such a Jesus existed. This Jesus is completely delusional, murderous, mentally deranged, impossible to exist in Israel. A Jesus like this, due to his disobedience, would have died at the hands of society. With all that Jesus had started, everyone in the city hated Jesus and his family. Soon we will see a vengeful Jesus, using all his power against anyone who dared to

Jesus of Nazareth

speak against him. Despite Joseph repeatedly questioning Jesus about his actions, Jesus told him that he would remain silent for Joseph but not for others. Nevertheless, we are told that all those who spoke ill of Jesus became blind to the point where everyone recognized the power that came from Jesus's mouth in his words. Conversely, we see an adult Jesus in *Matthew 12:32 saying, "Anyone who speaks a word against the Son of Man will be forgiven, but anyone who speaks against the Holy Spirit will not be forgiven, either in this age or in the age to come."* It's clear that the Jesus from the gospel used by the infancy writer is not a vengeful Jesus like the one seen in the authentic previous Gospels, nor is he one who curses. We see Jesus pronouncing judgments in the canonical Gospels, which are difficult to compare with curses, although some texts use the word "curse" while others use "rebuke," possibly a euphemism to portray Jesus as more compassionate. We see him acting this way against the people's unbelief, which are the portions where we see him act.

Matthew 11:20-22:

Jesus curses the cities of Chorazin and Bethsaida for their lack of repentance despite witnessing many miracles. He compares their unbelief unfavorably to pagan cities like Tyre and Sidon, suggesting that those cities would have repented if they had seen the same miracles performed in Chorazin and Bethsaida. Jesus implies that the judgment will be less severe for Tyre and Sidon than for these cities.

Matthew 11:23-24:

Jesus condemns Capernaum for its pride and lack of repentance despite witnessing his miracles. He compares Capernaum's unbelief to that of Sodom, stating that if Sodom had seen the same miracles as Capernaum, it would have remained to this day. Jesus predicts a harsher judgment for Capernaum than for Sodom on the day of judgment.

Matthew 21:18-19:

Alexander Frias

Jesus encounters a fig tree on his way to the city and finds it without fruit, only leaves. He curses the fig tree, saying, "May you never bear fruit again!" Immediately, the fig tree withers. This incident is often interpreted symbolically, illustrating Jesus's authority and the importance of bearing fruit (evidence of faith and righteousness) in one's life.

These three canonical portions are where we see Jesus cursing and pronouncing judgment, but it's very important to understand that in each of these instances, Jesus is not specifically referring to a single individual. Jesus is speaking to the peoples who have been closest to Him, the peoples who have seen God's works through Him but have ignored and rejected the great opportunity God has given them to believe in the salvation sent by God, which was present among them at that very moment. This privilege was not shared by many cities. Jesus clarifies that if all those cities had had the privilege of having the Savior present, performing all the miracles done in the neighboring cities where Jesus was, they would all have repented of their evil and sin.

Jesus' judgment as the prophet of God in this instance was a clear call to repentance; otherwise, they would be brought down and ruined. We see this fulfilled when the Romans, in the late first century, unleashed their fury against the Jews throughout Israel, continuing with the Jewish persecution under Emperor Hadrian, who renamed Judea and Samaria to Palestine, expelling and killing a majority of Jews in Israel.

The curse of the fig tree is clearly a dual teaching for every reader. The cursing of the fig tree, a kind of parable, is also theologically a solemn warning for us, at least in two senses. Throughout the Old Testament, Israel is described as God's vineyard, tree, or plantation, as seen in some verses like Isaiah 5:1-7; Jeremiah 12:10; Ezekiel 17:2-10; 19:10-14. *As any Israelite or Jew dedicated to agriculture knew, the first fruits of the harvest belonged to God (Exodus 23:19;* Numbers 10:35-37), signifying their relationship with God—they were His special planting and vineyard, expected to bear spiritual fruit as a covenant people (Psalm 1:3; Jeremiah 17:8-10). Israel's

Jesus of Nazareth

fertility, whether literal or not, formed the basis of their relationship with God, as God was the one who blessed fruitfulness in Israel and the land (Deuteronomy 7:13; 28:4). The lack of fruit was a sign to the ancients of God's provoked wrath or curse upon the people for their rebellion (Deuteronomy 11:17). The time had come for God's people to bear fruit that would bless the world (Isaiah 27:6).

Repeatedly, the prophets depict God examining Israel for early figs as a sign of spiritual fertility (Micah 7:1; Jeremiah 8:13; Hosea 9:10-17), but finding none. Thus, in the two exiles—the Assyrian for Israel and the Babylonian for the Jews—God poured out His wrath in the curse of sterility, as seen in Hosea 9:16, and Israel became a rotten fig (Jeremiah 29:17). Through the prophets, God promises that one day He will replant Israel and produce healthy figs again (Joel 2:22; Amos 9:14; Micah 4:4; Zechariah 8:12; Ezekiel 36:8).

With this background of imagery in mind, Jesus' disciples would have envisioned Israel's past stories when Jesus cursed the fig tree. *The fruitless fig tree reminds us of earlier accounts when Israel was called to produce spiritual fruits (Matthew 3:8-10; 7:16-20; 13:8; Luke 3:7-9).* Nevertheless, the fig tree representing Israel itself failed once more, first by not recognizing and accepting the Son of God and Messiah, Jesus of Nazareth.

The Passover celebration, the tumult, the crowds, the chants—all are a spectacle. Jesus enters God's house of prayer and finds it a den of thieves—much action, much noise, but no justice. Leaves, but no fruit. Therefore, upon inspecting the fruitless tree, Jesus pronounces divine judgment through two symbolic acts: the future act of cursing the temple and the metaphorical curse on the fig tree. In other words, the fig tree, representing Israel—the tree that was meant to bear fruit for the whole world—was withered; Israel was about to see God's judgment both upon the people and the temple.

Theologically, we must understand that as children of God, we represent those fig trees that must always bear fruit for the world. Sometimes we bear the title of Christians but do not live or testify as Christians. The genuine and true Christian will always symbolically exude a pleasant fragrance, imitating Jesus and loving their neighbor as themselves, bearing fruit like a tree. Otherwise, when Jesus returns in His second coming, any Christian found dry and fruitless will suffer judgment and condemnation, just as Israel and Judah suffered for not valuing God's justice.

Returning to Jesus' childhood in the Infancy Gospel of Thomas, there's a scene where Joseph grabs Jesus by the ear and Jesus becomes enraged. Joseph tries to correct Jesus, who demands that Joseph look at him and says not to touch him. The author then portrays Jesus as fully divine, telling his father Joseph, *"You do not know who I am, and if you knew, you would not contradict me, because even though I am here with you, I have been created before you."* This suggests that even at the age of five, Jesus knew where he came from and that he was older than Joseph. This narrative seems to draw on John the Baptist's words: *"He who comes after me is preferred before me, whose sandal strap I am not worthy to loose."* Or perhaps it refers to Jesus' statement to the Pharisees: *"Truly, truly, I say to you, before Abraham was, I am."*

We don't know exactly where the author got the idea of a created Jesus existing before his father Joseph, but it aligns closely with the belief in a created Jesus, which reached its peak in the 4th century as Arianism. During the formation of Christianity, this heretical Christian movement called Arianism became a headache for orthodox Christianity. The orthodox Christian belief from the first century onwards was that Jesus was begotten by God, not created. The idea of a created Jesus may have originated with the Ebionites, who early on viewed Jesus as merely a man until becoming divine in his resurrection.

We don't know the exact origins of this idea, but we see it very early in the Infancy Gospel of Thomas, dated to around 150 AD in the eastern parts of Rome. Summarizing Jesus' childhood experiences in this gospel, we see Jesus entering school, where a teacher named Zacchaeus tries to teach him letters. Joseph opposes this, saying no man can teach Jesus; only God can teach him. Jesus continues, telling his teacher that he has been the Lord before all men, given the glory of the ages, and that nothing has been given to men. Jesus says he knows the days of his life and that he will be exiled.

This Jesus is portrayed as proud and disobedient. Finally, Zacchaeus asks Joseph to take the child away because no one can teach him anything he doesn't already know. This child would be capable of mastering fire and sea, becoming a teacher, a Lord, or even an angel. Jesus' response upon seeing Zacchaeus again was that he had come so that those who did not believe would believe, those who did not understand would understand, so soldiers could hear, and the dead could be resurrected.

We see this Jesus resurrecting children, healing another child's foot, and at six years old, going to fetch water. He breaks the water jar and carries the water in his clothing to his mother. We see Jesus planting wheat with his father, then harvesting and distributing it to the poor, widows, and orphans. At eight years old, we see him assisting his father Joseph in carpentry, stretching a short piece of wood to the required length.

Jesus is repeatedly taken to school to be educated, but the teacher becomes increasingly angry with Jesus, often hitting him on the head until Jesus curses him and he falls to the ground dead. Finally, Jesus is taken to another teacher who sees him differently, recognizing God's gift in Jesus and asking Joseph to take him home because only God will be his teacher. Jesus rejoices at hearing this and causes the dead teacher to come back to life.

This writer must have written this entire gospel by mixing stories from the canonical gospels, as we often see this supposed child Jesus speaking with a wisdom identical to that seen in the canonical gospels, but already as an adult. This Jesus, from two to eight years old, is nothing like the Jesus we see in the canonical gospels. He is entirely indescribable, lacking love and compassion, proud, and seemingly unaware of his purpose, because instead of loving the world, we see him cursing and causing children and adults to die.

I believe that for all our readers, after reading this brief introduction to Jesus' childhood in the Infancy Gospel of Thomas, there will be no doubt as to why it was never accepted into the biblical canon. To learn more about this gospel and broader events in Jesus' infancy, I recommend "*Los evangelios Apócrifos*" Volume 2 of Literary Criticism, by Juan Bautista Bergua and Edmundo Gonzalez Blanco.

THE BIRTH, CHILDHOOD, AND INFANCY OF JESUS IN THE PROTOEVANGELIUM OF JAMES, OR THE GOSPEL OF JAMES:

Firstly, we must not confuse this gospel with the Epistle or biblical letter of James. While there are some similarities between them—for instance, both begin with a dedication to the twelve tribes of Israel—it appears that the second writer was aware of the first letter and used it as a basis for writing. We do not know with certainty who wrote the Epistle of James in the Bible. Tradition suggests that the author could have been either of the two Jacobs present: the son of Zebedee or the brother of the Lord. Generally, the Christian Church attributes the authorship of the letter to the brother of the Lord. However, this is not a historical fact and there is no evidence supporting it. Since the early Church, it has been assumed that it was composed around 45 AD, marking it as the first book written in the New Testament. This assumption is highly questionable among scholars and historians today, as many have shown a strong possibility that the Apostle Paul was the first to write a letter to a church or community, with his first letter to the Thessalonians being the earliest book composed in the New Testament. It is notable that in Paul's thinking, justification is by faith in Jesus Christ, not by works. While Paul never abandons or belittles works, it is clear that he considered himself a laborer and preacher full of works. If we were to describe Paul's life, among all the apostles, he accomplished and did the most for his Lord. It is said that almost 70% of the New Testament can be attributed to Paul alone. Many scholars have come to the conclusion that almost every letter in the N.T with the exception of James and Jude were written with or under Pauline though. This idea accepted by some American and European scholars and Christians dedicated to biblical study has not yet been fully accepted or very openly explained with details in conservative evangelical Christianity of the Hispanic branch since it has remained in the tradition since ancient times 13 letters to Paul without much added question or explanation. The academic biblical study has come to the conclusion that between 6 or 7 are authentic letters of Paul and the rest were written by direct disciples of Paul in Pauline schools or communities. As for tradition, this was the thought and teachings received from the fathers of the church and has remained that way until today. I won't touch a lot on this subject because is not time or space for it but some respected philologists, scholars and historians like Antonio Piñero, James Tabor and many more have even argued that the other narratives letters and books in the N.T not attributed to Paul were written in response to or in agreement with Paul's theological ideas. In other words, before writing they must have read or were influenced by Paul's theology. Therefore, it is important to clarify that if the Epistle of James, as seen in chapter 2:24, shows a significant interest in emphasizing that man's justification is not by faith alone, as clearly expressed in Paul's thinking in his letters and also to the Romans, it raises questions about whether Paul had read or heard the biblical James and wanted to centralize salvation and justification as the free gift given by God to men through the unique sacrifice of Jesus the crucified, not by any man's works. We also see this type of Justification by faith much later in the gospel of Saint John and others. Generally, Jews upheld the law and believed that complete adherence to it was essential for justification or salvation. While Jesus never abolished the law, it is also clear that this was said before his death and resurrection, showing clearly that Jesus himself lived subject to and under the law. This does not imply that the law died or disappeared after his resurrection because Paul himself, on other occasions as a Jew, clearly upheld his tradition and the law, despite the fact that in the book of Hebrews, which was early on attributed by a majority to Paul, it is evident that with a new covenant, a new priest, everything changes, including a new law known as the law of Christ. This new law operates in the freedom from condemnation that the same law imposed on man. We do not conclude that the book of Hebrews belongs to Paul, but there are many indications supporting his authority. In any case, what stands out here is the clear evidence, both from God and from the apostles in the biblical texts, of God's different treatment of the Gentiles. I do not believe it necessary to elaborate on how God's treatment of the Jews concerning the Mosaic law was the same as for the Gentiles. For Paul, it is clear that even if a man keeps the entire law, he still cannot be justified, because according to his letter to the Galatians, the law cannot justify anyone. This issue seems to have displeased James, assuming he had heard or read Paul in Romans or Galatians, which were early letters from the mid-1st century.

The vast majority of historians have concluded that Paul wrote before James and that James did not agree with Paul's thinking regarding salvation or justification. It is clear that James is an epistle to Jews, which aligns with the early days of Jesus of Nazareth's followers, who were mostly Jewish. If the letter had been written after AD 50, one would expect some reference to the Gentiles who were being added to the circle of traditional Messianic Jews—Nazarenes, Ebionites—until becoming a fully Gentile Christian community. Nonetheless, our interest is not to dwell extensively on these two books. The overall purpose is for us to understand that both the apocryphal gospel we are using on this occasion and the Epistle of James in the Bible are different, and in both, Jesus of Nazareth is portrayed differently.

In the Biblical book of James, Jesus is mentioned as Jesus Christ about twice. We also see him mentioned at other times but not as Jesus, rather as the Lord. This view of Jesus is entirely theological in terms of faith because the purpose is to present him as a servant of Jesus Christ, calling the twelve tribes of Israel to remain in the faith of Jesus Christ, to have their faith placed in the glorious Jesus Christ, and then to continue to await the second coming of the Lord, which refers to Jesus Christ himself. In this epistle, we do not see James emphasizing much about the earthly life of Jesus of Nazareth, much less any details about his infancy.

However, when we read the Proto or apocryphal gospel of James, it contains information that I believe is important to share regarding the infancy of Jesus. Scholars believe that the Infancy Gospel of James (also known as the "Gospel of James" or the "Proto-Gospel of James") was written in the 2nd century, between AD 140 and 170. It was very popular in its day. The earliest copy of the Infancy

Alexander Frias

Gospel of James is a text discovered in 1958 and dated to the 4th century. The manuscript describes the birth and life of Mary, her pregnancy, and the birth of Jesus and is also classified among the apocryphal gospels.

The gospel begins with what would be Jesus' grandfather, a man named Joachim, who was extremely wealthy, and his offerings were for all the people. He officiates in atonement to the Lord for all his offenses until the Lord would show himself propitious, having arrived at the great day of the Lord. We are not exactly sure what the great day of the Lord refers to since in the Old Testament this phrase was used for different purposes. However, it tells us that on this day the children of Israel brought their offerings.

A man named Reuben stood before Jesus' grandfather and said to him, "It is not lawful for you to offer your offerings because you have not begotten." Joachim was quite saddened because he had been unable to have children. Searching through past records, he recalled how God had promised a son to Abraham and how he had answered him. Joachim, feeling very distressed, had withdrawn to the desert, pitching his tent, fasting for forty days and forty nights, saying to himself, "I will not eat or drink until the Lord, my God, visits me. Prayer will be my food and drink."

The grandmother of Jesus was named Anna. She wept for her double affliction, declaring herself a widow thinking that her husband would die, but also because she was barren. Anna also seems to remember how God gave Isaac to Sarah when she was advanced in age and barren. She found her refuge in the hope that God would answer her amid the curse she was under. An angel of the Lord appeared to her and called her name twice, saying that God had heeded her plea, that she would become pregnant, and that her progeny would be talked about throughout the earth. Anna had promised to dedicate the child, whether it be a son or daughter, entirely to the service of her Lord God. Joachim had had the same experience in the desert with an angel of the Lord, as had been told to Anna by two messengers.

Jesus of Nazareth

Immediately, we see the attitude change both in Anna and in Joachim. Apparently, even before becoming pregnant, they were already celebrating the word that the angel had given them. These stories are quite similar to the stories we already have in the Bible, although this one does not appear because the Bible, in none of the gospels or genealogies of Jesus, tells us about the grandparents of Jesus, the parents of his mother Mary.

There is such a great similarity between the grandmother of Jesus, Anna, and the mother of the prophet Samuel, who was also named Anna. Both were barren, both cried and felt unfortunate. We also see other barren women in the Bible who experienced a similar event, although all these experiences or stories are different; the point to highlight here is the equality between the names and the barrenness of both and the same promise between both. Samuel's mother, Ana, had promised to dedicate her son to the complete service of her God every day, as did the mother of Mary, Ana.

Sometimes these stories with so many congruence and similarities note that later writers, seeing a similar environment to the one Israel once had previously in the Bible, use or are influenced by and use the ideas found in the previous stories in the Bible. For example, it is clear that during the time of the judges there was no king in Israel, there was no prophet, and everyone did as seemed right to them. The Israelites or the children of Israel lived in what is known as the time of the cycle where for a moment God was with them, and at another time, God delivered them into the hands of their enemies. For almost 250 years they lived in this cycle where we see the stories of all the judges until the arrival of the prophet Samuel, where the people enter the era of the monarchs and the time of the kings. With the arrival of Samuel, the figure of the king would also come to Israel. This Joachim hoped to beget someone important who could be part of God's plan for Israel, but Anna also received a very similar message to what the angel Gabriel gave to Mary her daughter. Anna was told that her progeny would be talked about throughout the world, but Mary was told that she would be blessed among all women on earth.

We see a clear similarity between both Anna's, that both were barren, both became pregnant to bring into the world someone who would mark and save the nation of Israel from its enemies. Ana brought Samuel the prophet who found David and anointed him as the Lord's anointed, and also Anna, the mother of Mary, brought her into the world so that she too would be the womb that would bring into the world the savior Jesus of Nazareth. It is important to see these clear intentions in the writers when the moments or environments in which they find themselves are similar; generally, writers used to use a previous narrative to write their own. We see this intention very clearly in the writer of this gospel.

In order to comprehend the glorious infancy of Jesus as we see in Matthew and Luke, this apocryphal text reveals a slightly broader background prior to the birth of Jesus. This gospel, as we have seen, presents the parents of Mary, who would be the grandparents of Jesus, but now it will show the birth of Mary, who would later become the mother of Jesus of Nazareth.

In this gospel, it is evident that the writer tried to maintain the story with fewer supernatural events than we see in some of the other gospels. When Anna's months were completed, at the ninth month, she gave birth to a girl. As the legal days passed, Anna washed herself, breastfed the girl, and named her Mary. At six months, something slightly unusual, although most likely normal, happened: the girl took about seven steps walking. After this, Anna decided to lift her, take her, and separate her from anything that could contaminate, stain, or make her impure.

When the girl reached one year old, the priests, scribes, and elders blessed the girl, praying to God over her, asking Him to grant her a name that would be repeated for ages and generations. Obviously, here we are already seeing that before Jesus, the birth of Mary is also glorious. The biblical text does not emphasize the birth of Mary because the purpose of the gospels is to point to the history of man's redemption through the anointed one and Messiah Jesus of Nazareth. We see special attention and blessing on Mary since the same angel tells her that she will be very blessed among all women.

Jesus of Nazareth

We do not know how much this apocryphal text can be certain, but it is worth saying that if we see many apocryphal sources used in the canonical texts, for the mother of the savior of the world to be something special, it would have to be.

Especially from the sons of David or from the tribe of Judah, from which both Joseph and Mary come, who would be king over Israel. These are part of the reasons why in the universal Christian church, Mary is viewed with great esteem. From the early centuries in Orthodox Christianity, Mary became more and more an object of admiration and veneration, to the point that some have even worshiped her. Mary was seen as the mother of God or God incarnate in Jesus the Word from as early as the 3rd century. By this early age of the church, we find prayers, devotions, or hymns to Mary as seen in the "*Sub tuum praesidium.*"

Not everyone saw Mary as the mother of God; many saw her as the mother of Jesus the man but not the mother of the divine part or the Word of Jesus, which would be equal to God. In the Council of Ephesus in 431, we see the issue arise due to the confusion among the bishops, which is what we know as the problem between Nestorius, Patriarch of Constantinople, and Cyril, Patriarch of Alexandria, whether Mary would be seen as the mother of Jesus or the mother of God "Theotokos" or if she would be seen as the mother of Jesus the man "Christotokos."

This question was quite confusing since the Nicene Creed established showed Jesus as of the same substance as the Father, begotten and not created, and God of God. Jesus was already seen as the same God and one with God, so the question arose if Mary was the mother of this Jesus, then she would also be the mother of God, as Jesus was seen as God. In the end, Cyril's view, as originally established by the Nicene Creed, prevailed, granting Mary the title "Theotokos."

Later, over the centuries, we see in the Second Vatican Council that Mary is pronounced as the mother of the Church. All these councils established up to some of the last dogmas established in the Catholic

Church about Mary, for example, the "Assumption of the Blessed Virgin Mary" by the Catholic Church, whose doctrine was defined as a dogma of faith by Pope Pius XII on November 1, 1950, which establishes that the mother of Jesus Christ, having completed the course of her earthly life, was taken up body and soul into heaven.

As we see, Mary's figure among the many centuries of the Church's existence evolved more and more into a figure, if possible to say, also divine along with Jesus, since flesh and blood cannot inherit the kingdom of God. Jesus himself said that no one had ascended to heaven, nor do we have any credible textual evidence that shows that Jesus' mother had ascended body and soul into heaven. With all due respect, I do not agree or believe, along with many serious historians and scholars, in this kind of evolutionary veneration or view towards Mary that the Catholic Church has given her since they have been invented by themselves over time.

These are the reasons why from very early on not all Christians saw Mary in the same way as the universal church saw her. It is clear in my opinion that the evolutionary veneration towards Mary by the universal Christian church has been at fault and has been part of the reason why most Protestants do not render her any kind of veneration or the same importance that Catholics do to the mother of our savior.

Many Protestant Christians see Mary as a common womb without special attention. Personally, I choose to adhere to what the canonical text offers us, and it is also that Mary was not just any womb, as some suppose. This young woman clearly, as the canonical text of Luke tells us, was highly favored. I believe that it can be said that there was no woman in the entire 1st century and the centuries to come with the gift that was given to her, giving life to the most extraordinary man who has ever existed on our earth.

We see an elderly woman who was also blessed in this same 1st century, and it was Elizabeth, the mother of the prophet John the Baptist, who will canonically be the one who will pave the way for Jesus of Nazareth. The synoptic indicate that this John will be the one to baptize Jesus in the Jordan. An interesting piece of information, and a question that we sometimes tend to ask ourselves is why biblical characters were given the names they received, and why they all end their lives fulfilling the meaning of the same name they received at birth. It is true that the "prophecy" story is believed to have been inspired and revealed before what was written as the biblical text says in;

2 Peter 1:21:

"For no prophecy was ever produced by the will of man, but men spoke from God as they were carried along by the Holy Spirit." (ESV)

2 Timothy 3:16:

"All Scripture is breathed out by God and profitable for teaching, for reproof, for correction, and for training in righteousness." (ESV)

According to religious confessional thought, God himself inspired the prophets and writers as we see or interpret in the biblical text. This is the broader reason that shows us that the names given to biblical characters were given to them to fulfill a function that was previously predicted in God's plan. Some scholars have said that the vast majority of people in the Bible were not called by the names the text calls them, but the names were given scripturally according to the purpose fulfilled in their lives.

As an example, let's use a name that we know was a real and true name from archaeology. Suppose King David's real name was not actually David, but there was indeed a youngest son among eight in the household of a man named Jesse, who later became king in Israel, becoming the beloved and favored one. When writing the story of this character, the writers or authors would give him the name David because he fulfilled the characteristics of what the name means. This is just one example used to show how historians think biblical characters may have received their names.

Consensually, David is a historical figure, and we know this from the evidence that archaeology has found with his name and his house inscribed on very ancient stones dated to the 13th and 9th centuries BCE. For more complete information, you can search for "The Tel Dan Inscription" and find more information.

With this said, regarding the name given to Mary by her mother Anna, some information that sheds a little light on why Mary's naming appears in the Protoevangelium of James is shared in "Literary Criticism" in its first volume of the apocryphal gospels by Juan Bautista Bergua. In one of the comments, it says the following:

"It is curious and worth observing that all the women near Jesus, out of admiration or worship towards him—Mary Magdalene, Mary the sister of Martha, Mary his mother, etc.—all have the same name in the story. It is true that this name could have been quite common or well-known in the 1st century. Moreover, in Asia, the mother of a god (especially if he was a redeeming god) almost always had a name that began with the syllable 'ma,' among others mentioned by the orientalist Jensen: Mary, Mariamna, Maya (the mother of Buddha), Maritala (the mother of Krishna), Mary of Mariandinio of Bithynia, and Mandane (the mother of Cyrus), whom the Jews considered as the Lord's messiah, as in Isaiah 45:1, we read the following:"

Isaiah 45:1 *(RV1960):*

"Thus says the Lord to his anointed, to Cyrus, whose right hand I have grasped, to subdue nations before him and to loose the belts of kings, to open doors before him that gates may not be closed:"

This verse from Isaiah 45:1 refers to God's message to Cyrus, calling him His anointed one (or His chosen one). God speaks of taking Cyrus by the hand to empower him to conquer nations and defeat kings. The imagery of opening doors that remain open symbolizes divine favor and success in Cyrus's endeavors.

This Mary of Nazareth, daughter of David, will be much greater than those who came before her in previous stories because she will bring into the world the mighty Jesus of Nazareth. This shows us the likely reason behind the Proto-Santiago author's thinking and the importance of Mary's naming by Anna, with the present inclusion of the Lord and His angels as seen from the beginning in her sterility and advanced age. Both Anna and Joachim remember the story of Abraham and Sarah while they are separated in different areas, where an angel appeared to them announcing a child (Isaac). We see this same congruence as soon as Joachim and Anna recall the story of Abraham and Sarah. Clearly, Santiago is using the story of Abraham and Sarah, first for the similarity in age and sterility, but also to announce that something great would come from the loins of Anna and Joachim—the true fulfillment of God's promise made to Abraham in Genesis. Santiago is announcing the imminent arrival of the great promise—the birth of Mary but more importantly, that of Jesus of Nazareth.

The birth of Jesus could not be an ordinary or common birth, especially if it would herald the arrival of the most anticipated Messiah in all of Israel. We see that in all the births of revered figures before Jesus in different historical accounts, their births were in some way glorious. Jesus's birth would not lack glory, however humanely the writers might attempt to narrate it. Some of the most powerful nations would have to be involved in this matter since this Jesus will be the savior of the whole world. Babylon and Persia, known as the East, both nations where the Jews were in captivity for many years, are where the great hope of a true Messiah who would bring them peace and true freedom emerged. Therefore, with the arrival of this child, the announcement would have to reach these nations where many Jews had remained in Babylon or Persia since the 6th century, not returning to Israel.

With the arrival of the Magi (wise men) from the East (possibly Persia or Babylon), we clearly see the announcement and fulfillment of the "messianic era" that the Jews themselves had been awaiting since the exodus from Babylon and Persia. Before delving into the important birth of Jesus in this proto-gospel, there are some important points I would like to share. The author indicates that at Mary's two years, Joachim wanted to take her to the temple to fulfill the promise made to the Lord to dedicate her to temple service.

Anna, her mother, suggested waiting until she was three years old. By the time Mary reached three years old, the story progresses until Mary is a young adult of 12 years old. It is no coincidence that this gospel, like the canonical gospels, and as previously mentioned regarding Jesus at 12 years old in the temple, portrays Maria at 12 years old as quite mature and ready for marriage. In traditional Rabbinic Jewish thought from the early centuries of our era, it is known that a young girl is considered Bat Mitzvah at 12 years old, and a boy at 13 is Bar Mitzvah. But do we know why these ages were established? In principle, psychologically and biologically, the ages of 12 and 13 mark the entry into adolescence for young people. Moreover, in ancient times, their emotional maturity and societal role were considered adult-like at that age. The priests, seeing that Mary was of marriageable age, compelled her to enter the Holy of Holies to petition the priest Zechariah on her behalf. Apparently, this priest will likely be the same father of John the Baptist, as we will later see him struck mute, as recounted in the Gospel of Luke. While Zechariah was in the Holy of Holies, an angel of the Lord appeared to him, instructing him to gather all the widowers of the town, and the Lord would perform a sign to choose a companion for Mary. It is at this point that Joseph the carpenter appears, setting aside his tools to join the priest and other widowers. Each widower held a rod, and after some prayers, the priest collected and then returned the rods. It turned out that a dove had emerged from Joseph's rod and flew over his head. These signs James mentions were well-known in biblical narratives to many of the chosen. For instance, the rod's significance is reminiscent of God's interaction with Moses, who was instructed to gather rods from each of the Israelites' households; among the 12 rods collected, only Aaron's had sprouted flowers and almonds, indicating God's public priestly election among his people. James uses these same symbols to signify Joseph's selection.

However, James does not just use the rod; he also notes Mary's age of 12 years during Jesus' temple encounter at the same age. This gospel highlights two significant differences in Catholic and evangelical thought: James suggests that Joseph was a widower, which is not found in the biblical text, and that Joseph was old, which is plausible, assuming the brothers or siblings mentioned in the biblical text could have been Joseph's children from a previous marriage. This is why the universal Catholic Church upholds the doctrine of Mary's perpetual virginity—before, during, and after Jesus—despite most Protestant Christians believing that Mary had other children after Jesus.

While Mary was in the temple, fetching water, a voice said to her, "Hail, Mary, full of grace, the Lord is with thee; blessed art thou amongst women." Startled, she returned home, where an angel of the Lord appeared to her, reassuring her not to fear because she had found favor with the Lord. Mary responded, questioning how she could conceive, to which the angel replied that she would conceive by the Holy Spirit, and the child would be named Jesus, who would save his people from their sins.

James's narrative closely mirrors the biblical account with few differences. Notably, Mary hears a voice before encountering the angel at home, which differs from the Bible, where there is no prior voice but an encounter with the angel. It's interesting that James doesn't initially name the angel in his narrative, unlike the biblical text, where the angel is identified as Gabriel from the outset.

From an early stage of Mary's pregnancy, close relatives recognized the child's significance. When Mary visited Elizabeth, she greeted Mary as the mother of her Lord, acknowledging the greatness of the child within her. James portrays Mary's conception similarly to the Synoptic Gospels, attributing it to the Holy Spirit. During Mary's labor, a bright cloud enveloped her, and the attending midwife witnessed miraculous signs heralding the Savior's birth in Israel. The midwife, astonished by the light, couldn't believe a virgin had given birth until she examined Mary's virginity, which when doubted, led to her hand being consumed by fire, a punishment from God. Seeking forgiveness and healing, she was visited by an angel who directed her to take the baby Jesus, promising health and joy.

James repeatedly emphasizes Mary's virginity, a point highly regarded in the Catholic Church. He also begins to reveal the identity of the one who will bring healing and salvation to the unbelievers and the sick—Jesus. We see Jesus performing miraculous healings from childhood, hinting at his extraordinary nature. While the reliability of James's proto-gospel may be questioned, it underscores that true healing and salvation come only through Jesus of Nazareth, the most extraordinary man on earth. As the midwife named Salome cried out to God for healing, she was directed to Jesus, symbolizing the need to approach Jesus in faith for healing and restoration in all areas of life.

The infancy narrative of Jesus concludes in this book with the entry of the priest Simeon into the temple, guided by the Holy Spirit, as seen in canonical texts. Mary and Joseph bring the child to be presented, and Simeon asks to be dismissed by God after witnessing the salvation of all Israel with his own eyes.

THE BIRTH AND CHILDHOOD IN THE ARAB GOSPEL OF THE INFANCY OF JESUS

This gospel is traditionally believed to have been written using some other apocryphal texts, along with some canonical ones, especially that of John. Some portions are plausible and align with parts in the canonical gospels, while others clearly appear exaggerated and depart significantly from common ideas and timelines. This is a rather lengthy gospel of around 55 chapters; we will focus only on some of the miracles concerning the birth and infancy of Jesus. Otherwise, to read it in full, you can obtain it elsewhere.

Jesus speaks from the cradle:

This gospel begins by telling us that these words were found in the book of Josephus, the high priest who existed at the time of Christ; some had said it was Caiaphas. Caiaphas (Joseph Caiaphas) was a contemporary high priest of Jesus, cited several times in the New Testament. The Jewish historian Flavius Josephus states that Caiaphas assumed the high priesthood around the year 18 AD, and according to the gospels, Caiaphas was the high priest when Jesus was condemned to die on the cross. In this gospel about the infancy of Jesus, we see Jesus from his childhood displaying incredible abilities and knowing from infancy that he was the Son of God. To begin with, we see Jesus, while in the cradle, already speaking and saying to his mother, *"I am the Word, Son of God, whom you have borne, as the angel Gabriel announced to you, and my Father has sent me to save the world."* Stories and depictions of Jesus like these were among those that led to the destruction or burning of such apocryphal texts. It is true that there were Gnostic Christian communities that used such gospel stories among themselves, but these stories were so exaggerated that their clear intent was to diminish Jesus' full humanity. If indeed Jesus spoke from infancy in the cradle, what would be the purpose of his growth or even being born as a child with adult consciousness? We can understand why the authors of this gospel wanted to depict Jesus speaking from the cradle. Firstly, the composition of this gospel dates back to the 5th or 6th century, and secondly, this Arabic gospel is believed to have been written in Syria. Some scholars suggest that the gospel may have circulated as an oral tradition centuries earlier, but its composition in Greek dates to the mentioned late centuries. With that said, by the 5th and 6th centuries, we see the rise of Islam in the Middle East, which is why the Islamic Quran contains some stories similar to those in this apocryphal Arabic gospel and others. What strikes me as quite possible is that while these authors were writing, they did so with the intention of competing with stories or births of other gods or deities. Considering that Buddhism reached Europe by the 3rd century BC, it's not improbable that many Buddhist stories could have passed through the Middle East to the West. It is said that there was contact between Europeans and Buddhists around the time of Alexander the Great's conquests in northern India. If this is true, how impossible would it be that some 700 or 800 years later, these Christian writers used even Buddhist religious sayings in their books to exalt Jesus above all other beliefs? With this in mind, I share one of the miracles attributed to Siddhartha Gautama, known as the Buddha and traditionally considered the founder of Buddhism.

It is said that immediately after his birth, he stood up and said:

"I am the firstborn,

The most ancient in the world,

Above all, I am in the world.

This is my last birth.

There is no more becoming.

There is nothing more to achieve."

It is also said that wherever the child Buddha stepped, a lotus flower bloomed. It is also said that he was born from an immaculate conception through a dream in which his mother saw a white elephant, indicating a voluntary transmigration.

Jesus of Nazareth

https://en.wikipedia.org/wiki/Miracles_of_Gautama_Buddha

I'm not entirely sure if this thought is common in Buddhist tradition or religion, but it's clear that from the childhood of this figure who was born around 500 years before Jesus, he was born with teeth and speaking like a full adult. I see the intention behind this miracle or attitude in Jesus as a complete hyperbole that was not authentic or true. We cannot say that the authors' intentions were malicious or to discredit Jesus of Nazareth, because they likely tried to create miracles and events to exalt Jesus of Nazareth from birth. However, I believe that being a complete human being, Jesus was subject to each stage, process, and normal life like any other human being. Jesus was the perfect example in life for humanity; from a child, he was born humbly in poverty. The reason we do not have all the stories of Him is precisely because it was not until He recognized His great responsibility in the world, revealing the reality that He had to wait like everyone else and before Him to begin fulfilling His purpose on earth. I believe that if this Jesus had known everything as we sometimes assume, disregarding His humanity, He would have written everything down from the beginning to avoid confusion among those who are confused about Him. The infancy gospel, despite having many similar stories to the canonical gospels, contains a very important detail that we do not find in the canonical gospels, and that is as follows,

The Magi come to Jesus

On the very night that Jesus was born in Bethlehem of Judea, this gospel tells us that a guardian angel was sent to "Persia". This angel appeared to the people of Persia in the form of a very bright star that illuminated the entire land of the Persians. The writer tells us (this date was the same as the feast of Christ's birth) on the 25th of the first Kanum. Throughout the centuries, we know that this date changed several times. We know that Jesus was not born on December 25th as commonly celebrated, but it is extremely important to pay attention to what was celebrated and carried out in the Persian world during this time. The celebration of "Mithra" took place during this period.

Mithra was a solar god of Persia, whose cult eventually spread to India and throughout the Roman Empire. According to the Belgian writer Franz Cumont, in his study published in the early 20th century, the origin of Mithraism can be traced back to ancient Persia (modern-day Iran). The origin of this Persian deity can be traced back to the 2nd millennium BC; his name is first mentioned in a treaty between the Hittites and the Mitanni, written around 1400 BC. Mithra in the Avesta means 'contract' or 'alliance'. He was the god responsible for providing protection during attacks, protecting the faithful and punishing the unfaithful. He was also depicted in a chariot drawn by white horses. Mithra was the possessor of truth. His act of killing a bull was a cosmogonic act comparable to the slaying of the dragon Vritra carried out by the god Indra, an epic first mentioned in the Rig-Veda (the oldest text in India, from the mid-2nd millennium BC). By 62 BC, Roman legionaries adopted Mithra as a god, adding non-Persian characteristics and creating a religion called Mithraism that rapidly spread throughout the Roman Empire and competed with nascent Christianity until the 4th century.

Scholarly consensus in Zoroastrianism identifies a connection in the origin of the deity Ahura Mazda with the prototypical gods Mitra and Varuna (Varuna), but there is no established consensus on whether Ahura Mazda is one of the two, a syncretism of both, or even superior to both. (https://en.wikipedia.org/wiki/Mithra_(Persian_deity).

This detail shared by this gospel about the birth of Jesus is extremely important because it takes us back to when the Jews were in Babylon and also in Persia for many years. It was there that they learned a great deal of the cultures, languages, and religious forms of Second Temple Judaism. When the Jews returned to Israel (Jerusalem), they carried with them all the hopes of a Messiah who would one day liberate them and bring them everlasting peace. With the return of all those who came back, and also with all the Jews who remained

Jesus of Nazareth

in Babylon and later Persia, the hope of someday seeing the long-awaited coming of this savior to the world, as prophesied by the prophets, especially "Isaiah," remained in their thoughts for all those centuries. Persia had much to do with the arrival of this Messiah "Jesus" because with the large number of Jews who remained in Babylon, they would never have heard the news of the long-awaited Messiah's birth if somehow the God of Israel had not sent this angel to the wise men in the East and the people in Persia. The reason this long-awaited news reached the wise Persian "magi" was that they had known it from about five centuries earlier. Some theologians and traditionalists say that these Persians came to know these prophecies and the coming of the Son of God through the wisdom and astrological schools of the prophet Daniel, on whom rested the Spirit of the God of Israel, which for the Persians would have been very similar to Ahura Mazda himself. We know that Daniel was an apocalyptic prophet and prophesied extensively about the Son of Man, who is the same image and typification of Christ in the canonical gospels. We see a strong possibility that through the Jews, the Persians themselves viewed this arrival as the visitation of the Son of Ahura Mazda, who was to them the creator God of light and fire. This writer goes further in the data he shares; he tells us that Zoroaster, who was the greatest of the prophets of Ahura Mazda in the Persian religion of Zoroastrianism, predicted and prophesied the coming of Jesus of Nazareth, the Son of God. This religious union between Persia and Israel (Jerusalem) is quite obvious. We cannot ignore how much sense it makes that this angel reached Persia to announce this great event. If this gospel, among all the miracles mentioned of Jesus, manages to capture the reader's attention, I believe that the most important piece of information in this gospel is the one we just shared about the news of the arrival of Jesus the Messiah through the angel to the wise men of the East "Persia," as also mentioned by Matthew. With that said, I believe we also have some reasons to validate why December 25th is used as the date on which the birth of Jesus of Nazareth, the Son of God, is celebrated. There are other historically significant reasons why the birth of Jesus is celebrated on this date according to Roman Christian tradition. I will not go into detail because it is not the focus at the moment, but I will say that when Christians chose a date for a celebration like this, it was not to conceal other festivals or celebrations to other gods. It is clear that on this date, pagans had their festivities for whatever gods they worshipped. In Rome, there were a considerable number of festivals celebrated throughout the year. A book I recommend for more information about Roman festivals is "The Roman Festivals of the period of the Republic" by W. Warde Fowler; there you will understand the Roman calendar and the many festivals held throughout the Roman year, with about 354 days by 165 AD, there were about 135 days of festivals dedicated to an emperor, a god, or some imperial reason in the culture. With that said, it is obvious that among Roman Christians, the celebrations they once had in their pagan and social world were changed to Christian celebrations. Generally, not only the Romans, but all nations, peoples, and tribes, when they migrated to foreign territories as captives or were exported in one way or another, their cultural and religious customs changed, mixed, or were reformed more and more over time until they became totally different from what they once were. This idea is seen in the Roman pagan world, with the celebration called "Saturnalia" dedicated to Saturn, which there is evidence continued to be celebrated in the Roman Empire for another century before the Roman Empire became Christian during the same period or around the celebration of Jesus' birth in December. However, I must clarify that Roman Christians never intended to celebrate or commemorate the "Saturnalia" festival; rather, they celebrated the birth of Jesus as a better and greater celebration of the arrival of the Son of God, the Christ, while pagans continued their festivities until Christianity dominated the entire empire and gradually the Saturnalia festival disappeared, leaving only the unique celebration of the glorious birth of Jesus of Nazareth as Christmas.

Jesus of Nazareth

The diapers of Jesus free the possessed

Since Mary and Joseph went to Egypt, as Matthew tells us, because of Herod's massacre of the children, we hear a story. As soon as they arrived in Egypt, the story goes that there was a priest who lived near idols to serve them, and a demon spoke to him from inside a statue. This priest was well known in Egypt, and whenever someone wanted to know something, they went and consulted the priest. He was the one who answered all the divine oracles for the people in Egypt. He had a son of about thirty years who was possessed by various demons. When the demons seized him, he would tear his clothes, walk around naked, and attack people with stones. Immediately, we see a tradition that was likely taken from the Gospel of Mark or Matthew, mentioning the famous Gadarene demoniac who walked naked among the tombs.

When Mary and Joseph arrived in Egypt, it seems the priests recognized their arrival due to a supposed earthquake. The priests said that an invisible and mysterious god had arrived, who had hidden within him a son similar to himself, and the passage of this son had shaken our land. The arrival of the child Jesus in Egypt disturbed all the priests, especially the one everyone admired. The arrival of Jesus in Egypt caused this priest to say in his own words, "We must adopt the worship of this invisible and mysterious god. He is the true God, and there is no other to serve, for he is truly the Son of the Highest."

We see that the authors are beginning to show what the presence of Jesus would provoke upon arrival in different places. Egypt was one of the largest empires in all of history, and the people of Israel had almost all their history and formation there. It is clear that what Israel could never accomplish with its presence there for over 400 years in all its history, now with just the arrival and presence of the child Jesus in Egypt, all of Egypt would change to worship only the one God and Father of Jesus Christ. The author's intention is to show us that the presence of Jesus contains all the absolute power to transform the earth and human beings.

One day, the demon-possessed son of the priest passed by where Mary, the mother of Jesus, was hanging Jesus's washed diapers. The possessed young man took one of Jesus's diapers and put it on his head. The moment the young man put Jesus's diaper on his head, the demons that were over his life left, and the young man was free and healed. The young man began to praise and thank God for restoring his health.

From this point on, we begin to see a series of miracles happening only with Jesus's diapers. We see him liberating travelers captured by bandits, a possessed young woman who could not bear any clothes on herself—walking naked all the time—and breaking chains and living in the wilderness. This life is not far from many young people whom we see daily with a complete lack of self-esteem; some feel despised. These chains speak of the weight of oppression and pressure they receive from such an opulent society or from a world that truly does not value them.

The knowledge of real evil, which we see running and increasing every day in humanity or life without Jesus, led both men and women to feel the inner shame of their spiritual and physical nakedness. We cannot doubt that possibly the first humans never wore or covered themselves with anything until their consciences were seduced or incited to know the shame of guilty evil. This was known when, through ignorance, one part allowed itself to be seduced and empowered the evil one to show the manifestation and inner feeling of guilty shame, which would then fall upon both, which feels it later to do what should never have been done.

We live in a time where this guilty shame has disappeared; everything seems normal, both good and bad are no longer valued. So much so that even those influenced by evil generally have no way to solve it unless through the same substances provided to temporarily calm the attitude and character of human beings. Jesus is the living example and the best encounter for changing a life. Jesus can change and heal people, characters, attitudes, habits, young people, adults, the elderly, families, marriages, weaknesses, or any situation in life that is willing to look at Him and give Him a chance to become the best friend anyone could ever have.

One of Jesus's diapers was placed by Mary on the possessed young woman; instantly, the demon, cursing and screaming, left that woman, freed from her afflictions, she returned to herself, confused by her nakedness, avoiding people, she covered herself with Jesus's diaper, running home, she dressed, and told others her story.

It is true that Jesus's diapers are not and were not the means of power; the power is Jesus himself. It seems that this same belief is seen among Christian communities very early on in the Acts of the Apostles:

Acts 19:12

"so that even handkerchiefs or aprons that had touched his skin were taken to the sick, and their illnesses were cured and the evil spirits left them." NIV

Luke 8:43-46

"And a woman was there who had been subject to bleeding for twelve years, but no one could heal her. She came up behind him and touched the edge of his cloak, and immediately her bleeding stopped. 'Who touched me?' Jesus asked. When they all denied it, Peter said, 'Master, the people are crowding and pressing against you.' But Jesus said, 'Someone touched me; I know that power has gone out from me.'"

If we see that people or the early Nazarene Christians believed they could be healed, cured, and even freed from demons by the handkerchiefs or aprons of the apostles, how much more would they be liberated by the very cloths or garments of Jesus? One of the most preached and dramatized miracles in the Christian church is that of the woman with the issue of blood. Jesus, now an adult in a crowded place, is approached by a woman who, with just a touch of the edge of His garment, is instantly healed to the extent that Jesus Himself was unaware of who had touched Him. We see the intention of Luke clearly as he wrote this passage in his gospel. Luke is telling us plainly that the power of Jesus operates in two parts: first in Jesus

Himself, and secondly in the faith within the sick woman. She had tried and spent everything, and everything was getting worse for her, but upon hearing about Jesus, she took the courage to approach Him in faith, believing that something could come from Him. Our faith in Jesus, whatever form it may take, however minimal we may think of Him, can enable miracles and grant us the freedom we need. For a long time, men have tried to manipulate how God through Jesus and His Spirit can perform works and wonders, but in this work it is clear that men have no power and cannot manipulate or limit the faith that God has given us. Jesus' words were clear when He said, "If you can believe, all things are possible to him who believes." Jesus can perform the miracle in the life of anyone who believes in Him and puts their faith in Him.

This woman had come out of the deserts, representing solitary, open, or secluded places away from human presence. Jesus' interest in our lives is not for us to live isolated in solitude from the world or people. God created us in the perfect image of His Son Jesus, and just as He sent Him into the world to be seen and saved by Him, He has now revealed the same image of Jesus in us so that we can be like a mirror to the world, upon which they too can receive the revelation and enlightenment of the truth that they were not created to live in depression, oppression, loneliness, or sadness, but rather in joy, peace, love, and happiness above all circumstances they may face on this earth, living through the words that Jesus Himself left us when He said:

Matthew 11:29;

Take my yoke upon you and learn from me, for I am gentle and humble in heart, and you will find rest for your souls. For my yoke is easy and my burden is light. (RV1960)

John 14:27;

Peace I leave with you; my peace I give you. I do not give to you as the world gives. Do not let your hearts be troubled and do not be afraid. (RV1960)

Jesus of Nazareth

John 16:33;

I have told you these things, so that in me you may have peace. In this world you will have trouble. But take heart! I have overcome the world. (RV1960)

Jesus asks us to learn from Him, and we will find rest, as He Himself is the peace in this world where there is no peace; only He can give us complete peace. Jesus, by His example, taught us that even when the yoke or burden of life is great, it can be carried easily and lightly on our shoulders. This is a sign that the peace, strength, and hope He gives us can surpass anything that comes against or upon our lives. The peace Jesus offers is not momentary, temporary, or hypocritical like that offered by the world and its armies. In its environment and context, Rome and the emperors offered a false peace by conquering other nations, killing, and through military force, thinking they would have the power to rule over all the earth without knowing that in just one day the entire empire would fall into the hands of another empire. This is because all empires raised by humans have a day of beginning and also a day of downfall; all will fall before the only empire that has not fallen and will not fall—the empire of Jesus the Christ—because it is not an empire created by humans and even less by human government. "My kingdom is not of this world." Even the mystical rabbinic Judaism offered a supposed peace, but neither the Roman Empire nor any mystical religion can give the peace that only Jesus of Nazareth offers to the world. He can offer it because He has it and has conquered it. Jesus said all these things, letting His followers know, just as He had said everything before they happened. He warned them not to forget to manifest the peace He would leave them when He ascended to the Father, so that we never doubt the victory He gave us, making us conquerors together with Him.

Jesus liberates a mute young woman

One day, as Mary and Joseph were walking with Jesus in their arms, they passed through a village where a wedding celebration was taking place. Among the crowd gathered there was a young woman who had been struck mute by the cunning of the demon and the actions of wicked enchanters. Her ears and tongue paralyzed, the young woman had lost all memory of using speech. When Mary carried Jesus in her arms and the young woman saw the child, she took Him, kissed Him, and pressed Him to her chest. The child exhaled upon her, immediately causing her ears to open and her tongue to move (to speak). In this miracle, we see something somewhat similar but not entirely the same as the canonical stories where a mute young man was freed by Jesus.

There has been speculation as to whether this young woman was truly demon-possessed. Science, with the evolution of knowledge, has revealed that muteness or deafness has nothing to do with demons, as there are thousands of faithful believers in God who have these difficulties. First, we must understand the worldview and how people viewed life in past centuries, in this case, the 1st century of our era in the Middle East. Generally, it was believed that all human afflictions were somehow caused by the divine; whenever something occurred in nature or human life, some god was involved in the matter. This kind of thinking is seen from the Old Testament to the Roman Empire, including all nations or empires that existed in between. With this said, Jesus, being a product of His time, was well aware of the prevailing thoughts of His era. Jesus did not come to change the earthly worldview of human thought on things; it is obvious that over time, all things change—cultures, languages, tongues, names, places, religions, humans themselves, etc. We do not know the past life of this mute and deaf young person; the writers do not provide much information. It is very possible that the cause of her muteness or deafness was not directly caused by a demon, but the demon could influence the cause. There are natural causes in life, but once damage occurs, I see the possibility that the evil one can influence thoughts, making the young person believe that her situation will never improve, draining and demotivating her, which can lead to further complications. The influence of the evil one on natural conditions often leads a soul to complete oppression or depression. What we mean by this is that the evil one is not depression or oppression, but the instigator who influences the

Jesus of Nazareth

emotional and earthly manifestations of human beings. It is very possible that Jesus knew the situation well. If it were not a demon involved, He would have said, as He once did, "Neither this man nor his parents sinned, but this happened so that the works of God might be displayed in him." However, we do not see these words from Jesus on this occasion. In this young person's situation, we see Jesus rebuke the demon, and immediately she regains her hearing and speech.

Any interpretation we attempt to make will only be a personal reinterpretation, as we do not have the original thoughts of the writer. It was believed that this young person's condition was somehow related to the presence of a demon in her life, whether directly or not. The important thing is that when Jesus arrives, the evil one must depart; when Jesus arrives, everything must change. This young person was mute, indicating she could not speak, and especially deaf, indicating she could not hear—the most important way to know God's word and have the necessary faith to serve and draw near to God is through hearing and hearing the word of God. If Jesus gives us the power to speak and also to hear, I believe the purpose is for us to speak of Him and also to hear from Him, to put all our senses in Jesus. This young woman was similarly liberated and healed by Jesus; she praised God, and there was great joy among the villagers, and they believed in God. Jesus can fix our vocabulary, our ways of speaking, and also change our hearing to listen to better things that can edify us and do good for us. In addition to the many miraculous liberations we see Jesus perform in this gospel, we also see a wide range of other miracles. We have Jesus performing a number of miracles on children, even curing them with the water used to bathe Jesus. People would take this water in which they bathed Jesus to wash other children, and they would be healed. It also contains a large number of healings of lepers, including Thomas and Judas Iscariot, who will later become His closest apostolic disciples. To this Thomas, Jesus in His childhood heals him from a deadly disease, and to Judas Iscariot, Jesus, at only 3 years old, liberates him by expelling a demon from him. With this said, it seems that these disciples had already known Jesus for a long time before; in reality, the Bible does not show us how long they had known each other before their canonical encounters. In addition to all these miracles, healings, liberations, and resurrections performed by Jesus, there are many more that the reader can continue reading about in this apocryphal Arabic gospel of the infancy of Jesus. It also shows how Jesus, from His childhood, supposedly already knew that one day He would die crucified alongside two thieves who had known Him well, whom the writer calls Tito and Dumaco. The general tradition has different names for these two thieves; the Bible never tells us what they were called, although it is quite possible that at least one of them was known—the one called the good thief, who reached paradise. When the one on the left asks Jesus, "Aren't you the Messiah? Save yourself and us too," the one on the right rebukes him, saying, "Don't you fear God? We are receiving the due punishment for our deeds; but this man has done nothing wrong." These words spoken by this character were probably not improvised, simply because there are commentators who tell us that these two thieves could have belonged to the circle of Jewish rebel zealots who had Barabbas the evildoer as the head of their sect. They were known as dangerous Jewish rebels who carried sharp daggers under their sleeves and, as soon as they had the opportunity to harm a Roman soldier secretly, they would do so. Later, the Jews would ask Pilate to release Barabbas instead of crucifying Jesus, as was customary every year, releasing one prisoner, and on that occasion, they asked Pilate to release the thief and put to death the only righteous man, Jesus of Nazareth. Some commentators tell us that this good thief could have walked with Jesus in His life, could have heard much from Him, just like the other who asked Jesus if He was the Messiah. In any case, we see the degree of internal justice in the life of this evildoer who recognizes exactly the extent of his wickedness for which he suffers crucifixion. In the world, there are many kinds of people, but this kind of internal recognition that we see in this man God will never overlook. This is akin to the parable that Jesus once shared when He said:

Luke 18:10-14;

Jesus of Nazareth

"Two men went up to the temple to pray, one a Pharisee and the other a tax collector. The Pharisee stood by himself and prayed: 'God, I thank you that I am not like other people—robbers, evildoers, adulterers—or even like this tax collector. I fast twice a week and give a tenth of all I get.' But the tax collector stood at a distance. He would not even look up to heaven, but beat his breast and said, 'God, have mercy on me, a sinner.' I tell you that this man, rather than the other, went home justified before God. For all those who exalt themselves will be humbled, and those who humble themselves will be exalted." (NIV)

Repentance and acknowledgment are the greatest keys to entering the kingdom of heaven or the kingdom of God. The call and preaching that John, Jesus, and His apostles most emphasized was that of repentance for the forgiveness of sins. Finally, we see this thief, standing to the right of Jesus on the cross, become a support for Jesus Himself. We see him repentant, suffering death alongside Jesus (the place that Paul would later desire), acknowledging Jesus as righteous and as the one who will come alive in His kingdom. This thief becomes an example for all of us, showing us the possibility of having had a good family and good people around him at some point in his life due to the degree of justice and repentance we see on the cross. Jesus did not overlook his repentance; even in the last minutes or moments of his life, he was found in favor by Jesus.

We can all go through problems in life, we can be the worst people in life, but if we repent wholeheartedly before God the Father, God will forgive us and justify us solely through the merits of Jesus of Nazareth and His sacrifice on the cross of Calvary. We have seen so many people commit so many atrocities because of a horrible past, or because of parents who did not pay enough attention to their children—abandoned, orphaned, for whatever reason they end up opting for harmful things and the worst decisions in their lives. For these kinds of people, there is still a solution. If somehow you are reading this, I want to tell you that all is not lost for you; there is still a life full of love and purpose in God for you. This Jesus who once stood beside this thief on the cross is alive today and still offers life together with Him to anyone who desires and thinks they can't go on. Like this thief, it's time for us to surrender to Jesus and ask for His love and mercy, which will have compassion on us, forgive us, and save us with Him.

We do not know the degree of authenticity of this apocryphal gospel. It is clear that for a likely Gnostic Christian community in the early later centuries, it held esteem. We have used it to show how some believed they saw Jesus from His childhood and how He was exalted from the beginning of His arrival and held in high regard—something quite doubtful and questionable by scholars, both academic and Christian theologians, who do not believe that the narrative, although it may have some historical basis, was likely borrowed similarly from the canonical gospels; the majority of it was not historical.

THE BIRTH AND CHILDHOOD IN THE PSEUDO MATTHEW GOSPEL OF THE INFANCY OF JESUS:

The Pseudo Matthew gospel, considered apocryphal, also belongs to the "infancy of Jesus" genre; formerly known as the book of "The Origin of the Blessed Mary and the Infancy of Jesus." In this gospel, we see several events from the birth of Jesus until the age of 12. It is believed that this gospel was composed around 600 AD to 800 AD, using some of the canonical gospels as well as the Proto-James and the Gospel of Thomas, which we have previously described. This gospel is among the later apocryphal infancy gospels, and its authenticity has been greatly discredited by the Christian Church, historians, and theological scholars.

The reason we have included the infancy of Jesus from the Pseudo Matthew gospel as a non-authentic source is due to some portions and events that provide valuable information for readers to understand how the figure of Jesus of Nazareth was viewed or thought of among certain Christians in the Middle Ages. The narrative or author of this gospel is generally anonymous within the church, although it appears in a list of writings among some of the early church fathers, such as Jerome and others. They were aware that Jerome had translated a Hebrew volume concerning the virgin birth of Mary and the infancy of Jesus.

Despite this gospel sharing the same name or title as the canonical Matthew, it is highly doubtful that Father Jerome was the author of this book. There are many reasons to question this, and considerable conviction that Jerome is not the author of this work. With that said, I find it difficult to believe that Jerome translated this book, given that its composition dates almost two hundred years after his death. Some early church fathers in their writings, such as Papias, Irenaeus, and even Eusebius himself, tell us that Matthew wrote his gospel in Hebrew or Aramaic, and then the disciples translated it into Greek. This Hebrew gospel of Matthew mentioned in tradition and the writings of the early fathers is believed by some academic scholars to have never existed because there is no evidence of this Hebrew or Aramaic Matthew.

One thing we are certain of, whether or not this Hebrew or Aramaic Matthew existed before the Greek version we have, is that I find it very unlikely that this Pseudo Matthew was part of or associated with the canonical Matthew we possess. It is hard to believe that Jerome translated the Hebrew or Aramaic Matthew into Greek, for which we have no clear evidence. What is clear is that Jerome translated the Old Testament from Hebrew and the New Testament from Greek into Latin with the famous "Vulgate Latin," the Bible that the universal church used for many centuries.

Once again, personally, I have not seen any of the apostles, early church fathers, apologists, philosophers, or theologians, including Jerome himself, Origen, or even Augustine the greatest writer of all, authentically speak, write, or mention this Pseudo Matthew, let alone its events. They all spoke of the Greek Matthew we have in the canon, but none ever mentioned the stories we see in the following text.

The Annunciation of the Child Jesus

It begins by telling us about the appearance of the angel Gabriel to Mary. He tells her that she is highly favored and that God has prepared her womb as a sanctuary for the Lord. He says that a light from heaven will come and dwell within her, radiating out over the whole world. Mary, trembling with fear, is reassured by the angel not to be afraid because she has found favor in the eyes of God. He tells her that she will conceive a king who will rule not only on earth but also in heaven, prevailing for all eternity. We see a conversation between the angel and Mary that is somewhat more extensive than what we find in the Bible.

Later, we see Joseph taking the pregnant Mary to his homeland due to the decree of the census and registration ordered by Caesar Augustus. While they are on the way to Bethlehem, Mary seems to have a vision. In this vision, she sees two peoples: one is the Jewish people, and the other is the Gentiles. One group is in tears, and the other is rejoicing. Joseph initially dismisses Mary's words as meaningless, but then he sees a child dressed in magnificent attire who tells them that Mary has seen how the Jewish people will weep for having turned away from God, while the Gentiles will rejoice for drawing near to the Lord, according to the promise made to our father. The child explains that the time has come for all nations to be blessed through Abraham.

It is clear that the author of this gospel must have been familiar with Paul's letters for several reasons. Firstly, the revelation of salvation or communion with God for the Gentiles is a theology we see in Paul. In all the gospels, Mary or Joseph never know this mystery that is only revealed to Paul. We never find Mary or Joseph proclaiming this good news or sharing this news with the Gentiles. It is Paul who, in most of his letters like Romans, Galatians, and others, mentions God's promise to Abraham for all nations. We see very little mention of Abraham and this promise in the gospels. When Jesus himself mentions Father Abraham, it is to the Jews to remind them to behave as the children of Abraham they are, not to show them that in this promise, which they reject, the Gentiles will have a part.

Theologically, we can interpret certain passages where Jesus shows that he has other sheep that are not of the fold he is speaking to at that moment, referring to the Gentile people outside the Jews. We also see many instances where Jesus welcomes people from other nations into his fold, such as Samaritans, Syrophoenicians, Greeks, and more. But it is clear that the apostle Paul is the one who makes and shows the complete distinction between Jews and Gentiles and is more concerned than anyone else with welcoming these Gentiles into the kingdom of God through the promise made to Abraham, as seen in the following verses:

Galatians 3:14;

"So that in Christ Jesus the blessing of Abraham might come to the Gentiles, so that we might receive the promised Spirit through faith." (ESV)

Acts 13:46;

"And Paul and Barnabas spoke out boldly, saying, 'It was necessary that the word of God be spoken first to you. Since you thrust it aside and judge yourselves unworthy of eternal life, behold, we are turning to the Gentiles.'" (ESV)

Galatians 3:6-9;

"Just as Abraham 'believed God, and it was counted to him as righteousness.' Know then that it is those of faith who are the sons of Abraham. And the Scripture, foreseeing that God would justify the Gentiles by faith, preached the gospel beforehand to Abraham, saying, 'In you shall all the nations be blessed.' So then, those who are of faith are blessed along with Abraham, the man of faith." (ESV)

Clearly we see that there is no doubt that Paul is the first to show the mystery and revelation of salvation and the inclusion of the Gentiles into Abraham's family through faith in Christ Jesus. This faith of the Gentiles in God and Jesus would make them directly children of Abraham by faith, children of God, and co-heirs with Christ Jesus. This author's vision placed on Mary in this gospel is a sign that the author knew or was taking directly from Pauline writings. The author's primary purpose in this gospel is to show the fulfillment of the prophecies previously spoken by the prophets, fulfilled in Jesus of Nazareth. Once Mary successfully gives birth to Jesus, the story continues by telling us that from the moment Jesus was born, angels surrounded him, saying, "Glory to God in the highest, and on earth peace among those with whom he is pleased." In the canonical gospels, we see that during Jesus' ministry, he was always strengthened by them in one way or another. Jesus did mention angels, but we do not find the presence of angels involved in Jesus' birth in the canonical gospels. This gospel does not say that Jesus' birth was so glorious and different from others that Mary brought him into the world without pain. Once Jesus is born, a great star shines all day over the cave or place of his birth. The shepherds who visited, mentioned by Luke, declared that they heard angels singing

Jesus of Nazareth

hymns saying, "The Savior of all, the Christ is born, and all Israel shall find its salvation." All the prophets in Jerusalem said that the star indicated the birth of the Christ, who must fulfill the promises and prophecies made, not only to Israel but to all nations. Surprisingly, we never see even a single prophet besides John the Baptist, the priest Simeon, and the prophetess Anna announce Jesus of Nazareth as the savior of all nations. Jesus never mentioned any other prophet, with John being the last of the law to prepare the way for him. Hardly outside theology is it believed that even John the Baptist mentioned the word "world" in a global term as including the Gentiles in the forgiveness of sins by the Lamb of God, this because we do not see him calling any other people such as Samaritans, Romans, or Greeks. We see this later when the apostles reach the Gentile world because of the persecution of Stephen. Scripturally, the first Gentile we see converted to Christ and baptized in the waters is the Ethiopian eunuch of Candace's court, and then Cornelius, the centurion of Caesarea. We do not know chronologically which of these two came first, but this is how we see it in the biblical order. Therefore, it is believed that John's call to repentance in the Judean desert was solely for the Jews, as it tells us that many Jews were coming to be baptized by John. Later, we also see Apollos mentioned arriving in Ephesus, powerful in the scriptures, as a knowledgeable follower of John's baptism, a Jew from Alexandria, Egypt, and likely a distant disciple of John himself. With this said, the vast majority of all disciples we see of John were all Jews. We never see John the Baptist calling Gentiles to his baptism or to repentance because in the law, it was very difficult for the promise made to Abraham to include Gentiles, especially if John came from the Jewish sect known as the Essenes, who lived in Qumran, and who did not view Gentile pagans favorably; rather, they saw them as children of darkness who would ultimately be destroyed. Above all, the text tells us that his preaching says that Jesus is the Lamb of God who takes away the sin of the world. This word "world" in Aramaic or Hebrew is known as "Tevel" or "Tebel"; when translated into Greek as "Cosmos," it directly refers to the entire human race. This obviously indicates that

John was familiar with many books of Isaiah, for the following reason: Isaiah is the one who mentions that a voice would come in the wilderness calling Israel to turn to the Lord.

Isaiah 40:3-5 (ESV):

"A voice cries:

'In the wilderness prepare the way of the Lord;

make straight in the desert a highway for our God.

Every valley shall be lifted up,

and every mountain and hill be made low;

the uneven ground shall become level,

and the rough places a plain.

And the glory of the Lord shall be revealed,

and all flesh shall see it together,

for the mouth of the Lord has spoken.'"

When the Jews sent priests and Levites from Jerusalem to ask John who he was—whether he was the Messiah, Elijah, or a prophet—John clearly answered that he was none of these; he was simply the voice of one crying out in the wilderness, telling them to make straight the way of the Lord as the prophet Isaiah had said. John did not think he was Isaiah or Elijah, but we see that he knew the scroll of the prophet Isaiah well. Knowing this scroll, his preaching could be completely in line with the scroll of Isaiah, and if his preaching was conscious of the scroll of Isaiah, we clearly see in many of the chapters of Deutero-Isaiah from chapter 45 onwards that salvation to all nations is being spoken of.

For example, in Isaiah 52:10 (ESV):

"The Lord has bared his holy arm

before the eyes of all the nations,

and all the ends of the earth shall see

the salvation of our God."

This baring of the Lord's arm by Isaiah clearly refers to the plan created by the very hands of God in the eyes of the whole world with the coming of Jesus of Nazareth as the perfect plan for the salvation of all nations that believe in the Lord. The fact that the arm has been bared shows that all nations will be able to see God's hand and favor toward them. John the Baptist would have to know all these prophecies spoken by Isaiah, not only directed to Israel but rather to the entire human cosmos. If this were so, it is very likely that he used the term "world" as Deutero-Isaiah also saw it, as the hope and forgiveness of sin for all, although the Gentiles were not seen in his baptism. In Christian tradition and Western interpretation, definitely John's call and preaching were toward Jesus of Nazareth, the Lamb of God sufficient for all humanity without distinction of people or race, color or size, as we will later see in the same vision, preaching, and thought of the Apostle Paul and also of Peter upon seeing the Holy Spirit descend upon the Gentiles as it had descended upon the Jews at Pentecost.

Jesus and the Dragons:

In chapter 18 of this gospel and those that follow, we begin to see the most unusual events and the reasons why this gospel never entered the biblical canon. It so happened that while Mary and Joseph were on their way with Jesus, they arrived at a cave, and suddenly a multitude of dragons came out of the cave. Everyone with Jesus was terrified at the sight, but Jesus, descending from his mother's knees, stood before the dragons, and they worshiped him and then departed. The writer tells us that this happened to fulfill David's prophecy when he said: "Praise the Lord from the earth, you great sea creatures and all ocean depths." The author is first showing Jesus' superiority as God Himself, whom David invites the irrational creatures to praise. Another word the Bible uses for these dragons is sea monsters or Leviathan, which we see mentioned in Genesis, Isaiah, Job, and the Psalms. In the Psalms, it's almost evident that whenever the psalmist uses these creatures, the narrative is poetic. In Psalms 74 and also 104, there's mention of these monsters or the supposed Leviathan, but it's clear that the interpretation of this creature, as most theologians and commentators tell us, signifies and is a symbol of the Pharaoh of Egypt. For example, in Psalms 74:12-14, where the psalmist mentions the dragon or sea monsters, he begins by declaring God as the King from of old, the One who works salvation in the midst of the earth. You divided the sea by your might; you broke the heads of the sea monsters in the waters. You crushed the heads of Leviathan; you gave him as food for the creatures of the wilderness. Clearly, the psalmist poetically speaks of God's victory over Pharaoh in the desert, dividing the sea for his people and causing the Pharaoh, symbolized by Leviathan, the sea monster, and his army to perish in the deep sea in the desert.

We could also add the academic scientific thought to the figure of sea monsters or Leviathan as gods or evil divinities of other peoples and nations, which the God Yahweh defeated in the past. Here, the psalmist knows that Yahweh, the God of Israel, his own God considered the creator of all things, whom we see in Genesis creating all sea monsters, those which humans fear and dread, David lets them know that everything that breathes must praise the one creator and mighty God. Therefore, this gospel and its author are showing that just as David invites the dragons (sea monsters) to praise God, these same creatures, in the presence of the child Jesus, fear and worship Him, just as they do before Yahweh, the God of Israel. As soon as everyone sees how these dragons worship Jesus, He tells them all not to see Him as a child because He has always been a man made, and it is necessary for all beasts of the forest to be tamed before Him. With these words, we are beginning to see a Jesus greater and superior to Adam himself, who could not stay with the beasts in Eden.

Jesus Among the Lions:

It is also said that the lions and leopards worshiped him and accompanied him in the desert. The synoptic Gospel of Mark tells us something very similar, with little explanation, which I think this author used to elaborate on this companionship of beasts with Jesus:

Jesus of Nazareth

Mark 1:13:

And he was in the wilderness forty days, being tempted by Satan. And he was with the wild animals, and the angels were ministering to him. (ESV)

After being baptized in the waters by John, Jesus was led by the Spirit into the desert to be tempted by Satan, and after overcoming each temptation after the 40 days and 40 nights, Mark tells us that angels and even wild animals served him. We won't delve into many interpretative details, but it is clear that the message that Mark and the author of this gospel are giving us is that Jesus represents both the new Adam and the new Israel. Both the first Adam and Israel failed to overcome their temptation in the places they inhabited: Adam was overcome with the beasts in Eden, and Israel was overcome by tempting God with their hunger as soon as they entered the desert, desiring to return to Egypt to eat the food they had there. Jesus, as the second Adam, unlike the first and Israel, was tempted in all things and by everyone, but He was never overcome. Instead, He overcame the world and death, becoming the true Anointed One and chosen by God to save and justify whoever He chooses. The message we understand from this whole passage is that Jesus is God and has control over all creation. Just as all creation praises and worships God, so does all creation—whether above (angels, principalities, or birds) or below (humans, animals, fish, or sea monsters)—praise and worship Jesus of Nazareth. The way Jesus walked among the lions, all kinds of wild animals, oxen, and donkeys harmed no one; they also walked among the wolves, and no one suffered any harm, and the lion and the ox ate together. The author reminds us, as always, that this fulfills what Isaiah said:

Isaiah 11:6-9:

The wolf shall dwell with the lamb, and the leopard shall lie down with the young goat, and the calf and the lion and the fattened calf together; and a little child shall lead them. The cow and the bear shall graze; their young shall lie down together; and the lion shall eat straw like the ox. The nursing child shall play over the hole of the cobra, and the weaned child shall put his hand on the adder's den. They shall not hurt or destroy in all my holy mountain; for the earth shall be full of the knowledge of the Lord as the waters cover the sea. (ESV)

Isaiah 65:25:

The wolf and the lamb shall graze together; the lion shall eat straw like the ox, and dust shall be the serpent's food. They shall not hurt or destroy in all my holy mountain," says the Lord. (ESV)

For evangelical Protestant Christianity, these prophecies have not yet been fulfilled; it is believed they will be fulfilled in Jesus' millennial kingdom when He returns for the second time. The earth will be liberated, restored, or made new; everything will return to what is thought to have been like in the beginning in Eden—the paradise where everything was innocent, without evil, sorrow, or suffering but in a completely spiritual dimension, where all animals coexisted without devouring each other. Some preterists believe that all these prophecies were somehow fulfilled in the past history; for this gospel, it seems that this was the idea and thought since it showed their fulfillment while Jesus was on earth in His first coming.

"The trees obey Jesus."

Another miracle we see in the infancy gospel concerning nature and trees is found in chapter 20. Mary, feeling tired and weary, told Joseph that she needed to rest a little. Joseph led her to a palm tree, where she sat down. Looking up at the palm tree filled with fruit, she expressed her desire to have some of the fruit, but the palm tree was too tall and difficult for elderly Joseph to climb and fetch it. Then the child Jesus, while sitting on his mother's lap, said to the palm tree, "Tree, bend down and feed my mother with your fruits." Upon these words from Jesus, the palm tree bent down to Mary's feet, offering fruits for her needs. After taking all the fruit she needed, the tree remained bent, awaiting the command of the one who had made it bow. Then Jesus instructed the palm tree to straighten up, regain its strength, and be the companion of all trees in the paradise of His Father. Jesus then commanded the tree to send its roots to the underground spring and bring forth enough water to quench their thirst. Immediately, the tree straightened up and caused clear, fresh, and sweet water to flow from its roots. Everyone who saw this water rejoiced, drank from it—including all the pack animals—and gave thanks to God.

In the synoptic Gospels of Matthew and Mark, we see a similar miracle involving a tree, specifically a fig tree, but with a different outcome:

Matthew 21:18-20:

In the morning, as Jesus was returning to the city, he was hungry. Seeing a fig tree by the road, he went up to it but found nothing on it except leaves. Then he said to it, "May you never bear fruit again!" Immediately the tree withered.

Upon seeing this, the disciples marveled and asked Jesus, "How did the fig tree wither so quickly?"

Mark 11:12-14:

The next day as they were leaving Bethany, Jesus was hungry. Seeing in the distance a fig tree in leaf, he went to find out if it had any fruit. When he reached it, he found nothing but leaves because it was not the season for figs. Then he said to the tree, "May no one ever eat fruit from you again." And his disciples heard him say it.

These accounts in Matthew and Mark show Jesus' power over nature, specifically demonstrated through the withering of a fig tree as a sign of judgment. The tree in these accounts did not respond by offering sustenance like the palm tree in the infancy gospel but instead withered as a result of Jesus' declaration. The symbolic meaning and lesson behind each of these miracles convey different aspects of Jesus' authority and the consequences of spiritual barrenness or disobedience.

Here we see two miracles that are very similar but with some characteristics unique to Jesus, in the Pseudo-Matthew gospel. While Jesus is still a child, we see him displaying power and authority over the nature of trees. This gospel likely had to use two biblical sources for its narrative. Suddenly, we hear that Mary was weary or fatigued, and she is taken to a palm tree for rest. This reminds us of the miracle of the same plant that God created for the rest of the prophet Jonah. In contrast, we see that after Mary's rest, the next day God orders the plant to wither. We witness the complete authority of God the Creator over the genus of plants and trees. Moreover, we see Jesus with complete authority over the palm tree itself; at his word, it bends down to provide its fruit to the people. The author's intention seems to be showing us Jesus's complete authority over nature, just as God commanded the appearance of a plant for the prophet's rest and then its withering. Similarly, we see Jesus commanding the palm tree to bend down, straighten up, and also provide water for everyone's thirst. We are faced with a series of comparisons that demonstrate Jesus's superiority even over Moses himself.

In the Old Testament, we see Moses making water gush from a rock for all of Israel to drink using his staff. Here, too, we see Jesus with the power of his word speaking to the tree, and it produces water for everyone to drink.

Now, let's look at the broader picture of the miracle from a mystical and spiritual perspective. It's clear that any tree that doesn't bear good fruit or provide shade for rest is cut down and used as firewood. Jesus likely desired to eat figs, but the clear message in this prejudicial miracle by Jesus is as follows: Jesus knew this fig tree bore no fruit. He wanted to show his disciples a message about the condition of Israel. Therefore, he had to pass judgment on this innocent and poor fig tree, expecting fruit from it when it wasn't even the time, or more likely, it was an early fig tree, indicating that it was alive and in full view, full of leaves but dead for not bearing fruit. This is likely a creatively crafted narrative by the synoptic gospels to convey a message about a people's condition. It's possible this miracle never happened exactly as conveyed because it would be impossible for God, a completely just God, to create trees subject to his laws to bear fruit as established in Genesis, trees that bear fruit in due time according to their species as established. However, we see that some trees are naturally affected in one way or another, perhaps innocently due to the fault of their own planters, so they don't grow and bear fruit successfully like others. This fig tree was completely innocent, but Jesus used it as an example.

Moses himself said that God is slow to anger and abounding in steadfast love, forgiving iniquity and transgression, but by no means clearing the guilty. Here, Moses is clearly talking about the human race, but God's justice is the same for all of his creation. How could this innocent fig tree be guilty and receive such a severe judgment from Jesus of Nazareth? God has appointed this Jesus as Judge of all things, especially people. The message the synoptic gospels wanted to convey through Jesus was this: In this miracle or curse of the fig tree, the issue is not that it can't bear fruit or that the time hasn't come for it to bear fruit. Instead, it's an early fig tree, full of leaves. Its appearance and impression are so admirable, but its reality or essence is not. Everyone approaches it expecting to receive what it openly promotes, but when everyone who approaches seeking satisfaction finds complete disappointment. At this point in spring, the fig trees had not yet produced figs, but what caught Jesus's attention was that it was full of leaves. Jesus is about to enter the city founded by King David, the great Jerusalem, mentioned directly and symbolically more than 800 times in the Bible. The prophet Jeremiah, in chapter 3:17.

"At that time they shall call Jerusalem the Throne of the Lord, and all the nations shall be gathered to it, to the name of the Lord, to Jerusalem. They shall no longer follow the stubbornness of their evil heart." For almost all the prophets and all the people of the Lord, Jerusalem, as well as the Jewish people of Israel, represented the kingdom and throne of God established on earth, despite Jesus establishing the true kingdom of God, the true Israel, in his new covenant, with his new law. Jesus approaches this fig tree representing both Israel and the great city of Jerusalem. In the Old Testament, Israel is described as a vine, the tree or plantation of God, as seen in the following verses (Judges 9:8-15; Isaiah 3:14; 5:1-7;

Jeremiah 12:10; Ezekiel 17:2-10; 19:10-14). Like any dedicated or knowledgeable Jewish Israelite involved in agriculture, they knew that the first fruits of the harvest belonged to God according to (Exodus 23:19; Nehemiah 10:35-37), showing their special relationship with God as His chosen vine, expected to be an example and bear spiritual fruit as a covenant people (Psalm 1:3; Jeremiah 17:8-10). Israel's fruitfulness or multiplication is not the basis of its relationship with God or what it can do for Him, as it is God who gives fertility and blessing (Deuteronomy 7:13; 28:4). The lack of fruit is a symbol of God's curse for their rebellion as seen in (Deuteronomy 11:17). This foundational allegory of Israel's spiritual life flourishes vividly in the time of the prophets. It had come time for the people of God to bear fruit that would bless the world (Isaiah 27:6). Several times the prophets describe God inspecting Israel for early figs, as a sign of spiritual fertility (Micah 7:1; Jeremiah 8:13; Hosea 9:10-17), but He finds neither early figs nor what He desired. The people of Israel were called to always bear fruit of blessing to the world. It is true that earthly figs or fig trees will not always produce out of season, but this is a clear sign that even amidst all the exiles, both of the people of Israel and the Jewish people, they were always called to represent the kingdom of God and His covenant among all nations. Fulfilling this was to demonstrate and give God's fruit to the world. During both exiles—Assyrian and Babylonian—they failed to keep the covenant, the law, and its ordinances. It was then that due to Israel's complete ingratitude, God poured out the curse of barrenness (Hosea 9:16), and Israel became a rotten fig (Jeremiah 29:17).

With Jesus's arrival in the great city Jerusalem, we see that before dying, he establishes what will be judgment for all, including the Jews and the ungrateful, who, after knowing God and receiving all blessing and fullness to become channels of blessing for the needy, poor, and prisoners, turned back to vanity, evil, and the pagan world that rejected God. The religious leaders and sects present during the first century, as Josephus tells us—the Pharisees, Sadducees, Essenes, scribes, and others—had become corrupted by greed and their traditional religiosity, more concerned with their own appearances like the leaves of the fig tree, but rotten, full of wickedness, and cruelty, abusing the people by imposing burdens and debts they themselves could not bear. Jesus had declared in Luke 21:5-6 the destruction of Jerusalem, the seemingly most beautiful city, but also the one that killed its prophets, the one that also saw the Jews clamoring for the crucifixion of the only righteous and faithful one approved by God. Jerusalem was destroyed just as Christ had predicted in AD 70, dried up like the fig tree never to be the same again for almost 2000 years, bearing the same fruit it once did.

In this metaphor, miraculous parable, we see the fig tree representing first and foremost Israel and secondly Jerusalem. There is a plausible dual application to its interpretation; there is a third interpretation, but this is more a matter for theological commentators, about which it is said: just as sin entered the world interfering with communion between humans and God, creating separation, the fig tree and its leaves used by Adam and Eve to cover themselves represent the species known as religion or law, the forms created by humans to try to approach God as it was in the beginning. They were naked before God, but then felt they had to do something on their own to appease God's feeling and to make themselves accepted by Him. This work, law, or religion is established as a means of coverage to revere so that man can somehow approach God again. When Jesus approached the fig tree full of leaves on his way to Jerusalem, the place of his death, seeing all the leaves, he remembered that what Adam and Eve used as guilty shame to approach God were the leaves of the fig tree. Jesus, by drying up the fig tree which had leaves but no fruit, showed that the same religion, in this case "traditional Judaism," which was killing the people of Israel, beautiful on the outside and admired by the Romans, yet a rotten Judaism full of laws and traditions invented by men and not by God. This religion made them think that through it their lives would be saved and justified before God. "Jesus came to dry up all the religions created and invented by men, which, although beautiful in appearance, are full of evil, enslavement, division, abuse, machismo, racism, greed, and rules of men that serve no purpose other than to create the same separation between the Creator and His creation." With this gesture of judging the fig tree and drying it up forever, Jesus is putting an end to the religious systems created by men, which serve to boast and enrich themselves, never bearing fruit for the followers or congregants living near or among them; what matters to them is that these see in them all their beautiful leaves. Jesus has opened a new way to the Father, better and greater than that of Adam and Eve at the beginning; He has given us all things, especially His Holy Spirit, so that we may always approach Him confidently, the true tree, always bearing fruit no matter the occasion, and at all times finding true fruit, always eating and being full of Him, without the need to approach confusedly or try dried trees only for appearances, dead and dry religions that do not justify and do not save man. Jesus is the only tree of life, the way to salvation and to the Father. Jesus came before that fig tree once, but He will come again a second time and hopes that it not only has leaves, but is also full of fruit, as we see in (Joel 2:22; Amos 9:14; Micah 4:4; Zechariah 8:12; Ezekiel 36:8). In this gospel and its infancy about Jesus, like some other apocryphal texts, we see a Jesus at times restless, cursing, disobedient to adults, avenging with evil even to the death of other children who somehow bothered Him out of envy or accidentally tripped Him in His path. Sometimes Jesus played with sand and made water channels; other children obstructing His work received curses from Jesus until death. We see a restless and proud Jesus in the schools, showing teachers greater wisdom than theirs, with tricky questions. Seeing His wisdom, His teacher would exclaim before everyone, praising Him. We see Him raising a dead child after falling from a terrace, at 6 years old, going on his way to a spring with a vessel to fetch water for Mary; a child smashing His vessel, Jesus miraculously collected the water with the mantle He was carrying. These and many more until the age of 12, we see Jesus acting in this apocryphal infancy of Jesus Pseudo-Matthew."

Jesus of Nazareth

THE BIRTH AND CHILDHOOD IN THE ARMENIAN GOSPEL OF THE INFANCY OF JESUS:

This Gospel is dated to around the 6th century AD and is considered entirely dependent on the Protoevangelium of James and also the Gospel of Thomas. In addition to the infancy of Jesus, it includes a lengthy discourse between the angel Gabriel and Mary when he visits her to announce the birth. When the angel of the Lord arrived with closed doors, he appeared incorporeal but presented himself in the likeness of a corporeal being, similar to what we see in Luke. The conversation is so extensive and lasts so long that apparently due to her fear and incomprehension, Mary continuously asks many questions—how will this be? when will it happen? etc. The angel explains to her that it will not happen as she had thought or imagined, because Mary assumed and said, "I have never slept with a man and have never known a man," implying that she thought divinity would somehow engage in a sexual act with her. The act of Mary's pregnancy was so miraculous and inexplicable that she was clearly told she would not lose her purity or her virginity, and would maintain it forever, hence the universal Christian dogmas known as "The Virgin Conception" and "The Perpetual Virginity of Mary." The doctrine of Mary's virginity was established at the Council of Ephesus in 431 and the Council of Chalcedon in 649, emphasizing its triple character before, during, and after the birth of Christ. It is one of the four Marian dogmas of the Catholic Church and is also upheld by Eastern Orthodox Churches in Eastern Christianity, and by some Lutherans and Anglicans in Western Christianity. In this encounter, when Gabriel visits Mary, she momentarily even thinks the angel might be a representation of the disguised devil trying to tempt her, similar to what happened with Eve and the serpent in the beginning. The angel continues to comfort her until we see the event unfold. This gospel contains a series of curious information and events about how Mary became pregnant with Jesus. The author tells us that the day Mary became pregnant was the 15th of Nisan, which would be April

6, a Wednesday, at the third hour of the day. Nisan means "bud, first sprout," and is the first month of the biblical Hebrew calendar, which begins its count from the Israelites' departure from slavery in Egypt; with this, we see the author's significant purpose in sharing with us the importance of the established date. By commemorating this date coinciding with the freedom from slavery of the Israelites in this month, precisely in it arriving in Mary's womb the great liberator who will save not only Israel but the whole world, mentioning this date shows that just as God freed his people from Egypt, liberating them from the punishment and oppressive slavery of the pharaoh, with the arrival of Jesus, God would liberate the world from the punishment and oppression of sin and the devil.

The Arrival of Jesus in Mary's Womb:

After the Virgin Mary was convinced by the announcement of the angel Gabriel, Mary, in response, concluded with the following words: Mary said, "If things are as you have explained, and the Lord Himself deigns to descend to His slave and servant, let it be done to me according to your word." And the angel departed from her. As soon as the virgin had spoken those words of humility, the divine Word penetrated her through her ear. The way in which the author tells us that the Word penetrated through her ear was and remains somewhat alarming, even for the early fathers of the Church. This matter was not widely discussed or accepted as a dogma of faith in synods or ecumenical councils. The phrase "the divine Word penetrated through her ear" was not universally interpreted by all the fathers, but there are some explanations that help us understand why it was written and said in this way.

This sexual symbolism of the ear can be traced back to the early history of Christianity: A heretic named Elian was condemned at the Council of Nicaea for saying, "The Word entered through Mary's ear." However, the Church, preferring not to delve too deeply into this matter, did not pronounce dogmatically and allowed Enodius to adopt Elian's thesis. The Salzburg Missal also appropriated two verses from the poet: "Rejoice, Virgin Mother of Christ, who conceived through the ear." The Breviary of the

Maronites, adds Remy de Gourmont, also contains an antiphon where one can read: "The Word of the Father entered through the blessed ear." The sexual interpretation here ignores another meaning: the ear symbolizes obedience to the divine word; by hearing, in the full sense of understanding and accepting the annunciation sent to her, Mary freely conceives the Messiah. The ear is here the organ of understanding. The piercing of the ear is a very ancient form of commitment and appropriation. It is found in the Old Testament: "If your slave says to you: I do not want to leave your house, because he loves you and your house and it goes well with you, you shall take an awl and pierce his ear against the door, and he shall be your slave forever." In the East, the dervishes of the Bektashi brotherhood, who took vows of celibacy, also pierced one ear and wore a hoop by which they were recognized. The European tradition of sailors piercing one ear and wearing an earring to signify their engagement and commitment to the sea undoubtedly has the same origin. (Article borrowed from https://siento22mundos.wordpress.com/orejas/) by: Jean Chevalier.

From that moment on, Mary became pregnant. Universal Christian high Christology asserts that at that very moment, the Word took complete control of Mary, sanctifying her entire life, including her flesh, womb, blood, organs, and all twelve limbs, purifying her like gold in the fire, creating from her womb the dwelling place for Jesus of Nazareth, the Word of God. Some commentators, when addressing Mary's sinful nature as a daughter of David and descendant of Eve, wonder how Jesus was not tainted by Mary's blood. The theological answer shared by the majority is that when the Word entered Mary, it was not she who sustained him; rather, the Word of God sustained her. In other words, Mary's blood did not contaminate Jesus; instead, the blood of Jesus, the Word, sanctified Mary throughout the entire nine months he was there.

The Magi and Their Gifts:

Upon the arrival of the Magi, this gospel, unlike other apocryphal texts, tells us that the Magi from the East had left their country nine months prior and arrived on the 23rd of Tebeth, which corresponds to January 9. This suggests that they likely received the message and vision of the star long before the event. They also brought with them a large army and arrived in the city of Jerusalem. These kings of the Magi were three brothers. The first was Melchior, king of the Persians; the second was Gaspar, king of the Indians; and the third was Balthasar, king of the Arabs. They camped outside the city where they stayed for three days with the princes of their respective kingdoms. Although they were brothers and sons of the same father, armies of diverse tongues and nationalities accompanied them.

Traditionally, it is believed that the first king or Magus, Melchior, brought gifts including myrrh, aloes, muslin, purple cloth, linen ribbons, and also books written and sealed by the finger of God. The second king, Gaspar, brought gifts of spikenard, cinnamon, and frankincense in honor of the child. The third king, Balthasar, brought gold, precious stones, fine pearls, and valuable sapphires. These gifts all hold spiritual and symbolic significance: gold symbolizes divine kingship, frankincense symbolizes divinity, and myrrh signifies that the Son of Man must die.

These gifts, also mentioned in the canonical Gospel of Matthew, have a clear interpretation. Matthew is depicting the birth and gifts received by the new Messiah, presenting a description of who Jesus of Nazareth truly is and his life. Some representations from the 3rd century show only two Magi, while by the 4th century, there are depictions of two to four Magi. By the late centuries, it was even believed that there were six, twelve, or even up to sixty Magi who arrived in Bethlehem. Based on the three gifts cited by Saint Matthew (gold, frankincense, and myrrh), it is supposed that there were three Magi who came to worship the Child. The first Christian theologian to assert this definitively was Origen (185-253). The same number appears in other apocryphal texts such as the Armenian Gospel of the Infancy (XI, 1) from the 6th century (the same text referenced here), and the Arabic Gospel of the Infancy (VII, 1) from the 7th century, which was mentioned earlier. The first text adds that they were kings and brothers, provides their names, and specifies the offerings they presented to the child. In some representations of the Adoration of the Magi, there is also a presence of a large entourage or at least one accompanying figure.

Interpretation of Jesus' Gifts by the Church Fathers:

The Church Fathers interpreted the gifts as follows: gold symbolized the signumregis, alluding to Christ's royal nature; frankincense represented the signum Dei, referring to his divinity; and myrrh symbolized the signumsepulturae, signifying his mortality and hence his humanity. According to Pope Saint Gregory I the Great (540-604), gold is offered to Jesus Christ when he is revered as the king of the world, incense when he is adored as true God, and myrrh when his humanity is commemorated. A different interpretation comes from Don Juan Manuel (1282-1348) in his Book of the States (1330): "the gold they offered signified that the whole world was under his power, and his great nobility; the incense symbolized the sacrifice that would be made in his body; and the myrrh, which is very bitter, signified the bitterness of his death." However, the interpretation by Bernard of Clairvaux (1090-1153) is quite different: "the Magi offered gold to Christ to assist the poverty of the Blessed Virgin; incense to counteract the bad smell in the stable; and myrrh to anoint the Child, strengthen his limbs, and prevent parasites and insects from approaching him." This interpretation is considered less accurate in tradition. Western religious tradition eventually related these gifts to the Holy Trinity: the gold from the Glorious Father; the myrrh, used as a funerary ointment since ancient times and associated with death and resurrection, from the Son; and the incense, a purifying element, from the Holy Spirit.

Jesus and the Miraculous Circumcision:

After eight days, as prescribed by the Law of Moses, Joseph and Mary kept the child hidden from any threats, but it was necessary for Jesus to be circumcised. Joseph decided to go to Jerusalem and seek out a wise man named Joel, who was well-versed in divine laws. When he arrived at the cave where the child was, and applied the knife to cut the flesh of his foreskin, miraculously no cut was made on Jesus' body. Witnessing this prodigy, Joel was astonished and exclaimed, "Behold, the blood of this child has flowed without any incision." The child was named Jesus, as the angel messenger of God had instructed. We do not have a clear explanation for this miraculous circumcision, but it is likely that the Word in Jesus retained his blood for the appointed time of crucifixion, or the circumcision was painless. It is not surprising to encounter a story like this, considering that even Moses was not circumcised. Rabbinic Jewish tradition tells us that Moses was born circumcised, which was seen as a sign that he would be the great liberator of Israel. Therefore, it is highly probable that just as Moses miraculously did not require circumcision, having been born already circumcised by God, Jesus, who is far superior to Moses but born from a womb subject to the same law as Moses, was miraculously circumcised without needing any healing. As time passed, we are told that the child Jesus grew, progressing in grace and wisdom.

Jesus in Jerusalem for the First Time:

After about 40 days, when no one was seeking the child's life anymore and all threats had ceased, Joseph took the gifts brought by the Magi and brought the child Jesus to be presented in the city of Jerusalem. After presenting the child to the priests, they offered the necessary sacrifices at the temple, as was customary, a pair of turtledoves or two young pigeons. It was there that we see the elderly priest Simeon, mentioned by Luke in his Gospel. Directed by the Holy Spirit to come to the temple that day, Simeon had received from the Holy Spirit the promise that he would not die before seeing the Savior born. When he encountered the child in the temple with his parents, Simeon took the child in his arms and blessed him. After taking and seeing Jesus, Simeon blessed Mary and, after a prayer to God, asked to depart, having seen the salvation of Israel with his own eyes.

Jesus at the Age of 5:

Having grown up, at the age of 5 Joseph decided to take the

child and his mother to Syria. When they arrived, the power emanating from this child was so great that upon entering the city gates, statues of demons, upon seeing him, cried out and proclaimed the arrival of a king, a great monarch, who would upheave the entire city. We do not know if Jesus in his ministry ever visited Syria; however, we are certain that Matthew tells us his fame had spread throughout Syria, and all who had various afflictions, including those possessed by demons, were brought to him.

Mateo 4:24;

"And his fame spread throughout all Syria, and they brought to him all who were ill, those suffering from various diseases and pains, demoniacs, epileptics, and paralytics; and he healed them." (RV1960)

Archaeology has uncovered numerous statues of gods and deities in Syria, indicating the strong presence of pagan spirituality in the region since ancient times. It is plausible that during Jesus' ministry, many people from Syria sought him out for healing, liberation, or miracles. However, we cannot verify the authenticity of Jesus' visit to Syria at the age of 5. It is unclear whether the author intended to convey a message to Syria through his gospel in that context.

Upon Jesus' arrival in Syria, the demons decided to leave the city and avoid Jesus' presence. This type of narrative involving the clash of powers between gods or deities is also found in ancient stories. For example, when the Israelites lost the Ark of the Covenant, representing Yahweh's presence among his people, to the Philistines, they placed it in the temple next to the god Dagon. Dagon was severely damaged and humiliated before Yahweh's presence, prompting the Philistines to return the ark to Israel due to the afflictions they suffered. Here, we see demons fleeing from this child.

At the same age, Jesus was playing with many friends when one got lost and died. Before judges, Jesus raised him from the dead, only to let him sleep (die) again later. At the age of 6, Jesus was seen making clay birds, blowing on them, and animating them to fly. He was also seen playing with dust, turning it into flies. Upon returning to Israel, Jesus entered schools to learn letters and was accepted by the king to study under a certain Gamaliel.

The exact identity of this Gamaliel mentioned by the author is unknown, but it is likely the same teacher who instructed the apostle Paul. This would be incredibly improbable, considering that Paul studied under Gamaliel for 14 years without meeting Jesus in person, or at least without walking with him. If Jesus had been a disciple of Gamaliel, it is likely that Gamaliel, when addressing the Jews in the biblical text, would have been aware of Jesus and the Nazarene sect following him. Gamaliel did not directly defend Jesus or the movement but requested that they be left alone, stating that if the movement was from God, nothing could stop it. In this case, we would have seen Gamaliel speaking with knowledge of Jesus as his student, something that all of Israel, including rabbinic Judaism, would have known.

Jesus performed healing miracles on lepers, including one instance where he told a leper that he never needed to consult a doctor because he knew someone better than earthly physicians, someone who raises the dead and gives life. The leper, crying and praying to God for healing, was told by Jesus that he would be healed. Jesus took him by the hand, and immediately he was cleansed and healed of his leprosy. When the healed man asked Jesus what to say if someone asked who healed him, Jesus replied, "A child, the son of a physician, who was passing by, saw you, had compassion on you, and restored your health." The healed young man then joyfully bowed at Jesus' feet before returning to his mother. Jesus continued performing many miracles and wonders throughout his childhood in Israel.

Jesus declares who He is:

To conclude Jesus' childhood and infancy in the apocryphal texts, a final and very important event is seen in the last chapter 28 of this gospel. It tells us that at a moment when Jesus had decided to reveal himself more to men, on the road he encountered two soldiers, who were quarreling violently. Jesus, intervening between the soldiers, asked them why they wanted to kill each other. They were so enraged and uncomfortable that they did not respond to Jesus. As they sat by a well continuing to insult each other, Jesus sat among them. One of the soldiers, looking calmly at him, asked him some questions: "Where do you come from, child? Where are you going? What is your name?" Jesus replied, "If I tell you, you will not understand." The soldier asked Jesus if his parents were still alive, and Jesus replied, "My Father lives and is immortal." The soldier retorted, "How can he be immortal?" Jesus replied, "He has been immortal from the beginning. He lives, and death has no dominion over Him." The soldier persisted, "Who is the one who always lives, over whom death has no dominion, since you claim that your father is assured of immortality?" Jesus said, "You could not know Him or even grasp the slightest idea of Him." Then the soldier asked, "Who can see Him?" Jesus answered, "No one." The soldier continued asking, "Where is your Father?" Jesus replied, "In heaven, above the earth." The soldier asked, "And how can you go to be with Him?" Jesus answered, "I have always been with Him, and even today I am with Him." Jesus spent a long time preaching and explaining mysteriously to the soldiers how he had an earthly mother but an immortal Father, indicating in this gospel that Jesus knew clearly from his childhood who his true Father really was and who had begotten him. This idea is highly debatable; theology could demonstrate that Jesus knew well who his Father was, where he had come from, and who he was. Clearly, the Pharisees told Jesus that they knew who his father was, but they did not know where he had come from or even who his father was. They also said that Jesus came from illegitimate birth. While many others said, "Is this not Jesus, the son of Joseph the carpenter?" Anyway, personally, I believe that Jesus was indeed a human being, born, lived, and died entirely as a human being, understanding theologically the plan established by God in Jesus the Christ, conceiving His Son in the womb of Mary, miraculously intervening in history through His Spirit and the Word, incarnating Himself in human form and servant, living subject to the law, obedient unto death, tempted in every way, yet without sin—not as God, but rather as a faithful and integral son to God, raised by His own power, by the Holy Spirit and the Father in resurrection, saving all who believe in Him, giving them life in abundance and eternal life.

THE BAPTISM OF JESUS AND HIS PUBLIC LIFE

Part 4

It has been said and demonstrated that one of the most questioned acts, within and outside of Christianity, is the great question: why did Jesus of Nazareth have to be baptized? According to the Bible, Jesus of Nazareth was without sin. We know that He was tempted in everything but absolutely without sinning. Immediately after His baptism, He entered the desert to be tested, and as we have explained, all His temptations in the desert were reflections of all the temptations that both Adam in Eden and the people of Israel in the desert could not overcome, to show themselves worthy and fit to be both chosen by God to fulfill the great purpose of redeeming and saving humanity.

Just as sin and death entered the world through a human being, Adam and Eve, and just as sin and death continued to dominate the world after God gave the Torah "instruction" at Sinai to His special treasure, the people of Israel, so that they might live by it and be the holy chosen people of God so that all nations might also turn to God the Creator and serve Him together with Israel. Neither Israel nor the kings, priests, or prophets chosen by God could fully accomplish the purpose of redeeming and saving humanity. Although God, the eternal, does not need to plan because He knows and understands all things from eternity, Peter tells us in his first letter that His plan in Christ Jesus existed before the foundation of the world but was manifested at the appropriate time out of love for humanity. All humanity was in grave need of being redeemed and regenerated. The time had come for God to show all His compassion and love for His greatest creation, which was lost in transgression and death.

For this, He could not come entirely in Spirit, invisible, or with all His power, because no one would see Him and even less understand Him. He had to come in the flesh, completely human to the world of human beings. The problem is that God, being eternal, can never and could never deny Himself; He could never cease to be God, always existing as God, without beginning and without end. Therefore, His word, thought, knowledge, wind, and all essence known as the Word, from the Greek word "Logos," which means divine principle and reason, creative order, or the principle expressed in rational words.

Philosophically, the word, the saying, the sound, and the manifested knowledge. In the first chapter of John's Gospel, we see the evangelist using the same Greek term "Logos," which is "Word" in Latin, a word generally used in the vast majority of biblical translations into Spanish. John introduces the Word as being with God in the beginning and being God Himself since it is impossible for everything that this Word of God signifies and represents to be separated or distanced from Him. God is one with His thought, His word, and His consciousness. Therefore, in John's thinking, he begins with the same example of Genesis of the cosmos, the earthly creation, but with a completely spiritual revelation of the true essence and origin of Jesus of Nazareth. While in Matthew and Luke, we see a completely human origin and birth, in John, we see an origin without a beginning. This does not mean that John rejects or denies the human birth or humanity of Jesus. Later, we will see him doctrinally declaring the recognition and duty to believe that Jesus came completely in the flesh, fully man and fully God. We will explain this in more detail later.

God never wanted to save humanity without becoming an example for it. For humanity to be redeemed and remain in that state of true freedom, it would need that great example manifested visibly. That is when we see God, the Word, whom no one has ever been able to see and hear and remain alive, manifesting in the flesh in full palpable view before humanity as a complete man. This Jesus was born as a man, grew up, lived, and went through all the processes of life as every human being. Paul tells us in his letter to the Galatians, "But when the fullness of the time had come, God sent forth His Son, born of a woman, born under the law, to redeem those who were under the law." This Jesus was completely subject to and under the law. He was, like every practicing Jew, part of His tradition and culture, celebrated all the feasts established in the Torah, and kept all its customs. At eight days old, He was circumcised like every Jew, receiving His name Jesus, "Yeshua," "Yeshu," or "Ischo" in Aramaic, Jesus' primary language. Generally, each year He visited the city of Jerusalem for the Passover festival, fulfilling the custom established as law since the return from Babylonian captivity, and also visited the synagogue of His community every Sabbath, "Shabbat." The Pseudo-Matthew Gospel gives us an interesting detail that we do not doubt about Jesus' normal and public life in His family. As a cultural Jew, He was always with His family, being the first to pray and bless the food in His house. It seems that no one ate or drank until Jesus first blessed the food. In the case of Jesus' special baptism, we will first explain the origin, practice, and different purposes of it, and thus we can better understand why Jesus had to enter the waters.

Baptism

The history and origin of water baptism do not begin in the New Testament with John the Baptist, nor is it a rite solely associated with Christianity. Water baptism can be traced back several thousand years before Christ. The association of water with internal spiritual cleansing was not unknown to early human civilizations. From Mesopotamia onward, water was sanctified and then sprinkled on the person. This rite was an act of purification and preparation for a new purpose and a new stage in life. Purifying baptism was conducted outside or away from sanctified places or temples. People could only enter the temple or sanctuaries after being baptized (purified).

The Egyptian civilization practiced about four different religious customs and ideas of water baptism. Newborn children were washed, immersed, or sprinkled with water to be cleansed of all internal impurities from the womb. Among these practices, baptism in Egypt was also practiced as a new birth, rebirth, or new stage in life. Baptism was also practiced as a rite of healing and exorcism for those with evil spirits in their lives. Another baptismal practice in Egypt was that baptism prepared you for entering the very presence of a god or prepared you to receive that god internally in your life. In the Greek world, there is some evidence of baptism in certain sanctuaries, granting humans immortality. However, in most cases, water baptism was usually practiced as a purifying rite and a preparation for a larger, specific ritual purpose.

In Mosaic law, where we see the beginnings of original Judaism, the purification rite was also practiced. Water was used for the purification of people and also for the purification of the elements (utensils) that the religious priests used in worship, sacrifice, or service to God. In the case of the children of Israel arriving in the desert after the exodus from Egypt, it was there that they received through Moses all the ordinances and purification rites to be able to present themselves before God. The washing in water is continuously seen as an ordinance established by God to Moses for the people in the books of Exodus, Numbers, Leviticus, Deuteronomy, and others. Whenever God wanted to present Himself to the people, He demanded days in advance that everyone wash to avoid dying in their impurities.

Each nation or people had a set of waters or a place where purification baptisms were carried out. In the case of Mesopotamia or Babylon, we see the two great rivers known as the Euphrates and the Tigris; in Egypt, the great source of water is the Nile, from where Moses was drawn; and in Israel (Canaan), the famous Jordan River. Historically, it was believed that the land of Canaan or Israel itself was a holy land chosen by God (Yahweh) where He would bring His holy people to dwell. This land had the symbolic title of being the land flowing with milk and honey, a land of sustenance and sweetness of life. The Jordan River has historically and anciently been known as one of the dirtiest rivers on earth, but simply by being in Israel (holy land), it contains the highest level of purification for life. In the biblical book of 2 Kings, we see one of the first purifying baptismal rites in the thinking and era of the prophets in Israel.

2 Kings 5:1:

"There was a man named Naaman, commander of the army of the

king of Syria, highly regarded and favored by his king, because the Lord had given victory to Syria through him. But this man was a leper." (RV1960)

2 Kings 5:9-10:

"Naaman went with his horses and chariot and stopped at the door of Elisha's house. Elisha sent a messenger to say to him, 'Go, wash yourself seven times in the Jordan, and your flesh will be restored and you will be cleansed.'" (RV1960)

The tradition of the prophet Elisha historically dates back to around the 9th century before Christ, showing that the ritual act of immersing or washing in purifying waters is very ancient and practiced in Israel, especially in the Jordan River. This practice and custom can be seen long before Christ. It is also important to understand that the baptismal act as a rite was not necessarily solely for the forgiveness of sins. In the case of Naaman, we do not see it as an act for the forgiveness of his sins, but as an act of inner healing, cleansing, and purification from his incurable disease, leprosy.

We can see more broadly that the traditional, cultural, or religious baptismal practice was an ancient one with different purposes depending on the civilization, nation, people, or tribe. However, all of them had a similar spiritual degree since each nation, people, tribe, or empire, over time, through multiplication, migration, and land conquests, became increasingly intermixed, procreating new ethnicities, races, peoples, tribes, and nations with adopted and reformed cultures. As a tribe returned to its land or procreated, it had to establish an ordered list or social-religious constitution type creed of belief that showed its own identity for all who wanted to be part of or integrate into the people, nation, or tribe.

Having explained the origin of baptism, in the next part, the general focus is to show where and with whom water baptism begins in the Judeo-Christian thought that we see Jesus practicing.

The Essene Community of Qumran:

With the discovery of the Dead Sea Scrolls between 1947 and 1954, found in 11 caves in Israel, dating from the 3rd century BCE to the 1st century CE, these scrolls have led scholars, historians, archaeologists, theologians, and academics to thoroughly study and reconsider the history of the Jews and Judaism in Israel during the Second Temple period. Thanks to these scrolls, we have been able to understand the significant differences in Judaism and Jewish culture from the return from captivity, through Greek Hellenization, to the rise of Jewish Christianity. With the return of the Jews from Babylonian captivity, although we know they maintained baptismal practices as a purification rite, the intertestamental biblical text does not emphasize the baptismal rite as its general focus is on the rebuilding of the Temple. With the division of the Greek Empire after the death of Alexander the Great among his four generals, the Ptolemies and the Seleucids controlled and dominated almost the entire Middle East. The Jews were forced to rise in revolts and create the well-known Maccabean rebellion, and later the Jewish Hasmonean Empire under the famous Judas Maccabeus "The Hammer".

The empire did not emerge instantly with Judas but was founded by one of his brothers named Simon about two decades after Judas defeated the Seleucid army. Judas had been the first to revolt against the Seleucids, especially against their general Antiochus Epiphanes IV, after trying to introduce pagan practices and sacrifices of pigs dedicated to the god Zeus into the Jewish temple, which was clearly forbidden among the Jews. A Jew had offered to sacrifice a pig in the temple; this immediately ignited the wrath of a priest named Mattathias, who was the father of the founder of the Maccabees, and also of Simon, the founder of the Jewish Hasmonean Empire. This Mattathias was from a rural priestly family from Modi'in.

Like all capable priests, he served in the Temple in Jerusalem. Son of John and grandson of Simeon, from the priestly order of Joarib. After the Seleucid persecutions began, Mattathias returned to Modi'in. In 167 BCE, when he was asked by the Greek representative government of King Antiochus IV to offer sacrifices to the Greek gods, he not only refused but furiously killed the Jew who had offered to make the pagan sacrifice in the temple to the Greek gods with his own hands. He also killed the Greek government official presiding over the act. This crime by Mattathias sparked great revolts among the Jews and the Seleucid Greeks. Immediately, Mattathias sought refuge in the Judean desert with his five sons, Judas, Eleazar, Simon, John, and Jonathan, and called on the Jews to follow him, many of whom did. These Jewish revolts, following their victories, became an army that took full political control and the worship of the temple in Israel. With this victory by the Jews, the priests who were present in the current service decided to seek a king from the Davidic line as established. The Maccabees, after winning a war that lasted more than 30 years, saw this idea of the priests as unjust against those who had sacrificed themselves fighting for so long and decided they would not appoint any descendant of David as king. This idea created a divisive split between the Maccabees and the original priests currently serving in the temple.

Ignoring the priests' idea, the Maccabees resolved to keep themselves as the kings of Israel with political control and power. This decision by the Maccabees led to the temple priests being expelled or leaving on their own to the desert to create and establish their own community known as the "Essenes." These Essenes chose to move from Jerusalem to the desert to live a monastic life of strict diet and celibacy entirely for God. It was a solitary place that granted them privacy and separated them from the corrupted Jewish political world. These practices would later be adopted in Christianity. In the desert, they had all the freedom to practice their traditions and religious rites without interference or interruption from anyone. In ancient Jewish thought, deserts were considered the most prominent places to approach and commune with God. From the patriarchs, kings, and prophets, including the nation of Israel, all in some way lived or passed through the desert. It was the place where God led each of them to know Him.

This was the reason why these original priests moved to the Qumran desert. Previously during the Davidic and Solomonic monarchy era, there was a priest named Zadok, whose name means "righteous and just" or "Righteousness and Justice," a descendant of Eleazar, and son of Aaron, who helped David and also establish Solomon, David's son, on the throne. It was believed that the true temple priests were the sons of this Zadok, known as the Zadokites, righteous and just priests. With the departure of the original temple priests, the Maccabees installed the Sadducee sect in place of the original priests. These were not legitimate priests, having probably bought the title that belonged to the true priests, sons of Zadok. They had become extremely corrupt and a large majority had paganly Hellenized.

They were placed there because of their economic position among the people. These false Sadducees were addicted to the regime of the Maccabees, who had appointed them as the new temple priests. It was thought that these Sadducees or the title given to them came from this righteous and just priest Zadok from the times of David and Solomon. However, with the discoveries of the Dead Sea Scrolls, this idea of thought revealed a great need to re-evaluate and re-analyze well the origin of these supposed imposter Sadducees and who the true righteous and just priests deserving of the title Sadducee really were. This famous and probably false Jewish sect known as the "Sadducees," impostors, false or corrupt priests, who were known among the wealthiest Jewish families of their time, is believed to have numbered around 6,000 Pharisees and some 4,000 Essenes.

This would reduce the number of Sadducees to much fewer. Later, with the conquest by the Roman Empire, these same Sadducees would become addicted to the Roman regimes as previously to the Maccabees and enter into mutual interest ties with them. These famous Sadducees were also known as the "Sanhedrin," the judges in charge of solving all social, political, and religious problems and issues of the people. These Sadducees are the same ones we see in the Gospels against the Pharisees and Jesus of Nazareth, denying the existence of angels, the resurrection, and other doctrines. Until the discovery of the Dead Sea Scrolls, it was believed that these

Sadducees were the true direct descendants of the priest Zadok, hence the title was granted to them. However, it turns out that the true sons of Zadok, righteous and just, were the original priests who had moved to the desert known as the Essene community. We do not know to what extent or if among the falsely called Sadducees or those who adopted the title there were true priests and sons of Zadok, who possibly existed but had become corrupted, Hellenizing themselves, or deciding to stay in Jerusalem separating themselves from the true priests, or for some other reason.

The problem arises when one of the other Jewish sects known in Israel as the "Essenes," briefly mentioned by some 1st-century historians, Flavius Josephus, Philo, and Pliny, until then we did not have enough data on this sect. With the discovery of the Dead Sea Scrolls, this whole idea would change. In one of the scrolls, the same community describes the corruption of the supposed corrupt Sadducees present in Israel, saying that they had contaminated the city and also the temple.

These scrolls, written by the same Qumran desert community, whom the mentioned historians call the "Essenes," declare themselves to be the original true priests to whom the title of Sadducees as the sons of Zadok, righteous and just, priests of the Eleazar line, son of Aaron himself, truly belonged. This is found in the scroll called "The Sectarian Scrolls" and in a portion titled "The Manual of Discipline." These false Sadducees were called "Manasseh" and the Pharisee sect was called "Ephraim."

The Jewish Baptism of the Essenes and John:

These original priests who had left Jerusalem to form their own community, later known as the Essenes, meaning "pious" or "holy," continued with their services, rites, and religious practices. It is among this Jewish community in the Qumran desert where we see, for the first time or initially, the baptism similar to what we see in the New Testament texts. These Qumran Essenes introduced the rite of baptism but with a purely external and moral sense, with an idea of external purification. It is believed that they could practice baptismal rites once or several times a day and continuously, interpreting the prophets in this way:

Ezekiel 36:25-28,

"I will sprinkle clean water on you, and you will be clean; I will cleanse you from all your impurities and from all your idols. I will give you a new heart and put a new spirit in you; I will remove from you your heart of stone and give you a heart of flesh. And I will put my Spirit in you and move you to follow my decrees and be careful to keep my laws. Then you will live in the land I gave your ancestors; you will be my people, and I will be your God."

It has been believed or thought that John the Baptist came from this very sect, and there is also the possibility that Jesus himself may have been or at least visited the desert Essenes. Some few theologians disagree, but the vast majority of scholars and academics agree on the high possibility that John could have come from the Essenes, and they also agree that many of Jesus' teachings originated from the Essenes themselves. It is true that John's baptism was an original one, especially with a different purpose from that of the Essenes, who customarily practiced continuous ritual baptism for the external purification of the body.

John's baptism was completely different; in the Essene community, baptisms were not only external purification rites, but also the one entering the waters was immersed by himself, baptizing himself without the presence of others. In John's baptism, no one baptized himself; John was the first to become the baptizer, the one who baptized others. He was the first to take on the dedicated office of baptizing others. John's baptism, similar with water but completely different in purpose from the Essenes' rite, was accompanied by the call to repentance and preparation for the entry into the Messianic kingdom that was among them or soon to come. John had established himself on the other side of the Jordan near Bethany, with Jericho and Jerusalem on the other side, representing a key place in Israel's history. This is similar to when the Israelites were about to enter Canaan, the promised land, with Joshua leading them

Jesus of Nazareth

as their leader and savior. When they were at Shittim about to cross, all the enemies, Amorites, and giants in Canaan were disheartened upon hearing how God had divided the Jordan and led all His people through it. After crossing, they reached Gilgal, where they were circumcised by Joshua, and after celebrating Passover, they entered victoriously into the first city of the promised land, Jericho in Canaan, "Israel."

With this said, the prophet John the Baptist had arrived in the Judean desert, establishing himself in Bethany, quite close to the ancient Shittim on the other side of the Jordan River, where Joshua also brought the people before entering Canaan. Through God, Joshua had called them to purify themselves and prepare because Jehovah would soon do wonders among His people. This is the same call of John, established in the same place where Joshua and the people were before crossing the Jordan. John would be the voice calling the Jews from the other side of the Jordan to not avoid the Jordan (Repentance and purification) to enter Jerusalem or the land of Israel by any other means than crossing the Jordan, which also symbolically represents the "baptism" to reach Jerusalem or Israel as the people once did, being baptized in the Jordan with Joshua and the priests before entering the promised land. John the Baptist knew that the time and moment had come for a promise much greater than the conquest of the land of Canaan.

He knew the time for the true Kingdom of God to come to earth had arrived, the fulfillment of the true promise made to both Abraham and King David, when God said, "Moreover, I will make your dynasty stand firm, and your kingdom endure forever." Until that moment, Israel had not had a true king, a descendant of David, because all the kings from the construction of the Second Temple until the 1st century were not true descendants of David or from the tribe of Judah. John, as a priest, had received the call to turn the heart of Israel back to their God, to prepare to receive the one whom he was not worthy to untie the strap of his sandal, the true King of Kings, Jesus of Nazareth, the Lamb who would take away the sin of the world. John not only called the Jews from the desert; the biblical text says that his fame was so great that all of Jerusalem went out to his baptism, and many were baptized by him. This is a representation of the necessary return to repentance needed by all the Jews, Pharisees, and sects in Jerusalem. The same fear we see among the Amorite enemies of Israel, upon hearing how God had divided the Jordan, the waters of purification, being immersed, would be symbolically baptized, representing purity and cleanliness, and preparation for the purpose of conquest. This fear we see in King Herod, who killed John, and many of the priests of Jerusalem towards John, represents the same fear and dread that the Amorites and enemies in Canaan had towards Joshua and the people of Israel.

The Baptism of Jesus in the Waters

One of the entirely historical events believed to have happened to Jesus was his baptism in the waters by the prophet John the Baptist. The synoptic gospels all agree that Jesus was baptized by John the Baptist. Matthew adds that when John saw Jesus coming to him, he opposed it, saying that he himself needed to be baptized by Him. But Jesus of Nazareth, opposing this suggestion, told John to baptize Him because it was necessary to fulfill all righteousness. The book of John avoids directly saying that Jesus was baptized by John. The text tells us that the next day, John saw Jesus coming toward him; we do not see any mention of the Jordan or the waters, but it is here when John said, "Behold the Lamb of God who takes away the sin of the world. This is he of whom I said, after me comes a man who is preferred before me, for he was before me." John did not know Him, but for His sake, he had been brought to the desert to baptize with water.

The One who had sent him to baptize had said, on whom you see the Spirit descending and remaining, this is He who will baptize with the Holy Spirit. Mark originally gives us an important detail, also appearing in other gospels, that the Spirit's descent on Jesus was in the form of a dove. In the section where we discuss John's testimony about Jesus, we touch on this but not in as much detail. For this reason, I am eager to share a very important detail for understanding the meaning of this dove. When scholars study Mark's text along with the other Gospels, an important and critical detail is to separate each gospel by its writer and its audience, because each writer writes for a different people with different thoughts. For example, to a Roman, a dove would not have the same meaning as to a Jew, especially in the biblical text. Therefore, historians and scholars say that to understand this dove in Mark's text, one must look at what a Roman thought to understand the context and its meaning when reading or hearing this part of Jesus' baptism. Among the Romans, divination through birds was very widespread. It was also believed that their flight brought a message from the gods, and on occasions, there were priests trained to interpret their divine message. The bird that the Romans admired above all others was the eagle. Pliny the Elder, a Roman writer and historian, tells us that the eagle was the noblest and strongest of all birds.

He describes it as a hunter, swift, precise, and deadly. The eagle was the most important symbol in Rome; the legions carried them on their standards and insignia. Suetonius, a Roman historian of the 1st century, shares an important detail about the descent of the eagle in Rome. In the lives of many of the emperors, an eagle would suddenly descend to where they were, and this represented an ascent to power. We see this with Octavian Augustus (27 B.C. to 14 A.D.), when, as a simple general, an eagle descended on the tent where he was, and the Romans saw this as a sign that he would be the one to ascend the throne. With Tiberius (14 A.D. to 37 A.D.), it is said almost the same thing happened: an eagle of a different species also rested on the roof of his house, and this was interpreted as his ascent to power. With Claudius (41 A.D. to 54 A.D.), it is said that when he presented himself on one occasion to the Romans, an eagle rested on his shoulder, and the Romans interpreted this as his being destined to become the emperor. There were many others who received this sign in Rome in the same way, that a bird resting on or visiting someone meant they would be the next emperor. With this detail, we can better understand why Mark used the image of the dove resting on Jesus in view of all. While the eagle was the most powerful, feared, and deadly bird, the dove was the most sublime, gentle, peaceful, and defenseless, representing peace. With this message, what Mark would be conveying to his Roman readers is that a new emperor had arrived, but not like the ones they were used to seeing.

This new emperor or government would not need weapons, swords, or shields to conquer, because he would conquer through love, gentleness, and peace. This new emperor would not use violence to defend himself; like the dove, he would remain humble and gentle before all his enemies. This new emperor was more than an emperor; he was the King of kings, initiating and taking his position in Israel. The Romans, through this news, would understand that someone new had risen under this familiar sign but different in this instance. This is Mark's message to all of Rome, telling them that a new King and government had been appointed by God for Israel and the entire world.

Continuing with the baptism of Jesus, among a great number of scholars, it is believed that Jesus had entered the baptismal waters to receive forgiveness for the natural sin engendered by Adam as the father of all humanity. Others have said that just as there are unconscious sins in humans, Jesus as a man, not knowing all things in his imperfection, most likely his baptism was for unconscious sins in his life. Another opinion says that just as Jesus taught his disciples to pray the Lord's Prayer, telling them to ask the Father for forgiveness for all offenses committed, most likely Jesus himself prayed, asking the Father for forgiveness for any offense committed. The last hypothesis says that just as Jesus, being a Jew and a son of his time, was fulfilling his ritual of external purification as once practiced by the Essenes.

All these rational hypotheses, although in a certain sense some plausible, are far from the truth and theological reality of why Jesus of Nazareth entered the waters to be baptized by the prophet John the Baptist. Jesus of Nazareth, entirely human as the expected Messiah, until the day he came to John at the Jordan, had not yet begun his public ministry as the Messiah of Israel. The baptism of Jesus was the public evidence of the beginning of the messianic era, the start of his dedication to fulfilling the purpose for which the

Father had sent him. All the time before his baptism, we see him living in Nazareth. From his baptism onwards, we never see him returning to live in Nazareth. From then on, Jesus decided to dedicate himself entirely to the needy, to the point where he didn't even have a pillow to lay his head on, as the biblical text tells us. From then on, he dedicated himself to depending completely on his heavenly Father and not on the monetary social work he once probably had. The baptism of Jesus is the full capacity and aptitude before his Father, determined and firm to enter another level of purpose known as the door and entrance to the new messianic era. As the first fruits, being the first in the messianic era, he set the example for all who would later enter this messianic era through Him. The baptism of Jesus was the acceptance of the suffering he would have to undergo to redeem the world. Before many entered into glory, one had to be baptized in suffering and death.

The baptism of Jesus also served as a sign to the prophet John and all generations of believers who would serve him in the future. John had received the word to see the Spirit descending on Him, and he saw it fulfilled. Jesus was determined to put his hand to the plow and never look back, and this was demonstrated when he was submerged in the waters. It was at his baptism that some Church Fathers tell us he truly descended into hell to rise from the dead, this Jesus being the visible image of the invisible God, upon whom all the fullness of God dwelt. Being in the form of God, he did not consider equality with God something to be grasped, but made himself nothing, taking the form of a servant, being made in human likeness. And being found in appearance as a man, he humbled himself and became obedient to death, even death on a cross. For this great cause, the best of men, Jesus of Nazareth, entered the waters to be baptized. The baptism of Jesus is found in the biblical text, but we also find it in some apocryphal texts like the Gospel of the Ebionites or the Nazarenes. Scholars date this gospel to the early 2nd century onwards. The complete gospel has not been found, but fragments and a number of verses have. The version of the Ebionites, who were Jews and are believed to have been some of the original primitive Christians, tells us that when Jesus entered the

Jordan to be baptized by John, after being submerged, the heavens were opened, a voice spoke saying, "You are my beloved Son, in whom I am well pleased," and again, "Today I have begotten you." The Holy Spirit descended like a dove, but it also says that the Spirit entered into Him, something that many early Christians probably believed, as it would be very likely that the Spirit was with Him and in Him as the Church received it.

This is not what the canonical text tells us, but it does say some interesting things, such as that once the Spirit entered Jesus, the writer says that a light or a great radiance rested over the whole place where they were. When John saw this, he asked the Lord, "Who are you, Lord?" The voice spoke again, responding once more, "This is my beloved Son, in whom I am well pleased." John immediately fell at his feet, praying, "Lord, I deserve to be baptized by you." Since the baptism of Jesus in the waters, this ceremony has remained one of the ordinances and sacraments in Christianity. Some organizations teach that to attain salvation, in addition to confessing the Lord, it is also necessary to enter the baptismal waters, according to the Gospel of Mark. Personally, I do not believe that water baptism excludes a person from the free gift of salvation given by God, as it is really a public and completely symbolic ceremony.

All our sins are forgiven immediately when we confess Christ into our lives. Paul shows us that the true baptism is not the ceremony but being immersed by the Spirit into Christ through union with Him, which is received when we confess and recognize that his blood shed on Calvary's cross as the perfect sacrifice is sufficient for the forgiveness of our transgressions against the Father. Now, allow me to say that there is nothing more beautiful, in my personal opinion, than following the master's steps. To be like Jesus or imitate Jesus would be the most beautiful example in a Christian or a common person. Following his steps, as Peter tells us, is the goal. Paul tells the Corinthians to be imitators of him as he is of Christ.

All who followed Christ also entered the waters. The gospels tell us that Jesus and all who were united to Him came repenting and were baptized in the waters. Therefore, every Christian should desire to enter the waters, especially when the true purpose and meaning of the public ceremony is understood. Dear reader, friend, I would like to ask you a question. Were you ever baptized in the waters? What happened to your life after you made that decision? It would be good to reanalyze whether the same attitude, conviction, and firmness that Jesus had after being baptized, to never look back and dedicate himself to fulfilling his Father's purpose until his last day, also convinced us to fulfill that purpose and the Father's will in our lives. Are you fulfilling the decision you once made after entering the waters?

Today I invite you, if you have stayed on the path, if you have taken your hand off the plow and turned back, or if in some way you feel you are not the same, I pray to God that through the merits of Jesus of Nazareth and his Spirit, you may have the necessary strength to stand firm and continue with the determined purpose you had on the day you entered the waters, where the old man and the old woman, the old life, without goals and without purposes, stayed. Coming out of the waters filled with strength and life to fulfill the calling that God has given and continues to give you each day. This Jesus, being in the form of God, made himself nothing, becoming an example for you so that you may know that just as he was able, even with all the sufferings and obstacles in his path, he was able to fully accomplish the purpose of his life, pleasing the Father and becoming the approved man and man of sorrows by God, an example forever for all humanity. If Jesus did it, he did it to show you that you can do it too. Father "Theodore of Heraclea" said of Jesus, in his baptism he identified with humanity and with all that pertains to human nature. "John Chrysostom" said, Jesus was not baptized for his own benefit, but rather for our benefit, fulfilling all righteousness. "John Chrysostom" also said, Jesus came to end the curse that pointed to the transgression of the law, and he ended it by fully complying with the whole law. "Hilary of Poitiers" said, in Jesus we contemplate a whole man, through his obedience to the Holy Spirit, the body he assumed, fulfilling in him all the sacraments of our salvation, though he had no need to be baptized. On the contrary, through him, the waters of the Jordan were sanctified for all men who were later baptized by John. "Origen" said, through Jesus' baptismal act, we see true humility and lowliness of heart, approaching those who were inferior to him, and humbly complying with all established order until his death. This demonstrates that not everyone who baptizes is greater than the one who is baptized.

This baptism in the waters of Jesus, followed immediately by the baptism of the Holy Spirit, was the beginning, the great example, and the very representation of the two baptisms that every believer in Jesus would also experience upon entering his kingdom: one representing suitability and aptitude, determined to die to the desires of this world to live a life dedicated, clean, and pure in the sole service of God, and the other representing the fullness, guidance, and power of the Holy Spirit in life, for service to humanity and to God.

The baptism of the Holy Spirit in Jesus

This kind of baptism or anointing with the Holy Spirit upon Jesus is completely unique and distinct from the other previous baptisms or what could have been theologically a representation of the coming of the Holy Spirit upon a people or an individual set apart for divine purpose and service. Why do we think that the baptism or anointing of Jesus with the Holy Spirit is completely different from the others? Jesus is the one who baptizes others with the Holy Spirit, although biblically we see that the promise of the Holy Spirit for the world is given by the Father, it is only granted through the merits of Jesus of Nazareth. Jesus is the means by which the world receives the promise of the Father. Therefore, no one can receive this promise of the Holy Spirit without first receiving Jesus.

Jesus in his anointing by the Holy Spirit comes to be the unique means by which after Him all who believe in Him will also receive this baptism of the Holy Spirit. It is true that this baptism of the Holy Spirit upon Jesus is somewhat different from the receiving of the Holy Spirit in the life of the believer, since immediately Jesus receives His anointing, He is enveloped in the power of the Holy Spirit to be tested and tempted in everything, and to fulfill His purpose before the Father, although all believers, upon receiving the promise or gift of the Holy Spirit to also dedicate ourselves to the service of the Father and Lord Jesus Christ, the true baptism of the Holy Spirit in believers, besides the gifts or signs that may occur, is that which Paul mentions when he tells the councils "one and the same baptism". For by one Spirit we were all baptized into one body, whether Jews or Greeks, whether slaves or free, and we were all made to drink of one Spirit. Through our sincere confession and unique faith in Jesus of Nazareth, we are taken by the Holy Spirit and immersed, and grafted or woven into the body and blood of Jesus, making us one in Him, under complete communion, so as never to be outside or separated from Him. This is Paul's thought when he explains in reality what the Baptism of the Holy Spirit represents for the believer. All other manifestations and the fruit of the same Spirit are accompanied by this baptism or anointing of the Holy Spirit. Now we cannot confuse the person of the Holy Spirit with the gifts and with the fruit.

The Holy Spirit is not the gifts, nor the fruit. The Holy Spirit is the one who produces and generates the gifts and also the fruit in the life of the believer. Every believer needs to understand that with the receiving of the baptism or anointing of the Holy Spirit in life, this act, although received only once, is not a matter of thinking that it was received only for that time. Nor should we think that the external manifestations that we see today inside and outside the church are directly produced by the Holy Spirit, something of which I am completely convinced is that the Holy Spirit will never manifest or do anything for entertainment, and less so that men may be glorified among themselves. The Holy Spirit has a work to do in the life of the believer, and generally, we do not see it working. Many churches, organizations, and people have been so mistaken and confused that they have not truly understood who the Holy Spirit is and what His ministry is for the body of Christ, the church. The Holy Spirit is the one who transforms, regenerates, vivifies, strengthens, and changes the life of man when he receives Jesus the Christ into his life. His work is to convince the whole man until he is perfected in the image of Jesus of Nazareth himself. As previously mentioned, the receiving or anointing of the Holy Spirit in life is a one-time experience, but this does not indicate that this experience ends there. This reception is the beginning of a new life, regenerated, which will be full of experience with God. From there, the Holy Spirit through our lives, conscience, souls, and strengths, will begin to educate us, guide us, show us, transform us, speak to us, and increasingly perfect us until the whole purpose of God is complete and fulfilled in us.

In contrast to the Holy Spirit in the Old Testament, who would come and go as He pleased upon the life of a person, it was believed that only prophets and kings could receive the special anointing or the unction of the Spirit. Kings were anointed as sons of God to fulfill their purpose, and prophets were also anointed to be the bearers of God between Him and His people. We see a kind of anointing that can also represent the same Holy Spirit and it is upon the priests of the people; they had to be anointed and set apart for the service of the temple, and to intercede on behalf of the people before God. In other cases, we see the Holy Spirit in the Old Testament as the very presence of Yahweh or His glory among His people Israel. When they came out of Egypt, we see a representation of what could symbolize or demonstrate the anointing of this people as being guided by God Himself with a cloud by day and a pillar of fire by night to illuminate and guide them on the right path. Jesus said that this same Holy Spirit, the Comforter, would guide us into all truth, so it is a clear comparison, just as God with His presence was with and guided His people for 40 years in the desert, in the same way, in the baptism of the Holy Spirit, or the anointing of the same, taking us out of death and the world of death, He continually guides us to Christ, and in the process perfects us through His consolation. To conclude this part of the anointing or the baptism of the Holy Spirit, the word used in the Old Testament for Spirit is "Ruaj" or "Ruach." This word in Hebrew thought has at least three uses: "wind", "breath", or "spirit". The Old Testament always associated the Holy Spirit with life, as the one who restores or gives life. In the creation of Adam, God breathes the breath or breath of life into him; this breath was the only means for Adam to awaken or become a living being. In ancient times, the only way to know if a person was alive or dead was through their breathing; they could be with their eyes closed, possibly without any movement, and the only way to certify if the person was alive or dead was if the air, wind, or breath, went away or moved away from the person. In ancient thought, it was believed that when someone stopped breathing it was because the divine essence within man left him and left him alone; he was considered dead. The Hebrews associated the Spirit of Yahweh or Yahweh Himself with His power over the winds, as His breath. This is the idea we see in the prophet Ezekiel when God asks him to prophesy to the Spirit of the four winds to come upon the dry and dead bones that represent the state of death without hope of Israel, captives and prisoners in foreign lands, to come upon them and give them life again. The prophet saw that it was almost impossible for these bones to come back to life, but the "Spirit" wind of God, the same that breathed upon Adam, had come upon Israel "Judah" to give them life again in the midst of their death, to regenerate them, and give them a new life. The Hebrews or Jewish Israelites also saw the catastrophic judgments of the earthly winds, both in the deserts and in the cities and places where they lived, as the punishment and wrath of Yahweh upon His people and also upon their enemies depending on the case. In this way, the ancients associated the winds with the Spirit of God, manifested in wrath. A final comparison of the Holy Spirit can also be seen as the winds of blessing upon the people; when the people obeyed their God, He came upon them as the dawn rises, and He came upon them as rain, like the spring rain that waters the whole earth. These were the words of the prophet Hosea to his people. These winds that watered the rain on the earth, which produced a better fruit for life, were also likened and seen as the very Holy Spirit of God. In the New Testament, we see a very similar arrival of the same "Spirit" wind upon Jesus in the form of a Dove, to represent the security and salvation of the world, just as a dove uses the wind to enter and exit Noah's ark, it came and went until it found a tree branch and did not return anymore, resting on the tree in a sign of salvation and security, likewise, it descended as a dove upon Christ the Spirit, remaining on the tree of life, or the true vine Jesus of Nazareth, letting the world know that He is the chosen one, the peace, security, and salvation of the world. After Jesus had risen, appearing to His disciples, He ordered them to go to Jerusalem and not to leave there until they were invested with the Holy Spirit. As we see throughout the chapter.

Acts 2:1-29

When the day of Pentecost had fully come, they were all with one accord in one place. And suddenly there came a sound from heaven, as of a rushing mighty wind, and it filled the whole house where they were sitting. Then there appeared to them divided tongues, as of fire, and one sat upon each of them. And they were all filled with the Holy Spirit and began to speak with other tongues, as the Spirit gave them utterance.

From this moment, the promise of the gift of the Holy Spirit for all, which the Father had promised to Jesus for humanity, had been fulfilled. It was from that moment that we saw the first event or reception of the baptism of the Holy Spirit, or the same anointing on all those who were in the upper room, for the service to God with power as witnesses of Jesus. After all these disciples were under tremendous fear for their lives, since Jesus had been put to death, the Jews and perhaps the Romans would also come out to kill His followers, these, in the midst of the festivities, were all hiding and terrified, but when they were baptized, vested, and filled with the Holy Spirit, they were all transformed to become men with strength, authority, and power before all those who sought their lives. Without fear, they began to preach boldly and demonstrate the same power of the Holy Spirit. This wind that had filled the whole house had been the sign of the advent of the Holy Spirit as a blessing for each one in that place. From the day of Pentecost, the Holy Spirit has not ceased to move and work over humanity. It still continues to work and move like the wind over the lives of all who long and wish to accept Christ and dedicate themselves to the service of God, just as the great teacher and perfect example Jesus of Nazareth did when He was baptized or anointed by the Holy Spirit.

Jesus of Nazareth

Acts 8:14-17

Now when the apostles who were at Jerusalem heard that Samaria had received the word of God, they sent Peter and John to them, who, when they had come down, prayed for them that they might receive the Holy Spirit. For as yet He had fallen upon none of them. They had only been baptized in the name of the Lord Jesus. Then they laid hands on them, and they received the Holy Spirit.

The Public Young Life of Jesus

This session continues and includes a part where we previously could not stop while talking about the growth and development in the life of Jesus. Here, we pause a bit to explain in detail what the public life of Jesus at a young age could have been like, and what it was really according to the biblical text the beginning of his public life. Hearing that his friend John, who preached in the desert, was imprisoned, Jesus decided to continue preaching where John had finished. It is from his public baptism by John the Baptist that Jesus dedicates himself to a completely public and communal life.

It is true that the life of Jesus is quite mysterious. Many have tried to fill all those dark areas of the unknown life of Jesus, and we have to recognize that we do not have authentically or historically faithful written texts about the so-called lost or unknown years of Jesus' childhood, adolescence, and youth. Personally, some years ago, an interest began in my life to delve deeper and get to know this Jesus of Nazareth, the man, the Jew who walked, slept, ate, talked, cried, rejoiced, felt sadness, got angry, suffered, had friends, enemies, and also died. I set out to annually visit the land where this Jesus was born and lived to learn more about the life and customs, which are very possibly still practiced in Israel. We cannot deny that we are in quite deep and dark waters since over 2000 years of history have passed, and with so much time, almost everything changes.

Anyway, with the help of many teachers, historians, scholars, both inside and outside of Israel, I have tried to create and elaborate on the public human life of this Jesus, using customs, traditions, upbringing, growth, foods, languages, practices, Jewish rites, and thoughts, etc. Firstly, the entire environment of the first century in Israel was deeply influenced by a completely religious worldview. There was no common or single thought in first-century Judaism. There were a large number of sects, as we have mentioned, and all these sects had different thoughts regarding ordinances and necessary practices. Each city had its own synagogue. Every Saturday, Jews would go to the synagogues, and after leaving, they would return home with their families. Jews were accustomed to celebrating all the culturally established festivals in the Torah and the Tanakh. Mothers were the housewives, while fathers were the providers of the household with their social work.

In the case of teachers or Rabbis themselves, some were wealthier than others. They had schools and meeting rooms, while the less wealthy and less affluent dedicated themselves to teaching on the road, sometimes in squares, deserts, mountains, or under shady trees. Students usually paid a small fee to the Rabbis or teachers who taught them. At this time, the Roman Empire had absolute control over all the land of Israel. The Romans collected all the taxes from the Jews. To go to the temple, Jews had to pay a due tax, and every year, Jews also had to pay a tax to the Romans. The Romans hired the wealthiest and most educated Jews to be the tax collectors instead of doing it themselves.

The most popular language in Israel during the first century was Greek. There were some other languages used, such as Aramaic, Hebrew, and Latin. There could have been some other dialects present, from Phoenicians or Jews who had emigrated from other parts, as Jews from all over the world came to Jerusalem and Israel with different languages. Most scholars tell us that in the first century, 97% of people in Israel were illiterate, who could neither write nor read. The profession of scribes was extremely important. The only known Jewish schools were in Jerusalem.

At this time, the two most famous rabbis, from whom the majority of all the rabbinic disciples emerged, were Shammai and Hillel. From these two came most of the first-century Pharisees, although the Pharisees had existed long before them. In the New Testament,

Jesus of Nazareth

we have some individuals like Simeon, Gamaliel, and Paul, who were at some point disciples of the schools of Shammai or Hillel themselves. It has been shown with ancient texts the great probability that many of Jesus' sayings and parables were taken from the same rabbi teachers, Shammai and Hillel.

It was in this time and environment that this humble Jew Jesus was born. The biblical text tells us that he was born in the small town of Bethlehem in Judea, where the most important kings of the tribe of Judah had been born, especially King David, from whom it is believed that Jesus himself came. Studies question whether Jesus was actually born in Bethlehem. Some suggest that he most likely was born in the city of Nazareth, but Matthew, using Bethlehem in his gospel, and Luke, after investigating the texts and traditions well, possibly took the birthplace of Bethlehem from Matthew as well. Matthew in his gospel continually shows Jesus as the King and the anointed one. For him to be a king in reality, even if he probably came from the tribe of Judah like David, he had to have been born in Bethlehem, the city of kings.

In any case, these ideas that have arisen to try to create a historical Jesus, whom we know existed but not in the hypothetical manner that many historians, in some cases skeptical, agnostic, and even academic atheists, have tried to create, and grow as absolute truth their own hypotheses, rejecting or completely ignoring the possibility of the text. No serious theologian or academic scholar of biblical sciences will ever study the biblical text to take away its veracity, authority, or the general purpose of its message for which it was inspiredly written. In the end, I believe what a teacher once said: I prefer to believe in the authority and veracity of a biblically archaeologically found verse on a piece of papyrus than in all the hypothesis books that may come out trying to hit and create as truth the histories and knowledge of the biblical text.

We believe that it is indeed possible to recreate many biblical things. Legitimate academic and serious theological study of the Bible has taught us a great number of errors we have had regarding the thought of the text in the past. But in no way should the text be studied to distort it with hypotheses or imaginative ideas as if the opinions of men of this century have more authority or veracity than the biblical text itself, which is still the most read and sold in all of history.

Historically, it is believed that if Jesus had been the firstborn of Mary, he had to have been delivered to God and left in the temple for the service of the priests. It was established that every firstborn male who broke the womb would be dedicated to the Lord. But we see that Jesus did not serve the priests nor the temple. Similarly, there was a special class of offering in the law that parents could pay as a ransom for the child and take him back, so that he would grow up at home and be dedicated to helping both father and mother. As Joseph and Mary lived in a town in lower Galilee, they returned with Jesus to Nazareth, where he was raised, grew up, lived, and worked alongside his foster father Joseph the carpenter or artisan.

There were no schools in Nazareth. To this day, no school has been registered or found in Nazareth, and it is highly doubtful that Jesus would have studied in the schools of Jerusalem. First, due to the great distance from Jerusalem to Nazareth. Second, because honestly, Jesus nor his parents had the kind of income for him to study at the height of Jerusalem's studies. And third, because if he had studied there, all the Pharisees of his time would have known him quite well and would never have questioned so much who he was and where he came from as we see in the biblical text. It is believed that Nazareth was a small town in the first century, so much so that it does not appear in the Old Testament, nor in any of the traditional Jewish literature such as the Mishnah, Gemara, or either of the two Talmuds.

The title Nazarene is not known if it was really taken because of a special vow or because he was from Nazareth. The general thought is that Jesus was titled the Nazarene because he belonged to Nazareth. Matthew tells us, "He came and dwelt in a city called Nazareth, that it might be fulfilled which was spoken by the prophets, 'He shall be called a Nazarene.'" But it is not known to which prophet Matthew was exactly referring. Generally, Matthew uses Isaiah a lot. If so, some think it could refer to chapter 11 where one of the Hebrew words for branch appears, which is "netzer." It is used in Isaiah 11:1 in reference to the Messiah and derives from the root natzar. The Greek word translated as Nazareth is "Nazara."

Some scholars believe that "Nazara" is the Greek form of "natzar" and is the justification for Matthew saying that calling Jesus a Nazarene was a fulfillment of the prophecy of the Old Testament. It sounds quite outlandish to us, but it likely made much more sense in the original languages. Jesus must have had a very interested life in the scriptures. We know that Jesus studied the scriptures to some extent, although we do not know where he studied, nor where he received such excellent training. In Jewish homes, mothers were dedicated to instructing their children in all the knowledge of the Torah and the Tanakh. We do not know the extent of Mary's knowledge. All apocryphal sources indicate that she had lived in the temple throughout her youth until the priests dismissed her to fulfill her purpose as Joseph's wife. We also cannot pretend that Jesus was the only child in the house. We see that Jesus had more brothers, and even a sister. We know that he grew quite close to them because they would later be with him in his public ministry. In Matthew and Mark, we see that when people heard him speak, they said, "Is this not the son of the carpenter? And his mother is Mary, and they mentioned each of his brothers, as if they knew them all." Generally, in Israel, the family, parents, and children remain together in one house. Education was important, almost obligatory, although as in all times, some children opted for banditry and criminality, which was punished with death, as we see with the two thieves crucified alongside Jesus. Children would dedicate themselves to learning their parents' trade or profession. In Jesus' case, his father was a carpenter, and he also learned carpentry. He was most likely a carpenter himself, as Mark 6:3 tells us, "Is this not the carpenter... etc.?" Those who dedicated themselves to study would go to study at the feet of their masters when they were ready. Those who decided to marry, after getting married, would move to their own homes. Jewish marriage in the first and second centuries of our era was different in certain aspects from ours in this 21st century. At that time, there was only one marriage ceremony. There was a minimal engagement act, in which the man would ask his intended if she wanted to marry him, and with an engagement ring, the relationship became more serious until a date was set for the wedding. Once married, they would then join and move in together. In the case of Jesus' sister, we know almost nothing, only that he had a sister because that's what the biblical text tells us. It is believed that Jesus had many religious relatives nearby, so if this is correct, then it could be entirely normal for him to have had extensive knowledge in some way. Some traditions have even said that Joseph of Arimathea was Jesus' uncle. In a highly recommended book by Juan Marcos Bejarano Gutierrez called "The Judaism of Jesus' Followers," we are given a list of all 15 brothers or direct cousins of Jesus who were left in charge of the church in Jerusalem after the apostles died. Many Christians also fled to Pella, a city in Perea, a Roman province. The list includes James, Simeon, Justus, Zacchaeus, Tobias, Benjamin, John, Matthias, Philip, Seneca, another Justus, Levi, Ephres, Joseph, and Judas (not Iscariot). This list is also shared by the Church Father Eusebius of Caesarea in his book "Church History," where he tells us that it was provided by the church historian Julius Africanus, who lived from the mid-2nd century to the mid-3rd century. For more information on each of these relatives of Jesus, you can read the recommended book above. Religious traditionalist Jews are so zealous about their religious practices and beliefs that they have a tradition where they believe children begin to hear and read the Torah after 40 days in the womb. It is believed that on the 40th day, the soul enters the child, giving them the capacity to begin hearing the Torah. Between 3 to 5 years old, they begin reading the Torah, between 8 to 10 years old they begin reading the Tanakh, which is the compendium of additional books to the Torah known as the Pentateuch. Between the ages of 12 to 13, they have their Bar Mitzvah; in Judaism, it is considered that a male individual stops being a child and becomes a man when he turns 13. This age is not chosen arbitrarily; there are written references in the Torah indicating that 13 represents the beginning of adulthood for males. To celebrate the transition from childhood to adolescence, Jews hold a celebration, the Bar Mitzvah or Bat Mitzvah. When a boy becomes

Jesus of Nazareth

a man, it implies that he is an adult and must assume responsibility for his actions. Therefore, before the age of 13, a child's responsibilities lie with their parents, and from this age onwards, the young person must begin their journey as an adult man, with duties and obligations. At this age, the young adult is responsible for keeping all 613 commandments, all traditions, holidays, and deeply studying the Mishna, the Gemara, and both Talmuds, Jerusalem and Babylonian. In the case of girls, they have their Bat Mitzvah at age 12, as females develop earlier than males. This is partly why Jesus, at the age of 12, could likely be alone in Jerusalem. Besides the apocryphal texts, this is also a reason why it is believed that Mary was given to Joseph at age 12 and also found herself pregnant at or near this age. Many of these traditions, although quite ancient, such as the study of traditional rabbinic literature and some ceremonies, were not practiced during Jesus' time. These were added from the 2nd century onwards with the rise of rabbinic Judaism. For more information and a clearer comparison of what was practiced and not during Jesus' time, studying the Talmud would be helpful, as it was composed between the 2nd and 6th centuries.

From the age of 15 onward, if an adult had not yet married, they had the decision to marry and dedicate themselves to procreating children, to work in agriculture, fishing, or in the construction trade with their father or a relative. It's clear that Jesus never married. The late and highly dubious sources about whether Jesus married Mary Magdalene or had children with her are absolute unsubstantiated inventions. Serious scholars haven't even bothered entertaining these absurd hypotheses, for which there is no evidence or authentic legitimate texts. This Jesus dedicated himself to working in carpentry or joinery, as construction in Israel primarily involved stones rather than wood. There were some scholarly adults between the ages of 15 to 18 who, at 18, interested and dedicated solely to the study of the Torah, sought out a Master or Rabbi to enter into study, aspiring to one day become a teacher of the law or even a doctor of it. At the age of 30, this student would receive the absolute authority bestowed by their master or Rabbi to become and receive the honorable title of teacher or Rabbi. They could then open a school or their own center and receive students, eventually turning them into their own disciples. Later, these elderly Rabbis or teachers, at a certain advanced age, had the decision whether to retire and leave one of their disciple-teachers in charge of the school, or to continue teaching for as long as they wished. We see this entire educational order reflected in Jesus' public life. Jesus, as a Jew of his time, had to go through all these steps before reaching his 30th year at the Jordan to be baptized. The greatest distinction between Jesus and other Rabbis was that Jesus never truly belonged to the known religious' circle of his time; rather, he was more of a Rabbi of the people. We'll delve into this information further in Jesus' life as a Rabbi.

Once Jesus began his public ministerial life, possibly only briefly in Nazareth but soon deciding to go to Galilee, where he would start with the company of his closest friends and students, as shown in Luke. Some commentators have helped us understand why Jesus had to start his ministry and his public life in Galilee and not elsewhere, which might have been more religiously or spiritually significant, such as Jerusalem, where the great masters and the best disciples sought good rabbis. In Jewish gematria, known as the science and study of biblical numerology, numbers have always had a symbolic and spiritual value. Each number appearing in the biblical texts is not there just for the sake of it; they all have some sense of spiritual purpose. Some numbers were specific and counted literally, especially the smaller numbers, from 1 up to probably 12 or some other possibly countable number. But others were hyperbolically used to show the magnitude or greatness of an event. For example, in 2 Kings 19:35, we see the angel of the Lord striking down an army in one day, killing 185,000 people. When we see such almost impossibly large numbers, even in the 21st century, when there is a large death toll, science typically does not provide a specific number unless there is an exact count of the dead, which often takes a long time with the technological investigations available today. It is possible that in antiquity, there were ways of keeping some kind of count or tally, but in a figure like the one seen here, it is highly probable that the number is not specific; rather, the message is that it was a large army or a significant quantity. Above all, it's unknown who was there to count the dead. With that said, we don't deny the inspiration of the text or claim it was an error or mistake; rather, we refer to it as a narrative form to show the greatness of the event. Sometimes the numerous could even be rounded to a lower or higher number. Another example is regarding the people of Israel in the desert. For a long time, it has been believed that they spent exactly 40 years in the desert, as seen in the books of Joshua, Exodus, Acts, and others. This was what most storytellers adopted and had to use as they wrote according to the received oral tradition, which they also used existing texts or books to continue writing from the provided sources. The number 40 has long been used to symbolize a generation. For this reason, in the New Testament, we see an example: Jesus prophetically announces the coming judgment on Jerusalem without that generation passing away. Luke tells us that Jesus was about 30 years old, indicating that the temple in Jerusalem was destroyed exactly about 40 years later, in 70 AD, which shows the fulfillment of a generation as symbolized by this number for the Jews. Until today, biblical numerology holds significant value in the study of the Torah or the Tanakh. With this said, I must clarify that it wasn't necessarily exactly 40 years for the stay in the desert of the people of Israel. The entire process could have been a bit longer, maybe 42, but the actual time spent in the desert could indeed be less, like some 38, as seen in Deuteronomy 2:14, where it tells us that the number of years they lived in the desert was 38 years, as the Lord had said. The book of Deuteronomy was a second clarified and arranged reinterpretation, much more accepted than the traditions found in the others. We know this because with the great reform of King Josiah, the book found in the temple by the priest and the scribe was the book of Deuteronomy, known as "the book of the law" in its initial compositions of some 9 to 16 chapters, as told by great scholars, both theologians and academics. Later, during this reform, the book of Deuteronomy continued to be elaborated until its final composition by the Deuteronomic priests alongside Ezra, Nehemiah, and those who returned from the Babylonian captivity, once again through the book of the law of Moses, "Deuteronomy," re-establishing the identity of the people of Israel as it once was in Israel, especially in Jerusalem and the temple. The vast majority of traditional sources, literature, along with commentary by great Jewish sages, agree that it wasn't necessarily or exactly 40 years, but rather tell us that this number was rounded for its symbolism and significance. Again, this does not diminish the purpose of the message or imply biblical errors. Our intention is to show the thought and idea of how it was written and also the general purpose of the transmitted message. The reason the exact number 40 was used is found in Numbers 14:31-34, because of the number of days the spies spent spying on the promised land when they were sent by Moses. God had told them that because of their disobedience and slander of the promised land, they would wander and pay for each day a year in the desert before entering it.

This is why the narrators always used 40 as the years the Israelites spent in Egypt. But we must understand that these numbers, though very countable unlike the much larger number of 185,000, were often used symbolically for their meaning and purpose. To understand a bit more about the numerical symbols in the Bible, for example, the number 40 appears around 158 times in the Reina Valera translation. This number generally symbolizes or represents a period of testing, process, or judgment. It also represents the number of a human generation, which can last more or less according to the time or period lived in the cosmos. In times of war, it may be shorter, but in times of peace, it may extend longer. This ideal is used because it is the average during the time of exile in the desert, where the place, life, and food are completely different, and thus the number can vary. In this case, the representation is used in the number 40 as a generation of man. In the life of Moses, the prophet and liberator of the children of Israel, he left Egypt at 40, lived in Midian and the deserts of Midian for 40 years, and at 80, God sent him to Egypt to free his people, where we also see the 40 years during the desert journey with the people of Israel. To add a bit more, he went up to Sinai for 40 days and 40 nights to receive the Torah, sent 12 spies, one leader from each tribe as a representation of the totality of the people of Israel divided into 12 tribes, to the land of Canaan, which they would later receive as a fulfillment of the promise made to the patriarchs. They spent 40 days spying on the land, the same number of days it rained upon the earth in Noah's flood. The book of Exodus, meaning "Exit" or something similar to "Way out," has 40 chapters. We could continue with this number throughout the Bible, and we would find that the significance of this number clearly in the thoughts of the writers speaks of the life, time, and condition that Israel had to pass through to enter Canaan. All other narratives, including those of the New Testament, truly show why the writers used this rounded number for the biblical stories. It is clear that the use of biblical numbers is not a coincidence; they are there not just as numbers or quantities but rather for their symbolism, meaning, and purpose in the story. This numerical study can be done for all other biblical numbers. I recommend a book titled "Numbers in Scripture" written by the Anglican theologian. Bullinger, which is written with the purpose of understanding the study and value of numbers in the Bible. There you can consult and investigate further the idea of rabbinic Jewish gematria or biblical numerology. Jesus goes up to Galilee, and at this time, Jesus is 30 years old, as previously mentioned according to the text of Luke. Knowing that this was the age when ministers were required to assume their special service in the tabernacle, as we see in Numbers 4:3; "from thirty years old and upward to fifty years old, all who enter the company to do the work in the tabernacle of meeting." This age in Jesus' ministerial initiation was not a coincidence for Luke; it was the age when service in the temple to God began. Jesus never dedicated or served in the current temple in Jerusalem. His calling and purpose were much greater than simply serving in a temple, firstly because it was made by human hands where he knew his Father did not reside, and secondly because he knew his purpose and vision were not only for the Jews, and even less for Israel as the religious leaders of his time thought. Jesus is the man called and chosen by God, with a limitless, broad vision for the whole world. Some say that Jesus' original human interest as a Jew was only for Israel, based on some verses where he prohibits the disciples from preaching in gentile cities and other occasions where he says he was not sent but to the lost sheep of the house of Ephraim, which was known as "Israel."

In any case, these few verses require thorough investigation according to the context and purpose with which they were written and spoken. We clearly see a Jesus interested in the whole world. I think it would be somewhat ignorant to say that the purpose of this Jesus was only for Israel as a people or nation, and by coincidence, the plan did not work out as the Eternal originally thought, resulting in over two millennia of more than 2 billion Gentiles serving and worshiping Him week after week around the world, and this is just referring to Christianity, not to mention all the other religions or traditional cultures that in one way or another believe in God and His purpose with Jesus on earth.

We see the many encounters with this Jesus in different places and lands in the Gospels. Then, in the Pauline letters, we see God's favor clearly reaching Asia Minor and all of Europe. The very ancient Christian tradition of the early Fathers tells us where each apostle died as a martyr, and the great number of all these who died preaching in other Gentile nations. What were they doing from Paul onwards, all these centuries preaching outside of Israel if the purpose was really only for Israel? We do not doubt that for many years Jews and Israelites often migrated or were expelled to different lands and nations and then became mixed, but it cannot be possible that the only and Eternal Creator was interested solely in a small people, a minority, among the many nations created, for such a grand and magnificent salvation and plan.

It is clear that God chose some patriarchs, from whom arose a nation titled "The children of Israel." God took this people among the many and freed them from the Egyptian empire, without them doing absolutely anything; God did everything for them. He gave them land, law, and kings, but they themselves rebelled against their God every time. This does not mean that God was exclusively and solely the God of this people; the writers called Him "The God of Israel," but there were many other nations where this God was also worshiped, and we see this in the same books of the biblical prophets. God had taken this people and its monotheistic and sometimes henotheistic prophets to be the light and example to other nations, so that they would stop being polytheistic and turn back to the one and only true God, the creator of all things. This people failed in their task and mission, as we see throughout their history, but this was part of the perfect plan and purpose of the Eternal Father, because when this people had lost all their dominion and prestige, including land, law, and kings, they found themselves, as they had previously and many times before, as slaves and vassals of the greatest empires on earth. It is the perfect time when the Eternal has to introduce His plan for humanity, sending His only Son out of love for the world, Jesus of Nazareth, to earth.

The plan was so perfect that even today, after over two millennia since Jesus came into the world to save mankind, bringing the empire of the Kingdom of God, starting with the Roman Empire, which fell prostrate at the feet of Christianity itself, converting to Christianity, even to the Islamic Ottoman Empire, all throughout history have tried to destroy and stop it, yet it remains unstoppable and indestructible. Therefore, seeing Jesus Himself go to Tyre and Sidon, Samaria, and all His encounters with Greeks and Romans, who were not Jews, clearly shows us that His purpose and that of God was much greater than just one nation. Jesus' last words to His disciples and apostles were clear, *"Go into all the world and preach the gospel,"* He also said to them, *"You shall be witnesses to Me in Jerusalem, and in all Judea and Samaria, and to the end of the earth" (Acts 1:8).*

According to:

Luke 4:14-15:

"Then Jesus returned in the power of the Spirit to Galilee, and news of Him went out through all the surrounding region. And He taught in their synagogues, being glorified by all." (NKJV)

We see Jesus in Galilee, and he tells us that he dedicated himself to teaching in the synagogues there. Also, Luke mentions that it was there where his fame initially began to spread throughout the surrounding land, while he was glorified by all. Investigative studies of the city and province of Galilee during and after Jesus have shown us that the time when there was the most advancement in religious education was during the second century AD, with the destruction of the temple in Jerusalem at the end of the first century. The title of the Pharisees began to disappear, until the successors, the Tannaims, at the end of the first century, the sons of the Pharisees already titled Tannaims, moved to the city of Jamnia, Israel, where they established their school and council. After the destruction of the temple in Jerusalem, the sages again became a list of sacred books and the canon of the Hebrew Bible, what we call the Old Testament. By the second century, many sages also moved and arrived in Galilee where they also began to establish religious schools. It has been shown that in Galilee, each city had its own synagogue, and each synagogue had its own attached school of religious education. Each synagogue and school had a leader, a rabbi teacher, hired for the same. There, as we have already said, elementary education began from ages 3 to 4. Each student had to learn to memorize long portions of the Torah, there was no luxury of having many books in the synagogues, some had only the Torah, the five scrolls of Moses, others more affluent had the Tanakh, an abbreviation for the "Pentateuch, the historical, and the complete prophets", and the poorest ones contained only some pieces of inscriptions of the scrolls from some books. (The book titled "The Jewish Bible and the Christian Bible" by the Hebraist, Julio Trebolle, one of the best professors in Hebrew and Aramaic language, highly recommended, shares with us how the synagogues operated, the uses of the scrolls, and which ones were used). This is the reason why in Israel it was more important to memorize and continuously repeat the Torah and the Tanakh to children, reciting to them in the morning, afternoon, and evening the law of Moses, as Moses was commanded from generation to generation in Deuteronomy chapter 6. This shows the great value that oral tradition holds for the Jews. There is no people where oral tradition is more valued and important than the Jewish people. Every so often, with the many exiles by other nations they experienced, in many ways they lost the written texts, either by getting lost, or by being burned and destroyed by their enemies. Other nations knew that Hebrew texts were always sacred to the Jews, we see this in Flavius Josephus himself, in his books, The Jewish Wars, and Antiquities of the Jews, where he tells us that while the Greeks cared more about their lives than their texts, the Jews hid them, preferring their own deaths rather than the sacred Hebrew texts being burned or destroyed. This shows us why all the Dead Sea Scrolls, and the other books found in the deserts, were hidden, precisely because they preferred to lose their lives by the Roman sword, rather than the texts being consumed. The greatest example we see from the second century onwards, with the new idea by the Tannaims, who were the Jewish rabbinic sages, who succeeded the Pharisees, among whom there were relatives of the same, to these arose the idea of putting in writing all the social laws and oral traditions, that anciently they practiced among the Jews, since ancient times. It was believed that all these oral laws, which had never been written, were essentially important along with the Torah. The Jews believed that these oral laws had been given by God to Moses at Sinai, and then received by him. These are known as the 613 Mitzvot. To these Tannaim sages, the Amoraim succeeded, this is where we see the beginning of the written composition known as the "Mishnah" which means "the study of repetition," in other words, the study and review. All these oral laws were first put in writing, the problem arose when writing the list of each law, but without its proper interpretation or way of how each one had to be kept. To this Mishnah was added the "Gemara," this was a composition where the laws were divided into separate groups, this was done to make it easier to understand in its reading, it contained the interpretive thoughts of a large number of different rabbis, explaining their point of view, regarding the same law, this gave the reader an idea of how to keep and fulfill the oral law that it was. After this Gemara, with the many multiplication of rabbis, and sages, they began to write with a broader vision, not only the interpretation of oral laws, they had also decided to put in writing all discussions and debates with different thoughts, and perspectives of each one among them, including the testimonies and stories of respected older rabbis who orally knew. They also added mystical rabbinic interpretations, of all the biblical stories of the Torah and the Tanakh. To this long and broad composition of many volumes, and thousands and thousands of pages, it was known as the "Talmud." The only thing that results is that there is not only one Talmud, there are two different versions of the Talmud, one is known as the "Babylonian Talmud" and the other the "Jerusalem Talmud." The reason for these writings is because one is the traditional history of the Jews who remained in Jerusalem and also those who returned during and after the Babylonian captivity, and the other is the tradition of the Jews who remained in Babylon. Among all these distinctions, and both places Jerusalem "Israel" and Babylon arose great schools of sages, to whom some were called by the title Rabbi, and others by the title Rav, the teachers in Israel were called Rabbi, while the Babylonian teachers were called Rav, this has an explanation, but we will continue since the essential point has been explained.

Therefore, with Jesus' preaching throughout Galilee, he knew that despite the limited education in Galilee among all the poor who dedicated themselves to hard work, they all, as a norm and part of their culture, had read and knew the Torah from childhood. It is worth mentioning that some were more intellectual than others, that some were more intelligent than others, somehow some could memorize the Torah more than others, although it is difficult to believe, but very speculative also that there might have been a few, most likely those who were more interested in work and life than reading. Among the Jews, religious life was the most important because their entire dependence for life, from waking up to going to bed, was placed on the Creator. They depended on God for everything, from rain to harvest, everything depended on God, to all this I add the most important thing, and it was that everyone was awaiting the most anticipated Messiah, the one of whom "Moses himself had spoken," none other than Jesus of Nazareth. Galilee is mentioned 67 times in the Bible, of these 64 times in the New Testament, the rest in the Old Testament, its territory was divided

Jesus of Nazareth

among the tribes of Naphtali, Asher, Issachar, and Zebulun, later the tribe of Dan had moved to the territory of upper Galilee, these mentions are found in 1 Chronicles and the historical book of Joshua. Galilee was quite important and well-known for its great agriculture, olive trees, vineyards, and fishing. Galilee had export areas for all these productions, normally students and disciples sought a rabbi, in the case of Jesus it was a bit different, before he called and chose his disciples whom he called his apostles, according to Luke, Jesus having started his ministry alone, after having preached in Nazareth and Galilee, with his fame growing everywhere, already had many people and disciples following him, although he had not chosen anyone. In the Gospel of Luke, Matthew or Levi, son of Alphaeus, is the first to meet Jesus and tell him to follow him, this calling to Matthew had not yet been to be an apostle, Jesus had not yet chosen anyone, this calling was a call to change his life, and to enter the kingdom of God, alongside Jesus. After this, we see Jesus going up a mountain to pray, with this gesture of prayer he showed that he did nothing on his own, Jesus was a leader who showed a lot of interest in prayer to God, after having prayed all night to God, then he knew that the time had come to choose by calling all his disciples, who were very likely many, from all these he chose 12 to be with him, to give them authority, and so that as his apostles they would be prepared to preach. Here we see once again a very symbolic and purposeful number, the number 12 represents all the tribes and the complete people of Israel, it turns out that after King Solomon died, his son Rehoboam succeeded to the throne, the people were quite exhausted by the high taxes that his father Solomon had imposed on the people for the construction of the Temple, and some other things. The elders who worked alongside Solomon and had served as his counselors after his death spoke in counsel to his son Rehoboam, telling him that if he lowered the taxes on the people he would reign over them and have a people, forever. Rehoboam decided to seek advice among the young men who had grown up with him, and he had appointed them as his advisors. He decided rather by the advice of the young men, who had told him to tell the people that if his father Solomon was strong and tough, he was compared to the little finger of his hand, which indicated that he would be tougher with taxes and the burden of the people. Solomon had a very intimate old friend, whose name was Jeroboam, a very faithful servant of Solomon, who, out of fear of God and having received the word from a prophet that he would reign over 10 of the tribes of Israel, and Solomon would lose his throne, passed to his son Rehoboam, he would reign over only one tribe, that of Judah, also counting that of Simeon which was within that of Judah. He would remain with only one out of love for God to King David, and for his promise that from his sons, he would raise up one in whom his throne would be firm and stable forever. For this reason, Jeroboam had fled to Egypt, until Solomon died. According to the texts, God had been responsible for dividing his own people, putting 10 tribes in the north into Jeroboam's hands and the two in the south into Rehoboam's hands, once these tribes were divided, they never united again, there was no longer unity in the nation of Israel, from this division onwards, with the arrival of empires, both by the Assyrians, and then by the Babylonians, all the tribes were dispersed. This Jesus called and chose 12 men, representing that he would reunite all the people of Israel, who were scattered throughout the world, it is true that this number represented all the tribes of Israel, but more than all the tribes of Israel, it represented all the world (Humans) who wanted to be part of the people of God, and enter the kingdom of heaven, which had come near to the earth, as the prophet John had said in the desert.

With the arrival of Jesus, the kingdom of God had come. Wherever he went, with him came the kingdom of God. His general and fundamental message was repentance and entry into the kingdom of God. Anyone who accepted this call to a 180-degree change in consciousness immediately entered the kingdom of God by following Jesus wherever he went. This kingdom is and was for everyone; Jesus never excluded anyone. He offered the kingdom of God to the most wretched sinner and also to the wealthiest. The number 12 represents "everything, the totality" of the people of God, among the Israelites and also the foreigners and Gentiles who also joined as one people for God, according to the promise made to

Abraham, which was for all those in his household, among his children, his slaves (Gentiles), and also his foreigners (Gentiles), even if they were not direct descendants of him. We see this from the Old Testament throughout the New Testament. If this promise was made to Abraham for all those of his, inside and outside his household, and we saw its fulfillment in the children of Israel and the other nations that came from his lineage when they entered the land of Canaan, fulfilling a part of the promise, since it would reach all the nations of the earth, how much more would the plan established in Christ Jesus reach the whole world when Peter said, "He was prepared before the foundation of the world, but has been revealed in these last times for your sake." This promise would be the culmination and spiritual fulfillment of the promise made to Abraham. God made it to Abraham, began to fulfill it with Jacob, and concluded it completely through Jesus of Nazareth alone. This Jesus came to fulfill the entire promise made to Abraham, and he fulfilled it. On the cross of Calvary, his last words were:

John 19:30;

So when Jesus had received the sour wine, he said, "It is finished!" And bowing his head, he gave up his spirit. (NKJV).

Of all the disciples that Jesus called, these were the names of each one: Peter (fisherman), Andrew (fisherman), James, son of Zebedee (fisherman), John (fisherman), Philip (?), Bartholomew, also known as Nathanael (Israelite, mercenary), Matthew, Levi, son of Alphaeus (tax collector), Thomas (?), James, son of Alphaeus (?), Thaddeus, Judas (?), Simon (the Zealot), and Judas Iscariot (treasurer). If you are interested in learning more about the lives of each of these men, I recommend the book "Twelve Ordinary Men" by pastor and theologian John MacArthur. If we observe closely, all of these were common people from the town, most were fishermen, others were rebellious militants, and one was a tax collector. It is true that thinking a company of men like these—fishermen, common folk, and uneducated—could achieve anything seems highly unlikely. Only God could fulfill His plan with such men. We must understand that each of these disciples knew the Law and the Torah, but none had dedicated themselves to studying the Torah as a student. This likely means that most of these men, at an early age, had devoted themselves to working with their fathers, as in the case of the sons of Zebedee, who had a fishing business and whose sons helped and worked with him. The same goes for the others who also devoted themselves to work; none had the privilege of deciding to go to Jerusalem to study at the feet of a Rabbi. By age 8, it was already known if a child was going to be a Rabbi or if they would dedicate themselves to social work. In the case of all these men, none were found with the capacity and qualifications needed for study. Additionally, in Israel, 97% of the inhabitants, especially the Jews, had some kind of debt to the Romans, and they had to devote themselves to hard work to pay off their debts. This is why we see Jesus in His public ministry speaking extensively about debts. When each of these disciples received the call and the opportunity to be chosen to be beside and walk with a Rabbi, the privilege was quite significant since they had previously lost the opportunity, most likely due to economic need and possibly also due to the intellectual incapacity required for the study and dedication to the Torah. Only the most capable students could study in Jerusalem. Josephus tells us that there were 1,100,000 people in Israel; some scholars say this figure is an exaggeration and most likely quite high, but there were many people in Israel. Josephus also tells us that there were only 6,000 Pharisees (devoted or separated ones); these were the doctors and scholars of the Torah. Some Rabbi teachers tell us that even this number is quite high; if there were fewer, imagine how difficult it was to achieve a (paraphrasing) doctorate in Jerusalem or a Rabbi title at that time. This gives us an image of the capacity and who Paul of Tarsus or the Apostle Paul really was, as he studied at the feet of Master Gamaliel, the Pharisee. Returning to the disciples chosen by Jesus, they made good use of the opportunity Jesus offered them, leaving everything to follow Him. Leaving everything to follow a Rabbi guaranteed them a greater reward. We will explain this detail better in Chapter 2, in the part about Jesus as Rabbi. Jesus, at all times and for everything He did, depended on His Father. Therefore, when choosing each of these disciples from the many He had, He later tells us that they did not choose Him; He chose them. In John 17, while Jesus was praying, He said the following:

John 17:9-12;

I pray for them; I do not pray for the world, but for those whom You have given Me, for they are Yours. And all Mine are Yours, and Yours are Mine, and I am glorified in them. Now I am no longer in the world, but these are in the world, and I come to You. Holy Father, keep through Your name those whom You have given Me, that they may be one as We are. While I was with them in the world, I kept them in Your name. Those whom You gave Me I have kept; and none of them is lost except the son of perdition, that the Scripture might be fulfilled. (NKJV)

Here we see that each of those whom Jesus chose were not chosen by His own accord; they were chosen because God His Father had given them to Him. That being said, Jesus had so much passion and love for humanity that, receiving from the Father the lowest, the foolish, and those without eloquence or preparation, Jesus fulfilled His purpose in each of them. He took each of these vile men, prepared them, transformed them, and made them into men and leaders who turned the world upside down for their Lord. As it is written:

1 Corinthians 1:27-31;

But God has chosen the foolish things of the world to put to shame the wise, and God has chosen the weak things of the world to put to shame the things which are mighty; and the base things of the world and the things which are despised God has chosen, and the things which are not, to bring to nothing the things that are, that no flesh should glory in His presence. But of Him you are in Christ Jesus, who became for us wisdom from God—and righteousness and sanctification and redemption—that, as it is written, "He who glories, let him glory in the Lord." (NKJV)

It is worth asking and imagining what people publicly thought of Jesus when they saw Him walking and sharing with these kinds of people. At first, it is to be assumed that many did not take Him seriously and did not believe in Him, or perhaps saw Him as just another common teacher. But when they began to see the authority with which He spoke, the wonders, signs, and expulsions of demons—not like the Pharisees and scribes, who lacked authority and these signs—everyone, including the apostles, wondered who this man was and what new doctrine this was that even the demons (unclean spirits) obeyed Him and were cast out.

Publicly, Jesus was a man, a friend, a brother, and a human being loved by both the poor and the rich. There was not a single person in the time of this Jesus of Nazareth who did not love Him, except perhaps the religious leaders of His time and those who envied Him in some way. Jesus loved sinners, ate and shared with them, went to parties when invited by them, and participated in community events and weddings. Jesus was a healer to many sick people, always compassionate towards the poor and needy. He wept when He lost a friend, His words were full of comfort when He spoke to those who had lost a loved one, He did favors for His friends and also for His enemies, walked a mile with the needy and if He had to walk two, He did so. He was struck by His enemies and never defended Himself out of love. He called all who were thirsty and hungry to come to Him and fed many in Galilee with whatever little He had.

As if that were not enough, this Jesus of Nazareth, who could have lived for Himself, chose to leave His own home after His baptism to dedicate Himself to preaching the Kingdom of God to all, without even having a pillow to rest His head on. Many turned their backs on Him, other disciples left Him for riches, but Jesus never abandoned His love and passion for others. Publicly, Jesus prayed for His enemies, publicly forgave them, and while everyone else distanced themselves from the poor lepers, Jesus not only approached them but also touched and healed them. While many of the wise always tempted Him, Jesus never tempted anyone and always responded with questions. His words were full of blessings for all.

With His attitude and words, Jesus always gave hope to others. At one moment, He said, "You are the salt of the earth," and at another, "You are the light of the world." We rarely see Jesus uncomfortable or angry, although He had every right as a human and man to be angry. His love was so great and compassionate that, instead of anger, His love surpassed all things. It is almost as if we are talking about the same God of whom Moses said, "Slow to anger and abounding in mercy." This was just a minimal part of the image and attitude of the life and public ministry of Jesus of Nazareth.

The best source and book I can recommend for you to continue reading and to know more details about the life and public ministry of Jesus is "the Bible." I do not believe there has ever been a human being as extraordinary, excellent, and unparalleled as Jesus of Nazareth, without a doubt the best and perfect example to follow.

Hebrews 12:2;

looking unto Jesus, the author and finisher of our faith, who for the joy that was set before Him endured the cross, despising the shame, and has sat down at the right hand of the throne of God.

Alexander Frias

JESUS OF NAZARETH, THE RABBI
Part 1

John 3:2

"This man came to Jesus by night and said to him, 'Rabbi, we know that you have come from God as a teacher; for no one can do these signs that you do unless God is with him.'" - RV1960

In Israel, there have been teachers and rabbis for a long time. We will use the term "Rabbi" for now as an interpolation since during these early or ancient times, the word rabbi did not exist. It is believed that during the era of the patriarchs, especially Abraham, the wise Job, contemporary to him, was among the first wise rabbis. Some 500 years later, in the biblical text, we see nations that had schools or systems of religious education. Life and culture were tied to the same religious thought. We see Moses being educated in all the wisdom of the Egyptians. In Israel, the responsibility of educating and teaching children fell to the parents, as seen in the biblical Exodus. The elders passed the law to the parents, who then passed it to their children. Later, in the era of the monarchy (Kings), with the prophets present, such as Samuel, Elisha, and Elijah, there were prophetic schools and they were the teachers who presided in Israel. "But when they saw the group of prophets prophesying, and Samuel standing as their leader, ..." or "Then the sons of the prophets who {were} at Bethel came out to {meet} Elisha..." It is during this same era between the prophets and the kings that Jewish rabbinic tradition tells us that the idea of the first rabbi in its current form and sense arose. This first rabbi would be King Solomon himself, to whom God would give wisdom for all things. Hence, the tradition believes that Solomon may have composed and written more than 3000 parables, including Proverbs, Ecclesiastes, and the Song of Songs. Job was considered a wise man before Solomon, but Solomon composed more parables than Job, and God gave him more wisdom than all the men of the earth. It is also said that many of the parables Solomon composed were used throughout Israel and continue to be used today in rabbinic schools. In a certain sense, all the prophets, major and minor, were considered teachers and rabbis, as they all educated, prophesied, and taught through parables. Scripturally, in later translations, it is believed that the last prophet and book of the Old Testament was Malachi, but historically, according to studies by academic historians and the vast majority of serious theologians, the conclusion is that the last book of the Old Testament composed in its history among the wise men and prophets of Israel was Daniel, with a date around the mid-2nd century B.C., with scenes and historical events from the 6th century B.C. In the more conservative Christian tradition, it is believed that this book of Daniel was possibly composed by the prophet Daniel himself, around a date between 605 and 536 B.C. There is also the idea that Daniel himself may have begun its composition by writing most or some of the chapters during this early date, and later some disciples or students could have finished writing the remaining chapters, especially 10-12, where it speaks of Alexander the Great and also Antiochus Epiphanes IV, which has been considered part of the intertestamental period. This idea arises because it is believed that Daniel may have had schools and wise disciples in Babylon. In any case, the idea is that this book of Daniel is the last to mention all these historical events in Israel during the intertestamental period. It is precisely during this same intertestamental period that 1 Maccabees 9:27 tells us, ("Since the time when the prophets ceased to appear, Israel had never suffered so much") that there were no prophets present in Israel, at least among those who wrote and prophesied wisely to the people. Between 170 and 160 B.C., when it is believed that at least the last chapters of Daniel were composed, we see the rise of the sect that would become the great teachers and scholars in Israel, known as the "Perushim," separated ones, or "Pharisees." These Pharisees were those zealous and ultra-religious Jews, also known as doctors of the law. They were sometimes found together with the scribes, who were the ones holding the pens to write and reinterpret the sacred texts. These Pharisees were the largest sect of scholars in Israel. By the time of Jesus, there were almost 6000 Pharisees. They were in charge of the synagogues in the cities, were always around the temple, and were the originators of the known traditions of the elders, which were private reinterpretations added to the rules established in the Torah. During the time of Hellenization, the Jews were increasingly becoming Hellenized. These Hellenized Jews wanted to maintain their strict Judaism but gradually freed themselves from overly strict practices in Judaism. Many Jews, with the Greek conquests by Alexander the Great and Hellenization, soon adopted many Greek customs and set aside the interest in the original Judaism that they had once received from Ezra and the priests who returned from Babylon to Jerusalem. This mixture between Jews and Greeks greatly troubled the Pharisees to the point that whenever it was necessary to tighten or make the law stricter, they added additional rules to those already established. It has been thought that there were so many among the thousands of traditions of the elders, or the additional rules to the Torah, that there was not a single person who could bear the burden of this heavy law imposed by the Pharisees on the people. For this reason, Jesus said: "For they bind heavy burdens, hard to bear, and lay them on men's shoulders; but they themselves will not move them with one of their fingers. But all their works they do to be seen by men." The burden of these traditions was so heavy that Jesus also said to them: "Woe to you, scribes and Pharisees, hypocrites! For you travel land and sea to win one proselyte, and when he is won, you make him twice as much a son of hell as yourselves." Among all these Pharisees, we also need to clarify that not all were the same; there were about seven different groups of Pharisees in Israel, mentioned in the "Treatise Sota 22b – Soncino translation of the Babylonian Talmud."

Treatise Sota 22b – Soncino Translation

The Pharisee Shikmi, the Pharisee Nikpi, the Pharisee Kizai, the "Mortar" Pharisee, the Pharisee who constantly exclaims: "What is my duty that I may perform it?", the Pharisee out of love [for God], and the Pharisee out of fear.

The Pharisee Shikmi: he is one who performs the action of Shechem

Jesus of Nazareth

[shikmi = shoulder, meaning he performs his actions on his shoulder for everyone to see].

The Pharisee Nikpi: he is one who knocks his feet together [i.e., he finds excuses to postpone and not do good deeds].

The Pharisee Kizai - R. Nahman b. Isaac said: "He is one who causes his blood to flow against the walls [i.e., he walks towards the wall to avoid looking at or having contact with a woman]."

The "Mortar" Pharisee - Rabbah b. Shila said: "His head is bowed like a pestle in a mortar [i.e., he constantly presents himself as humble]."

The Pharisee who constantly exclaims: "What is my duty that I may perform it?" This is not a virtue! What he means is: "What other duty is there for me to perform?" [i.e., constantly calculating good deeds against bad deeds].

The Pharisee out of love [i.e., serves God out of love].

The Pharisee out of fear [i.e., serves God out of fear of punishment].

(information borrowed from: https://weekly.israelbiblecenter.com/es/los-siete-tipos-de-fariseos-talmud)

All these groups of Pharisees were considered the wise men, teachers, and doctors of the law in Israel. Among all these different groups, not all hated and were enemies of Jesus. Many of the different Pharisees were friends of Jesus, and we know he had friendships with them because these Pharisees were the same ones who helped him escape when others came to stone or kill him. Having journeyed from the beginning to the first century with the education of teachers in Israel, we have reached the most important point, which is to present Jesus of Nazareth as the "Rabbi." A question that remains without conclusion and without a concrete answer among philologists, academic scholars, and theologians, about which there is no consensus, is whether the term or word "Rabbi" was used during the early first century, the time of Jesus, as we see in the gospels. A significant portion says that it was already used because it appears in biblical texts dating to the late first century. Another significant number of scholars say that the word is an anachronism in the early first-century texts because this title was used for teachers of the rabbinate, or the group of rabbis that was formed after the destruction of the temple in 70 A.D. From then on, the most outstanding wise teachers in Israel, and the authors of the Mishnah, Gemara, and the Talmud, were titled and called "Rab" or "Rabbi." Today, the title is still used internationally for Jewish teachers who have reached the study and capacity in all necessary areas of Hebrew life, tradition, and culture. These are recognized as "Rabbis." It is believed that this title was not used for Jesus since his death was around 33 A.D., and the title had not yet been invented. However, there are many different opinions. In any case, we see that the function and title of teacher were known, with high respect and admiration, almost like that of a master or excellency to his servant. This idea is seen in some of Jesus' parables, for example, when he says:

"No student is above his teacher, nor any servant greater than his master. It is enough for the disciple to be like his teacher and the servant like his master." And he also said to them:

"Which of you, having a servant plowing or tending sheep, will say to him when he comes in from the field, 'Come at once and sit down to eat'? Will he not rather say to him, 'Prepare my supper, get yourself ready and wait on me while I eat and drink; after that, you may eat and drink'? Does he think that servant because he did what was commanded? I think not. So you also, when you have done everything you were told to do, should say, 'We are unworthy servants; we have only done our duty.'"

These parabolic metaphors were used by Jesus to illustrate his relationship with them and also his communion with God. In the time of Jesus, there were many different kinds of teachers. There were teachers like the Pharisees, who had studied extensively and undergone a long process under their teachers' tutelage until they became professional teachers both within and outside Jerusalem. Jesus was a different kind of teacher; he taught all kinds of people—

Jesus of Nazareth

children as well as the elderly, the poorest people as well as the richest, the greatest sinners as well as the most religious. He had many different ways and methods of teaching, and two things always accompanied his teachings: truth and authority. Jesus was a teacher of justice, committed to teaching the truth at all costs without fear, even at the cost of his own life.

Jesus is called "teacher" 90 times in the gospels, and of these, 60 times he is called "Rabbi." He was called "teacher" by his followers, disciples, apostles, Pharisees, scribes, himself, and others. Rabbis customarily taught using various methods. Jesus taught through questions, parables, stories, metaphors, allegories, and more. In the biblical text, we see him teaching and instructing for the first time at the age of 12 in the temple in Jerusalem. This was where most of the rabbis and elder teachers were found. There, they shared and debated the wisdom they had and also recruited their students. Many commentators suggest that being a child, as Luke calls him ("When they had finished the feast, as they were returning, the boy Jesus stayed behind in Jerusalem. His parents did not know it"), every rabbi who heard him would have wanted to have him as a disciple.

However, it is crucial to understand that even though Luke refers to him as a child, this Jesus, despite being called a child by Luke, was not a child. An important fact is that Luke wrote his gospel for a Gentile audience, most likely Greeks. In the Greek world, an adolescent entered adulthood at the age of 20, indicating that an adolescent at 12 was still considered a child. Luke was a Greek doctor, not a Jew, and he thought that at this age, Jesus was a child. Therefore, in his gospel, he referred to Jesus as a child so that when any Greek Gentile read his gospel, it would make sense according to their culture and they could understand it. In reality, in this scene, for any Jew, this Jesus at 12 years old, teaching as he was, would be considered an almost mature disciple among the rabbis. We see him sitting among the doctors of the law, listening to them and asking them questions. And all who heard him were amazed at his understanding and his answers.

In Greek and Roman cultures, teachers taught standing up, but in

Jewish culture, rabbi teachers sat to teach. The act of sitting indicated that the teacher was assuming all his teaching authority. So to speak, he was speaking ex cathedra. For the disciples, it was as evident a sign that he was about to impart some teaching as it is today when someone stands in a congregation. Sitting is the typical posture of Jewish teachers for teaching and instructing. Sitting is the bodily position that most facilitates concentration for teaching and, incidentally, for listening. This is how the teacher, the judge, and the one with authority would sit. Jesus presented himself as a teacher and taught, solemnly sitting, a new doctrine, and he taught with authority (Mark 1:27); unlike standing, which he used especially to proclaim something (John 7:37). And his seat (his chair) was, for example, a fishing boat, his school was in the open air, and always open to everyone. People saw in Jesus a teacher (Rabbi) because he was always teaching; we always see him surrounded by a crowd, by followers whom Jesus taught a lifestyle similar to his own because he announced the coming of the Kingdom of God.

In Jewish thought, the teacher had the highest authority in education. Jesus was a teacher with much authority but even more humility, and the act of sitting symbolized lowering himself to the same level as his audience and listeners. This showed that Jesus' interest was never to use his mastery to dominate, much less to feel greater and higher than others. Jesus' greatest interest was for each of his disciples, regardless of their level of knowledge, to reach his same position and be like him. What Jesus, as a teacher, always taught was that no one would be greater or higher than his teacher. He did this with the intention that all would remain united at the same level, so that when he was absent, no one would feel superior or exercise lordship over the other, as he taught them by saying:

"No student is above his teacher, nor any servant greater than his master. It is enough for the disciple to be like his teacher and the servant like his master."

Matthew 20:25-28 (RV1960)

Then Jesus, calling them, said: You know that the rulers of the nation's lord it over them, and those who are great exercise authority over them. But it shall not be so among you; rather, whoever wants to become great among you shall be your servant, and whoever wants to be first among you shall be your slave; just as the Son of Man did not come to be served, but to serve, and to give his life as a ransom for many.

Jesus was not just any rabbi like the others; he was a human being just like everyone else, but his intuition was special, something no other teacher of his time had. His experience and authority went beyond those of the teachers in Israel. He did not only operate in the physical and earthly realm of people; through the finger of God and the Holy Spirit upon him, he ordered and commanded demons and unclean spirits. Despite teaching to educate, his teaching also liberated people from their oppressions and illnesses. This kind of authority was completely new both for the people and for the doctors of the law and the scribes.

The Jews believed in unclean spirits and also in exorcisms. During the intertestamental period, Jews practiced exorcisms by invoking Beelzebub, who was believed to be the "Lord" or god of the flies. There was a belief in a kind of divine duality. For the Jews, God never had a rival or an enemy on his same level, but during their time in Persia, they adopted the belief in a good divinity and an evil one. They thought that the god of evil or destruction was called "Angra-Mainyu" and the God of fire, the creator of all things, was known as "Ahura Mazda." From that point on, the Jews adopted this belief in the Creator God and the antagonistic spirit of evil.

However, with the introduction of Greek thought into the Jewish world, alongside the Persian influences they already had, Jewish teachers and doctors of the law continued to adopt and reinterpret texts with the thinking of these present cultures. This is why we see God or even Satan, the devil, with so many different names in the Bible because each time the text was reinterpreted, different names and attributes were added to the divinity in question.

Beelzebub is the Greek form of the name Baal-zebub, a pagan

Alexander Frias

Philistine god worshiped in the ancient Philistine city of Ekron during the times of the Old Testament. It is a term that means "the lord of the flies" (2 Kings 1:2). Archaeological excavations at ancient Philistine sites have uncovered golden images of flies. After the time of the Philistines, the Jews changed the name to "Beelzeboul," as used in the Greek New Testament, which means "lord of the dung." This name refers to the fly god who was worshiped for relief from the wounds caused by that insect. Some biblical scholars believe that Beelzebub was also known as the "god of filth," which later became a name of bitter contempt on the lips of the Pharisees. As a result, Beelzebub was a particularly despicable deity, and the Jews used his name as a descriptive term for Satan. The word has two parts: Baal, which was the name of the Canaanite gods of fertility in the Old Testament, and Zebul, which means "majestic dwelling." By putting the two parts together, they formed a name for Satan, the prince of demons. The Pharisees used this term for the first time when they described Jesus in Matthew 10:24-25. Previously, they had accused Jesus of casting out demons "by the prince of demons" (Matthew 9:34), referring to Beelzebub (Mark 3:22; Matthew 12:24). Information borrowed from: (https://www.gotquestions.org/Espanol/beelzebu.html).

The Jews in the intertestamental period believed that to relieve people in their exorcisms, they had to appeal to the prince of unclean spirits so that another higher authority could cast it out for a while. It was also believed that these exorcisms were only temporary or momentary. Sometimes the Jews had rites and procedures for the practice of their exorcisms. In the Deuterocanonical Apocrypha "Book of Tobit," which was part of the translation and version of the LXX "Septuagint," two cases are mentioned in the New Testament where reference is made to this intertestamental book. The situation is that there was a woman with an evil spirit so strong that every time she got married, that same night she killed her husband. She ended up having 7 husbands until her last one, Tobias, receiving from an angel some necessary procedures to scare away and expel the demon tormenting his wife. Tobias did everything the angel asked him to do, and once fulfilled, the demon would be scared away and expelled. This abbreviated story is seen in two different cases, the first in this case where the wise Jews accused Jesus of receiving the authority for these liberations he performed through the prince of demons, as their wise sons used to practice and believe in ancient times. The second case is seen in a Sadducee who comes to test Jesus, saying;

Matthew 22:25-29

Now there were seven brothers among us. The first one married and died, and since he had no children, he left his wife to his brother. The same thing happened to the second and third brother, right on down to the seventh. Finally, the woman died. Now then, at the resurrection, whose wife will she be of the seven, since all of them were married to her?" Jesus replied.

In this case, the Sadducees did not believe in the resurrection, and they used this story as a pretext to see if Jesus would confuse or discredit himself in his doctrine of resurrection. Jesus, as a teacher and Rabbi, had come not only to teach but also to truly liberate man from the slavery of sin and the enemy of souls, which was believed to be Satan, the prince of darkness and malignant spheres.

Jesus and His Teaching Methods:

In his youth, Jesus had acquired a lot of skill and experience in the field of construction, carpentry, and building. We see him using all this experience in his teaching and preaching. Like a good builder, he mixed all the experiences he had with his teachings, which caught people's attention. His greatest message and his greatest interest was the kingdom of God; all his parables, metaphors, and allegories were connected with the kingdom of God. Jesus is also considered an apocalyptic rabbi; his teachings were prophetic and also mixed with events that would later come true in history. Jesus was the only rabbi teacher who could truly reveal God, unveil, and show His essence without any veil, who God is. Today we know the Creator Father thanks to Jesus of Nazareth. Today we have communion, knowledge, and peace with God only through that rabbi from Nazareth. Another way he taught was through questions; sometimes he showed his high and superior ability over the doctors of the law when even the most respected ones couldn't answer him. They were uncomfortable with the degree of wisdom and intelligence he taught with. Some of the questions he asked were as follows:

***Matthew 22:41-46;*ns**

Then, surrounded by the Pharisees, Jesus asked them a question: "What do you think about the Messiah? Whose son is he?" They replied, "He is the son of David." Jesus responded, "Then why did David, speaking under the inspiration of the Spirit, call him 'my Lord'? For David said, 'The Lord said to my Lord, sit in the place of honor at my right hand until I humble your enemies beneath your feet.' Since David called the Messiah 'my Lord,' how can the Messiah be his son?" No one could answer him, and from that day on, no one dared to ask him any more questions.

***Luke 10:26;*ns**

Jesus replied, "What does the law of Moses say? How do you read it?"

***John 8:10;*ns**

Then Jesus stood up again and said to the woman, "Where are your accusers? Didn't even one of them condemn you?"

***Luke 18:8;*ns**

I tell you, he will grant justice to them quickly! But when the Son of Man returns, how many will he find on the earth who have faith?

***Luke 12:57;*ns**

"Why can't you decide for yourselves what is right?"

***John 6:61-62;*ns**

Jesus knew within himself that his disciples were complaining, so he said to them, "Does this offend you? Then what will you think if you see the Son of Man ascend to heaven again?"

***John 3:10;*ns**

Jesus of Nazareth

Jesus replied, "You are a respected Jewish teacher, and yet you don't understand these things?"

Luke 6:46;

"So why do you keep calling me 'Lord, Lord!' when you don't do what I say?

These and many more were questions Jesus used as a teacher to teach. A chapter, a book, or even a lifetime would not be enough to fully encompass the kind of teacher Jesus was. Jesus used nature, divinity, all kinds of earthly work, food, construction, agriculture, governments, and whatever was according to his surroundings to show the kingdom of God. His grace and intuition were so special that there was nothing Jesus couldn't use to convey the message of the Kingdom of God, and this gift was the reason he could teach anyone regardless of their ability. To conclude this part, I will share two last points of utmost importance, which show why Jesus of Nazareth was not only a good rabbi but the best and most excellent of all rabbis. It has been said that every good teacher is known by what others have been able to retain from him. Today we have more information and writings of Jesus than of any other ancient historical figure that ever existed. Everything we have today and what we have retained about Jesus' teachings, we have because those who heard him received the best example of a teacher from him. This survey has been done to see the level of retention in human life; it has been used to measure Jesus. Let's see its result.

90% of people and adults retain teachings when they teach them to others: "Teaching them to observe all things that I have commanded you; and lo, I am with you always, even to the end of the age. Amen."

Matthew 28:20

75% of what they learn when they put it into practice:

"He sent them to preach the kingdom of God and to heal the sick. And they departed and went through the towns, preaching the gospel and healing everywhere."

Luke 9:2,6

50% of what they share with others:

"When Jesus came into the region of Caesarea Philippi, He asked His disciples, saying, 'Who do men say that I, the Son of Man, am?' So they said, 'Some say John the Baptist, some Elijah, and others Jeremiah or one of the prophets.' He said to them, 'But who do you say that I am?' Simon Peter answered and said, 'You are the Christ, the Son of the living God.'"

30% of what they see demonstrated:

"But Peter, standing up with the eleven, raised his voice and said to them, 'Men of Judea and all who dwell in Jerusalem, let this be known to you, and heed my words.'" Acts 2:14

20% of what they see and hear:

"And they watched Him, and sent spies who pretended to be righteous, that they might seize on His words, in order to deliver Him to the power and the authority of the governor. Then they asked Him, saying, 'Teacher, we know that You say and teach rightly, and You do not show personal favoritism, but teach the way of God in truth: Is it lawful for us to pay taxes to Caesar or not?' But He perceived their craftiness, and said to them, 'Why do you test Me? Show Me a denarius. Whose image and inscription does it have?' They answered and said, 'Caesar's.' And He said to them, 'Render therefore to Caesar the things that are Caesar's, and to God the things that are God's.'"

10% of what they read:

"Search the Scriptures, for in them you think you have eternal life; and these are they which testify of Me." John 5:39

5% of what they learn in a lecture:

"So He got into one of the boats, which was Simon's, and asked him to put out a little from the land. And He sat down and taught the multitudes from the boat."

In this statistical summary of retention in people's lives, we see that in each of them, Jesus of Nazareth was able to achieve his goal in his students and disciples. Finally, we will share a (abbreviated) list of some of Jesus' parables and teachings in the Gospels.

Parables only appearing in the Gospel of Matthew:

- The wheat and the tares (13:24-30)
- The hidden treasure (13:44)
- The pearl of great price (13:45-46)
- The dragnet (13:47-50)
- The unforgiving servant (18:21-35)
- The laborers in the vineyard (20:1-16)
- The two sons (21:28-32)
- The wedding feast (22:1-14)
- The wise and foolish virgins (25:1-13)
- The talents (25:14-30)

Parables only appearing in the Gospel of Mark:

- The growing seed (4:26-29)
- The doorkeeper (13:32-37)

Parables only appearing in the Gospel of Luke:

- The debtors and the creditor (7:40-47)
- The good Samaritan (10:25-37) (my favorite)
- The friend at midnight (11:5-8)
- The rich fool (12:13-21)
- The faithful and evil servants (12:35-48)
- The barren fig tree (13:6-9)
- The unfinished tower (14:25-34)
- The lost coin (15:8-10)
- The lost son (15:11-32)
- The unjust steward (16:1-13)
- The rich man and Lazarus (16:19-31)
- The persistent widow (18:1-8)
- The Pharisee and the tax collector (18:9-14)
- The minas (19:11-27)

Parables appearing in Matthew and Luke:

- *The two builders (Mt 7:24-27; Lk 6:47-49)*
- *The leaven (Mt 13:33; Lk 13:20-21)*
- *The lost sheep (Mt 18:10-14; Lk 15:1-7)*

Parables appearing in Matthew, Mark, and Luke:

- *The lamp and the measure (Mt 5:15-16; Mk 4:21; Lk 8:16)*
- *New cloth on old garments (Mt 9:16; Mk 2:21; Lk 5:36)*
- *New wine in old wineskins (Mt 9:17; Mk 2:22; Lk 5:37-39)*
- *A house divided against itself (Mt 12:25-29; Mk 3:23-27; Lk 11:17-22)*
- *The sower (Mt 13:1-23; Mk 4:1-20; Lk 8:4-15)*
- *The mustard seed (Mt 13:31-32; Mk 4:30-32; Lk 13:18-19)*
- *The wicked vine-dressers (Mt 21:33-41; Mk 12:1-12; Lk 20:9-18)*
- *The fig tree (Mt 24:32-35; Mk 13:28-31; Lk 21:29-33).*

Matthew 23:8

But you, do not be called 'Rabbi'; for One is your Teacher, the Christ, and you are all brethren.

JESUS AS A PROPHET

The Major and Minor Prophets:
Part 2

The word "prophet" is the transliteration of a compound Greek term derived from "pro" (before/towards) and "phesein" (to say); thus, a προφήτης (prophḗtēs) is someone who conveys messages from the divine to humans, occasionally including predicting future events. In the Bible, prophets were presented with various functions. Firstly, prophets served as representatives of God's divine voice to the people of Israel, and they were also representatives of God Himself. Prophets had the utmost authority to anoint kings, priests, and other successor prophets of the people. In the study of the panorama of the Old Testament or its introduction, the category of prophets is divided into two classes: one called "the Major Prophets" and the other "the Minor Prophets." The major prophets contain 5, and the minor prophets 12; they are called this way due to the duration of their ministries and the volume of prophecies they received. The total number of all the prophets was 17. It is worth saying that in the history of the people of Israel there were hundreds of prophets and possibly even thousands, the (sages) wise men in the Talmud tell us that from Moses until the destruction of the temple of Jerusalem in 70 A.D there were approximately one million prophets in Israel, a fairly high or hyperbolic figure but the truth is that the biblical ones were the most outstanding, and their stories were written in sacred texts. It is believed that from ancient times, from the return from the Babylonian captivity until the end of the intertestamental era, all the books of the prophets were united or considered a separate group from the Law of Moses, "The Torah," known in Greek as the "Pentateuch." Each prophet had their own role; generally, they called the people to repentance when the people disobeyed or turned away from God. In times of war, kings consulted the prophets to receive advice or the voice of God in direction for the wars. In good times, prophets also prophesied blessings for the people. Prophets generally tended to walk alone and live separated from the people, with the exception of some who worked in the political palaces of kings. Some lived in the deserts, others in cities with established prophetic schools.

The Messianic Prophets:

In Israel, there existed a time known as the golden era, the best of times in Israel. It is believed to have been during the time of King David, who conquered all the lands of Israel's enemies dating back to the time of Moses and Joshua. King David conquered Jerusalem, also known as Zion, among many other biblical names. During the reign of King David, he reinstated the Tabernacle of David, which consisted of the worship of Yahweh in all its proper order and splendor, and there was also political control by the Davidic dynasty. It was a time when Israel had no worries about enemies because they had all of Israel under control. God made a promise to David that from his descendants, He would raise up a son whose throne would be established forever, which we know in no way was Solomon as some academic scholars say and think. Solomon died and his throne was greatly divided, as previously explained. After David, there was never a king in Israel like him. Sometimes kings from the tribe of Judah, sons of David, would rise up, but none were like David. Josiah, Hezekiah, and others were very good, but never like him. Through David, the Messiah ("anointed one") of Israel would be initiated, the Messianic era, or the Messianic kingdom. About two hundred years after David, the kingdom of Israel fell and was taken captive by the Assyrian Empire in 722 BC, then a century later the kingdom of Judah fell captive to the Babylonians, Jerusalem was destroyed, and the temple of David and Solomon was consumed by fire until it was destroyed. The view and hope of the Messianic kingdom, and the same awaited Messiah by traditionalist Jews and practitioners of Judaism, is not the same as the Messiah and the Messianic kingdom for Christians and Messianic Jews. For Christians, Jesus is and was the Messiah, the son of David, the Son of Abraham as Matthew says. Traditionalist Jews and practitioners of rabbinic Judaism still await a Messiah who will bring them justice, save them, enable them to build a third temple in Jerusalem, and give them peace from all their enemies. In this case, we will only focus on Jewish Messianic thought and Christianity, because we know that Jesus of Nazareth is the true and only Messiah, the son of David, whose empire has not been destroyed for over 2 millennia and continues to grow worldwide. The prophet Isaiah was the one who initiated direct and historical prophecies about the coming of a promised Messiah. Conservative Christian theological tradition continued to use what was known in the apostolic and patristic era, the typology of Christ the Messiah, in the prophecies of the Old Testament, starting from Genesis onwards to Daniel and Malachi, throughout the history of Israel, until the fulfillment with the arrival of the last prophet in the law, John the Baptist, paving the way for the welcome of Jesus of Nazareth.

Jesus as a Prophet:

After a brief history of the prophets of Israel, we can now focus on the general purpose of this section. Jesus, although he was a prophet, was much more than a prophet. Jesus as a prophet surpassed all the signs and miracles that all the prophets before Him performed. Among the most respected and well-known prophets of the north, such as Elijah and Elisha, who raised the dead, brought down fire, and multiplied oil, Jesus was superior to them. Jesus multiplied the 5 loaves and 2 fishes to feed 5000 people, not counting women and children, and after everyone had eaten their fill, there were 12 baskets left over. Jesus resurrected several dead, healed lepers, gave sight to the blind, a miracle that no prophet had done throughout history, raised the paralyzed, and freed many from demons. There is no book that can contain all the signs that Jesus did as the Son and prophet of God. Not all prophets in Israel performed miracles, but it was highly expected that prophets would perform signs, and their prophecies would be fulfilled.

We see Jesus in the encounter with the Samaritan woman, telling her about her past marital life. It was quite unlikely that Jesus knew this woman beforehand; he was Jewish, and she was Samaritan. Not only did they not know each other, but culturally Jews and Samaritans did not get along well. After Jesus predicted her life, she, astonished, replied, *"I perceive that you are a prophet" (John 4:19)*. In Luke 7:11-17, Jesus resurrects the only young son of a widow in the city of Nain. Once he is resurrected, the people say the following, *"A great prophet has appeared among us!" and "God has visited his people!" (Luke 7:16)*. The people knew and believed that Jesus was such a prophet that at one point, in *Matthew 16:13-14, when Jesus asked his disciples who people said he was, they replied, "Some say John the Baptist, others say Elijah, and others Jeremiah or one of the prophets."* All of these mentioned were among the most powerful prophets with the greatest authority. The prophet Elijah was considered the father of the prophets, and Jeremiah was the greatest and most excellent preacher prophet in Israel.

Jesus as a prophet not only turned the hearts of his people back to God but also reconciled the world to God, reuniting humanity with God as it was in the beginning. The saddest day, in present times for rabbinic Jews, was prophesied by Jesus of Nazareth. *In Matthew 13:1-2, Jesus predicted the destruction of the temple in Jerusalem, "Truly, I say to you, there will not be left here one stone upon another that will not be thrown down."* This great destruction occurred in 70 AD by the Romans, and it remains marked in Jewish history forever, even to this day. Jesus prophesied many other things as a prophet, and his fundamental message was a continuation of the same call to repentance that all the prophets made to Israel. This repentance, which indicated turning back to God and turning away from the world, a 180-degree turn and change of consciousness, was what Jesus came to continue and fulfill as a prophet of God.

We see the image of Jesus as a prophet more clearly through Dr. Luke and the writer of the book of Hebrews when they compare Moses to the superior Jesus of Nazareth. *In Acts 3:22, Dr. Luke records Peter's speech on Solomon's Portico, where Peter says, "Moses said, 'The Lord God will raise up for you a prophet like me from your brothers. You shall listen to him in whatever he tells you'" (Acts 3:22)*, showing that these words were fulfilled in Jesus, calling him a prophet just like Moses. Later, *in Acts 7:37, we see Stephen in his great speech to the religious Jews citing the same words spoken by Moses in Deuteronomy 18:15,* saying that these had been fulfilled in Jesus. The Jews by accusation and the Romans by crucifixion killed Jesus, the prophet of whom Moses had said that God would raise up among his brothers. The message of the prophet Jesus was twofold, first in the style of the prophet Isaiah from chapter 39 onwards, especially in chapter 61:1-3:

Isaiah 61:1-3

"The Spirit of the Lord God is upon me, because the Lord has anointed me to bring good news to the poor; he has sent me to bind up the brokenhearted, to proclaim liberty to the captives, and the opening of the prison to those who are bound; to proclaim the year of the Lord's favor, and the day of vengeance of our God; to comfort all who mourn; to grant to those who mourn in Zion— to give them a beautiful headdress instead of ashes, the oil of gladness instead of mourning, the garment of praise instead of a faint spirit; that they may be called oaks of righteousness, the planting of the Lord, that he may be glorified."

Secondly, not only preaching like Isaiah, but rather fulfilling what he himself said;

Luke 4:18-44;

"The Spirit of the Lord is upon me, because he has anointed me to proclaim good news to the poor. He has sent me to proclaim liberty to the captives and recovering of sight to the blind, to set at liberty those who are oppressed, to proclaim the year of the Lord's favor." And he rolled up the scroll and gave it back to the attendant and sat down. And the eyes of all in the synagogue were fixed on him. And he began to say to them, "Today this Scripture has been fulfilled in your hearing."

We see widespread recognition of Jesus as a prophet. The apostles called him a prophet, the deacons, the people, and even the Samaritans knew him as a prophet. They did not believe in or expect just any prophet; they awaited another Moses, which alludes to someone greater than a prophet. Moreover, he fulfilled all the requirements of a prophet. He came as a messenger of God to bring the message to his people, performed many signs and wonders equal to or greater than all others before him, prophesied many things, some of which have been fulfilled and others yet to be fulfilled. He referred to himself as greater than a prophet, and everyone called and knew him as a prophet. In Jesus's final declarations in his last days in Jerusalem, referring to all who had come as the voice of God just like him, knowing that his time was short, he looked upon Jerusalem and said;

Matthew 23:37;

"O Jerusalem, Jerusalem, the city that kills the prophets and stones those who are sent to it! How often would I have gathered your children together as a hen gathers her brood under her wings, and you were not willing! See, your house is left to you desolate. For I tell you, you will not see me again, until you say, 'Blessed is he who comes in the name of the Lord.'"

After Jesus had wept over Jerusalem and its abuse against its prophets;

"When he entered Jerusalem, the whole city was stirred up, saying, 'Who is this?' And the crowds said, 'This is the prophet Jesus, from Nazareth of Galilee.'" **(Matthew 21:10)**

JESUS OF NAZARETH THE SHEPHERD
Part 3

God the Shepherd of Israel:

The idea of shepherding, specifically by God Himself as the Shepherd of Israel, is a theme found throughout the Bible, from the beginning in Genesis 48:15 and 49:24 where we see Jacob on his deathbed describing how God had been his Shepherd throughout his life up until then. In Revelation 7:17, with reference to the saints who came out of the tribulation, standing before the throne of God, the Lamb who is in the midst of the throne will shepherd them and guide them to springs of living water, and God will wipe away every tear from their eyes. The theme of the shepherd in the Bible is quite significant; it appears at critical moments during the life of the people of Israel. Shepherding sheep is one of the oldest jobs and dedications known in biblical lands and throughout the Middle East. God allowed men and writers to show and compare Him as the Shepherd of His people. Shepherding, in this case, sheep, was very common in the Middle East. The patriarchs and tribe leaders were all shepherds: Abraham, as the father of all Hebrews, was a shepherd; Moses, the great liberator of Israel, was also a shepherd; the greatest of the kings of Israel, David, was also a shepherd of sheep. It was in the pastoral field of sheep that the news of the birth of Christ was first revealed. In Israel and throughout the Middle East, sheep and goats were raised a lot, but sheep were more special. There was not an abundance of pastures and sources of restful waters for them due to the vast desert, but the shepherds knew how to find them and lead their sheep to these so they could eat, drink, and also rest. Annually, the shepherds would prepare the places and the desert fields in advance, so that in due time, these would be ready when they brought their sheep, and they could be well. Generally, among the children, everyone had a time to shepherd. If there was only one firstborn, he would be the shepherd of the house along with his father. If there were eight, as in the case of David, each would take turns until the youngest was left with the task of shepherding the sheep. In the case of Cain and Abel, the youngest was a shepherd of sheep. Jacob, a twin by day but younger in time, was also a shepherd. The comparison between God as a shepherd and Israel as sheep is the closest comparison that can exist among all the other comparisons we see of God in the Bible. We see God as a Potter, Doctor, Architect, King, and many other characteristics, but none surpasses the figure of the Shepherd. Israel is the weakest and most defenseless people among the nations in the entire Bible; it is the people who travel the most in the Bible, and it is the people who experienced the most slavery. Just as sheep are so weak and defenseless and need a shepherd at all times, so did the people of Israel. God, as the good shepherd, took them, liberating them from the hands of bad shepherds like the Pharaohs, who were put in charge of them for a period of time. But these being bad shepherds, God the good shepherd saw them, heard them, and went out for them, leading them through the desert as shepherds do without lacking anything until He brought them into the land of Canaan, where they would have everything. Just as sheep do not know where they are going, Israel did not know where they were going either, but God, through Moses, led them as the shepherd leads his sheep. This title of shepherd was not only exclusive to Israel or in Israel; among other nations, the title was used for kings. In the case of Babylon, King Hammurabi called himself a shepherd, and Homer, as a regular Greek pattern, also called himself the Shepherd of the people. For this reason, we see in Jeremiah 49:19 and also 50:44, Yahweh Himself making a call to all the shepherds to see who could resist Him. God was calling all these kings and their shepherds to show that none is like Him, the true Shepherd of Israel. Shepherds had instruments for shepherding, the general instrument being a rod. With this, they guided the sheep and also sustained themselves on the way. In the case of Moses, we see him perform many signs through his pastoral rod. Theologically, this rod is compared to the word of Yahweh and the creative power of His word. The figure of the shepherd also came to represent the symbol of protection, power, and absolute authority.

Isaiah 53:6;

"We all, like sheep, have gone astray, each of us has turned to our own way; and the Lord has laid on Him the iniquity of us all."

It continually reminds us that we are Yahweh's people, like His sheep, always disobeying and straying from His ways. But He, being the Good Shepherd, faithful to His sheep, after they have strayed from Him and His path, wandering alone in the desert of this dark and lost world, decided to go after them (us), to find them, call them, heal them, return them to His path and His safe fold. Only the owner and Shepherd of the sheep Himself could go in search of them, incarnating, becoming a man like everyone else, and went to rescue them.

Isaiah 35:4;

"Say to those with fearful hearts, 'Be strong, do not fear; your God will come, He will come with vengeance; with divine retribution He will come to save you.'" (NIV)

Ezekiel 34:11-12;

"For this is what the Sovereign Lord says: I myself will search for my sheep and look after them. As a shepherd looks after his scattered flock when he is with them, so will I look after my sheep. I will rescue them from all the places where they were scattered on a day of clouds and darkness."

Jesus the Good Shepherd:

There are two places in the Bible where we can see exactly what the Good Shepherd represents: in the Psalms and in Jesus of Nazareth Himself. An example of the failed and bad shepherd is seen at the beginning of Ezekiel 34, where God had appointed shepherds to care for His own sheep. Similarly, in the New Testament, God had appointed sedentary shepherds (Pharisees and Scribes) to shepherd the people, but they became hired hands and thieves, abusing the sheep, taking all their wool for their own interests, neglecting them, without caring for them or feeding them. Jesus spoke to these as the protector of the sheep when He said:

John 10:10;

"The thief comes only to steal and kill and destroy; I have come that they may have life, and have it to the full." (NIV)

John 10:8;

"All who have come before me are thieves and robbers, but the sheep have not listened to them."

To see the direct cause of why the Pharisees and Scribes were bad shepherds, you can read the entire chapter 23 of the Gospel of Matthew, which is dedicated to them and all their judgment for becoming bad shepherds of Israel. Making a parallel comparison between the Shepherd Jehovah of Psalm 23 and the Good Shepherd Jesus of Nazareth in John 10, we will see why Jesus is the Good Shepherd and has all the qualifications to truly be called the Shepherd.

David, as the composer of the most famous poem and hymn of the Old Testament, decided to call Yahweh "Jehovah" his Shepherd because, as the Creator, he knew that even if all men left or abandoned him, God would never fail or abandon him. David knew he could put all his trust in God and knew that God was so real that despite his life being in constant danger, fleeing through all the deserts in Israel, hiding in all the caves, with no one to trust. It is under these circumstances and at this moment in his life that David decides to call Yahweh his Shepherd. Jesus, through whom all things were created and exist, on one occasion, after having healed a man born blind as the Good Shepherd, the blind man (sheep) is interrogated by the religious Pharisees (bad shepherds), prohibiting his healing and discrediting the work of the Good Shepherd Jesus. Jesus defended the blind man and, as the Shepherd, confronted the Pharisees, showing them their own spiritual blindness. Once He finished speaking with these bad shepherds, He turned to the people (the sheep), saying publicly, "I am the Good Shepherd. The good shepherd lays down his life for the sheep." The religious teachers and leaders did not care about the lives of the needy, but Jesus came to give and lay down His life for the people of God. As their Shepherd, His followers never lacked anything while they were with Him. They all abandoned their lives and resources to follow Him as sheep, and during the entire time they were with Him, they lacked nothing.

Luke 22:35;

Then Jesus asked them, "When I sent you without purse, bag, or sandals, did you lack anything?" "Nothing," they answered. (NIV)

John 17:12;

"While I was with them, I protected them and kept them safe by that name you gave me. None has been lost except the one doomed to destruction..." (NIV)

Just as God found David among the sheep of his father Jesse and then appointed him to shepherd His sheep Israel, Jesus found each of His disciples and apostles and, like Peter, appointed them to shepherd His sheep. God, as Shepherd, fed the people of Israel by making "manna" fall from heaven for them to eat fresh every day. This Jesus, as Shepherd, offered Himself to all the people, saying, "I am the bread of life; whoever comes to me will never go hungry, and whoever believes in me will never be thirsty," and confirmed to them that He was that Bread and manna that God sent from heaven:

John 6:31-35;

"Our ancestors ate the manna in the wilderness; as it is written: 'He gave them bread from heaven to eat.'" Jesus said to them, "Very truly I tell you, it is not Moses who has given you the bread from heaven, but it is my Father who gives you the true bread from heaven. For the bread of God is the bread that comes down from heaven and gives life to the world." "Sir," they said, "always give us this bread." Then Jesus declared, "I am the bread of life. Whoever comes to me will never go hungry, and whoever believes in me will never be thirsty."

David continues by saying that Yahweh would make him lie down in green pastures, leading him beside still waters, restoring his soul, and guiding him in paths of righteousness for His name's sake. We see all this in the unique Good Shepherd, Jesus of Nazareth. Jesus said:

John 4:14;

"But whoever drinks the water I give them will never thirst. Indeed, the water I give them will become in them a spring of water welling up to eternal life." (NIV)

And He also said:

Matthew 11:28-29;

"Come to me, all you who are weary and burdened, and I will give you rest...and you will find rest for your souls." (NIV)

Here we clearly see who David's shepherd was, whom he had prophetically known as his Lord when he said in Psalm 110:1, "The Lord says to my Lord: 'Sit at my right hand until I make your enemies a footstool for your feet.'" This Shepherd of David would guide him in paths of righteousness, being Jesus Christ Himself the righteousness and the only righteous way to the Father, the one who would establish the way of righteousness, as Paul tells us in Romans 3:22, *"This righteousness is given through faith in Jesus Christ to all who believe. There is no difference between Jew and Gentile,"* declaring and telling Thomas in front of everyone else, *"Jesus answered, 'I am the way and the truth and the life. No one comes to the Father except through me.'"* This path of righteousness by which David desired his Shepherd to guide him is the same path that Moses had asked God to show him in the desert when they did not know where to go. God then said, *"See, I am sending an angel ahead of you to guard you along the way,"* but Moses replied, *"If your Presence does not go with us, do not send us up from here."* This same righteous path of God for the salvation and freedom of man is Jesus of Nazareth the Christ, and His Gospel, as the only way to true freedom and righteousness that leads man to the Creator Father.

Jesus of Nazareth

David continues, *"Even though I walk through the darkest valley, I will fear no evil, for you are with me; your rod and your staff, they comfort me."* The Hebrew word translated as "shadow of death" is "salmawet." It is a word that most often appears poetically. The best translation would probably be "the valley of the deepest or darkest shadows." The Septuagint (LXX), which is the Greek translation of the Old Testament, translates the phrase as "skiasthanatou" (the shadow of death). I would say that this verse can apply to death, and perhaps death or the prospect of death was at the forefront of David's mind. There is an explanation that caught my attention greatly by the great preacher Charles Spurgeon, which gives us a cultural and historical interpretation as follows:

The Valley of the Shadow of Death exists and is a place located south of Jericho. For many years, it was believed that the figure of the "Valley of the Shadow of Death" was simply an allegorical concept used by David to refer to physical death. However, today we know that between Jericho and the Dead Sea, there is a gorge known as the "Valley of the Shadow of Death." Recent research into the ancient customs of Jewish shepherds has shown, as Wallace states in his article published by Reader's Digest, that ancient Jewish shepherds knew it and used it for transhumance. It is located south of Jericho, towards the Dead Sea, and is about 7.5 kilometers long. Its rock walls reach heights of up to 500 meters in some places, and in some parts of the path, it is only two or three meters wide. There are bends where the usable space is so narrow that the sheep cannot even turn around. Additionally, it is extremely dangerous because it is filled with crevices and internal ravines. The climatic conditions of the country and the location of pastures in Palestine make transhumance necessary, which forced most flocks in David's time to pass through this valley at least once a year. It is impossible to cross it during the day due to the unbearable heat. Therefore, it must be done either at dawn or at dusk, which significantly increases the danger. Although there was no established law, it seems that due to the lack of light, there was a verbal agreement among the shepherds that flocks should pass through it in one direction in the morning hours and in the other direction in the evening. The shepherd skillfully used his staff as a persuasive tool to force the sheep to walk, jump over crevices, and avoid getting close to the precipice; nevertheless, it was easy for a sheep to slip and get caught in a crevice two or three meters off the path. When this happened, the shepherd would use his staff to encircle the neck of the larger sheep or the body of the smaller ones, pulling them up, lifting them, and helping them return to the path. (Excerpt from the book "El Salmo 23," by C.H. Spurgeon, published by Clie.)

According to this interpretation, when we make a comparison, we see that Jesus fulfilled everything by caring for His own like sheep, leading them on the path even unto His own death. He was with them and never abandoned them during all the days of danger, including after His death when they were all hiding, locked away, and filled with fear like sheep whose Shepherd had been wounded. Three days after His resurrection, He came out to seek His sheep, knowing exactly where they were, like the Good Shepherd who knows where His sheep are and where they go. Finding them together, He said, "I will not leave you as orphans; I will come to you... Peace I leave with you; my peace I give you. I do not give to you as the world gives. Do not let your hearts be troubled and do not be afraid... And surely I am with you always, to the very end of the age." Jesus, as the true shepherd of His sheep, promised to always be with them. He went to prepare a place for each of them but did not leave them abandoned and uncared for. He sent the Comforter, the Holy Spirit, who is one with Him. The Spirit would stay in representation of Him and in absolute care of His sheep until the appropriate time when they would reunite with the Good Shepherd.

David ends his poem and hymn by confidently stating that his Shepherd, as a king, would prepare a table before him in the presence of his enemies, anointing his head with oil, and making his cup overflow. All the enemies of the apostles witnessed Jesus' favor upon each of them. After Jesus' resurrection, on the day of Pentecost, all His disciples were anointed by the Holy Spirit, symbolizing the anointing oil of the sacred unction that kings and priests received from the Spirit of Yahweh for their spiritual function. They received the Holy Spirit and the anointing in the presence of all their enemies and the religious Jews who were against them. The cup and the wine, representing the death and blood of Jesus, were poured out over them, forgiving and cleansing them of all sin and offense against God, justifying them and giving them a place in the kingdom and at the table of God with Christ. This also represents their union with Jesus and their spiritual richness that would overflow in them, in front of their enemies. As we see later, the world was turned upside down by the grace of Christ overflowing in them.

The word "Pastor" appears in the New Testament about 18 to 20 times, referring to pastors and shepherds. Of these, 15 times are direct references to Jesus of Nazareth, one reference is to the shepherds who came to Bethlehem at His birth, and the rest refer to those whom God calls and chooses as pastors for His church. Concluding this part, we see Jesus as the shepherd known among His people for His care and guidance of His followers, leading them on the right path, the path of righteousness, protecting them from all evil and danger. This clear image of Jesus emphasizes His role as the Good Shepherd, who loves, cares for, protects, and has compassion for all His sheep, fulfilling His spiritual purpose in each of them. Finally, it is clear that Jesus is the Good Shepherd, not only because of all that He did and fulfilled but also because He fulfilled His role as a shepherd, laying down His life every day, even unto death, in rescue for His sheep.

John 10:11:

I am the good shepherd. The good shepherd lays down his life for the sheep.

Alexander Frias

JESUS OF NAZARETH THE KING

Part 4: From Theocracy to Monarchy (Kings of Israel and Judah)

In the Old Testament, there were three essential roles or functions: prophet, priest, and king. Jesus Christ fulfilled all of these roles. In this part, we will focus on the role of the king, and in the next part, we will discuss His role as a priest. The first thing we need to understand is that Jesus' role as king will have two different realms: the earthly physical realm and the spiritual realm. With that said, we will first focus on Jesus' reign in His earthly realm and then conclude with Jesus' spiritual kingdom.

Before the nation of Israel entered the era of their monarchs or kings, God was their ruler, which is known as "Theocracy," meaning "divine government." Since Israel had left Egypt, Moses and Joshua were the servants and leaders that God appointed as His representatives to guide the people into the Promised Land. Once they were established in Israel by tribes, they still did not have kings; God was their king. They went through a period of almost 355 years where they were judged by judges that God raised up among the tribes. This number is calculated from when Joshua conquered the land (1398 B.C.) until Eli and Samuel judged before the establishment of the monarchy (around 1043 B.C.).

The problem arose when the Israelites saw that all the other nations had kings governing them. The Israelites became envious of the other nations and then asked the prophet Samuel to appoint a king for them like the other nations had. This decision of the people disturbed the prophet Samuel because he knew it would kindle God's anger against His people, since God had been their only King from the beginning. When the news reached God through Samuel, God told Samuel not to worry because He knew this demand was not Samuel's fault, but that of the people. After God spoke with Samuel, Samuel conveyed God's message to the people, telling them that God would give them what they asked for—a king like the nations—

but warned them that when they faced problems, this king would not be able to resolve them as God had. Samuel gave them what they asked for, anointing the first king of Israel, Saul, from the tribe of Benjamin.

After Saul reigned for 40 years, he did evil in the sight of God, and his kingdom was taken from him and given to someone after God's own heart. Samuel had to fill the horn he used for anointing kings once more. God had given orders to go to the house of Jesse in Bethlehem, for there He had provided a king for His people. It is evident that God loved Saul, but from the story, it seems as though He had chosen Saul until David grew and was ready to be anointed as king. We see that God waited until David was king to give him the greatest promise ever given to anyone in the Old Testament, excluding Abraham, who was the father of the descendants and progenitor of all.

Saul was much older than David. Initially, we see that David becomes the best friend of Jonathan, Saul's son, indicating that David was so young he could have been Saul's son. In the story, we see David being adopted by Saul, who took him in and did not let him return home. At first, Saul was fond of David's prudence, but later we see the other side of the coin where Saul himself attempts to kill David twice and pursues him for almost 13 years until he finally dies in a battle against his enemies. After being wounded, he decides to take his own life.

The prophet Samuel had previously anointed David to eventually reign over his people. Once Saul was dead, the tribe of Judah, to which David belonged, saw the prophet Nathan appear to David, telling him to go up to Hebron, a city in Judah, because there he would be crowned king of the tribe of Judah. Seven years later, all of Israel, the ten northern tribes, sent for David to anoint and install him as their king. This indicated that now David was king over all the land of Israel.

David was the most special king in Israel. God gave him a promise that He had never given to any other king. To read all the promises made to David, they can be found in 2 Samuel 7, but among all these promises, God tells him;

"When your life comes to an end and you go to rest with your ancestors, I will place one of your own descendants on the throne and establish his kingdom. He will be the one to build a house in honor of My Name, and I will establish the throne of his kingdom forever. I will be his Father, and he will be My son... Your house and your kingdom will endure forever before Me; your throne will be established forever."

God had promised David that one of his descendants would be established to uphold his kingdom, and this descendant would have to build a house in honor of his God's name, but his kingdom would have to be established forever. Then He says that his house, family, kingdom, and throne would endure forever, without end. Academic scholars generally say that this son of David referred to by the prophet Nathan in all this prophecy promised to David refers to his son and king Solomon. But it turns out that in no way could this refer to Solomon. Firstly, because the only thing Solomon did, if all this prophecy is referring solely to an earthly kingdom, was to build a house in honor of Yahweh, which lasted for about 400 years until it was burned and turned to ashes by the Babylonians. Solomon's throne only lasted about 40 years, and God never considered him as His son nor called him His son.

Since David's death, there were 42 kings in Israel and Judah, and none of these promises were fulfilled in any of them, except the only Jesus of Nazareth, a direct descendant and son in the flesh of David. Here is a list of all the kings who reigned in order over Judah. The kings of Ephraim (Israel) or the northern tribes would not be of great interest since the promise had been made to David, for one of his sons ("Jesus"), descendants, kingdom, throne, and house. Despite this, Jesus, being the king of the Jews, found all the lost sheep of Ephraim (Israel's ten tribes), liberated them, and taking them, made both the people of Israel and Judah one united people, as it had originally been, subsequently calling them "Israel His Church."

Jesus of Nazareth

- *Rehoboam (son of Solomon)*
- *Abijah (son of Rehoboam)*
- *Asa (son of Abijah)*
- *Jehoshaphat (son of Asa)*
- *Jehoram (son of Jehoshaphat)*
- *Ahaziah (son of Jehoram)*
- *Athaliah (Queen of Judah) – The only queen of Judah*
- *Joash (son of Ahaziah)*
- *Amaziah (son of Joash)*
- *Uzziah (Azariah) (son of Amaziah)*
- *Jotham (son of Uzziah)*
- *Ahaz (son of Jotham)*
- *Hezekiah (son of Ahaz)*
- *Manasseh (son of Hezekiah) – Longest reign: 55 years*
- *Amon (son of Manasseh)*
- *Josiah (son of Amon)*
- *Jehoahaz (Shallum) (son of Josiah) – Reigned for 3 months*
- *Jehoiakim (Eliakim) (son of Josiah)*
- *Jehoiachin (Jeconiah or Coniah) (son of Jehoiakim) – Reigned for 3 months*
- *Zedekiah (Mattaniah) (son of Josiah)*

Jesus, the King of the Jews (according to the flesh):
Matthew 2:2-4:

"Where is the one who has been born king of the Jews? We saw his star when it rose and have come to worship him." When King Herod heard this he was disturbed, and all Jerusalem with him. When he had called together all the people's chief priests and teachers of the law, he asked them where the Messiah was to be born.

These were the words narrated by Matthew, about the Wise Men from the East who arrived in Israel during the time of Jesus' birth. Herod, troubled, and all Jerusalem with him, filled with fear and dread, summoned all the chief priests and scribes to see where the prophecies said the Christ (the Anointed One) would be born.

Because Herod knew first and foremost that he was not Jewish, and also not legitimately a king. He had been placed there by his father Herod the Great, who had been appointed by the Romans, who had usurped the power to appoint and anoint kings in Israel, being ancestrally the kings among the sons of Judah and the house of David.

In this part, we won't talk about the Wise Men or Herod since we previously shared enough information about them in the infancy of Jesus. Entering the topic, Matthew in his gospel is very interested in showing Jesus as King and Messiah (Anointed One). It's not just a coincidence that he begins with Jesus' genealogy, starting with David as the initial head, then follows with Abraham onwards until Jesus Himself, showing a total of 42 generations divided into 3 groups of 14 generations each. The first from Abraham to David, the second from David to Jeconiah, also known as Joachim, and the third from Jeconiah or Coniah to Jesus.

Matthew does something very interesting; he starts Jesus' genealogy by calling Him the son of David first, instead of calling Him the son of Abraham, who was before David and the progenitor of the Hebrews, from whom the Israelites and then the Jews came. But it turns out that investigating the thoughts of the early Church fathers, in their ancient Christian commentaries on Matthew, and why he placed David before Abraham in his genealogy, the reason was said to be because the authority and position as the son of the king were above and more important than birth by Hebrew patriarchal descent. In other words, being born of Abraham was something good, but also something very common; all Israel had been born of Abraham. Now, being born as the son of the direct descent of the most excellent king in Israel was something different and much more special. With this, Matthew's intention at the beginning of his gospel is to show that this Jesus who has come, a direct descendant of the tribe of Judah, is directly the son in the flesh of the lineage of King David.

It is clear that if this Jesus was born in Bethlehem, the house of the kings of Judah, where King David was born, and He comes from the

Jesus of Nazareth

same lineage, as Matthew shows us, and also Luke in the list of his genealogy for Jesus, then Jesus was the king of the Jews. Sometimes the question arises: how could this Jesus be the son of David, if David had lived almost 1000 years before Jesus? There are two plausible reasons. The first is as follows: in Israel, there was always a list of citizenship and the tribe to which people belonged. When a person wanted to move to another tribe, they had to add their name to the census that was taken to be registered among the people and the tribe to which they were transferred. It is true that with the great wars and exiles, this information was lost each time they reunited as a people and a nation; they took a census to know to which tribe or people the individuals belonged. A second reason is that usually, people who lived in a tribe rarely moved or moved to foreign territories or long distances outside the territory of their own families, unless it was to emigrate to other nations.

A third reason is if this Jesus were not a direct descendant of David, historians from the 1st century onwards, like Josephus, Philo, Pliny, or some of the Romans themselves who wrote about Jesus, and others from the same generation as Matthew, who were alive to see and read Matthew's gospel, which traditionally and mainly was considered the first among all, written in Aramaic or Hebrew, and then translated into Greek. We do not see any of all those writers refuting or saying with evidence that this Jesus of Nazareth was not the direct descendant of David. In the book of Romans 1:3, we see the apostle Paul, who was once a Pharisee of Pharisees, the greatest scholar and researcher among all who wrote, writing and being the paternal author of almost 70% of the N.T., mentioning and confirming for himself: "concerning his Son, our Lord Jesus Christ, who was of the lineage of David according to the flesh." All the apostles knew that Jesus had come from the lineage of David; even the biblical text tells us: "And the crowds going before him and those who followed were shouting, 'Hosanna to the Son of David! Blessed is he who comes in the name of the Lord! Hosanna in the highest!'" All Jerusalem knew that this Jesus was the son of David.

Another important case is that we never see any of the Pharisees and nor the scribes refuting His lineage, nor that He was a son in the flesh of David; everyone knew that He was the son of Mary and of Joseph, who were both of the lineage of David. Therefore, this shows that Jesus in terms of the flesh and earthly realm, politically speaking, was the legitimate King of the Jews and the whole house of Judah. This legitimate and earthly political reign of Jesus of Nazareth is also declared in the text of Mark 10:47:

Mark 10:47-48:

"And when he heard that it was Jesus of Nazareth, he began to cry out and say, 'Jesus, Son of David, have mercy on me!' And many rebuked him, telling him to be silent. But he cried out all the more, 'Son of David, have mercy on me!'"

Only God and kings could have and show mercy to poor beggars and prisoners on the road. Mercy is the capacity to feel compassion for those who suffer and to provide them with support. It comes from the Latin "misere," meaning "misery, need"; "cor, cordis," indicating "heart"; and "ia," expressing "towards others." The term mercy can be used synonymously with: compassion, pity, kindness, among others. But the term that comes closest to the context is the term mercy in Hebrew or Aramaic, in the Old Testament it is "rehamîm," which means "bowels" in a figurative sense expressing an intimate, deep, and loving feeling that binds two people. Bartimaeus was asking the Son of David not only to regain his sight but also to allow him to join his kingdom, to be one within his kingdom. When Jesus asked him what he wanted, Bartimaeus had asked to regain his sight to see who the true Son of David was. As soon as Bartimaeus regained his sight, the text tells us that he followed Jesus. This "followed" is Jesus' true mercy towards Bartimaeus. The miracle of sight was God's gift out of love for Bartimaeus from Jesus, but mercy is seen when Jesus allows him to follow Him to Jerusalem. For Bartimaeus, following Jesus meant belonging to the circle and kingdom of the Son of David, the king of Israel. So far, I believe there should be no doubt regarding the legitimate reign in the flesh of Jesus of Nazareth as a descendant of the tribe of Judah and a direct son of the lineage of David, through both Mary and Joseph. In

Jesus of Nazareth

conclusion, despite Jesus of Nazareth clearly knowing that He was the legitimate king, from the lineage of David, and that He could assume His position as king whenever He wanted, He was never interested in reigning over the earthly politics and governmental power of Israel.

John 6:15:

"When Jesus, therefore, perceived that they would come and take him by force to make him a king, he withdrew again into the mountain himself alone."

John 19:19-22:

"Pilate had a notice prepared and fastened to the cross. It read: Jesus of Nazareth, the King of the Jews. Many of the Jews read this sign, for the place where Jesus was crucified was near the city, and the sign was written in Aramaic, Latin, and Greek. The chief priests of the Jews protested to Pilate, 'Do not write "The King of the Jews," but that this man claimed to be king of the Jews.' Pilate answered, 'What I have written, I have written.'"

With this, we have concluded the first part or the earthly realm of Jesus' kingdom in terms of the flesh as a legitimate son and heir to the throne of David.

Jesus the King of kings (Spiritual Kingdom):

John 18:36;

Jesus answered, "My kingdom is not of this world. If my kingdom were of this world, my servants would have been fighting, that I might not be delivered over to the Jews. But my kingdom is not from the world."

With Jesus' triumphant entry into Jerusalem, riding on a donkey, many spread their cloaks on the road, while others cut branches from trees and spread them on the road, praising their king. They all shouted "Hosanna! Blessed is he who comes in the name of the Lord! Blessed is the kingdom of our father David that is coming! Hosanna in the highest!" This was one of the most crucial moments in Jesus' life. He knew that with this praise and proclamation of kingship in Jerusalem, acknowledging the arrival of David's kingdom, in front of the Jewish religious leaders and even worse, before all the Roman soldiers who were watching over Jerusalem, possibly with Pilate the governor nearby, this could be seen as treason against the Roman Caesar. This Jewish praise-filled entry was not normal; the scribes, Pharisees, and priests would soon understand the intention behind Matthew's writing. Matthew tells us that this entry would fulfill the words of the prophet Zechariah when he said, "Rejoice greatly, O daughter of Zion! Shout aloud, O daughter of Jerusalem! Behold, your king is coming to you; righteous and having salvation is he, humble and mounted on a donkey, on a colt, the foal of a donkey." (Zechariah 9:9). This would be the ultimate trigger for the Jews to pursue Jesus to his death.

The problem was quite significant. First, it's true that in Jesus, God's promise to David to establish his kingdom and throne forever through one of his sons, who God will be a father to, and he will be a son to God, is fulfilled. But very soon, all these Jews who praised, proclaimed, and shouted "Hosanna," making Jesus their king, would be disappointed and would initially be the culprits in Jesus' death when they realized that Jesus was not seeking an earthly, military, and political kingdom like David once had. These Jews thought that the moment had come when Jesus would proclaim himself king and confront the Roman Empire to liberate them from Roman slavery and oppression, but it didn't happen that way. Including all his apostles, they thought that by proclaiming Jesus king, he would lead a rebellion like the Jewish Maccabees and Hasmoneans had done during the intertestamental period, in revolts against the Seleucid Greeks and Antiochus IV Epiphanes. Throughout the intertestamental period until the time of Jesus' arrival, there was always a Jew who rose up, seen as a messiah figure, and promoted a rebellion against the oppressors, but each time the Romans ended up quelling the Jewish revolts.

In 4 BC, as Flavius Josephus recounts, in the province of Judea, a pastor of enormous physical strength named Athronges similarly

Jesus of Nazareth

took the royal crown, and with his four brothers, whom he appointed as generals, he subdued the entire region. The leaders of these revolts were supported by many Jews and gained great popularity. Firstly, because they were all Jews, and the people had longed for a native king; Herod was not Jewish but Idumean. Secondly, because all the leaders were of humble origin yet charismatic, much like the great king David had been. These leaders had managed to revive ancient hopes of a Messiah King who would come to liberate the people from foreign oppression. The appearance of these three leaders, proclaiming themselves as Messiah, created riots and enthusiastic revolts everywhere, and soon Palestine was ablaze and in need of liberation. Faced with this situation of widespread revolt, Rome's reaction was swift.

General Publius Varus, stationed at that time in Syria, lightly took three legions and marched against the rebels. First, he quelled Simon's movement, then crushed the rebels of Athronges in Judea, crucifying over 2,000 insurgents near Jerusalem. But the harshest punishment was applied in Galilee, the land where Jesus was from. There, Varus besieged Sepphoris, captured and killed Judas, set fire to the city, completely destroying all its buildings to ashes, and finally, its inhabitants, for supporting Judas, he made them sold as slaves. Shortly after Jesus was born, around 6 AD, this Judas of Galilee, a Jewish political leader, rebelled, leading an assault against the Romans in the city of Sepphoris, where the Romans later killed his two sons and scattered all the followers of this Judas. This was the same idea of all his followers; many scholars and experts have concluded that this was the main idea behind Judas' betrayal of the master. It is believed that he could have been or could have been involved with the rebel groups, anachronistically the Zealots, who were ultra-religious nationalists, or Jewish Sicarii who secretly attacked the Romans with daggers and remained silent to avoid being seen. It is thought that Judas Iscariot, as a nationalist and disciple of Jesus, after seeing his power in all areas, needed a way to publicly provoke or put Jesus against the Romans. According to Judas' thinking, this betrayal and imprisonment would somehow provoke Jesus to destroy the Romans, giving them freedom. In the end, it became clear that no one had understood what kingdom Jesus had come to bring to the earth.

The title King of kings appears 6 times in the Bible. Originally and historically, it is believed that this title was first granted to the Persian king Cyrus the Great, but we see it once applied to God the Father (1 Timothy 6:15), and twice to Jesus (Revelation 17:14 and 19:16), the other 3 times to King Artaxerxes, who was fifth after Cyrus the Great (Ezra 7:12), and lastly to Nebuchadnezzar, king of Babylon, which shows that the title had etymologically originated from Babylon and Persia (Ezekiel 26:7), (Daniel 2:37). Just as these were powerful men and kings over nations, with the authority to subject them under power, likewise Jesus the Son of God and King, would become the King of kings once he had faced the most powerful empires to which all other earthly empires had been subjected, the spiritual empire of the devil, and the empire of death. Jesus came with a completely different message from all the kings; the messages of the kings were earthly to attain vain earthly power, but Jesus was not interested in attaining earthly power, glory, or vanity. Pilate, during his trial, asked him if he was a king, and Jesus replied that his kingdom was not of this world. This answer made it clear that Jesus had never come to earth with the same mindset as all his followers. Jesus had come to earth to fulfill, first of all, an order and secondly to bring his Father's kingdom as a ransom for humanity. He had come to bear witness to the truth and to call the children of truth back to the truth. This truth to which Jesus was referring was the unbreakable covenant that God had made with Israel, the only thing that would remain firm forever, His word, but Israel had broken it, turning away from God, violating and breaking his commandments and laws. Jesus had come to renew the covenant of truth with Israel; he had come so that Israel, as God's bride, would return to Him and return to communion with her beloved. God had given Israel a bill of divorce because she had prostituted herself with other gods and mingled among the other nations, adopting their paganism and going after their strange gods. Once there was a bill of divorce, the bride could not fall back into adultery with her husband or another man while he was still alive, otherwise, the bride

Jesus of Nazareth

would remain in adultery. Jesus, being in the form of God, one with God, but not grasping to be equal with God, offered to come to earth and as the husband of Israel, die obediently, putting his life so that Israel would once again be the free bride she once was before entering the desert after leaving Egypt, where she met her Husband, the eternal God who took her for himself. Jesus' death, the incarnate Word, gave her that freedom again to be free from her adultery, but it also offered her a new covenant of grace, a new hope, to marry the groom once again. Jesus did not remain dead in the tomb; he rose again in resurrection. Ascending to the right hand of his Father, to make all the preparations and then return for her, to the great celebration of the marriage supper of the Lamb, where Israel (the Church) will forever be the bride of Christ. Israel is the same representation of the Lord's Church, all who believe in Him and confess Him as Lord of their lives, the Good Shepherd who pastors one people, in the end, will unite them all and will shepherd them forever. Jesus preached through parables, but each of these parables had its purpose and goal: to reveal the kingdom of God and what life is like in that kingdom. Jesus came to call the whole world to be part of that spiritual kingdom; this kingdom that Jesus would introduce to the earth was for both the poor and the repentant rich. Sinners entering this kingdom received an internal transformation of life; thieves stopped stealing, the sick received healing, the demon-possessed were liberated, the lunatics returned to sanity, the blind received sight, the lame and paralyzed, taking their beds, returned home healthy, the mute received their tongue, the deaf regained their hearing, the lepers were healed, and the dead returned to life. All these kinds of signs that Jesus did were part of the life of the spiritual kingdom to which he belonged; his preaching compared to the kingdom to which he belonged showed that it was a kingdom, full of justice, love, prudence, peace, joy, without selfishness, without sadness, and without weeping; this was and is the kingdom to which Jesus belongs and of which he is the true King. Jesus came as king, but while he was on earth, he had not yet become King of kings materially; it is true that theologically, in his pre-existence, we can say that he always was, but historically speaking, it was not until he had overcome death that he became King of kings. Paul tells us in;

1 Corinthians 15:27

For "God has put all things in subjection under his feet." But when it says, "all things are put in subjection," it is plain that he is excepted who put all things in subjection under him.

Hebrews 2:8

You have put all things in subjection under his feet." For in subjecting all things to him, he left nothing outside his control. At present, we do not yet see everything in subjection to him.

Ephesians 1:21-23

far above all rule and authority and power and dominion, and above every name that is named, not only in this age but also in the one to come. And he put all things under his feet and gave him as head over all things to the church, which is his body, the fullness of him who fills all in all.

Once Jesus had fulfilled his mission on earth and had risen, his resurrection became the highest and supreme power. Through his death and resurrection, he took all the power of every empire, including that of death, which was the most powerful and to which all men were subject from Adam to Jesus. God made Jesus King of kings, placing him above all things, whether principalities, powers, empires, or kings, subjecting them under his dominion, giving him all power in heaven, on earth, and under the earth. For this reason, Jesus is the author of this salvation and freedom, which he offers to all men, welcoming them into His kingdom. Pilate and all of Jesus' followers were far from knowing which kingdom Jesus belonged to; they thought it was an earthly kingdom that would bring them vindictive and selfish justice for one people. Jesus came not only for one people but for all peoples and all nations to enter into the kingdom of God and his righteousness. In Revelation, we see Jesus being called with the title of King of kings and Lord of lords. This second title is only granted to God Yahweh in the book of Deuteronomy 10:17 and Psalms 136:3. This is a clear comparison

Jesus of Nazareth

by John showing Jesus as King of kings and Lord of lords being one with the Father, of the same essence and equal in power and authority. These titles, according to the vision of Revelation, which means "to reveal" or "to unveil the hidden," indicate that previously this Jesus had not been revealed as he is now. These titles speak of his position in the end; it has been almost two millennia since this vision was written for the churches of Asia Minor, and we see the many rulers who have come and gone, but in the end, all who have remained will be conquered and abolished by the King of kings, Jesus of Nazareth the Christ, and only He will reign as the supreme King and Lord over heaven and all the earth.

To conclude this part, a very important final point that I believe we should separate and understand the differences between both reigns of the same Jesus, one was his earthly Davidic inheritance reign, but the other is his spiritual reign. Jesus was a Jewish king for the Jews; he was born as a Jew, lived as a Jew, and also being every man, he died as a Jew. With that said, Jesus rose, but he did not rise as a Jew, nor with the same corruptible body that he had before he died; he rose with a visible and palpable but completely spiritual body, which would be glorified by his Father. It is true that he appeared to his own and likely spoke to them in their Aramaic language, and also ate with them what was eaten before, this is most likely a symbolism or a representation for the hope of those who also believe in the resurrection and in the raising of the dead in Christ. John says that we will be like him, and Paul says that the corruptible body is buried and the incorruptible one is born, this corruptible will be clothed with incorruption, one are the earthly bodies without glory and the other are the heavenly ones with glory. The apostle Paul was the only one who saw Jesus in his final state of glory, in the heights, with the exception of John in Patmos, where through the Apocalypse he shows us the revelation of Jesus Christ, there we see Jesus Christ with a glorious and full image of all his attributes and roles, we see him as King, Judge, Lamb, Lion, and so on, this is a clear indication that the vision is not necessarily physical or earthly, what is being transmitted with the vision is his current condition and position, the highest authority, his absolute power, his purity, and his radiant holiness. Some traditionalist conservatives and literalists will think that this is his current state as described, even after the writer called it a vision, but throughout all time, there have always been our fundamentalist and literalist brothers who believe the text just as it is written. In any case, we cannot think that this is his literal current state, since the book is a vision and a revelation, which indicates a message, a purpose, and Jesus Christ's current position in absolute power over all things, both in this earthly cosmos and in the invisible spiritual spheres. I have seen many Messianic Jews and practicing Christians of Hebrew culture and roots who believe that because Jesus of Nazareth was our greatest example and left us his glorious gospel of which we are witnesses, and lived as a Jew observing all Jewish customs and Israelite feasts, they also believe that this same Jesus rose as a Jew, with Jewish blood, and returns as a Jew. Jesus of Nazareth died as a Jew, but Jesus Christ rose in a spiritual body without race or ethnicity because in his kingdom, neither flesh nor blood of this world enters or inherits; his kingdom is a completely spiritual kingdom for all.

2 Corinthians 5:16-21:

Therefore, from now on, we regard no one according to the flesh; even though we have known Christ according to the flesh, yet now we know Him thus no longer. Therefore, if anyone is in Christ, he is a new creation; old things have passed away; behold, all things have become new. Now all things are of God, who has reconciled us to Himself through Christ, and has given us the ministry of reconciliation; that is, that God was in Christ reconciling the world to Himself, not imputing their trespasses to them, and has committed to us the word of reconciliation. Now then, we are ambassadors for Christ, as though God were pleading through us: we implore you on Christ's behalf, be reconciled to God. For He made Him who knew no sin to be sin for us, that we might become the righteousness of God in Him.

JESUS THE PRIEST AND HIGH PRIEST
Part 5

The Priesthood in Israel from Adam to John the Baptist

No tabernacle of meeting is complete without the ministry of a priest. The very existential purpose of the tabernacle or place of meeting requires the presence of a functioning priest. The word "priest" is precisely the term used to translate the Hebrew words "kohjén" (priest) and "kohjén ha-gadol" (high priest), from the Latin "Sacer" (sacred) and "Dotis" (gift, inheritance), referring to one who possesses the inheritance of the sacred or "set apart" work of Yahweh. The priestly figure is quite ancient. In polytheistic religions, such as those of the ancient Greeks, Romans, Aztecs, ancient Egyptians, and others, the priesthood became specialized, with each deity having its own priests. Most likely, these originated in other nations long before the people of Israel existed. For example, in Genesis 14:18-20, we see Abraham, the father of the Hebrews, when the people of Israel had not yet existed, giving a type of tithe to the king and "priest" of Salem of the Highest God named Melchizedek, whom we will discuss further later.

From the days of Adam to the time of Moses, men and women lived under the patriarchal order of the Priesthood of Melchizedek. That is, they lived in a family order presided over by a patriarch during the patriarchal era. One could say the same patriarchs or heads of families acted as priests. For example, in the case of Noah, he was the one who raised the altars and offered worship to God. The same can be said of Jacob, and successively, these were the responsible ones as heads of families to intercede and offer worship to God on behalf of the family.

With the arrival of the covenant of the law and the delivery of the two tablets of the commandments to the people of Israel, we see Yahweh telling Moses to go up to Sinai, where He would reveal and give him the entire idea and dimensions of the tabernacle and place of meeting that they would build for worshiping Yahweh during their stay in the desert. Along with the orders for the construction of the tabernacle, Yahweh also gave the order and preparation for the anointing into the priestly ministry. In Exodus 30:30, God says the following: "And you shall anoint Aaron and his sons, and consecrate them, that they may minister to Me as priests." This Aaron would be the older brother of Moses and Miriam, descendants of the tribe of Levi. God had set apart the tribe of Levi for the complete service of the tabernacle and later the temple, with Aaron's sons to be His ministers in the strict priestly service, and the other Levites were to take care of everything related to the service of the tabernacle and later the temple in Jerusalem, in worship, praise, sacrifices, offerings, and more. During the tent tabernacle in the desert, these Levites would also be responsible for dismantling the tabernacle and transporting it to its next place. Moses would be like Aaron in the quality of high priest but with greater authority, as he would be the direct mediator between Aaron, the people, and God. Yahweh spoke to Moses face to face. This expression of God speaking to Moses face to face like two men talking has been one of the most debated portions and with the most different interpretations.

This was not the only time in the Bible that we see the expression of a man seeing God. There are other moments when it appears that people have seen God: *In Genesis 32:22-32, "Jacob wrestles with a man later revealed to be God. After the incident, Jacob understood the importance of what had just happened and felt overwhelmed: "So Jacob called the name of the place Peniel: 'For I have seen God face to face, and my life is preserved."* On a purely physical level, Jacob wrestled with a theophany, a personified manifestation of God in human form. In Judges 13:1-23, Samson's parents have a conversation with the angel of the Lord. They do not realize they are speaking with the angel of the Lord until the angel makes a sign and ascends to heaven before their eyes. At that moment, Samson's father becomes terrified and says, *"We shall surely die, because we have seen God."* In all these events, we see that in the minds of the people, they all thought they had seen God or the Lord Himself. It will never be known exactly what they saw or experienced. God is so sovereign that He has always manifested Himself to humanity and spoken in many different ways. One thing we are sure of is that there has never been a human being who has seen God in the flesh and lived. God is spirit. Paul confirms that no one can see Him in 1 Timothy 6:15-16: *"Which He will manifest in His own time, He who is the blessed and only Potentate, the King of kings and Lord of lords, who alone has immortality, dwelling in unapproachable light, whom no man has seen or can see, to whom be honor and everlasting power. Amen."* According to John 6:46: *"Not that anyone has seen the Father, except He who is from God; He has seen the Father."* And in 1:18: *"No one has seen God at any time. The only begotten Son, who is in the bosom of the Father, He has declared Him."*

Among the basic functions of priests, they had to know how to worship God through the correct forms of sacrifices before God. They had to impart teachings to the communities so that they kept the law of Moses and cultural traditions. As time passed, the structures of the priests acquired specific roles and became identified with specific families that performed all the important functions of religious service. At the end of the period of the judges and entering the era of the monarchy, we see some verses that show us that there were families that had inherited the priesthood. The same style that was once seen in the desert, where God spoke and was somehow present in the priestly anointings, was no longer frequently seen. 1 Samuel 18:30 shows us that there were priests from Moses' lineage still: *"Then the children of Dan set up for themselves the carved image; and Jonathan the son of Gershom, the son of Moses, he and his sons were priests to the tribe of Dan until the day of the captivity of the land."*

The problem was that the priests from Moses' lineage seemed to have become corrupted, erecting strange images. Other translations and the Hebrew Bible tried to change the name from Moses to Manasseh, most likely attempting to guard or conceal Moses' name and figure from being associated with idolatry or something strange. However, most scholars agree that these sons or grandsons of Moses could have been pagan idolaters.

During Saul's reign, once he rose against David, it seems the priests did not know what was happening between Saul and David. Saul had summoned all the priests, as stated in 1 Samuel 22:11-14:

"And the king sent for Ahimelech the priest, the son of Ahitub, and all his father's house, the priests who were in Nob; and they all came to the king. Saul said, 'Hear now, son of Ahitub.' He answered, 'Here I am, my lord.' Then Saul said to him, 'Why have you conspired against me, you and the son of Jesse, in that you have given him bread and a sword and have inquired of God for him, so that he has risen against me, to lie in wait, as it is this day?' Ahimelech answered the king, 'And who among all your servants is as faithful as David, who is the king's son-in-law, who goes at your bidding and is honorable in your house?'"

Saul thought the priests were against him and in favor of David. When he ordered his servants to kill all the priests of Yahweh in Nob, they refused. However, Doeg, Saul's military commander, turned and killed 80 priests who wore the ephod and linen.

There was a family known as the Zadokites, previously mentioned, which came from a priest named Zadok. This family had been in the priestly order for a long time. It is not known if this family had any direct contact with the tribe of Levi, most likely not, but it is not certain. There is a probability that many of these priestly families may not have come directly from Levi but from Aaron, his sons, or their descendants among the multiplying people. This Zadokite family was a priestly family during David's reign and Solomon's temple for a long time.

As time passed and the division between Jeroboam and Rehoboam occurred, we see that in the northern area, when the Assyrian Empire conquered Israel, they exiled many Jews to other parts outside Israel and brought in many Assyrians to populate Samaria and northern Israel. The problem arose when the Assyrians in Israel tried to worship Elohim, but they did not know how to do it. The Assyrian king sent for exiled priests of Elohim to teach the new inhabitants how to worship Elohim. With this mixture of Israelites and

Assyrians present, the Samaritans emerged, whom the Jews despised as impure pagans.

Many priests who fled the north emigrated to the south and are believed to have brought with them all the scrolls and traditions of everything that happened in northern Samaria, from Moses to the traditions of northern prophets like Elijah and Elisha. It is believed that these stories were brought by the northern priests when they fled to Judah. All these priests remained in Judah until Judah was taken captive. With the Babylonian captivity by Nebuchadnezzar, he took all the priests who were in Judah and those who had remained after emigrating from Samaria. We see this in Jeremiah 29:1:

"These are the words of the letter that Jeremiah the prophet sent from Jerusalem to the remainder of the elders who were carried away captive—to the priests, the prophets, and all the people whom Nebuchadnezzar had carried away captive from Jerusalem to Babylon."

The majority of historians, scholars, theologians, and many rabbis have concluded that these Jewish priests and those added from the north in Babylon were the ones who wrote many of the historical books and also reinterpreted the oral traditions that existed among the Jews, traditions they had received from the exodus from Egypt to the arrival in Canaan. The religious tradition, Judaism, and Christianity generally attribute the authorship of the Torah to Moses. However, this idea has recently remained only as tradition among these groups. Among the Jews themselves, most scholars and rabbis have accepted that Moses was not the author of the Torah. It is believed that Ezra and the priests in Babylon were the real authors who reinterpreted and wrote down the oral traditions they had before the captivity.

Now, it is not believed at all that Ezra and the priests wrote everything, but it is known that something written existed. For example, there are two distinct thoughts: first, with King Josiah's reform. Josiah began to reign as a child and, in his youth, wanted to organize and cleanse all of Jerusalem, including the temple, of all gods of Baal, Ashtoreth, and other images throughout the territory. He then ordered Shaphan, the priest Amasiah the governor, and Joah the secretary to repair the temple. They went to Hilkiah, the chief priest, and gave him all the money that the temple keepers had collected from the people of the tribes of Manasseh, Ephraim, and Benjamin, as well as from the people of Judah and Jerusalem, and the rest of the Israelite territory. The temple was in ruins because the kings of Judah had neglected it. The money was then given to the construction managers of the temple to pay the carpenters and builders. With the same money, they bought the wood and stones needed for the repairs.

The temple was in ruins because the kings of Judah had neglected it. The overseers of the temple's construction were honest men, led by the following assistants to the priests: Jahat, Aadiah, Zechariah, and Meshullam. The first two were descendants of Merari, and the other two were descendants of Kohath. The assistants to the priests supervised the work of the laborers and directed all the workers, regardless of the work they performed. Some assistants to the priests were very good musicians, while others were secretaries, inspectors, or gatekeepers of the temple entrances.

When they were taking money out of the temple, the priest Hilkiah found the Book of the Law of God, which had been given through Moses. Then Hilkiah said to the secretary Shaphan, "I found the Book of the Law in the temple of God!" And he gave it to him. Shaphan took the book to the king, along with this report. Once the king had heard all the law written in the Book of the Law of Moses, he tore his garments and asked that they consult God, who was most likely angry with his people.

Scholars believe that this book could be a part of the Book of Deuteronomy, which is thought to be the first in composition of the entire Torah (Pentateuch), although some of the traditions in the other books of the Torah may be older than those in Deuteronomy. Second, another thought among scholars and historians, which I doubt is plausible, is that the whole idea of a book found by the priest Hilkiah and the secretary Shaphan was their idea alone, or together with Josiah, as an invention or a way for Josiah to reform all worship to Yahweh, bringing it and allowing it only in the Temple of Jerusalem, canceling services elsewhere in Israel. It has been thought that they themselves wrote the book and brought it before Josiah. I find this latter hypothesis completely implausible and very strained; the other two are the most common among serious scholars.

With the return of Ezra, the scribe and the priests to Jerusalem from Babylon, they returned with almost the entire Tanakh (Old Testament). In Jerusalem, after having adopted part of the social and religious culture learned in Babylon, including language, dress, religious form, and many other things, they created a mix between both traditional religious cultures. This system was the true emergence of Judaism as a tradition among the Jews. It was there that Judaism began. It has been believed that Judaism was practiced from the days of Abraham, who is given paternity as an Abrahamic religion, but this is an error. The traditions practiced among the Hebrew patriarchs and the Israelites in the desert were all different; they never had an established religious system and lived according to tribal traditions.

The true father of Judaism as an initial religion is believed to be Ezra, although others attribute it to Abraham. He was the father of the lineage but not of Judaism as the official religion of the Jews. It is true that some believe Judaism existed from the beginning and went through different stages of reform, changing over time until Ezra gave it its final formation, becoming the official religion. It is worth noting that this Judaism did not last long before being reformed again because by the time of Jesus, the original Judaism of Ezra was far removed from all of Israel, with so many Jewish sects with different thoughts and practices. This would not last long either, because with the destruction of the temple, Judaism would be reformed again into Rabbinic Judaism. With the expulsion of the Jews from Israel by Emperor Hadrian between 129-135, they would have no option but to reform their thinking again. Judaism has undergone so many reforms that it is almost impossible to determine how many times it has really changed.

Returning to Ezra and the priests, with their arrival in Jerusalem, they continued reinterpreting all the scrolls of tribal laws that had been lost, which they carried in their memories, and all the oral traditions of pre-exilic and post-exilic stories learned in Babylon that they had adopted. Post-exilic, they composed all the other later books that we have in our Old Testament today. During the intertestamental era, with the arrival of the Greeks and the Jewish Maccabean and Hasmonean revolts, there would be a rupture that would cause a division among the priests in Israel.

The original priests had decided to withdraw from all of Jerusalem due to the contamination of the temple and the city, moving to the desert of Qumran. There, they established the communities known as the community of the Essenes, who are believed to be the authors of the Dead Sea Scrolls. In the desert, these communities continued composing and writing all the original books of the Tanakh (Old Testament), laws for the community, and also apocalyptic books. To understand this better, I invite you to read the Dead Sea Scrolls, and you will get an idea of the types of literature the Essenes wrote.

There is a hypothesis, which I find very plausible, regarding the translation of the LXX, known as the Septuagint, in its final state. There were a series of books, which were called apocryphal or deuterocanonical. Despite being part of and included in the Septuagint canon by Greek Jews, these books were never accepted as inspired or authentic. This was simply because they were never written in Paleo-Hebrew; the majority were written in Greek, with some strophes in Aramaic. This idea of having books written in Greek in the Old Testament was not well received by traditional orthodox Jews.

The reason I bring this up is that it is thought that among all these deuterocanonical books, there were apocalyptic literature books. This type of literature among the Jews is believed to have been composed only by priests and prophets. But with the disappearance of prophets during this time, it is believed that among this priestly division, one group could have written some of the apocalyptic books that were well received among many Jewish communities, especially the book of Enoch.

The other part of the priestly division were the famous Sadducees, who were placed in the priestly order and service by the Maccabees themselves. They have come to be known as false priests and usurpers of the true priestly ministry that belonged to the Essenes, who had vacated their positions by withdrawing from everyone. As previously mentioned, it is not known exactly if among these few Sadducees appointed by the Maccabees, there could have been some real priests who decided to stay in Jerusalem and continue with the orders of the new Maccabean kings. These would be considered false, traitorous, pagan, and completely children of darkness. These Sadducees and purely titular, completely corrupt priests were the elite during the entire time of Jesus until the destruction of the temple by the Romans, which caused the disappearance of these false Sadducees.

The Priesthood of John the Baptist (his brief life):

Luke 7:28:

I tell you, among those born of women there is no one greater than John (the Baptist); yet the one who is least in the kingdom of God is greater than he.

His name implies only a part of his life and his vocation; he dedicated himself to preaching under his message and call to repentance and preparation for the arrival of the anointed one and the kingdom of God. Establishing himself in the desert of Judea, he baptized all repentant Jews in the waters of the Jordan. These received baptism in water as a symbol of purification to enter the kingdom of God and as a way to receive forgiveness for their sins through Jesus of Nazareth, who was already present among them. To understand the greatness and importance of his priesthood, it is necessary to explain where he comes from and briefly his life.

The birth of John the Baptist, like that of Jesus, was miraculous, except that John came naturally through the marital union of a man and a woman. His birth, like that of Jesus, had been predicted by the angel Gabriel six months before Jesus' birth to Mary. His mother, Elizabeth, and his father, Zechariah, were very old and had never been able to have children (Luke 1:7). The angel Gabriel announced to Zechariah, who was a Levite priest from the tribe of Levi, that he would have a son. Zechariah received this news with disbelief. Gabriel had told his parents that the blessing they had regarding John: *"He will be great before God. He will be filled with the Holy Spirit, even from his mother's womb."* He told them that their son (John) would turn many of the children of Israel to the Lord their God. He will go before the Lord in the spirit and power of Elijah, to prepare a people ready for the Lord." Elizabeth, his mother, was also a daughter of the tribe of Levi, indicating that John was a true and pure priest by both parents.

John's birth and presence were so important because up until that moment, the true priestly ministry of Israel had not been presented, appeared, or manifested. It is believed that John grew up and learned in the desert among the community of the Essenes. Some believe he could have been part of the community and most likely separated from it at some point. We do not know for sure if this is true, although we do not deny some similarities in John that indicate he may have been or learned from the Essenes. The Essenes came from the true priests of Jerusalem. They also expected the return of two messiahs, one to restore the political government of Israel as it was with David and one to restore the worship, ending those who contaminated all of Jerusalem and the temple. The Essenes believed that the priesthood of Melchizedek was still valid since God had said that his priesthood would be forever, and it seems that one of the messianic priests they expected could be this Melchizedek, who would bring them peace and freedom. This is the idea in the thought of the writer of the book of Hebrews when comparing the priesthood of Jesus the Christ to that of Melchizedek. It is believed that for this reason, the Christians or the writer of Hebrews himself adopted or took this idea from the community of the Essenes, since they also saw Melchizedek as a messiah, just as the Christians saw Jesus as

Jesus of Nazareth

the high priest of a better covenant.

John was more than a priest; it is even thought that John was not just a priest but much more than a high priest. He was the voice that prepared the way for the Lord Jesus Christ, the incarnate Word of God. Theologically, his life is a mystery and a clear comparison to that of the prophet Elijah the Tishbite, the father of the prophets. Elijah was a rather mysterious prophet; it was not known where Elijah had appeared from and who his parents were, at least in the texts. But the Spirit of the Lord had come upon Elijah so powerfully that he, with authority and force, turned the heart of Israel back to their God.

John the Baptist would come filled with the same Spirit and authority, in a violent environment. **Matthew 11:12:** *"And from the days of John the Baptist until now, the kingdom of heaven suffers violence, and the violent take it by force."* We have no idea where John was raised and with whom. Now there is an apocryphal text, the "Protoevangelium of James," which theologically tells us with some historical possibilities how and why he came from the desert. This gospel tells us that at the time when Herod had ordered the massacre of the children, he was not only seeking Jesus. The text tells us that he was also seeking John's life. Zechariah, his father, as a priest, had remained in the temple; it was assumed that John, once of a certain age, would dedicate himself to the temple as a priest alongside his father to fulfill the established law that every firstborn would be dedicated to God. The text tells us that Elizabeth had hidden John so that Herod would not kill him, but unable to hide him any longer, she took him and brought him before a high mountain. Before this mountain, Elizabeth groaned and cried out loudly to God to open the mountain because it was very high, and her age no longer allowed her to climb it. After her prayer, the mountain opened and received the child and his mother. There was a great light that illuminated them, and an angel with them who guarded them.

Herod, seeking to kill John, had sent his soldiers several times to the temple. Finding Zechariah, John's father, they asked him about the child and his whereabouts to kill him, but Zechariah refused to give them any information, saying he knew nothing about the child because he remained in the service of the temple. When Herod returned to inquire without receiving any information, he ordered Zechariah to be killed in the temple. The next day, the priests, expecting Zechariah to exit the temple, waited too long and entered, finding all of Zechariah's blood on the floor. Spreading the news everywhere, they placed Simeon in his position, upon whom the Holy Spirit rested.

We see a very possible and real part of the text: Zechariah, as a high priest, could not abandon the temple; therefore, he could not have been with John during Herod's edict. Second, we do not know if Herod was actually seeking John, but it is very likely if he knew or had learned about the relationship between Mary and Elizabeth and their visits, or as some scholars say they were relatives or family. Then we see the possibility that they were also seeking John among the other children. And third, it is very likely that before this great massacre of children, this mother had taken her son, and knowing that the only place she knew where the child could be safe was in the desert of Qumran among the community of the Essenes, which she must have known being from the priestly circle. The Essenes adopted orphaned children or the children of widows. Elizabeth could have moved to the desert with John, where she would spend her last years, and John would be instructed.

The Essenes practiced celibacy, and we see no evidence that John was married, let alone had children. John was a Nazirite; from childhood, his parents had been instructed to separate him with the same vow seen in Samson, which meant he could not touch or consume anything related to the vine and could not cut his hair. This vow was a sign of absolute consecration to God. Anyone who wanted to take it had to abstain from many things. For more details, you can read Numbers 6, which describes the vow. His clothing and food are some of the reasons why it is doubted that he was part of the Essene community; they wore linen, but John "was clothed in camel's hair, with a leather belt around his waist; and his food was

Jesus of Nazareth

locusts and wild honey." These things seemed unique to John, but we see a symbolic theology with the prophet Elijah, as they were the only two with the same clothing and the same food. Camel hair was a coarse cloth, commonly worn by the poor, while the rich wore fine clothes made of silk or linen. As John was a Nazirite from birth, it is possible that he never cut his hair. Certainly, because of his clothing and appearance, it was clear that he lived a simple life, entirely dedicated to doing God's will.

Commentators have different interpretations and thoughts about what John's clothing and food represented or symbolized. What we do know for sure is that as a prophet of God, he lived separated from the rich, abundant, and vain life that the false usurping Sadducean priests of Jerusalem had. John proclaimed the coming of the Messiah to a people desperately in need of a Savior. He was the first priest-prophet God had called since the time of Malachi, some 400 years before. The coming of John was announced 700 years before by another prophet, Isaiah, who said, "A voice of one calling in the wilderness: 'Prepare the way for the Lord; make straight in the desert a highway for our God. Every valley shall be raised up, every mountain and hill made low; the rough ground shall become level, the rugged places a plain. And the glory of the Lord will be revealed, and all people will see it together. For the mouth of the Lord has spoken'" (Isaiah 40:3-5). John's ministry did not last long, only about six months of preaching before being imprisoned and killed by King Herod. But there was no prophet-priest with more fame than John the Baptist in Israel during the first century. When his disciples brought the news of his imprisonment to Jesus, Jesus praised John uniquely, saying that of all the children born of women, none had been greater than John; he would be the greatest of all... etc. Jesus did not say this about John just to say it. John was a true and very brave high priest of the royal line. Here is the most important detail: there was a significant difference between priests and high priests. The high priest could perform the work of regular priests, but ordinary priests could not perform the work of the high priest. Priests had to know how to take the sacrifices and bring them to the high priest, but only the high priest could inspect it and declare it legitimate for sacrifice. Only the high priest could enter the Most Holy Place once a year to intercede before God for the people. The high priest was the highest and most authoritative person in all the people. Everyone had to live in holiness, but the high priests were required to maintain a higher level of holiness than the rest of the priests.

The high priests were forbidden from coming into contact with any corpse unless it was a close relative. They were not to shave their heads or cut their beards. They could only marry Israelite virgins and could not perform their priestly duties if they had any physical deformities. This indicates that all had to be physically perfect (Leviticus 21). The high priest was the only one to whom God gave the word or message for those seeking God's direction. Besides Moses as a prophet and high priest, the only two we see with both callings as prophets and high priests are John the Baptist and Jesus of Nazareth. John the Baptist was entrusted with a unique ministry, but he is also an example for all of us, including you, dear reader. God has conferred upon you a ministry similar to John's, but with more power and much greater than John's. He preached repentance for the first coming of Jesus of Nazareth to earth as prophesied, but you have been called and chosen by God to prepare and preach the imminent second coming of Jesus Christ to earth for salvation. He will come with power and glory, and every eye will see Him. This second coming will be a much more powerful event than the first; if the first was with glory, the second will be with much more glory. The priestly life of John ended with him being assassinated, his head cut off by Herod.

Revelation 22:6-7:

These words are faithful and true. The Lord, the God of the spirits of the prophets, has sent his angel to show his servants what must soon take place. "I am coming soon!" Blessed is he who obeys the prophetic words of this book!

The Priesthood of Jesus of Nazareth;

Hebrews 7:21-28:

For those who were made priests without an oath; but this one with an oath by the one who said to him: "The Lord has sworn and will not change his mind: 'You are a priest forever, according to the order of Melchizedek.'" Consequently, Jesus has become the guarantor of a better covenant. And the other priests became many, because death prevented them from continuing in office; but this one, because he remains forever, has a permanent priesthood. Therefore, he is able to save completely those who come to God through him, because he always lives to intercede for them. For such a high priest was fitting for us: holy, innocent, undefiled, separate from sinners, and exalted above the heavens; who does not need to offer daily sacrifices like those high priests, first for his own sins, and then for those of the people. He did this once for all when he offered himself. For the law appoints men as high priests who are weak, but the word of the oath, which came after the law, appoints the Son, who has been made perfect forever.

The priestly order under the law had to come through the tribe of Levi. Jesus did not come through any priestly tribe, which indicates that His priestly order would be completely different from the order of Levi and Aaron. Jesus came through the tribe of Judah, and although at times due to the lack of priests, King David, without being a priest, consulted God by wearing the ephod, a task only the high priests could do. This foreshadows that among the sons of David, one without priestly descent would rise to be much more than a high priest of God. The writer of Hebrews gives us a broad view of which priestly order Jesus belongs to. It turns out that long before Levi, the son of Jacob, even existed, during the time of righteousness, when not even the covenant of the law with Moses had been established, there was a priestly order under whom Abraham, his great-grandfather, was subject. This priesthood never ceased to exist; the only difference was that with the people of Israel, God treated them differently and established a priestly order through the tribe of Levi. God had made Aaron, the son of Levi, the first high priest in the covenant given to Moses at Sinai for the people of Israel. This people, unlike the patriarchs, never lived or experienced the priesthood of righteousness under the order of Melchizedek, the king of Salem. Aaron's priestly order had a kind of glory, but the problem was that this glory would only be momentary and temporary. Aaron, despite being a high priest by title, was a sinful man, common to all others; he was even so sinful that he was the one who raised and made the golden calf, for which the wrath of God never turned away from Israel. Aaron had to enter the tabernacle with fear and trembling, and before entering, he had to go through all the processes that the priests went through before ministering to God. This meant he had to first sacrifice and purify himself before sacrificing for the people. The high priests wore special garments made of gold, purple, blue, and scarlet. These garments included a breastpiece, an ephod, a robe, a tunic, a turban, and a sash. A particular part of their special garments was the Urim and Thummim, precious stones with the names of the twelve tribes of Israel that the high priest had to carry on his breastpiece and shoulders: *"And Aaron shall bear the names of the sons of Israel in the breastpiece of judgment on his heart when he goes into the Holy Place, to bring them to regular remembrance before the Lord. And in the breastpiece of judgment you shall put the Urim and the Thummim, and they shall be on Aaron's heart, when he goes in before the Lord. Thus Aaron shall bear the judgment of the people of Israel on his heart before the Lord regularly"* **(Exodus 28:29-30).** Jesus fulfilled and embodied all these functions, garments, and symbolic colors of the high priest perfectly, thereby legitimately becoming a better high priest of a new covenant, much better than the previous ones. To see the comparisons of all these elements directly fulfilled in Jesus, I recommend the book "The Tabernacle of Moses" by Kevin J. Conner. Melchizedek, who was the king of Salem and a priest of the Highest God, to whom Abraham had given tithes, his name meaning King of Righteousness, and also King of Salem, which is King of Peace, had been made like the Son of God, taking part in a priesthood that would remain forever. This clearly indicates that what remained forever was the priestly order of the true Son of God, but not Melchizedek himself; he would also be subject to the true guarantor of the better covenant and priesthood, Christ the Word of God, who was much greater than Melchizedek.

Jesus of Nazareth

Jesus Christ improved this priesthood, as the writer of Hebrews tells us, because Christ did not enter a holy place made by hands, a representation of the true one, but into heaven itself, now to appear in the presence of God on our behalf, nor was it to offer himself repeatedly, as the high priest enters the Holy Place every year with blood not his own. Jesus, as the high priest of the new covenant, also offered Himself as the unique and perfect sacrifice. With His sacrifice, the veil of the Holy of Holies was torn, allowing people to have direct access to God by putting their faith in Jesus.

With that said, there wouldn't be another sacrifice equal to or more perfect than Himself, so in this new covenant and priestly order, there would be no need for any other sacrifice. This would indicate that all sins would be forgiven once and for all. The freedom and forgiveness that God would offer through the sacrifice of Jesus, and the intercession of this same High Priest, would be sufficient forever. The writer of Hebrews tells us: *"But when Christ came as high priest of the good things that are now already here, he went through the greater and more perfect tabernacle that is not made with human hands, that is to say, is not a part of this creation. He did not enter by means of the blood of goats and calves; but he entered the Most Holy Place once for all by his own blood, thus obtaining eternal redemption"* (Hebrews 9:11-13). This new high priest has also given us a new law called "The Law of Christ," which consists of complete freedom from the power and enslavement of sin and the devil. Through this new covenant, in which Jesus Christ is the only great high priest, Paul tells us, *"For you did not receive a spirit that makes you a slave again to fear, but you received the Spirit of sonship. And by him we cry, 'Abba, Father'"* (Romans 8:15). Neither the covenant of the law nor the high priest Aaron could do more than offer an animal sacrifice, with the expectation that it could temporarily cover man's sin, but it could never achieve what Jesus alone as the perfect sacrifice accomplished. This sacrifice before God the Father resulted in the heavens being opened and men not only regaining communion with God but also joining the "family in the heavens and on earth, so that according to the riches of his glory, he may grant you to be strengthened with power through his Spirit in your inner being, so that Christ may dwell in your hearts through faith—that you, being rooted and grounded in love" (Ephesians 3:15-17). Among all the seven covenants from the beginning and all the high priests present in them, there never existed a covenant and a high priest who could offer humanity all the benefits that this great High Priest Jesus of Nazareth officiated and gave; He was superior to all others. Aaron and his sons, including John the Baptist, the greatest, died, and their priesthood perished with them, but Jesus, made the guarantor of a better covenant, died and rose forever. Therefore, as long as He lives, His covenant, law, and priestly order will also live. This priesthood of Christ Jesus, through His blood, washing and purifying all men, made them together with the royal priesthood and holy nation, acquired by God, to proclaim as once the priests did the virtues offered by the Torah, we proclaim the virtues of the One who called you out of darkness into His marvelous light; through the holy gospel of Jesus Christ.

Hebrews 10:19-23:

Therefore, brothers and sisters, since we have confidence to enter the Most Holy Place by the blood of Jesus, by a new and living way opened for us through the curtain, that is, his body, and since we have a great priest over the house of God, let us draw near to God with a sincere heart and with the full assurance that faith brings, having our hearts sprinkled to cleanse us from a guilty conscience and having our bodies washed with pure water. Let us hold unswervingly to the hope we profess, for he who promised is faithful.

Now Jesus Christ acts as the sole mediator and great High Priest between men and God (1 Timothy 2:5). We do not have to turn to any leader or religious man to reach God or to receive forgiveness of our sins, but we rely on God's grace that we receive through faith in Jesus alone (Ephesians 2:8-10).

Hebrews 12:2:

"fixing our eyes on Jesus, the pioneer and perfecter of faith. For the joy set before him he endured the cross, scorning its shame, and sat down at the right hand of the throne of God."

Jesus of Nazareth

WHO DID JESUS SAY HE WAS
Part 1

How the early Christian communities saw Jesus and how we see Him today:?
Matthew 16:13;

"When Jesus came to the region of Caesarea Philippi, he asked his disciples, 'Who do people say the Son of Man is?'"

It has been traditionally assumed that Jesus, being preexistent as the Word of God, came filled with divine wisdom and knowing exactly who He was. This was and is the theological opinion that dominated and remained from the end of the 1st century in the early church, as we see in the Gospel of John. Undoubtedly, the first generation of Nazarenes, Ebionites, or those of the Way never saw Jesus as divine; they saw Him as a prophet, teacher, and the chosen Messiah of God, son of David. Then, during the late 1st century, with the second and third Christian generations onwards, and the entry of the apostolic, philosophical, apologetic, and theological fathers of the church, all these figures saw Jesus as so divine and spiritual that it seemed as if His divine deity had completely absorbed all His humanity, for many centuries. Some Orthodox theological fathers, especially those from Alexandria or those who had studied in the school of Alexandria in Egypt, saw a divine Jesus who knew everything from the beginning, including His own divinity, while others, like those who studied in the school of Antioch in Syria, saw a completely human Jesus who grew and developed in wisdom with God and men, a Jesus who did not know everything but who was later perfected in everything as the writer of Hebrews says. None denied Jesus's humanity, and all knew that He had been a man, but once resurrected, it was as if all attention to His humanity had lost interest. With the exception of a Christian community known as the Docetists, who believed that Jesus was not human; they simply believed He was a human image but of complete divine nature. This heresy was abolished by the Orthodox church and disappeared in the

3rd century. Over the centuries, with continuous growth and the formation of Christianity as an established imperial system, and the worship of Jesus, as the Nicene Creed says, of the same substance as God, one with God, begotten not created, the figure of Jesus became increasingly divinized, and His humanity became more disinterested, as if His humanity had lost all meaning. We see in the words of "Saint Athanasius" in his book "The Incarnation of the Word," known as the father of orthodoxy, saying that Jesus never got sick because He was the one who healed others' illnesses; he also tells us that the body that strengthened others' weaknesses could not weaken. This is not what we see in the Gospels, but we understand that he said this because, according to him, it was not convenient for illness to precede death so that weakness in His body would not be considered to exist. Athanasius believed this by alluding that the Word that dwelt in Jesus kept Him from all diseases or fevers that could exist in the world; it was impossible for Jesus as the Son of God to get sick. Today, this high theological Christology is dominant in the vast majority of Christianity, both universal and Protestant. I completely agree with the deity and this divine image of Christ; I also agree with the theology of His preexistence because it is biblical; I agree that Jesus is completely worthy of all worship because the Father exalted Him and placed Him above all things, subjecting them all under His feet, giving Him all power and authority in everything, except the one Father to whom Jesus Himself submitted, as Paul says, *"For he 'has put everything under his feet.' Now when it says that 'everything' has been put under him, it is clear that this does not include God himself, who put everything under Christ" (1 Corinthians 15:27)*. However, I do not agree with the disinterest that the Christian church has had for many centuries in the complete historical and Jewish human life of Jesus of Nazareth.

I think it's very important for us as faithful believers in Jesus Christ to maintain a true balance regarding His deity, which historically was all man and theologically all God, not only man or only God, but all man and all God, knowing well the Jesus who grew tired as the Gospels say but also the Christ who resurrected and now lives at

Jesus of Nazareth

the right hand of the Father. When we make a comparison and separate the harmony among all the Gospels, it has been found that the thought of the first three Gospels, Matthew, Mark, and Luke, contains a level of Jesus and a much more human low Christology than that of John, who shows Jesus as superior with a multitude of divine characteristics, beginning as the pre-existent Word of God, and then showing all the "I AM" statements. Of the four Gospels, it is believed that this was the last in composition by John and the Johannine community, most likely in Ephesus where tradition tells us he had moved and where he spent the last years of his life until his death. Finally, it is believed that this community had joined the Pauline Christian community, which was already the majority throughout Asia Minor and Europe; this Gospel and the Pauline letters have much in common, especially the high Christology that both Paul and John had of Jesus. These two saw Jesus resurrected in glory, John on Patmos, and Paul on the road to Damascus; both saw Jesus as the only begotten and divine Son of God. Something clear between both was the divinity of Christ over the carnal Jesus, without denying or diminishing His human purpose and importance because both agree that Jesus was all man and born of woman; even John goes a little further by declaring that if anyone does not confess that Jesus came in the flesh, he does not have the spirit of God and is antichrist. Both John and Paul were interested in the Jesus who had resurrected and salvation by faith in Him as the Son of God. Paul wrote most of his letters with this motive. As for John, tradition attributes to him 5 books, including his Gospel, the three Epistles of John, and Revelation. Although Christian tradition attributes authorship to the Apostle John for all of these, it is not known with certainty if he was the author of Revelation, 2nd and 3rd John; it is believed that their authors could have been disciples of the Apostle John or some Christian close to him, as the apostolic fathers did not have enough evidence to authentically attribute authorship to John with certainty. Many scholars agree that this high divine Christology of Jesus by both Christian communities could have been the main factor for which both communities ended up united, becoming the final form of the Church of Jesus Christ. Many of the Christians of the first generation who had fled during the persecution of Stephen had died in the midst of persecutions and Roman punishments; Nero put many of them to death, including Paul and Peter. Gradually, all the other communities that remained joined the Pauline and Johannine communities, including the Petrine ones, until they all ended up united, maintaining the same perspective and high Christology until today. By the 2nd century, we see Tacitus the Christian, a writer and disciple of St. Justin, composing for the first time in a single book the harmony of the 4 Gospels called the "Diatessaron." Matthew composed his book most likely in Antioch in Syria, one of the Pauline communities; Mark composed his in Rome, another Pauline and Petrine community; Luke composed his in Caesarea, and John composed his in Ephesus. The first 3 Gospels, known as the "Synoptics," which contain many similar stories or events among each other, with few distinctions and different variants. These Gospels show more of a Jesus of low Christology as a whole Jewish man, more human, and with less divinity. With this, we do not say that the Synoptics discard or reject the divinity of Jesus; these Synoptics also theologically show a high divinity of Christ, just not to as high a dimension as we see in the Gospel of John, where Jesus apparently carries His own cross and everything He does, He does knowing exactly what must be fulfilled, as if He knows everything; He dies absent from pain without any suffering, and at the hour of death, He bows His head and delivers His spirit. In this part of this work, our greatest interest is not the opinion of the writer, the reader, the church, the fathers, Christianity, organizations, religions, or any extra-biblical opinion; in this part, what is important is to see how and what titles Jesus self-claimed Himself. How He was seen and how He called Himself according to the Gospel writers, Matthew, Mark, Luke, and John.

TITLES AND NAMES USED BY JESUS HIMSELF:

THE SON OF MAN:

This name or title is the most frequently used by Jesus himself throughout the Gospels, mentioned approximately 60 to 85 times in the New Testament, and over 90 times in the Old Testament. This title is one of the most significant in the life of Jesus. Etymologically, this title appears in plural form many times in the Psalms, sometimes referring to humans who have found favor with God, but it also appears singularly, prophetically typifying Jesus as the anointed one. Later, we see God using this same title for the prophet Ezekiel; Ezekiel is called the son of man many times by God. Initially, this name for the prophet had nothing to do with divinity; God used it with Ezekiel simply to emphasize his humanity. In other words, this was God demonstrating his absolute authority over his servant, the human. Finally, in the apocalyptic book of the prophet Daniel, this title is given divinely and prophetically by God himself to Jesus the Christ. It's true that Daniel did not know Jesus, but the prophetic vision of the Son of Man only points to the unique Jesus Christ, who we also see paralleled in the canonical Apocalypse of John, and no one else. Later, in the apocalyptic text of 1 Enoch, which contains the continuous story after he was translated by God to heaven, Enoch begins to recount all the things he saw, and among them he saw the Son of Man and asked his angelic guide about him, and the angel answered: "This is the Son of Man to whom righteousness belongs, with whom righteousness dwells." The Son of Man is present here as a celestial being: though he appears human, he is a supernatural being, in a very special relationship with God himself. This text was widely used by the early Jewish Christians in all Christian communities because, although it was apocryphal or deuterocanonical, it pointed directly and solely to Jesus Christ himself. From then on, for all Jews from the 1st century onwards, this title was quite elevated and divine; every Jew knew that this title belonged only to the awaited Messiah and anointed one of God, who would come to bring justice, peace, and salvation. Therefore, one should not confuse this title with the prophet Ezekiel's "son of man," nor in plural form like the Psalmist's "sons of men." Although in some instances, it is prophetically typifying Jesus the anointed one, we cannot confuse all these titles with the unique "Son of Man" Jesus of Nazareth, who is also the only begotten Son of the Father. For this reason, there is no title more exalted for Jesus than the "Son of Man." Now, Jesus used this title for himself, and he employed it in three different ways as we have just explained. At times, Jesus called himself the son of man to show himself as a complete man, the son of God like everyone else, and also the son of Adam in terms of flesh, speaking humanly. Ministerially, he used it to show himself as the humble servant of humanity, to serve others. On another occasion, he used it to refer to and show himself as the savior, the one who was to die but would be resurrected on the third day, as he said, he would be raised from the dead. Lastly, we see him using the title to present himself as the judge of the world and creation. It is very important, with these three different expressions by Jesus himself, to interpret the exact sense of the verse according to the particular characteristic that Jesus is properly employing each time he uses the title throughout the biblical text. Here, I share with you three different verses illustrating the three ways in which Jesus presents himself as the Son of Man in the three different characteristics: "Minister," "Savior," and "Judge."

Mark 10:45;

For the Son of Man came not to be served but to serve, and to give his life as a ransom for many. (MINISTER)

Luke 9:22;

Saying, "The Son of Man must suffer many things and be rejected by the elders, the chief priests and the teachers of the law, and he must be killed and on the third day be raised to life." (SAVIOR)

Matthew 24:30;

Then will appear in heaven the sign of the Son of Man, and then all the tribes of the earth will mourn, and they will see the SON OF MAN COMING ON THE CLOUDS OF HEAVEN with power and great glory. (JUDGE)

I AM:

Sometimes I have encountered very eloquent, wise, and scholarly people who tell me that Jesus never claimed to be God. Mainstream Christianity maintains a hypostasis between Jesus and God; Jesus is the expressed and manifested word of God, the very thought of God, the visible form of God, the Son of God, one with God, and God himself. Outside of Christianity, most other major religions or traditions view Jesus as a prophet or a teacher who somehow became the foundation and leader of Christianity. Among Messianic Jews, thoughts vary; some see him as the Messiah, son of David, Son of God, sent by God to turn the hearts of men back to their creator. These Messianic Jews still uphold the Torah and its laws, so they view Jesus as the sacrifice provided by God for the salvation of humanity, but they do not see Jesus as God. Another faction does believe and see Jesus as the ultimate earthly expression of God manifested to mankind. Muslims strictly regard Jesus as a prophet and messiah but not as God. Lastly, Orthodox Jews, of Rabbinic Judaism, like the Hasidic Jews, practitioners of the Talmud and all Jewish traditions, view Jesus as a bastard and a "Mamzer," a foreigner, a person born of fornication or incest; Talmudic Jews do not look upon Jesus favorably. I remember on one of my trips to Israel, visiting Jerusalem, entering the Western Wall, I had tried to engage with the rabbis present; we were talking well until I asked them what they knew or thought about Jesus of Nazareth? Once I asked this question, I was shocked or suspended by the response I received about Jesus. Some sarcastically responded with a question, who was this character? This reminded me of Jesus' encounter with Nicodemus, who was a doctor of the law and a Jew like himself but did not know who this Jesus was, which is why he had gone to consult him. This showed me that many live in Israel and are wise in the Torah, but they do not believe in or read the "Brit Jadashá or Brit Hadashá," the New Testament; for many, it is a contaminated and false book, and all they know about Jesus comes from what little the Talmud says about him.

They prefer to ignore Jesus and are also bothered to talk about Him. Some responded to me with humor, saying that Jesus was the "Galilean Athlete," and when I asked why they saw him as an athlete, their response was because he was a Jew who walked a lot; it is believed that Jesus walked about 28 miles a day. Nonetheless, Jesus is generally not well received and viewed in Israel. While there is a large number of Christians, Jews, Catholics, Armenians, and Arabs, the number is a minority compared to traditional Talmudic Judaism. All these ideas and thoughts are simply religious opinions that will always vary over time. Now, what do the Gospel writers tell us, and what was the initial meaning when Jesus appears calling himself "I AM"?

THE 7 "I AM" STATEMENTS OF JESUS: The first time we see this name, which is not actually a name but a noun or a personal title of God himself, is in Exodus 3:14, when Moses encounters the representation of God in the burning bush. Moses asks God for his name, and God responds, *"I AM WHO I AM" or "I WILL BE WHAT I WILL BE."* This was the only personal response God gave to Moses. There are many commentators who give different opinions as to why God never gave an exact name. Clearly, God is eternal, and eternity has no name. This is why he is called "Hashem," which means "The Name" or "The One of the Name," but there is no name that the eternal one has that could limit him. Jesus appears seven times in the Gospels, especially in John's Gospel, and the way he self-identifies is clear evidence of his divine deity.

Here are the seven "I AM" declarations found in the Gospel of John:

"I am the bread of life" *(John 6:35, 41, 48, 51).* In this chapter, Jesus establishes a pattern that continues throughout the Gospel of John: Jesus makes a statement about who He is and demonstrates it with something he does. In this case, Jesus asserts that He is the bread of life just after having fed the 5,000 people, not counting women and children, in the desert. He also compares himself to what

Moses had done for the people: "Your fathers ate the manna in the wilderness, and they died. This is the bread that comes down from heaven so that one may eat of it and not die." Jesus is showing himself superior to Moses and also as the true bread that gives life. Who else can give life except God himself?

"I am the light of the world" *(John 8:12; 9:5).* This second "I am" declaration of Jesus in the Gospel of John occurs just before he heals a man born blind. The element that Jesus uses for this miracle is clear; the blind man lacked something in his life, which shows his imperfection and lack of a sense: vision. Jesus, showing himself as God on the sixth day, when he took clay to create Adam before breathing life into him, similarly spits saliva from his own mouth, mixing it with the dirt, and applies it to the blind man's eyes. We see Jesus as the same Potter that Jeremiah went to visit, the same God who created Israel. Jesus not only says that he is the light but also demonstrates it to everyone. The words and actions of Jesus bring us back to *Genesis 1:3: "And God said, 'Let there be light,' and there was light."* How can a mere human being give sight to another and be the light of the whole world if he is not God? In the apocryphal or deuterocanonical text of 1 Enoch 48:1, it tells us that the Messiah would be the image of light, and this light the staff of the righteous, upon which they will rest. He is the light of the Gentiles and will be the hope for all sick souls. Jesus also said to confirm this text, "For the Son of Man came not to be served but to serve, and to give his life as a ransom for many," just as Enoc tells us. This action of Jesus, upon pronouncing these words, discomforted the Pharisees because they were so extreme that they saw Jesus breaking the Sabbath in different ways. First, Jesus spitting saliva and making mud with dirt, they thought Jesus was building, which was forbidden labor. Then, putting it on someone's eyes to heal them was also prohibited. In the Mishnah, it is allowed to give water to animals to drink, so Jesus refutes their strict religious tradition invented by themselves because it was possible to do good to animals but not to human beings, who were much more important. Jesus did good, showing the light of life to the blind, just as he shows us all that he is the light of the world.

"I am the door" *(John 10:7, 9).* This "I am" declaration is a true metaphor for what it represents to enter the kingdom of heaven, for which there is no other means than Christ himself. Jesus' words in this passage are depicted in the image of a flock of sheep. He is the only way to enter the sheepfold. Here he tells us, "Truly, truly, I say to you, I am the door of the sheep. All who came before me are thieves and robbers, but the sheep did not listen to them." Who else is the shepherd of Israel, if not God himself?

"I am the good shepherd" *(John 10:11, 14).* With this "I am" declaration, Jesus shows all His love and care. He is the one who willingly protects his flock unto death. When Jesus called himself the good shepherd, he clearly took for himself one of the titles of God in the Old Testament: *"The Lord is my shepherd" (Psalm 23:1).* Jesus clearly portrayed himself as the shepherd (Jehovah) who appears throughout Psalm 23, and who is this shepherd in Psalm 23, unlike Jesus himself when he self-identifies as the Good Shepherd! if not only God himself.

"I am the resurrection and the life" *(John 11:25).* Jesus made this "I am" statement immediately before raising Lazarus, his friend, from the dead. It is true that many prophets had also raised their dead, but none called themselves *"The resurrection and the life."* He has *"the keys of Death and Hades" (Revelation 1:18).* By raising Lazarus from the dead, Jesus showed how he can fulfill God's promise to ancient Israel: *"Your dead shall live; their bodies shall rise" (Isaiah 26:19).* Without Jesus, there is no resurrection or eternal life. And who is the only one who can raise the dead but also give them life, only God.

"I am the way, and the truth, and the life" *(John 14:6).* This powerful "I am" declaration of Christ encapsulates great significance. Jesus is not simply one way among many ways to God; He is the only way. Scripture says, *"The sum of your word (Torah and covenant) is truth" (Psalm 119:160),* and here is Jesus proclaiming that He is the truth (Torah and covenant), confirming His identity as the Word of God. Only Jesus is the source of life; He is the Creator and Sustainer of all life and the Giver of eternal life.

Additionally, Jesus is the salvation path that God laid out for His people to enter into rest when He led Israel through the wilderness. But He is also the truth that David asked God to show him.

"I am the true vine" (John 15:1, 5). The final "I am" statement in the Gospel of John speaks of Christ's sustaining power. We are the branches, and He is the vine. Just as a branch cannot bear fruit by itself unless it abides in the vine, only those who are united to Christ as the true vine receive their power and strength from Him to bear fruit in the Christian life. Israel had been a vine that produced wild grapes, but Jesus is the "true vine" that produces good grapes. With this, the message is clear: humans do not produce anything good because our nature is inherently sinful, but God is the only good one, and He can produce good things. Therefore, Jesus is once again showing that while humans are wild trees, He as God is the only true good tree that sustains and nourishes the branch to always bear much fruit.

In the Gospel of John, there are two other declarations of Jesus as "I am." These are declarations of the name of God that Jesus applied to Himself. The first case is seen when Jesus responds to a challenge from the Pharisees. *"Truly, truly, I say to you," Jesus says, "Before Abraham was, I am" (John 8:58).* The verbs Jesus uses contrast with each other: Abraham was, but I am. There is no doubt that the Jews understood Jesus' claim to be the eternal God incarnate because they took up stones to stone him. Then we see them accusing him, saying, "We are not stoning you for any good work," they replied, "but for blasphemy, because you, a mere man, claim to be God."

The second instance in which Jesus used the name I AM occurred in the Garden of Gethsemane. When they came to arrest Jesus, He asked them whom they were seeking. They said "Jesus of Nazareth," and Jesus responded: "I am" (John 18:4-5). Then something curious happened, "When he said to them, 'I am,' they drew back and fell to the ground." This is immediately an attitude of reverence or respect, by those who knew this name. Jesus simply said, "I am." Applying the covenant name given to Moses by God to Himself, Jesus demonstrated His power over His enemies and showed that His surrender to them was entirely voluntary (John 10:17-18; 19:11) without a word, violence, or force. There is no doubt, after analyzing all these names and titles that Jesus uses for Himself in the Gospel of John, Jesus and God are one and the same substance.

"*I am the Alpha and the Omega*" *(Revelation 1:8).* Lastly, adding one more to the 7 "I am" statements of John, this title that Jesus gives Himself is traditionally seen by the apostle John in the book of Revelation, and it is a completely Greek title, representing an indication between the first and last letters of the Greek alphabet. With this self-designation, Jesus would be showing His complete divinity and hypostasis with God, His Father. We see this same title in Isaiah 44:6, where the prophet, speaking on behalf of Jehovah, declares Himself as the first and the last, which is a clear and identical proclamation by Jesus to His Father when He says that He is the Alpha and the Omega as the resurrected one, the beginning and the end, the first and the last. These were words in Isaiah to identify God as the one who has always been and will remain forever.

THE BRIDEGROOM:

In Matthew 9:15, we see Jesus referring to Himself directly as the bridegroom. This revelation is also seen of God as the Bridegroom of His people in the Old Testament, specifically speaking of His covenant of love. The covenant context is the intimate marital relationship and communion between God and His people Israel. Although we may be familiar with some passages pointing to this understanding of Jesus as the Bridegroom (Matthew 9:15, 22:2, 25:1, etc.), what may be new to us is that when Jesus proclaimed Himself as the Bridegroom in the New Testament, He was connecting Himself to an identity that was already in the minds of His people: the Bridegroom of the Old Testament, to whom Israel belonged (Isaiah 54:5) *"For your Maker is your husband, the LORD of hosts is His name; and your Redeemer is the Holy One of Israel, who is called the God of all the earth."* Then, at the end of times, we see Jesus, in His capacity as God, as the Bridegroom marrying forever His beloved Israel (the Church) in the marriage supper of the Lamb of God; *"Then the angel said to me, 'Write this: Blessed are those who are invited to the wedding supper of the Lamb!' And he added, 'These are the true words of God.'" (Revelation 19:9).*

THE MESSIAH:

On one occasion, as Jesus passed through Samaria, as we know, there was no good relationship between the Jews and the Samaritans, for many centuries. For the Jews, the Samaritans were seen as pagans. In Jesus' case, it is completely different because for Jesus, no Samaritan was less than anyone. He had come to seek the lost sheep of the house of Ephraim, and the Samaritans were from the house of Ephraim. Jesus encounters a Samaritan woman who had come to a well to draw water. Jesus, tired and seeking a way to talk to her, asks her for water to drink. The Samaritan woman finds it strange that this Jew is asking her. After a conversation, the disciples, being hungry, had gone to the city to buy food. In the conversation between Jesus and the Samaritan woman, after Jesus asks her for water, she refuses to give it due to the cultural differences between them. Jesus tells her that if she knew the gift of God and who was asking her for water, she would ask Him, and He would give her living water. With this response from Jesus, she immediately asks Him if He considered Himself greater than the patriarch Jacob. Jesus was beginning to show His divinity and superiority over Jacob to this woman, offering her better water than the inheritance Jacob had left for her. Jesus continues, saying that whoever drinks of this water will thirst again, but whoever drinks of the water He will give will never thirst, but it will become in him a fountain of water springing up into everlasting life. Here, Jesus is already comparing the earthly water that Jacob left them, which causes continual thirst, with the living water that springs up to eternal life that only He can give. With this proposal by Jesus, the woman eagerly desires to receive this kind of water from Him and asks for it. But before Jesus gives her the water, He asks her to call her husband and come back with him. After admitting she has no husband, Jesus replies that she has spoken correctly, for she has had five husbands, and the man she is with now is not her husband. This was the only word Jesus had to give to convince this woman. Moses had told the Samaritans that God would raise up a prophet (Messiah) after him, from among their own brothers. The problem with this is that it could not be just any prophet, for Moses was not just a prophet; Moses was the lawgiver and liberator of Israel. Therefore, Moses was speaking of someone very important. The Samaritans did not believe in mere prophets; they knew that among the Jews, they believed in and had prophets, but who they were expecting was more than a prophet. The word that the Samaritan woman uses toward Jesus as "Prophet" is because she sees Him as a Jew. Jesus continues to explain to her that neither in Jerusalem nor in Samaria was the true place to worship God; the hour had come, and it was already when the Father (God) would seek true worshipers in spirit and truth. Not knowing everything, she said to Jesus, "I know that Messiah (called Christ) is coming. When he comes, he will explain everything to us." And Jesus declared, "I, the one speaking to you— I am he." Here, it is clear that Jesus showed Himself and called Himself the Messiah, the Christ of God. With this declaration, Jesus was demonstrating that He was the one of whom all the prophets, including Moses, spoke, who would come to save Israel, and that is exactly what the Lord Jesus Christ did.

THE JUDGE

In John 5:22, Jesus said, "For the Father judges no one, but has entrusted all judgment to the Son." Jesus spoke these words after healing a paralyzed man on a Sabbath day. For the Pharisees, they had learned by tradition, before and during the era of the rabbinical school of Shammai, that it was not lawful to do any work on the Sabbath; for them, one could not even save a life on the Sabbath. What happened was that after this paralyzed man had been healed, Jesus asked him to pick up his mat and go home. The problem was not so much the miracle itself, but rather taking up the mat and walking more than necessary with it. This led the religious Jews to judge Jesus of Nazareth for the good he had done to this paralyzed man on the Sabbath. Jesus never broke a Sabbath; the problem lay in the man-made rules they had added to the Sabbath. One could not even give money to the poor on the Sabbath. The Pharisees had added so much burden to the rest that there was really no true rest. Jesus knew well how the Sabbath was to be kept and did so according to the original Torah (instruction). For this reason, Jesus called Himself the Judge, because the Father judges no one but has entrusted all judgment to the Son. God appointed Jesus as the ultimate Judge; what Jesus said, we later see the apostles saying: *"He commanded us to preach to the people and to testify that he is the one whom God appointed as judge of the living and the dead" (Acts 10:42).* None of us is qualified to be the Judge. Only the Lord Jesus is qualified, and all judgment has been entrusted to Him. The tribunal of Christ as Judge refers to a time in the future when believers will give an account of themselves to Christ. This is the clear teaching of the Scriptures: *"For we must all appear before the judgment seat of Christ, so that each of us may receive what is due us for the things done while in the body, whether good or bad" (2 Corinthians 5:10).* The warning is for Christians, not unbelievers. As Jesus taught in His parable, the king is going to return, and at that time, he will settle accounts with his servants (Luke 19:11-26). Jesus is clearly the Judge, and He called Himself so because the Father entrusted Him with the power to judge and justify whomever He chooses.

THE MASTER:

A title that Jesus used specifically with his disciples was that of teacher. One example of this is found in John 13:13-14. Before the Passover feast, knowing that his hour had come, while he was gathered with his disciples eating dinner, Jesus got up, removed his outer garment, took a towel, and tied it around himself. Then he poured water into a basin and began to wash his disciples' feet and to wipe them with the towel. Jesus, as a teacher, was teaching them by his own action, his own example, how they should treat and interact with each other. Jesus knew that the time would come when He would not be physically present with them, and it was necessary for them to learn from their teacher. Jesus said to them in his own words, "You call me 'Teacher' and 'Lord,' and rightly so, for that is what I am. Now that I, your Lord and Teacher, have washed your feet, you also should wash one another's feet. I have set you an example that you should do as I have done for you." Jesus called Himself a teacher, and He was not just any teacher; He was the greatest of all.

THE LORD

Jesus also called Himself the Lord. The title "Lord" is applied to God (Psalm 90:1, "Adonai"), and in the New Testament to the Lord Jesus, not only as a term of deference but also in recognition of His established Lordship (Acts 2:36; Philippians 2:11). In this title, there is also the idea of administration, which is of great importance to observe. As the Lord Jesus is the mediator between God and men, and receives blessings for them that are administered by Him as Lord. The same term in Greek is used many times in the Septuagint (LXX) translating the Hebrew name or tetragrammaton Yahweh written in the King James Version as Jehovah, then it passes to the New Testament as a proper name in the same sense of the same Yahweh (God), as we see in (Matthew 1:20, 22, 24, etc.) with the angel of the "Lord." In the New Testament, the name Jehovah, or Yahweh, or Yah, does not appear, although it is known that when the word Lord is used, it is referring to the same God. Jesus called Himself the Lord in the capacity of God Himself when He said, *"For the Son of Man is Lord of the Sabbath"* ***(Matthew 12:8).*** Jesus was showing His complete authority over the Sabbath, the holiest day for the Jews, created by God Himself, and established in the commandments as an obligation to remember and observe it. The Jews had idolized the day so much that they had placed it above the value of life itself, for which the commandment was created. Faced with this situation where they valued the Sabbath more than life itself, Jesus defended life, showing them that the day was created for man, not man for the day. With this, Jesus showed two things: first, that He is the Lord and creator of the Sabbath, and second, that the commandment was created for life, not life for the commandment. Jesus is Lord of the Sabbath and of all things.

THE TESTIMONY OF EYEWITNESSES OF JESUS
Part 2

John 5:32-35:

There is another who bears witness about me, and I know that the testimony he gives about me is true. You sent messengers to John, and he bore witness to the truth. But I do not receive testimony from any man; but I say this so that you may be saved. He was a burning and shining lamp, and you were willing to rejoice for a while in his light.

Isaiah 43:10-11:

"You are my witnesses," declares the Lord, "and my servant whom I have chosen, so that you may know and believe in me and understand that I am He."

The testimony of a witness is as important as the testimony itself. The words spoken and written by those who heard directly through the apostles were quite important, but more important was the direct testimony from the very lips of those who saw, knew, and personally walked with Him. Jesus Christ could not have chosen better witnesses than those He made part of His life; each one fulfilled their purpose and fearlessly spoke and testified about Him. Some sources of studies and research have shown that in the first three centuries of Christianity, there were about 100,000 witnesses of Christ who died due to Roman persecutions. Each of the apostles who were eyewitnesses of Jesus, tradition tells us, died as martyrs for the cause of the word and the testimony of Jesus. We could speak of all of them because, in some way, the traditional testimonies we have of each of the apostles are important, but we have chosen a number of about four witnesses whom we personally think most impacted and transformed the world with the testimony of Jesus Christ.

THE TESTIMONY OF JESUS BY JOHN THE BAPTIST:

John the Baptist, being a prophet and priest, was a highly feared and respected man, with more fame throughout Israel than Jesus himself. John had his own disciples, and Jesus had said that no one born of women was greater than John the Baptist. All Jerusalem went out to the desert to be baptized and to see John the Baptist. John the Baptist was the first eyewitness who truly knew who Jesus of Nazareth was. All Jews revered the prophets as the holiest among men, making John the most impeccable witness to recognize and declare the true identity of Jesus of Nazareth. According to Luke, when John's mother was six months pregnant, Mary, after receiving a visit from Gabriel with the announcement that she would conceive Jesus, went to visit Elizabeth. As soon as she entered the house and greeted her, the child John began to leap in the womb, and his mother instantly understood the message that her child was giving her about what Mary, just a few days pregnant, carried in her womb—the "Lord." God had given a sign to the prophet John, saying, "Upon whom you see the Spirit descend and remain, He is the one who baptizes with the Holy Spirit." After John baptized Jesus, when Jesus came up out of the water, the Holy Spirit descended upon Him like a dove. John himself says that he saw this and testified that this is the Son of God. The evangelist John, or the apostle who wrote, must have been present to see and hear John the Baptist testify about Jesus. If he was not there, his narration is so detailed that he must have received it directly from an eyewitness. All the Gospels mention and speak of John the Baptist, leaving no doubt about his historical existence. All serious scholars agree that John was a real prophet and that he testified about Jesus, the Son of God. All of John's disciples saw and knew Jesus, and some, even after John's death, became disciples of Jesus. For this reason, it is very likely that the things the apostle John wrote about John the Baptist, if he was not his disciple before becoming Jesus' disciple, were received directly from one of John the Baptist's disciples who ended up following Jesus.

JOHN THE BAPTIST KNEW WHO JESUS WAS:

During the time the apostles were with Jesus, none truly knew who He was until they were endowed with the power of the Holy Spirit.

Jesus of Nazareth

However, John the Baptist knew who Jesus was, although for a moment, while imprisoned, he was concerned and sent to ask if Jesus was the one they were expecting or if they should wait for another. John's faith was shaken because what he saw seemed contrary to what he expected from the Messiah. Did the Messiah not bring justice, freedom to captives, and salvation? John was as human as we are and seemed to expect God to act differently at that moment. He had his moment of uncertainty but turned to the one who could answer him, Jesus Himself.

Our Lord did not respond in the direct way John expected, but His response is astounding, as seen in Luke 7:22-23. The answer is doubly wonderful. First, Jesus explains to John that God's Messiah is doing what He came to do. Nothing has changed in the redemptive plan. Miraculous signs are being performed, and the gospel is being preached. Second, Jesus exhorts John not to find offense in the way He is carrying out the work of redemption, saying, "Blessed is the one who is not offended by me." Jesus was telling John that he had to understand and trust in God, even when we cannot fully understand His plan and hand.

Later, we see Jesus say, "Blessed are those who have not seen and yet have believed." It is true that John, as a human, would have loved to see more of the Messiah and perhaps to be with Him longer, but he was called only to prepare the way for the Lord. John had fulfilled his purpose, but his time of trial had come, just as it did for the prophets before him. This case was difficult because John knew who Jesus truly was, but like every Jew, he expected that after hearing he was imprisoned, the Messiah would probably come to rescue him or send someone else to free him. This may have been John's thought, but it was not God's will for him. John was not the only prophet to whom God hid certain mysteries. They were not God; they were simply prophets and messengers of God. Occasionally, God concealed the mystery from them, as in the case of Elisha, who said, "The Lord has hidden it from me and has not told me."

John the Baptist publicly clarified that he was not the Christ, nor was he Elijah. He said he was the voice of one crying out in the wilderness: "I am the voice of one crying out in the wilderness: 'Make straight the way of the Lord,' as the prophet Isaiah said." It is clear here that John, as a prophet, knew Isaiah's prophecies and understood upon whom they would be fulfilled. He calls Jesus the "Lord." To understand the context of this name, refer to the section on the names and titles of Jesus, where it is explained who the "Lord" is and to whom it referred when He was called "the Lord."

JOHN THE BAPTIST WAS NOT THE LIGHT, BUT A WITNESS TO THE LIGHT:

The apostle John tells us that there was a man sent from God, whose name was John. This man came for a witness, to bear witness of the Light (Jesus), so that all might believe through him. He was not the light, but was sent to bear witness of the Light (Jesus). That true Light, which gives light to every man, was coming into the world. John was chosen to see with his own eyes the true Light of the world. He saw it and himself became a light for others. Among all the extraordinary characteristics of John the Baptist, the greatest was not his calling as a prophet, nor his message in the wilderness. The greatest thing recognized by the apostle John about John the Baptist was that he had been sent from God and had come to bear witness to the Light.

THE 6 WAYS JOHN THE BAPTIST IDENTIFIES JESUS:
1. THE PRE-EXISTENT JESUS:

John 1:27:

"This is the one who comes after me, the one who is before me, whose sandal strap I am not worthy to untie."

John said, "This is the one who comes after me, the one who is before me, whose sandal strap I am not worthy to untie." In the Gospel, John the Baptist says that he is not worthy to untie the strap of Jesus' sandal. These words are often interpreted as a sign of humility. However, they have a much deeper meaning. The book of Deuteronomy (25:5-10) talks about levirate marriage, where the brother of a man who has died without children is encouraged to marry the widow. John the Baptist specifically refers to the law of levirate marriage. The sandal is a sign of the right to marry a bride. In the book of Ruth, Boaz acquires the right to redeem Ruth, the widow of a close relative, and marry her. He receives the deceased's sandal as a credential. John the Baptist does not even deserve to untie the sandal, so he is not accredited as the groom. There is only one groom, Jesus of Nazareth. John, instead, is His friend. Nor is he the one who has the right to redeem Israel (the church) from sin. He baptizes only with water for repentance and purification. There is only one Redeemer and Messiah: Jesus of Nazareth. The sandal also represents dignity. John, who is preparing the people for the coming of Christ, is not the Messiah, and this dignity cannot and will not be taken from Him. John showed such humility and respect before Jesus, knowing that he had much more fame and recognition than Jesus. His words to his own disciples were, "He must increase, but I must decrease."

2. THE LORD JESUS:

John 1:23:

He said, "I am the voice of one crying out in the wilderness: Make straight the way of the Lord, as the prophet Isaiah said."

John said publicly, "Make straight the way of the Lord," "KYRIOS," as Isaiah said. Here, the significant matter is that John is comparing this Lord to the very one Isaiah announced would come. When we consider the context of who this Lord was to Isaiah or whom he directly referred to when calling Him Lord, we can understand a bit more whom John was referring to when repeating what Isaiah said. In the first chapter of the book of Isaiah, the prophet tells us what he saw: "In the year that King Uzziah died, I saw the Lord sitting on a high and lofty throne, and the hem of His robe filled the temple." Here, Isaiah sees in a vision the Lord personified, sitting on a high throne. Throughout the Bible after the prophet Isaiah, there is absolutely no one else in heaven and no one sitting on a throne except God and the Lord Himself. But it is worth noting that in the Gospels and the Pauline letters, there is someone who passed through the heavens and sat at the right hand of God. The same John who writes Revelation tells us in chapter 4:10, *"The twenty-four elders fall down before the one seated on the throne, and worship the one who lives forever and ever, and they lay their crowns before the throne, saying: 'Our Lord and God, you are worthy to receive glory and honor and power, for you created all things, and by your will they exist and were created.'"* In Revelation 5:13, it is then confirmed who exactly this Lord and God is: *"And I heard every creature in heaven and on earth and under the earth and in the sea, and all that is in them, saying, 'To the one seated on the throne and to the Lamb be praise and honor and glory and power forever and ever.'"*

Isaiah means *"The Lord is my salvation."* He referred to the Lord as the God and savior of Israel. When John the Baptist called to make straight the way of the Lord as Isaiah had said, he was welcoming the same Lord and the only Lamb of God who takes away the sin of the world. The 24 elders bow down, worship, and cast their crowns before the Lamb of God, our only Lord and God, Jesus Christ.

3. **THE HOLY ONE OF GOD**

Matthew 3:14:

"But John tried to deter him, saying, 'I need to be baptized by you, and do you come to me?'"

When Jesus came to John in the wilderness, we know that John knew Him and knew who He was. The Synoptic Gospels show us a recognition by John the Baptist toward Jesus immediately, but in John, he says he did not know Him. Most likely, he had not seen Him for a while. We do not know exactly if they grew up together or how much time they spent together. What we can plausibly speculate is that even though John knew Him, perhaps due to the many Jews who came to be baptized by him, he did not recognize Jesus from a distance until He was close enough. No one doubts that John knew Him; it is even believed that they were cousins. When Jesus comes to John to be baptized by him, John tries to deter Him and again calls Him Lord. Here, John is letting Jesus know that he is His servant, that he knows His holiness is far above, and that Jesus does not need to be baptized; rather, John asks to be baptized by His Lord. We never see John being baptized by anyone, and this has a reason: as a prophet and high priest, these two callings or offices had no authority above them other than God. Therefore, no disciple could baptize his master, just as no son of a prophet could prophesy to his prophet master. The Lord was the only one who could baptize His servant John, and John asks the Holy Jesus to baptize him. But Jesus opposes him to fulfill all righteousness. John had been called for that office, and Jesus was showing that He had not come to exercise authority over anyone but to serve the world. John recognized his impurity before the holiness of the unique Jesus of Nazareth.

4. **THE LAMB OF GOD**

John 1:29:

"The next day John saw Jesus coming toward him and said, 'Look, the Lamb of God, who takes away the sin of the world!'"

Jesus is called the Lamb of God in John 1:29 and John 1:36 because He is the perfect and final sacrifice for sin. To understand who Jesus is and what He did, we must start with the Old Testament, which contains prophecies about the coming of the Messiah as a "sin offering" (Isaiah 53:10). The entire sacrificial system established by God in the Covenant of the Law served as a foundation for the coming of Jesus Christ. He is the perfect sacrifice that the Father provided as atonement (forgiveness) for the sins of the world (Romans 8:3; Hebrews 10). The sacrifice of lambs was very important in Jewish religious life and their sacrificial system. When John the Baptist referred to Jesus as *"The Lamb of God, who takes away the sin of the world" (John 1:29),* the Jews who heard him knew and could have immediately thought of any of the many significant sacrifices. With the Passover feast each year, which they were familiar with, the Jews could have thought of the sacrifice of the Passover lamb. The Passover feast was the first of all, one of the main Jewish feasts in remembrance of when God delivered the Israelites from slavery in Egypt. The blood of the lamb was taken and sprinkled on the doorposts of the houses (Exodus 12:11-13). This is a representation of the atoning and redeeming work of Christ on the cross. Those for whom He died are covered by His blood, protecting us from (spiritual) death. Another important sacrifice that included lambs was the daily sacrifices in the Temple of Jerusalem by the priests. Each morning and evening in the Temple, a lamb was sacrificed for the sins of the people (Exodus 29:38-42). These continuous sacrifices, like all the others, were a type and shadow of Christ Himself on the cross. Incidentally, the time of Jesus' death on the cross corresponds to the same time when the evening sacrifice was being offered in the Temple. It was precisely at this same hour that the veil was also torn from top to bottom. The Jews of that time would also be familiar with the Old Testament prophets Jeremiah and Isaiah, who prophesied and anticipated the arrival of one who would be led "...like a lamb to the slaughter..." (Jeremiah 11:19; Isaiah 53:7) and whose suffering and sacrifice would provide redemption for Israel. When John announced Jesus as the Lamb of God, all the Jews knew that this had to be someone quite special.

5. **THE ONE WHO BAPTIZES WITH THE HOLY SPIRIT:**

John 1:33

I did not know him, but he who sent me to baptize with water said to me, 'Upon whom you see the Spirit descending, and remaining on him, this is he who baptizes with the Holy Spirit.'

John knew that his baptism was good but at the same time temporary and only for the external purpose of bodily purification. In contrast and comparison to the baptism of the Holy Spirit, John knew that the baptism Christ was bringing was much more powerful than his own. John recognized that only Jesus of Nazareth could baptize and be the means for the gift of the Holy Spirit. The Holy Spirit is God's gift for all who acknowledge Jesus of Nazareth as their Lord and Savior. This gift, in the Old Testament, was quite limited, only by measure. Kings, priests, and prophets were anointed, upon whom the Spirit of God came at necessary moments to fulfill a function. But the promise that Jesus came to announce, that the Father would give us through Him alone, we see at Pentecost. He had told His disciples not to leave Jerusalem until they were clothed with the power of the Holy Spirit. No one knew what would happen, or when it would arrive, but exactly 10 days after Jesus had been with them for 40 days, which alludes to 50 days later, when the day of Pentecost came, they were all together, and suddenly, the Holy Spirit descended upon all who were in the house, and they all spoke in other tongues, as the Spirit gave them utterance. And all those who heard them speak said, are these not Galileans? Why do they speak our languages? This powerful baptism would give them absolute power over all things, make them true witnesses, and give them the power to testify before the whole world without fear of dying or losing anything for the cause of the testimony of Jesus of Nazareth. We see the lives of each of the apostles and disciples of Christ change powerfully, turning the world upside down for Christ, only after being baptized by the Holy Spirit that Jesus breathed on them. The Holy Spirit is God's gift to the world, which is received only through Jesus Christ.

6. **THE SON OF GOD:**

John 1:34

And I have seen and testified that this is the Son of God.

Jesus is the Son of God in the sense that He is God manifested in human form (John 1:1, 14). Jesus is the Son of God in that He was conceived by the Holy Spirit. During His trial before the Jewish leaders, the high priest ordered Jesus, *"I charge you under oath by the living God: Tell us if you are the Messiah, the Son of God" (Matthew 26:63). Jesus replied, "You have said so. But I say to all of you: From now on you will see the Son of Man sitting at the right hand of the Mighty One and coming on the clouds of heaven" (Matthew 26:64).* The Jewish leaders responded by accusing Jesus of blasphemy *(Matthew 26:65-66). Later, before Pontius Pilate, "The Jews answered him, 'We have a law, and according to that law he ought to die because he has made himself the Son of God'" (John 19:7).* Why would claiming to be the "Son of God" be considered blasphemy deserving the death penalty? The Jewish leaders understood exactly what Jesus meant by the phrase "Son of God." Being the "Son of God" means being of the same nature as God. The "Son of God" is "part of God." The declaration of being of the same nature as God, in fact, was "being God Himself," which was blasphemy to the Jewish leaders; therefore, they demanded Jesus' death, which conformed to Leviticus 24:15. *Hebrews 1:2-3 expresses this very clearly: "But in these last days he has spoken to us by his Son, whom he appointed heir of all things, and through whom also he made the universe. The Son is the radiance of God's glory and the exact representation of his being."*

Now, according to the worldview of the time, I believe that when we see Jesus as the Son of God, it is important to understand that for the Jews and the Greeks, the title Son of God could have been completely different. The gospels were written in Greek, according to a time when Greek dominated all aspects of life and culture. It is true that although many things were written in Greek, the thought behind them could be based on Jewish or Aramaic cultural thinking. This title Son of God, as we have previously mentioned, for a Jew could refer to a righteous human created by God like Adam, to a

Jesus of Nazareth

Hebrew son of Abraham, but they never saw it as Jesus expressed it, we could say almost biologically, although God does not have earthly biological children, the way Jesus expressed it was much more than simply a righteous one like Adam and Abraham. He expressed Himself directly as the Son of God. For the Greeks, this term was used in Greek mythology to refer to all men who had divine lineage. The Greeks believed that divine gods could have sexual relations with earthly women, these women would become pregnant by the gods, and the children born to them were considered demigods, small gods, part man and part god. Although many of the Greek conquerors had or were known to have earthly fathers, when these conquerors conquered with incredible, superhuman strength and courage, it was thought that they were sons of a god, and they adopted the belief that they were truly sons of the gods. For example, in the case of "Achilles," one of the greatest warriors of Homer's Iliad. The greatest of the Greek conquerors, his father was called Peleus, grandson of Zeus, and son of Aeacus, directly from Zeus who had impregnated Aegina. Peleus was a demigod king of the Myrmidons, a people in southern Thessaly through his father, while his mother was called Thetis, daughter of Nereus, one of the sea gods alongside Poseidon, and granddaughter of the Titans, whose parents were Uranus and Gaia, who was the goddess of the earth, and who was born from chaos (the great void). This Achilles was a great conqueror, and it is believed that from his childhood he was baptized in a river that would make him a divine being. Supposedly he had left a heel out of the water, which is why he died after receiving a wound from an arrow in his tendon, incapacitating him from continuing victoriously. For the Greeks, the gods were not eternal, the gods could die. In the case of Achilles, he died and was venerated throughout the time Greek mythology existed. Later, with the arrival of the famous Macedonian, Alexander the Great, he was the son of Philip II, king of Macedonia, and his mother was named Olympia. Alexander always admired Achilles and always wanted to be like him. After his father's death, rising to power, his mother had told him that his real father was not Philip, but Zeus. She seemed to have become pregnant by Zeus in a dream. Later, a prophetess confirmed that he was the son of Amon, an Egyptian god, who for the Greeks was the same as Zeus. Therefore, in Greek thought, when it was said that Jesus is the Son of God, it was most likely because the Spirit of Yahweh (God) had rested upon Mary, making her pregnant by the God of the Hebrews. This creature, according to the Greek vision, would be a son of the gods. Jesus is categorized as the only Son of Yahweh the Father and Creator. This could have been the Greek thought for titling Jesus the Son of God.

In Roman thought, almost identical to the Greeks, since the Romans adopted Greek thought when it suited them, they saw demigods as sons of the gods. For the Romans, the gods had the names of planets. They adopted the Greek gods but changed their names. For the Romans, emperors, once they died, over time, Rome deified them and declared them gods, then they were worshipped and sacrificed to. This was one of the biggest problems and reasons for the Christian persecutions in the early centuries. Christians did not worship and less sacrifice to the Roman emperors. In the case of Gaius Julius Caesar, after his death, he had been turned into a god. This would give the title of son of god to his adopted son Augustus, who later adopted the name of his father Julius Caesar, calling himself Augustus Julius Caesar. The Romans never served Yahweh, the God of the Jews. They knew and respected Judaism as one of the oldest religions or traditions, but they never took Yahweh into the empire as one of their gods. We see in the case of that Roman who, seeing the earthquake and the events after Jesus' death on the cross, had said, "Truly this was the Son of God." We do not know exactly if he was referring to the God of the Jews or which god exactly. For the gospel writers, they wrote the name of God with a capital letter, which in the narration would be the God and Father of Jesus Himself. But centurions normally did not serve the God of the Jews, until we later see the first convert to Christianity, Cornelius, with the arrival of Peter in Acts 10. We see some encounters and petitions from that centurion who asked Jesus to heal his servant with just His word. Most likely, some Romans followed and had heard Jesus speak of His God as the Father. For now, we stick with the main thought of the authors, who narrate the centurion recognizing that

Jesus was the Son of God the Father. All these points of view regarding the title of Jesus as the Son of God could have been seen in the first century. For John the apostle, in his Gospel of John, we have no doubt that Jesus as the Only Begotten Son of God is completely a divine title. As for John the Baptist, by calling Jesus the Son of God, we know that he prophesied that He was the Messiah of God, and as Jesus' cousin, he must have heard of His glorious and divine birth from his mother. If so, it would be quite credible that for John to call Jesus the Son of God, he did so recognizing His divinity, although many of the Jews expected a human Messiah. What we are sure of is that John gave the highest respect to Jesus, recognizing that He deserved to be baptized by Him. This fact alone, without counting the others, was enough to show Jesus divinely as the Son of God.

THE TESTIMONY OF SAINT PETER ABOUT JESUS AND HOW HE IDENTIFIED HIM:

Among all the friends and disciples of Jesus, it has been shown in the texts of the New Testament that Peter was most likely Jesus' closest friend. When Jesus arrived in Galilee to begin his public ministry, we see that from very early on, the trust with Peter was so great that Jesus stayed in Peter's house as if it were his own. We also see him taking Peter's boat to use it as a pulpit to preach to the crowds from there. Almost at the end of the book of John, who would also be among Peter's close friends, after Peter had denied Jesus several times, there is a very intimate and personal encounter between Jesus and Peter. Besides the name of Jesus in the gospels, the most mentioned name, Peter's name follows as the most mentioned, being referenced around 200 to 210 times. Let's look at the titles that Peter used for Jesus.

THE CHRIST OF GOD:

Matthew 16:16;

Simon Peter answered, "You are the Christ, the Son of the living God."

Among all the titles testified by Peter, that of the Christ "Hamashiach" as the Son of God is probably the most recognized in the gospels, because it marks one of the most important concerns in the life of Jesus alongside his disciples. Jesus took them to Caesarea Philippi, where it is believed the gates of Hades were, known today as Banias. "The place has always had religious/cultic significance and was frequented as a popular site for worship of Semitic deities. Baal, the Canaanite god, was worshipped there during Old Testament times (Joshua 11:17, 12:7, 13:5; Judges 3:3; 1 Chronicles 5:23). The Greeks later worshipped their god Pan at the same location, thus naming it Paneas or Panias, 'Deity of Pan.'" It is a place that has always been associated with pagan worship where practices included rituals of sexual immorality and even human sacrifices. "Centuries before the time of Christ, the residents of the region named the city Panias. That was in honor of the fertility god Pan, who also demanded human sacrifice. Each spring, the priests of Pan would throw a young virgin into the strong currents of water that flowed from the base of Mount Hermon. In Jesus' time, it was a Roman city. Herod the Great built a marble temple there for the worship of the emperor. Later, his son Philip renamed it Caesarea Philippi, naming it after Caesar and himself. It was there, in that strange environment, that Jesus decided to speak about His Church: '...I will build My church, and the gates of Hades shall not prevail against it.' [Matt. 16:18]... Today, the place is called Banias. It was there that Jesus took them, in full view of the most pagan place of the time, to truly see the maturity among his disciples, to see if they truly knew him and who he was to them. This question would indicate to Jesus if he could leave and entrust them with his church, faith, and path. With the answer given by everyone except Peter, this showed Jesus that none of them were actually ready to go out into the world and preach Christ. It has been questioned whether Peter himself, after his answer, was not ready either. It turns out that Messianism in Israel, from Isaiah onwards, has had different interpretations and different forms of the Messiah. There were completely political messiahs, but also some who tried to restore worship in Israel. The word Messiah, which in Greek is equivalent to "Anointed," is a common word in Israel for Jews, so to speak. For Christianity, there was only one true Messiah, and that is Jesus, but for the Jews, the word Messiah was someone chosen and anointed by a priest or prophet to fulfill the task that God had given them during that time. With that said, there were also many who claimed to be messiahs, or who were named messiahs by priests but were actually found to be false messiahs. When Peter answered Jesus that He was the Messiah of God, the Son of God, Jesus replied that this had not been revealed to him by flesh and blood, but rather by His Father who was in heaven. We know that Jesus is the channel of all revelation given by the Father, and then we see the Holy Spirit as the one who reveals Jesus himself. We never see the Father directly revealing anything to Jesus' disciples except on this occasion, but it turns out that after this magnificent revelation to Peter, shortly afterwards we see Jesus calling him "Satan" as the one who opposes. The moment Jesus tells Peter that he would have to die, Peter humanly says that this would never happen, theologically this would be an obstacle to Jesus' main purpose on earth. Therefore, it is believed that the kind of Messiah that Peter was seeing in Jesus was completely wrong. Peter was seeing a completely military Messiah, who would liberate them from the hands of Roman oppression. Peter had done the right thing in recognizing Jesus as the Messiah and as the Son of God, but his idea of the Messiah was more in line with the idea received by the political and military Messiah that had arisen during the intertestamental era by the Maccabees, Hasmoneans, and Pharisees onwards. But then after the crucifixion, and it is worth mentioning that this Peter, although he denied Jesus several times, as had been foretold to him, was the one who came closest to the crucifixion of Jesus. During Pentecost, and the experience of the Holy Spirit upon Peter, there we see him again mentioning Jesus as the Messiah and Son of God, the Lord of all, but in a different and correct way than he had previously confessed. After the resurrection of Jesus, Peter continued to call Jesus the Christ of God, during the more than 30 years he lived preaching until his death, which is traditionally believed to have occurred in Rome around 62-65 AD under the emperor Nero.

Alexander Frias

THE RABBI:

Mark 9:5-7

Then Peter said to Jesus, "Rabbi, it is good for us to be here; let us make three tabernacles, one for You, one for Moses, and one for Elijah." For he did not know what to answer, because they became terrified. Then a cloud formed, overshadowing them, and a voice came out of the cloud, "This is My Beloved Son, listen to Him!"

On the Mount of Transfiguration, we see Jesus taking his three most intimate disciples, John, James, and Peter. Mark tells us that while they are on the mountain, the three see Jesus being transfigured, his clothes becoming dazzling white. Matthew adds that not only his clothes but also his face shone like the sun. Obviously, Matthew always likes to show Jesus superior to Moses, and the Jews knew that when Moses ascended and descended from Sinai, his face shone so brightly that he had to wear a veil in front of the people. With Matthew mentioning the shining face, he would be telling the Jews that this Jesus was and is superior to Moses. For now, we will stick to the text of Mark, since traditionally the church fathers told us that Mark was Peter's secretary, which indicates that being a firsthand witness, Mark writes it directly from Peter's lips. Mark tells us that Elijah and Moses appeared to them, talking with Jesus. We know that the appearance of these two in the gospel narrative on the mountain with Jesus has a significant purpose. Firstly, both Moses and Elijah knew the heights in the mountains, especially Mount Horeb, where they sought the presence of God. Secondly, their appearance symbolizes Moses as the law and Elijah as the prophets. In Jesus of Nazareth, both the law and the prophets were fulfilled and also surpassed; Jesus fulfilled the entire law, and he was also greater than the prophets. The message is quite clear, but then we see that after this glory, the first to speak is Peter, calling Jesus "Rabbi" (Teacher). He asks Jesus to make three tabernacles for each of them. A tabernacle is a tent, booth, or hut, which was used as dwelling by people in ancient times. It comes from the term 'skene,' which translates to hut, pavilion, etc. To understand why Peter asked for this and why the vision disappeared afterward, we have to go back to ancient Israelite thought: when God ordered the people of Israel to celebrate the 'Feast of Tabernacles.' During this festival, the population had to live in booths for seven days as a way to remember their wanderings in the desert. The experience of leaving slavery in Egypt and the precariousness of their conditions is symbolized by the precept of dwelling in a booth or tent, with the purpose of not forgetting that they were strangers in the desert and that God was always with them. In Hebrew culture, it is mentioned that during the Feast of Tabernacles, the souls of the seven shepherds of Israel. That is, the patriarchs, leaders, and king such as Abraham, Isaac, Jacob, Moses, Aaron, Joseph, and King David, leave the Garden of Eden to participate in the presence of God dwelling in booths, caves, or deserts (tabernacles) with them. Each day of the festival, these seven souls are present in the thoughts of the Hebrews/Jews, united with the God of the living, but each one takes its turn to lead the others. Collectively, these visits are called 'ushpizín,' a word in the Aramaic language that means 'guests.' Mark says that Peter did not know what he was saying, most likely Peter showing his ignorance, but in my opinion, he did know what he was asking for, as these figures were almost venerated to the point of being idolized by the Jews. To be in front of Moses and Elijah was quite serious, to the point that after the vision, Jesus asks him not to tell anyone until the Son of Man is resurrected. A cloud had settled over them, and a voice said, *"This is my beloved Son, listen to Him."* Then, upon closer inspection, Moses and Elijah had disappeared, leaving only Jesus the Teacher. This was a clear sign that Jesus was the new Messiah, the new Savior, the Son of God, whom they had to listen to. In the apocryphal gospel known as the "Apocalypse of Peter," written later, around 170 AD, we see that there seems to have been a community that did not accept the narrative of the canonical gospels showing the appearance of Moses and Elijah alongside Jesus. Despite the gospels mentioning that it was a vision, it seems that many Christians did not agree that these two, who had been dead and resting for centuries before, did not take kindly to this idea. We see that the text of the Apocalypse of Peter recounts the event as follows:

Moreover, the Lord said: Let us go up to the mountain and pray. And going with Him, we, the twelve apostles, begged Him to show us one of our righteous brothers, who had died, so that we could see what kind of form he had; and taking courage, we might also encourage the men who listened to us. And when we prayed, suddenly two men appeared standing eastward before the Lord, whom we could not see. They emitted a ray like the sun from their faces, and their garments shone in a way never seen by human eyes. There is no mouth capable of expressing, nor heart able to conceive, the glory with which they were endowed, nor the beauty of their appearance. And when we looked at them, we were amazed, because their bodies were whiter than snow and redder than roses; and the red joined the white with such beauty that I cannot express it in words. Their hair was curly and shiny, and it fell elegantly over their faces and shoulders like a garland woven with aromatic plants and flowers of various colors, or like a rainbow in the sky. Such was their appearance. (Apocalypse of Peter 4.-10.).

In this version, the men do not have names, but what stands out is that the event, in one way or another, seems to have been historical, or at least well known among early Christian communities. In any case, Mark's text is canonical and more authentic than this Apocalypse of Peter. Peter testified, calling Jesus "Rabbi" (Teacher) many times.

THE MAN APPROVED BY GOD:

Acts 2:22;

"Men of Israel, listen to these words: Jesus the Nazarene, a man attested to you by God with miracles and wonders and signs which God performed through Him in your midst, just as you yourselves know—"

Peter begins by calling him 'Jesus the Nazarene,' and then his approval by God, since he was born and raised in Nazareth, where as an adult he had been expelled and rejected several times by the Jewish leaders in the synagogues of his city. Although he had also been rejected by the leaders of the nation, he was "a man approved

Jesus of Nazareth

by God." God indeed appreciated and approved of His Son's life. There was never a moment when Jesus did something He should not have done, nor did He ever fail to do what He should. He always lived in perfect obedience and dependence on His God, always saying, "I have come not to do my own will but the will of Him who sent me," not as an obligation but with complete delight in His heart. Many great prophets, kings, and men in antiquity accomplished feats through their faith in God, but they also had their flaws. Jesus of Nazareth was unique, having the full divine approval in everything He did and said. God confirmed it through His authentic authority over others of His time, the signs and wonders that Jesus performed among the peoples. Nicodemus, a prominent Pharisee of the Sanhedrin, understood this well, and he also expressed the thoughts of others when he said, *"We know that you have come from God because no one can perform the signs you are doing if God were not with him" (John 3:2).* The apostle Paul, later in his second letter to his son in the faith, urgently asks him to present himself before God as an approved worker, who has nothing to be ashamed of, who correctly handles the word of truth. It is true and very likely that there were different thoughts between Peter and Paul, but Paul, considered among the most outstanding apostles, also desired to be found approved by God, as we see; "I am not seeking the approval of men, but of God. I do not seek to please men. If I wanted to please men, I would not be a servant of Christ!" Paul knew that Jesus never sought the approval of men and even less that of the teachers and religious doctors of his environment; He sought only to please His God. This same ardent desire that was in Paul is what he sends to Timothy in his letter with all the certain things expected of a worker approved by God. The first thing he says is that the man approved by God must know how to correctly handle the word of God, something that the Pharisees, scribes, and Sadducees against Jesus did not know how to do. Jesus not only knew how to use and handle the word of God, but the authority He had over the people had never been seen before. Second, Paul mentions that he should be sanctified, set apart only for the service of his God; the holiness of Jesus was so secure and firm that He asked all His oppressors to point out or accuse Him of sin, and none could accuse Him of anything. Paul told Timothy, "The servant of the Lord must not be contentious, but gentle to all, apt to teach, patient; with meekness correcting those who oppose, perhaps God may grant them repentance to know the truth, and escape from the snare of the devil, in which they are held captive by his will." Jesus said, *"Take my yoke upon you, and learn from me, for I am gentle and humble in heart; and you will find rest for your souls."* Jesus was the most excellent example that God gave to humanity. Peter also said, "For to this you were called; because Christ also suffered for us, 'leaving us an example,' that we should follow in His steps; He who did no sin, nor was deceit found in His mouth; who, when He was reviled, did not respond with reviling; when He suffered, He did not threaten, but entrusted Himself to the one who judges justly; who Himself bore our sins in His body on the tree, so that we, having died to sins, might live for righteousness; and by His wounds you were healed" (1 Peter 2:21-24). Peter said that Jesus had been "A man approved by God" and he knew what he was saying, he said it with authority and with all certainty for several reasons. First, by the evidence and guarantee of seeing Jesus resurrected as He had previously told them; second, by the promise that Jesus gave them which they received from the Father, that they should remain in Jerusalem until they were clothed with power from on high, Peter as a present witness among those who were filled with the Spirit receiving the promise through Christ could speak with all certainty and firmness as he did. And third, because he was a witness not only seeing Christ ascend in a cloud until He disappeared, he was a present and ocular witness in most of Jesus' wonderful experiences. Peter, as we said previously, was present on the Mount of Transfiguration, where he saw Moses and Elijah, and the shining Christ, with the voice that clearly said to them, "This is my Son, listen to Him." Among all the apostles, if there was one who could say whether Jesus was approved by God or not, it was Peter, His best friend, and that's exactly what he did correctly without fear or hesitation.

Jesus of Nazareth

THE AUTHOR OF LIFE:

Acts 3:15;

"You killed the 'Author of life,' but God raised him from the dead. We are witnesses of this."

An author is someone who creates or initiates a work, usually a work of art, literature, or science. However, in its Latin origin, this word also pointed us to a producer, a creator, a father, or a founder, and in its Greek etymology, it also points us to an author, a commander, a chief patron, a captain, and also a prince. All of this was and is Jesus Christ. In reality, Jesus Christ was the author of all creation, as written by Saint Paul in (Colossians 1:16) *"For by Him all things were created, both in the heavens and on earth, visible and invisible, whether thrones or dominions or rulers or authorities—all things have been created through Him and for Him."* And also Saint John in *(John 1:3) "All things came into being through Him, and apart from Him, nothing came into being that has come into being."* We also see Jesus as the author of some other things; the writer of Hebrews in chapter 5:9, tells us that Jesus, having been perfected, became the author of eternal salvation for all who obey Him. There were people who saved others in many different ways; some saved others from physical death at a given moment, others saved from temporary difficult circumstances that came upon them. However, no one can save us from eternal damnation except Jesus Christ. Only and solely Jesus "came to be the author of eternal salvation for all who obey Him." The salvation that Jesus gives us is not temporary, that is, it is not a salvation limited to the time of our life here on earth. Jesus' salvation is eternal because Jesus is the "author of eternal salvation." No one could ever offer this kind of salvation; for this reason, Jesus is the author of it, and only He can offer it and grant it because He has every right as the author to do so. That is why it is impossible to compare any salvation with the salvation of Jesus because all human salvation is temporary and disappears with time or death. But it is not the same with the salvation of Jesus because Jesus is the author of a salvation that remains eternally forever, it is completely eternal and, therefore, has no limits. Jesus is also the author of abundant life, according to *(John 10:10) Jesus said, "The thief comes only to steal and kill and destroy; I have come that they may have life, and have it to the full."* Many, because of the many problems they face, sometimes say they do not have a life, referring to the amount of problems and scarcity they face and exclaim, "This is not life!" because they do not see the benefit or success they think they deserve. But Jesus did not come for scarcity but for abundance and prosperity in every sense of life because He said, *"I have come that they may have life, and have it to the full."* Having abundance means having a large amount, much, that remains of something; it is having prosperity in every sense of complete life. An abundant life is a full life, a fulfilled life, a joyful and happy life. Jesus came so that human beings could learn to live in joy and happiness. With this, we are not saying that in life there are no problems, difficulties, or situations that cause momentary sadness, but we do say that even with all these piled up, the life that Jesus offers is one full of abundance of peace, joy, love, happiness, and everything else correlated to prosperity and wealth for the soul and social life of man. Jesus is the author of this abundant life that only He can give. Jesus is also the author of the new spiritual birth or the regenerated life that all who believe in Him receive. (2 Corinthians 5:17) tells us "Therefore, if anyone is in Christ, the new creation has come: The old has gone, the new is here!" To be in Christ Jesus is to receive from Him a new birth, a complete transformation of consciousness and a new heart; the past life is regenerated, forgiven, and everything that was a consequence, through Jesus' death on the cross, is now turned into a blessing for life. They are no longer seen as consequences but rather as part of the plan that will help everything good to the purpose out of love for God of this new life in Christ and new birth of God. Jesus, through the sacrifice on the cross of Calvary, offered us and gave us a new life; this kind of life to feel, experience, and know, must be lived only in Him and for Him, as Paul says, "that those who live should no longer live for themselves but for Him who died and rose again for them." Jesus was the only one who knew exactly what humans needed to return to their original state of communion with God, and because He was and is the author of all things, He came and fulfilled exactly what was necessary for man to return to his original state in communion with his creator. This multitude, which we see before Peter in Jerusalem, declaring that Jesus is the author of life in this discourse, was the same multitude that a few days ago following Jesus to the gates of Jerusalem sang saying "Hosanna, Hosanna" blessed is He who comes in the name of the Lord, this was also the same multitude that stood before Pilate demanding with shouts the death of Jesus and the freedom of Barabbas the murderer and murderer, saying "Crucify Him, crucify Him!" but now they were astonished and surprised, feeling the rebuke by the Holy Spirit, seeing Peter, a common man without learning, completely regenerated, like a new person full of authority by the one they themselves had condemned to death, and also seeing cured and healed that paralyzed man raised by the same author of life whom they put to death, Jesus. Peter clarified to them that the miraculous healing was neither from nor by him; it was Jesus who healed him, he said, *"And the faith that is through Him has given this man complete healing in the presence of all of you."* They killed the author of life, and the author of life whom they had killed had given complete healing to a man paralyzed from birth. Jesus is the one and only true author of life.

THE PRECIOUS AND CORNERSTONE:

1 Peter 2:7-8;

For you who believe, this stone is precious; but for those who do not believe, "The stone the builders rejected has become the cornerstone," and, "A stone that causes people to stumble and a rock that makes them fall." They stumble because they disobey the message—which is also what they were destined for.

From ancient times, builders and constructors have used cornerstone stones in their construction projects. A cornerstone was the main stone, usually placed at the corner of a building, to guide the workers during their work. It was among the largest, most solid, and best crafted of all the stones in the building. It was also the one that supported all the weight of the others. We see it for the first time in (Psalm 118:22), Peter described Jesus as this cornerstone on which His church would be built, but also on which the whole nation of Israel was actually built. Theologically, we see stones, or rocks, being used comparatively and typologically many times with God or with Jesus both in the Old Testament and the New Testament. The title "the perfect Rock of Jacob" was given to the God of Israel because of His firmness and power, but we also see that in the New Testament, Paul makes a typological reference, referring to the rock that gave them water to drink in the desert to the people of Israel, was Christ Himself. We see that the commandments given to Moses at Sinai were written on stones, stones were also used for altars and sacrifices dedicated to the gods. This title that Peter also called "Cephas," which means "Stone," given to Jesus, most likely comes from the encounter Jesus had with Peter while in Caesarea Philippi, in front of that pagan area called the gates of hell. Jesus had declared that He would build His Church on "this" rock, and the gates of Hades (Gehenna) or (hell) would not prevail against His church (community) or (congregation). The universal Catholic Church has thought that this rock to which Jesus referred was Peter himself, but clearly we see that it was not so. The church was never built on Peter; he was an apostle among the 13 including Paul. Instead, the church of Christ was built on the one perfect and cornerstone, which is solely Jesus Christ. This is the reason why even today it still remains, being built on men would not remain, because everything that is built by men has its destructive end, whether empires or governments, all have fallen. We see that in the Gospel of John at the end Jesus asks him to shepherd His sheep, but then in the Acts we see that James the brother of the Lord is the bishop and apostle in charge along with the others of the church and the council in Jerusalem. We never see a unique hierarchy of Peter over all as the universal Catholic tradition supposes, although in the Gospels we see Peter first in the lists of the apostles when he was not the first to be called. This also does not mean that Peter was the head in government or hierarchy over the others or the Church, Jesus clarified very well before leaving, that none among them would be

Jesus of Nazareth

over another, and none would lord it over another, rather the greatest would serve the least. In (1 Peter 2:5-9), we see Peter take the prophecy of the prophet Isaiah in (Isaiah 28:16-17) where he compared the coming Messiah to this cornerstone. There he tells us in Peter's words referring to Isaiah; "you also, like living stones, are being built into a spiritual house to be a holy priesthood, offering spiritual sacrifices acceptable to God through Jesus Christ. For in Scripture it says: "See, I lay a stone in Zion, a chosen and precious cornerstone, and the one who trusts in him will never be put to shame." Now to you who believe, this stone is precious. But to those who do not believe, "The stone the builders rejected has become the cornerstone," and, "A stone that causes people to stumble and a rock that makes them fall." They stumble because they disobey the message—which is also what they were destined for." The people of God but you are a chosen people, a royal priesthood, a holy nation, God's special possession, that you may declare the praises of him who called you out of darkness into his wonderful light. Clearly Peter is saying that all who are part of Christ are living stones, and are part of the building, but none are the foundation, the base, the stone in Zion, the precious cornerstone, and neither the "cornerstone", which clearly shows here that it is only the Lord, Jesus Christ. He is the only one qualified to be called and known as the stone and the foundation that sustains all His Church, the world, and religions, as they were present at the gates of Hades, they could not and have not been able to stop or destroy the Church of Jesus Christ, which is sustained and built solely on and upon the precious cornerstone, Jesus Christ. concluding with this title, the apostle Paul makes a direct reference just like Peter, to the church of Ephesus and wishes the Christians of Ephesus to know Christ better by telling them: *"Consequently, you are no longer foreigners and strangers, but fellow citizens with God's people and also members of his household, built on the foundation of the apostles and prophets, with Christ Jesus himself as the chief cornerstone. In him the whole building is joined together and rises to become a holy temple in the Lord" (Ephesians 2:19-21).*

PASTOR AND BISHOP OF THE SOUL:

Alexander Frias

1 Peter 2:25;

For you were like stray sheep, but now you have returned to the Shepherd and Overseer of your souls.

The first thing we think of when reading the phrase "stray sheep" is possibly the danger it may face, such as the wolf or fierce animals and their lurking threats. And of course, this is part of it, but it also implies a misguided walk by those who stray from the presence of their shepherd, lives with poor resource management, without guidance or direction. It is not the same to walk blindfolded as it is to walk with your shepherd, and that is the function of the shepherd. One who watches over and sees the full picture, and leads not only to the best and most delicate pastures but also manages the pastures for their best use, ensuring that the sheep never lack food. Christ is the Good Shepherd who has given them the complete vision of eternal life and showed those who have that living hope the way to live. Of course, the emphasis in the verse is on protection and security, as we know by the use of the word overseer. An overseer in antiquity, a word used for pastors or elders in charge of a community, district, or town, was a watchman whose responsibility was to keep others safe, a guardian, or a respected teacher. In Jewish literature, God was known as the Guardian of His people. Remembering that Christ was their protective shepherd could be a great encouragement for those suffering unjustly, which is why He sought out everyone and called them to His presence. Christ was the example of the morality they should live by and also the Guardian of their lives. Jesus was actually more than an overseer, but Peter uses the term to encourage the present overseers in the church, so they would feel uplifted, as sometimes the sheep feel the encouragement and protection of the pastors and overseers, but they do not have protection from the defenseless, sensitive sheep. Peter tells both the church, the elders, and the overseers, that Jesus is the shepherd who guides them, but also the overseer, watchman, and teacher of their souls. In Him, they can have all the confidence and security that they will not lack sustenance. When the emperors wanted to take away their water and bread in persecutions, Jesus would sustain them, and no wolf or fierce animal, like the emperors or the enemies of the church, would harm them because Jesus would protect them and fight on their behalf. Jesus of Nazareth is our Good Shepherd and the Overseer par excellence.

THE TESTIMONY OF JESUS BY JOHN AND HOW HE IDENTIFIES HIM:

THE WORD:

John 1:1-4;

In the beginning was the Word, and the Word was with God, and the Word was God. He was with God in the beginning. Through him all things were made; without him nothing was made that has been made. In him was life, and that life was the light of all mankind.

The word "Word" from Latin is the word used from the Greek "Logos". John introduces it christologically to show the high divinity of Christ. For John, God the Creator, being one with the "Word", shows the absolute equality of both as the same being. For John, the Word (Jesus) of His same substance comes from Him, while being from Him, achieves in His divinity to become flesh, providing Himself with a terrestrial body to be seen and dwell among humans. Scholars have often tried to find in Hellenic Greek thought the source of John's concept of the Logos. For the Greeks, as we have previously explained, this Logos represented knowledge, thought, speech, reason, intelligence, harmony, or the very law of the infinite, eternal, invisible deity. When John gives this title to Jesus, it was because he was trying to show the Jews, but more especially all the Greeks, that Jesus is that Logos made visible, incarnated, and manifested to men. This hidden and concealed knowledge that they so loved, called philosophy, which some regarded as the goddess "Sophia" (knowledge and wisdom) upon which they relied for their salvation or security, John tells them that this Word (Logos) was found in the person of Jesus, the true knowledge, wisdom, and harmony of God. This same God had manifested Himself carnally before all. There was no longer a need to keep searching for human philosophical knowledge or wisdom from the Greek schools, which never fulfilled or satisfied the soul. In Jesus, the Word of God, was found all the fullness and the ultimate true philosophy of God, as stated by the Church Father Justin Martyr. Among the most prominent philosophers and apologists, upon finding Christ, he converted to Christianity, showing and declaring that Jesus is the true and highest philosophy of God. The terminology of the Word is only found in the literature of John, but the idea of this Word as Logos, etymologically, goes back to the philosopher Heraclitus (6th century BC). Heraclitus said that all things were in a continuous flow, that although nothing ever remains the same, while everything is in complete harmony. From the beginning of the universe to the end of all progressive creation with all constant changes, there exists an order. The Word is that creative word, the foundation of all that flows unceasingly, making the world a cosmos, an ordered whole. Jesus is that Word, that expressed creative word, through which all that exists and is seen above and below came to be, from nothing, and from what was not seen.

THE RESURRECTION:

John 11:25;

Jesus said to her, "I am the resurrection and the life. The one who believes in me will live, even though they die."

Having remained as the last living among all his closest brothers and friends, all the apostles had died except John. Tradition tells us that according to the same text of John, in his final chapter, after Peter asked Jesus what would happen with John, Jesus replied, "If I want him to remain alive until I return, what is that to you? You must follow me." This saying spread among the brothers that this disciple would not die. But Jesus did not say that he would not die; he only said, "If I want him to remain alive until I return, what is that to you?" With this saying, it is believed that John outlived all the apostles, while some scholars hold the opposite view and believe that the Apostle John also died earlier along with the other apostles. In any case, with the thought and weight contained by the church fathers and tradition itself, we see that John aimed to show Jesus not only as the Word but also as the "Resurrection and the Life." John dedicated two entire chapters to both the resurrection of the empty tomb and the resurrected appearance of Jesus to his apostles. Previously, he was the only one to show Jesus as the resurrection and the life, raising his friend Lazarus. Jesus demonstrated before Lazarus that he had all the power to give life to whom he wanted. Lazarus had been dead for four days; in Jewish custom, it was believed that as long as a body was within a tomb, the soul could hover around for three days with the possibility that the dead might come back to life. But we see that Jesus delayed until the fourth day, and this was on purpose, waiting for all human or cultural hope to disappear so that all could see and believe that He is the Son of God, the Resurrection, and the Life, and that only in Him is eternal life found. Jesus did not give Lazarus eternal life at that moment, but he did return his earthly life until the due time to later grant him eternal life in the resurrection of those who sleep in Christ. Jesus of Nazareth died, laid down His life, and with the power of the Father and the Holy Spirit, rose again from the dead, becoming the firstfruits of those who die and rise to never die again. He took the key of authority from the devil and the empire of death, to never die again and to give the same life to those who die in Him, so that they may also be resurrected in Him, finally destroying the last and ultimate enemy: death. Jesus Christ is the only one who can give life and life in abundance. It is clear that He is also the only one who has resurrected and today lives with power seated at the right hand of the Father. Therefore, no one else can say with authority as He did in the Revelation of John; *(Revelation 1:17-18) "When I saw him, I fell at his feet as though dead. Then he placed his right hand on me and said: Do not be afraid. I am the First and the Last. I am the Living One; I was dead, and now look, I am alive forever and ever! And I hold the keys of death and Hades."*

THE TESTIMONY OF JESUS BY THE APOSTLE PAUL AND HOW HE IDENTIFIES HIM:

In this part by the Apostle Paul, being the last among all the apostles, and probably the first and most prolific writer about Jesus of Nazareth, we will refrain a bit, as many of the titles used to refer to Jesus have already been touched upon by the other apostles. Some academic scholars and historians tell us that many of these previous titles we have mentioned could have originally come from Paul, and that in the narrative process, the authors were reading Paul's letters and taking ideas from him to write. Some philologists have gone so far as to say and support that all the writings of the New Testament were inspired by Paul's unique thought. Christian tradition does not support this idea, as it would be impossible for Paul to have known everything. We know that many knew Jesus in the flesh much more than Paul, many knew a great number of traditions and stories that Paul never knew. It is not surprising that Paul did not frequently write about the earthly life of Jesus, or what they called Him, because he never knew Him personally and did not walk with Him. Paul was more interested in writing about the resurrected Christ than the Galilean who walked the streets of Galilee healing and freeing the demon-possessed in His earthly ministry. Paul never disregarded the life of Jesus, but we clearly see how little he spoke of His ministry, probably because he did not know much about it. The most earthly aspect of Jesus that Paul used in reference to the forgiveness of our sins was the crucifixion of the crucified Jesus, His death, and resurrection, the powerful gospel for salvation.

THE IMAGE OF THE INVISIBLE GOD:

Colossians 1:15;

He is the image of the invisible God, the firstborn over all creation.

He is the exact representation of the Creator. Simply put, Jesus Christ makes God visible. Paul, John, and the writer of Hebrews said the same, not because it was a personal title they gave to Jesus. They called and testified of Jesus according to the same title that Jesus spoke of Himself. Jesus had said that He is one with the Father and that anyone who sees Him sees the Father. His life was the highest and perfect example of who the invisible God would have been if He ever clothed Himself in a body as He did in Jesus of Nazareth.

Jesus had asked for honor so that the Father would also be honored. He said He was before Abraham, even saying that Abraham had seen His days and rejoiced greatly.

While the church asked who Jesus really was in the first centuries of its existence, many great heresies arose from failed attempts to answer this question. Heresies like Docetism, Nestorianism, Apollinarianism, and primarily Arianism were completely anti-biblical formulations by some leaders and Christians. These proposals by these men were each time brought before councils, declared heretical, and subsequently excommunicated. The church, in its attempt to define, set limits, and defend the truths it proclaimed, formulated what we now know as the Christological creeds (the Nicene Creed and the Chalcedonian Definition). What we can say with certainty and security, according to the canonical and biblical text, is that for these three—John, the Hebrews writer, and especially Paul—Jesus was and is the image of the invisible God, the mirror of God for men on earth.

THE LORD JESUS CHRIST:

This is the title Paul used most for the testimony of Jesus in his writings, but as we have already detailed what it means, I suggest referring back to the title "Lord" "Kyrios" by John the Baptist and "The Anointed of God" "Hamashiach" by the Apostle Peter, as they are the same words with the same narrative meaning in Greek and Jewish thought.

Alexander Frias

THE TESTIMONY OF THE CHURCH FATHERS ABOUT JESUS
Part 3

The Church Fathers were of great importance due to their role in the development and definition of Christian doctrine, the ancient traditions collected and received from Jesus by the apostles themselves. The Church Fathers during the first centuries of Christianity played a crucial role in interpreting the complete Scriptures, formulating theological beliefs, and defending Christianity against heresies. Their writings and teachings helped establish the foundations of Christian thought, and their legacy has had a lasting influence on the theology, liturgy, and spirituality of the Church.

Regarding the thoughts of the Church Fathers about Jesus of Nazareth, there is a wide range of writings and teachings that demonstrate their deep devotion to Jesus Christ as the Son of God and the Savior of the world. They played a fundamental role in developing and articulating early Christian doctrine, including understanding the divine and human nature of Jesus, His role in redemption, and His relationship with God the Father. Their teachings have significantly influenced Christian theology throughout the centuries.

There are numerous writings by the Church Fathers that cover a wide variety of theological, doctrinal, and pastoral topics. These writings include sermons, letters, theological treatises, biblical commentaries, and other types of works. Some prominent Church Fathers whose writings have been preserved include Saint Augustine, Saint Jerome, Saint John Chrysostom, Saint Gregory the Great, among many others. The works of the Church Fathers are an invaluable source for understanding the evolution of theological, ecclesiastical, and Christological thought in the early centuries of Christianity. They provide profound perspectives on issues such as Christology, soteriology, ecclesiology, and many other areas of theology. Here we share some of the testimonies of the Church

Jesus of Nazareth

Fathers about who Jesus of Nazareth was.

POLYCARP OF SMYRNA:

The early Church Father Irenaeus (120-190 AD) wrote that Polycarp was "instructed" and "appointed" by the apostles and "conversed with many who had seen Christ ... always teaching the things he had learned from the apostles." Irenaeus also wrote that he clearly remembered "the accounts that [Polycarp] gave of his relationship with John and with the others who had seen the Lord. And recalling his words, and what he heard from them about the Lord, and about His miracles and teachings, having received them from eyewitnesses of the 'Word of life.'" Therefore, his view of Jesus is very important. In the Letter of Polycarp to the Philippians, he mentions "the God and Father of our Lord Jesus Christ" and "our Lord and God Jesus Christ."

__Polycarp:__ "Now may the God and Father of our Lord Jesus Christ, and the eternal High Priest Himself, the Son of God Jesus Christ, build you up in faith and truth and with all gentleness and with all freedom from anger, patience, constancy, and perseverance, and purity, and may He give you a portion and a place among His saints, and with us with you, and with all those under heaven who will still believe in our Lord and God Jesus Christ and in His Father who raised Him from the dead."

Polycarp agrees with the teachings of the apostles that Jesus is God.

IGNATIUS OF ANTIOCH:

Ignatius was the bishop of Antioch and wrote seven letters to the Churches while he was on his way to his execution in Rome around 107-110 AD. He was one of the apostolic fathers who also saw Jesus as the incarnate God. In Ignatius' letter to the Ephesians (18:2), *he tells us: "For our God, Jesus the Christ, was conceived by Mary according to the plan of God..."* And then he tells us in (19:3): *"Consequently, all magic and every kind of spell were dissolved, the ignorance so characteristic of wickedness disappeared, and the old kingdom was abolished, when God appeared in human form to bring the newness of eternal life..."* In (7:2) he says: "There is only one physician, who is both flesh and spirit, born and unborn, God in man, true life in death, both from Mary and from God, first subject to suffering and then beyond it, Jesus Christ our Lord."

For Ignatius, it is clear that Jesus was both man and God, and the incarnate Word. This vision did not come solely from him; like many of the Church Fathers, they saw Jesus as their God, worshiped Him, and sang hymns of worship from as early as the first century of the church. Some scholars reject or deny the veneration of Jesus as God from the first century, often saying it was impossible given the first commandment that Jews would worship Jesus as this could be seen as idolatry or blasphemy. While there were some sects like the Nazarenes or the Ebionites, who were among the first followers of Jesus and did not see Him as God, by the mid-first century and onwards, Jesus was worshiped and seen as God among Christians. The number of those who believe and know that Jesus was seen as God, and also worshiped by Christians, far exceeds those who deny it.

Praising the church of Ephesus at the beginning (1:1), *he says: "Being imitators of God, once you assumed a new life through the blood of God, you completed perfectly the task so natural to you." Finally, in his letter to the church of Smyrna, including Polycarp, bishop of the church of Smyrna and apostolic father, sharing the same vision of Jesus, he says in (1:1): "I glorify Jesus Christ, the God who made you so wise..."* Thus, it is clear that both Ignatius and Polycarp referred to Jesus as God.

JUSTIN MARTYR:

Justin Martyr was a great philosopher, apologist, and defender of the Christian faith during the second century (c. 110-166 AD). Justin Martyr recognized Jesus as "Our Christ" who spoke to Moses through the appearance of a burning bush. Without directly denying the Father, Justin said that the one who appeared or spoke to Moses in the desert was not the Father of the universe, but rather Jesus the Christ. This is seen in his Dialogue with Trypho where he says:

"That Christ being Lord, and God the Son of God, and appearing formerly in power as a Man and Angel, and in the glory of fire as in the bush, also manifested Himself in the judgment executed on Sodom, is demonstrated fully by what has been said." He also says: *"The Father of the universe has a Son; who also, being the Word begotten of God, is God. And in the old times He appeared in the form of fire and in the likeness of an angel to Moses and the other prophets; but now in the time of your reign, having, as we said before, become man by a virgin..."*

Here we see Him as the Almighty God, the same God of Abraham, Isaac, and Jacob. This was the God who told Moses that His name is "I Am," just as Jesus Christ named Himself because He was the same God revealed to Moses. In Justin's writings, we see a dual testimony about the deity of Jesus; we see Jesus as the Son of God, Messiah, Savior, doing what His Father commands, but we also see Him recognized clearly as God Himself. We see Jesus at times inferior to His Father, but also one with God and the same God. Justin was among the best Christian apologists and philosophers; for this reason, he could easily present a broad philosophical vision of Jesus, taking Christianity to a more interesting, acceptable, and credible level during the early centuries when Greek philosophical thought dominated philosophy. With the blending of Greek philosophical thought and Jewish Christian thought, the view of Jesus and who He was continued to expand until, later on, theology would have its final vision as we see it today.

One of the greatest struggles Christians faced with traditionalist Jews and rabbis was that they did not want to accept or see Jesus as equal to God. Trypho appears to be a Jew whom Justin sought to convert to Christianity, and finally, testifying about Jesus, he says: *"For if you had understood what was written by the prophets, you would not have denied that He (Jesus) was God, the Son of the only, unbegotten, and ineffable God."*

These testimonies from the Church Fathers, Ignatius of Antioch and Justin Martyr, among others, demonstrate their deep conviction of Jesus' divine nature. They contribute significantly to the understanding and development of early Christian theology and Christology, affirming the belief in Jesus as both God and man, which has become a cornerstone of Christian doctrine.

IRENAEUS OF LYON:

Born between 126 and 136 AD in Asia Minor, probably in Smyrna, Irenaeus grew up listening to the sermons of Polycarp in his home. As an adult, Irenaeus remembered Polycarp, the direct disciple of the Apostle John, saying he could still recall the place where Polycarp sat and disputed, his coming and going, the character of his life, his physical appearance, and the discourses he gave about his life. Irenaeus recounted how Polycarp remembered John's words and the things related to Jesus that he had heard from them, about His miracles and teachings, and how Polycarp related everything according to the Scriptures as he had learned from eyewitnesses of the Word of Life. Irenaeus recorded all these things in his heart. These words are found in Eusebius' Ecclesiastical History.

Irenaeus was the greatest theologian of his century, and in his writings, he maintained all the doctrines of the apostles quite clearly. In my personal opinion, I believe Irenaeus, like Polycarp and Ignatius, saw Jesus as God. But we see in his apologetics against heresies a very eloquent way of expressing the testimony of Jesus. Irenaeus often used the term "Word of God" for Jesus, and he also used His name, Jesus Christ. When discussing the knowledge of the Father by the Son, using the verse from **Matthew 11:27,** *"All things have been handed over to me by my Father; and no one knows the Son except the Father, and no one knows the Father except the Son, and anyone to whom the Son chooses to reveal him,"* Irenaeus shows his testimony towards Jesus by saying, "With this, He taught us what He Himself is and what the Father is...etc."

Defending the Father of our Lord against Marcion, Valentinus, Basilides, and Carpocrates, he says that the teaching he received from Jesus was, "No one can know God if God Himself does not teach him," meaning no one can know God except through God, even if He is known, it is also the will of the Father. Irenaeus also says, *"Therefore, the Father revealed Himself to all, making the Word visible to all; and in the same way, the Word, letting Himself be seen by all, manifested the Father and the Son.* Irenaeus says, *"Through the Word made visible and palpable, the Father was manifested."* And because of this, being present, all said that He was the Christ and called Him God.

Irenaeus was so illustrious and wise that he knew well how to explain the doctrine of the Father and the preexistent Word being of the same substance, with the same purpose, in different manifestations. Irenaeus saw the incarnate Word as the same God and Father visible to men, saying, *"From the beginning, the Word of God preannounced that God would be seen by men and would live and converse with them on earth, being present in the work of His hands to save it and make Himself accessible to it, 'delivering us from the hands of all who hate us' (Luke 1:71)."* (Some notes taken from Selected Works of Irenaeus of Lyon, by Clie)

CLEMENT OF ALEXANDRIA:

Clement of Alexandria, born around 150 AD and died around 215-216 AD, was one of the most prominent Christian theologians and philosophers of Alexandria, and the teacher of Origen and Alexander, who were well-known students in Christianity. He was the successor of Pantaenus and leader of the catechetical school in Alexandria, Egypt, where many bishops, priests, and Christian leaders attended.

In his work "Pedagogue," he says, *"What does the Pedagogue offer? Above all, an authentic model of life, which is none other than the very image of Christ imprinted on believers, as corresponds to Him who has created man, for Christ is God and, as such, is the creator of the world."* Clement clearly shows Christ as the same God. For Clement, Christ was the full realization of everything God had said. Confronting all the wise men, he refuted them by asking and declaring, *"Thus after the baptism of the Lord, a voice is heard from heaven testifying about the Beloved: 'You are my beloved Son; today*

I have begotten you' (Matt 3:17, Mark 1:11, Luke 3:22). Let us ask these wise men: Is the Christ who has been begotten today already perfect, or, which would be entirely absurd, does He lack something? In this case, He must learn; but it is impossible for Him to learn anything, because He is God. For no one could be greater than the Logos, nor be the teacher of the only Teacher."

Another testimony from Clement about Jesus was the following: *"The food, the Lord Jesus, the Logos of God, is spirit made flesh, celestial sanctified flesh."* John in his Gospel tells us through Jesus that God is spirit; therefore, here Clement calls the Logos of God spirit, calling the Logos spirit is calling Jesus Himself the Celestial Spirit in reference to the Father. Then Clement, countering those who thought that the righteous were not good, said, *"There is nothing, then, that is hated by God, and therefore, nothing is hated by the Logos. For both are God: In the beginning, the Logos was with God and the Logos was God (John 1:1), and if the Logos does not hate any of the beings He has created, it is evident that He loves them."*

These are just a few testimonies of Clement about Jesus Christ, the Logos of God, in his literature "Pedagogue." For more, one can consult his writings. With these few testimonies, we see that for Clement, Jesus Christ is clearly God, just as many of the Church Fathers saw Him. (Some notes taken from Selected Works of Clement of Alexandria, by Clie)

These insights from Irenaeus of Lyon and Clement of Alexandria highlight their theological contributions and their understanding of Jesus Christ as both divine and human. Their teachings, along with those of other Church Fathers, have been instrumental in shaping the foundation of Christian doctrine and Christology.

TERTILIAN

Tertullian was a Church Father and prolific writer during the latter part of the 2nd century and the early part of the 3rd century. He was born around 160 A.D. and died in 220 A.D. He is well-known for his theological writings and for establishing the doctrine of the

Trinity of God. However, some scholars believe he was not the first to use the term "Trinity." Theophilus of Antioch was the first to use the Greek term Τριας (Trias) in the mid-2nd century to express the union in God of three divine persons: God (the Father), His Word (Logos), and His Wisdom. From this term derived the Latin form Trinitas, used for the first time by his contemporary Tertullian in the early 3rd century, who recognized it as the three persons of God within the church. It was from Tertullian onwards that the Christian doctrine of the Trinity became an official part of Christian thought.

Tertullian did not receive the title of "saint" in the church due to a controversial decision to convert to Montanism, one of the early heresies. For this, he was considered a heretic by Christian orthodoxy. Nevertheless, his writings and teachings remain with us and have been quite useful for Christianity. Very little is known about his life, as he is only mentioned by Eusebius of Caesarea (263-339) and St. Jerome (340-420).

Tertullian's testimony about Jesus is as follows: Tertullian considers the Logos (Word) of God as God in a derived sense, being of the same substance as God; God coming from God, like a ray and the light of the sun come from the same Sun. For Tertullian, Jesus is of the same substance as God and is God Himself: "And we say that He has been pronounced by God and from such pronouncement is generated, and for this reason, He is called the Son of God and God by unity of substance; because God is spirit. Just as the ray is born from the Sun, a portion of that sum, while the Sun remains in the ray, because in the ray is the Sun, and the substance does not separate, but extends; so the spirit is born from spirit and God from God. Like the flame, though it kindles others, remains whole without being diminished, and the source does not lose its degrees, although from it originate other equal lights, which if communicated, are not diminished; so what was born of God is entirely God and Son of God, and both are one, Spirit of Spirit and God of God, in whom only the degree of generation makes a number, the mode of the person, not the majesty of the essence, which although born does not separate; like the branch, although born, does not divide from the trunk." (Apology against the Gentiles in defense of the Christians).

Moreover, refuting Praxeas, we see him say: "The heresy of Praxeas thinks it is in possession of pure truth when it professes that to defend the oneness of God, one must say that the Father, the Son, and the Holy Spirit are the same." (Apology against the Gentiles in defense of the Christians).

TESTIMONY OF JESUS BY FAMOUS MODERN WRITERS
Part 4

Besides the testimony of the Church Fathers, who were all Christians, the testimony of Jesus reached far beyond, impacting a host of thinkers, historians, writers, and leaders who, in some way, marked history. These men were also witnesses to Jesus of Nazareth and believers in the divinity of Christ. Let's consider some of their testimonies regarding Jesus.

Flavius Josephus:

Among the most important historians of the first century, Josephus testified about Jesus in his TestimoniumFlavianum, stating: "At this time there appeared Jesus, a wise man, if indeed one ought to call him a man. For he was the author of marvelous deeds, a teacher of people who receive the truth with pleasure. He won over many Jews and many of the Greeks. He was the Christ. When Pilate, upon the accusation of the principal men among us, condemned him to the cross, those who had first loved him did not cease. He appeared to them spending a third day restored to life, for the prophets of God had foretold these things and a thousand other marvels about him. And the tribe of the Christians, so called after him, has still to this day not disappeared."

William Shakespeare:

In his final words, Shakespeare said: *"I commend my soul into the hands of God, my creator, hoping and assuredly believing through the only merits of Jesus Christ my Savior."*

John Milton:

The famous poet declared that *"Jesus the Christ incarnate was both human and divine."*

Daniel Webster:

On one occasion discussing Christianity, after affirming his belief in the divinity of Christ and his reliance on the Savior's sacrifice, Webster was asked if he could comprehend how Christ could be both God and man. Webster responded that he did not understand it, saying that if he could, then Christ would not be superior to him. Not understanding it left Christ as his superhuman Savior. He also said, *"I believe Jesus Christ is the Son of God."*

Martin Luther King Jr.:

"Jesus Christ was an extremist for love, truth, and goodness."

Napoleon Bonaparte:

"I know men, and I tell you that Jesus Christ was not a mere man. Between Him and every other person in the world, there is no possible comparison. Alexander, Caesar, Charlemagne, and I have founded empires. But on what did we rest the creations of our genius? Upon force. Jesus Christ founded His empire upon love, and at this hour, millions of men would die for Him."

Albert Einstein:

"I am a Jew, but I have been captivated by the luminous figure of the Nazarene."

John Knox:

"No one else holds or has held the place in the heart of the world which Jesus holds. Other gods have been devoutly worshiped; no other man has been so devoutly loved."

Jean-Jacques Rousseau:

"Socrates died like a philosopher; Jesus Christ died like a God."

These testimonies from modern writers and thinkers, alongside the testimonies of the Church Fathers, highlight the profound impact and enduring belief in the divinity of Jesus Christ across various periods and cultures.

JESUS AND FAITH
PART 1
Hebrews 12:2
"Fixing our eyes on Jesus, the author and perfecter of faith, who for the joy set before him endured the cross, despising its shame, and sat down at the right hand of the throne of God."

As we believe that Jesus was fully human and fully God, we must understand that to become the example for all humanity, He had to, as God, empty or strip Himself completely of His divine attributes. This does not mean that Jesus ceased to be God or completely abandoned His divine attributes; rather, to fulfill His purpose on earth and become the author of faith and salvation for mankind, He had to overcome solely in the flesh, as 1 Peter 4:1-2 tells us: *"Since Christ suffered for us in the flesh, arm yourselves also with the same mind, for he who has suffered in the flesh has ceased from sin, that he no longer should live the rest of his time in the flesh for the lusts of men, but for the will of God."*

Chapter 11 of the Book of Hebrews is dedicated to all the Biblical heroes who made good use of and depended on faith. Among them, we know Abraham, the progenitor of the Hebrews, who is traditionally known or called the father of faith. We see that there were many before Abraham who also had faith in God. With Abraham, it is different because from chapter 12 of Genesis, known as the key chapter of the Bible, in the context of the history of the nation of Israel, God called Abram, who, after receiving a promise, had his name changed to Abraham. This Abraham, through the promise received from God, decided to believe and put all his faith in Him. This faith of Abraham in God was then counted to him as righteousness. Abraham played a very important role because through his faith, all his descendants would come to know the almighty God and would also place their faith and hope in Him. Now, in Abraham's faith, all nations would be blessed; his descendants would be exceedingly great, and they would receive all the land. This faith was rewarded as time went by.

However, the kind of faith we see in Jesus was much greater and superior to Abraham's faith. For the love of God, Abraham offered his son Isaac to God; a Jewish tradition tells us that for this reason, Sarah expired or died, unable to bear the test God gave Abraham. Abraham received Isaac back after seeing his own capability and faith towards God; this would later benefit him. But not so with Jesus. He was given up for the love of God to humanity. Jesus offered Himself in absolute love; no one had to ask Him to strip Himself of all His glory; He did it out of pure grace and love, giving His life, dying. Unlike Isaac, who was provided a substitute to avoid death, Jesus had no substitute. He gave His life, knowing and believing that He would save the world and receive a better reward from His Father. Jesus was the first and only one to give His life without reservations and without self-defense before God for humanity. As a man, His faith was unparalleled; I would even dare to say unsurpassable, being everything, He chose to live as a servant of His God and Father. Jesus is undoubtedly the author and perfecter of faith.

Next, we will see some of the many biblical verses that show the faith Jesus taught was necessary to have. We do not question whether Jesus had this faith and whether He put it into action since He taught it. We reiterate that we believe that Jesus, as a man and Son of God, not only taught faith but also believed it, showed it, practiced it, and fulfilled it completely, becoming its author for mankind.

Jesus asks us to have faith:

John 11:40:

Jesus said to her, "Did I not tell you that if you believed you would see the glory of God?"

Martha had faith in God, but the faith that Jesus expected from her in Himself was a greater and more personal faith, not just a faith of habit and culture. The faith that Jesus expected was one to see God manifested in the present, in the current moment, and not in the future or uncertain last day as they used to believe by tradition. Jesus was telling her that faith was not for the future; faith is for today, to see God manifested in our favor from today, not tomorrow. Tomorrow will bring its own trouble, and only God knows it. Let us put our faith in God today! and we will see His glory.

Mark 9:23:

Jesus said to him, "If you can! All things are possible for one who believes."

Faced with the disbelief of a father who had seen his son suffer continually from childhood due to what the text tells us was an unclean spirit trying to kill him, which even the disciples of Jesus could not cast out, this father asked Jesus for mercy and help. In response to this request, Jesus did not say much; all Jesus had asked was for him to believe. "Jesus said to him, 'If you can! All things are possible for one who believes.'" Immediately the father believed and asked Jesus to help his unbelief. All that Jesus asks of us is to believe in Him and the Father; believing in Him is all the sufficiency that God demands from us. Believing in God and Jesus amidst all our human unbelief will help us see all impossible things made possible by God and Jesus Christ Himself.

Matthew 21:22:

And whatever you ask in prayer, you will receive, if you have faith."

Jesus always prayed to the Father; in His ministry, everything He did, He did after praying. Scholars tell us that 90% of His ministry was spent in prayer. Jesus prayed more than He preached and taught; it is believed that everything He did and received from His Father, He acquired through faith and prayer to the Father. In addition to teaching His disciples to pray, He taught them to believe by faith that they would receive whatever they asked for. Sometimes we pray out of habit and routine, but we seriously need to believe by faith in our prayers to the Father. For Jesus, prayer was never alone; it had to be accompanied by faith. Let us pray believing...

John 6:35:

Jesus said to them, "I am the bread of life; whoever comes to me shall not hunger, and whoever believes in me shall never thirst."

Jesus, in His preaching, compared Himself to food and, comparing Himself to man's greatest trials, the struggle for the sustenance of bread and water, which produce and generate life, showed Himself as the bread of life and the water that would quench man's spiritual thirst. Jesus had enough faith to believe and know that everything He offered would be sufficient for man's life. All Jesus asked was for them to believe in Him; having faith in Jesus would be sufficient to never hunger or thirst spiritually. He went so far as to ask us to eat His flesh and drink His blood, which many have misunderstood, but His flesh is the word of God, and His blood the forgiveness of our sins. Believing and having faith in Jesus gives us access to the knowledge of the word of God; by receiving His sacrifice and valiant blood over our lives by faith, symbolized by the wine, we receive through the same faith the forgiveness of all our sins, receiving two things: first, reconciliation with the Father, and justification through our faith in Christ Jesus.

Matthew 17:20:

He said to them, "Because of your little faith. For truly, I say to you, if you have faith like a grain of mustard seed, you will say to this mountain, 'Move from here to there,' and it will move, and nothing will be impossible for you."

Unbelief is the greatest obstacle to faith. Jesus was continually surrounded by unbelief. In this case, the mustard seed, one of the smallest seeds at the beginning, grows into one of the largest and tallest trees. Jesus says that if faith were at least the size of a mustard seed, it would continually grow to be quite large, showing the possibility that by the power of faith, one could speak to the mountains and they would be moved. Obviously, earthly mountains do not need to be moved, but Jesus wants to show something. Some scholars tell us that Jesus was facing or in view of a mountain that Herod and his workers had managed to build in Bethlehem by bringing soil from a distant place. If men put their faith in earthly men and kings and achieve earthly things, how much more will those who put their faith in the creator of all things achieve? Jesus asks us to at least have faith in God present in our lives, a great faith is the best there can be, but if we at least have it small, let us allow it to progressively grow in God through our relationship with Him.

John 6:29:

Jesus answered them, "This is the work of God, that you believe in him whom he has sent."

Luke 8:50:

But Jesus on hearing this answered him, "Do not fear; only believe, and she will be well."

The Pharisee, and ruler of the synagogue, Jairus, may have been very learned and knowledgeable in the law, but faced with the need in his home with his daughter just 12 years old, who was sick while he had gone out for Jesus, in the meantime, she had just died. Upon hearing the news, one from his house had come out to tell him not to trouble the teacher anymore. It was under this impossible situation before Jesus hearing the news, Jesus asked Jairus to only have faith and believe, and his daughter would be saved (healed). Jesus shows us that faith placed in Him will change all human impossibilities into possibilities for God. Therefore, let us always put all our faith in Jesus no matter what need we have; let us do as Jairus did, let us go out or act in search of Jesus, through our prayer and His word, and let us ask in His name believing, and He is faithful to answer and reward each of His children.

John 20:29:

Jesus said to him, "Have you believed because you have seen me? Blessed are those who have not seen and yet have believed."

Blessed are those who can put their faith into action; the vast majority of humans say they have to see to believe, but Jesus here shows how blessed the one who does not need to see to believe is. Faith is God's attribute, which existed long before human reason or earthly vision; everything that is seen has its end, and by having its end, it loses its hope, to what end should one hope for what perishes. Therefore, what is unseen remains in hope; it is faith, the certainty of what is hoped for, the conviction of what is not seen. Without faith, it is impossible to please or satisfy God; God is Spirit, therefore to approach Him, it is necessary to believe that He exists, and to believe that He exists is to approach Him walking on the path established in His word, which can only be walked by faith and not by sight. Blessed is he who can nourish reason with his faith, and not his faith with reason, for the examples and heroes who have most marked history with their brave and firm faith have achieved it.

Jesus is undoubtedly the author of faith and its finisher; many participated in it, "According to faith, all these died without receiving the promises, but seeing them from a distance, and believing, and greeting, and confessing that they were strangers and pilgrims on the earth. For those who say this clearly indicate that they seek a homeland; for if they had been thinking of that from which they came out, they would have had time to return. But they longed for a better one, that is, a heavenly one; for which reason God is not ashamed to be called their God; for He has prepared a city for them".... And all these, although they obtained good testimony through faith, did not receive what was promised; God providing something better for us, so that they would not be made perfect apart from us. Thanks to the faith of the biblical heroes, especially our greatest example Jesus, today you and I can have and participate in this great faith, let us continue to show and give testimony of this faith in our Lord Jesus Christ, for those who are lost and for those who have not yet reached it, may it reach, heal, and save them.

Lastly, I believe Jesus would be deeply interested in our faith. In Mark 2:5, we see Mark telling us, "When Jesus saw their faith, He said to the paralytic, 'Son, your sins are forgiven you.'" The essence of Jesus' message was entry into the kingdom of God, and to receive this entry, forgiveness of sins was paramount. The faith of these friends of the paralytic was, in Jesus' eyes, the primary reason for the forgiveness and salvation of the paralytic. With this said, I believe it would be unnecessary to add more about how important and crucial faith was and is to Jesus of Nazareth.

Alexander Frias

JESUS AND TEMPTATION
Part 2

Hebrews 4:15;

For we do not have a high priest who is unable to sympathize with our weaknesses, but one who in every respect has been tempted as we are, yet without sin.

For Jesus to be perfected in all things and to become the author of salvation for humanity, he had to have been tempted in all things. For the writer of Hebrews, he could not have been perfected without first being tested in his life as every human being, for every human being. Jesus was tempted in all things, and he also experienced what temptation was directly from the evil one as well as from men who also tempted him, being influenced by the same. All of us in life have desires and different weaknesses as human beings. God created us with free will and has given us the ability to choose between good and evil. In the case of the biblical Jesus, it is a bit complicated because this Jesus that we see is a Jesus interpreted according to faith. We have to consider that everything we have about Jesus was written and reinterpreted many years after his death. Some church fathers, as we have shown previously, were so fundamentalist and confessional that they never saw the possibility of Jesus even getting sick. Some went so far as to say that it was impossible for Jesus to sin. Jesus had been elevated to such a spiritual dimension that what remained of his humanity to us was very little. The historical, real Jesus that we see in the Gospels was a completely human Jesus. He was born of a woman, grew up, ate, drank, slept, cried, suffered, felt, walked, and did everything that a normal human being does. Jesus had free will and also his own decision-making; he could have had all the possibility as a human being to sin and also to repent, but we know as the Son of the Father and servant of his God, he lived in complete obedience, without sin, to the point that he preferred to abandon all his will to fulfill that of His Father. Jesus had all the freedom to live like every human being, and he lived like every human being until the moment of his baptismal act in the waters of the Jordan, around his 30 years as Luke tells us. After his baptism, we see him solely dedicated to the purpose of his Father for his life for the next 3 years until his death. We do not authentically have a broad view of Jesus in terms of his daily life before his baptism, and this has made it a bit difficult to assimilate Jesus with the weaknesses that we human beings have. We do not see a Jesus laughing, enjoying delightfully, playing, or even entertaining himself with his friends. The lack of these characteristics in Jesus led the church to see a Jesus always serious or even angry, to the point that it was almost impossible for the world to see a smiling Jesus. The perceptual level of his holiness led him to be seen as a serious statue, which he never was. When the enemy or the evil one tempts a human being, he never tempts him with things that do not attract him, much less with things that were never his weaknesses. The enemy, when he tempts, does so knowing the things that can attract you and the things that once pleased you. With this said, we see Satan tempting Jesus at the beginning of his public ministry.

Jesus and Hunger:

Satan tempts Jesus with food because he knows that Jesus needs to eat. Jesus had been fasting for 40 days, and anyone would say, "What's wrong with eating?" Would it have been a sin if Jesus turned the stone into bread and ate? There are some things we need to understand before addressing this issue. Firstly, we must know that we do not know in what form Satan presented himself; possibly, this battle took place entirely in the conscience and mind of Jesus himself. Secondly, if Satan appeared in some kind of vision, I am sure he did not do so with horns and tridents as we are accustomed to seeing in Western images. And thirdly, what I find interesting is that it was not until Jesus felt hunger that Satan tempted him. He had not appeared before because he knew it would not be a temptation for Jesus. Jesus' response to this first temptation by Satan shows us whether it was a sin or not to eat. With this request by Satan to Jesus to turn stones into bread in the middle of the desert, he was trying to divert Jesus' dependent gaze from his Father and make him depend on himself for his own food and sustenance. The serious problem of Israel in the desert was that they had decided to tempt God by asking for food wickedly, as if God did not know and understand their needs. Israel provoked God by doubting their dependence on him in the desert to the point that they decided to return to Egypt after witnessing Yahweh's saving wonders. Theologically, Satan had influenced the conscience of Israel so much that he was now trying to do the same to Jesus against his Father. Turning stones into bread would only exacerbate hunger in the face of the discipline that Jesus was undertaking with his fast in the desert. The sin was not in eating; the sin was in using divinity for one's own benefit, which Jesus never did. If he had used his divinity for his own benefit, he would have failed and been disqualified from being the example for humanity. Jesus knew that he had been led by the Spirit into the desert, and perhaps he also suspected that he would face a series of temptations there. But what I am sure of is that Jesus knew that if God had led him there, he would not abandon him, nor would he let him die there. For this reason, his response was clear: "Man shall not live by bread alone, but by every word that comes from the mouth of God." Jesus knew that his Father had declared a word about him, and this was what gave him life. The confidence that Jesus had in his God and Father was too great to even consider sustaining himself with earthly bread at that moment by himself. And if he had this spiritual internal struggle with himself, we see him as a man overcoming temptation in the flesh.

Jesus and the Temple:

Jesus is taken, most likely in a vision or in an experience akin to a spiritual trance, where Satan asks him to throw himself down from a height, saying that God would send his angels near him, and they would support him so that his feet would not strike against a stone. Anyone would think or wonder if Satan was instilling some instinct of suicide in Jesus. It is not to doubt the possibility of it since we see great prophets under oppression asking God to take their lives. We see Job, Moses, and even Elijah asking God to end their lives. The burden that each one felt and the process each one went through was not easy. In any case, with Jesus, the main purpose was not to instill a suicide instinct because although at times due to diabolical influence, socially, we all have abstract and evil thoughts which are clearly from the evil one. Jesus was not exempt from all these thoughts that the enemy could have placed in him. If Jesus threw himself down, it is very likely that God would send an angel to rescue him, or perhaps miraculously he would have survived. The problem here is that if Jesus threw himself down, this was a great opportunity for all the Pharisees, Sadducees, priests, scribes, and elders of the people who worked in the temple to see that He was the true Messiah. This sign of throwing himself and supposedly being sustained by an angel, so as not to die, would have been the opportunity to be accepted by everyone once and for all. Perhaps as a human being, Jesus may have wanted this during all his time trying to prove that he was the true anointed one sent by God. Jesus knew that this thought was completely wrong because it was tempting not only God but also his own life. Sometimes the devil's temptations against our lives may seem and sound good as if there is nothing wrong behind them, but it is necessary to know clearly, as Jesus himself said, Satan is an adversary, a murderer, and the father of all lies. There is nothing good in him; therefore, his offers to our consciences and hearts, no matter how good they sound or look, will never be good. Jesus preferred that a few recognize him as the true Messiah rather than tempting against his own life and against God, caring less about what the religious contemporaries of his time thought of him, choosing instead to live according to what His Father thought of him.

Jesus and All the Kingdoms:

Fame, recognition, and worship, along with praise, have always been the greatest weakness that Satan offered to kings and emperors. All kings hungered to conquer the whole earth with their power. Jesus, being the true king, would not be an exception. Satan offers Jesus all authority over the kingdoms and the glory of this world if he would bow down and worship him. Jesus had come as the

Messiah, and if there was something he wanted, it was for his Father's Kingdom to be established lightly upon the earth. We must recognize that the kingdom that was in force and the most powerful one was the Roman Empire. The Kingdom of God was neither greater nor more famous than the Roman Empire. During the time Jesus was preaching, this kingdom was unknown to the common Jews of Israel. For the Jews, the concept they had was that anyone who kept the law and tradition was part of the kingdom of God. This kingdom that Jesus came to bring would have to be progressively introduced first, and then, after preparing some disciples, they would be sent to preach the kingdom of His Father. If something we know is that Jesus always wanted his Father's kingdom to advance rapidly on earth because he knew he did not have much time. This offer by Satan to Jesus, to give him all the kingdoms and their glory, was quite dangerous. If Jesus had accepted and succumbed to this temptation, he would have aborted the purpose of his death. If he had all the kingdoms and their glory, what he would later receive after his death and resurrection through his Father, he would have received from Satan without the need to die. Without death, there would be no resurrection, and without resurrection, he would have been just another common messiah like all those who came before and after him. What made the difference in Jesus' messianism was his death and resurrection, which gave the kingdom and glory of Christ on earth a firm and enduring touch for over two millennia. Jesus, as a man, could easily have accepted this offer since later in Gethsemane, we see him distressed and troubled, asking his Father if it was possible to pass the cup of his death. If he bowed down and worshipped Satan, supposedly, he would not have to die since he would receive all the kingdoms and have absolute control over the earth, and humanity would live under the dominion of his glory. Here we see and are faced with the true greatness of Jesus of Nazareth because, although it could have been easier and cut short the path, or even advanced it more quickly, he preferred to suffer to become the high priest of a better covenant for humanity, choosing to suffer with his life all the suffering and carry upon his life and body all the burden of the world to show us that he knows and understands all that we suffer. Therefore, we can approach with confidence knowing that we have a High Priest who first suffered for us and through that suffering that Satan did not want to happen, he knows how to understand and sympathize with us because he became the example for all.

What Jesus Asks of Us in the Face of Our Temptations:

Jesus becomes the greatest example for us, being tempted in every way, yet he loved obeying his Father so much that he never sinned or allowed himself to be carried away to fall into temptation. During the last moments of his life with his apostles and disciples, Jesus asked Peter something very specific, and it was to pray for at least an hour so that he would not fall into temptation. We see a series of ruins and falls that Peter had to face simply because he could not watch and pray for just an hour. Every time Jesus went to pray and returned to his disciples, he found them sleeping, waking them up and admonishing them to enter into prayer. But each time they remained asleep until it was too late. Peter acted so violently that when they went to arrest Jesus, Peter cut off the ear of a certain Malchus, who was the servant of the Jewish High Priest Caiaphas. At the crucifixion of Jesus, Peter denied him three times until he felt so guilty that he wept bitterly. After leaving everything for Christ, we see him returning to his old way of life. Peter was shaken by Satan as wheat is shaken, and he fell quite hard. Christ restored his life by forgiving him out of love, but he gives us and teaches us a great lesson, and that is that there is no more perfect antidote against temptation than prayer. Prayer will deliver us and give us the power, perhaps not to be tempted, but certainly not to fall into our temptations. This is a call to examine our lives, our weaknesses, and temptations. Sometimes we have to do a spiritual self-analysis and ask ourselves, why do we neglect ourselves? Or why do we fall so much into our temptations? I think the answer will probably be that we do not even pray enough to greet our Father. Prayer should be the bread of every child of God. If we see a strong and firm Jesus, it was not because he was divine, but because of the life of prayer he led. Let us pray while we can, let us pray at all times, let us pray without ceasing because the effective prayer of the righteous can accomplish much.

JESUS AND HIS MESSAGE
Part 3

Mark 1:14;

After John was imprisoned, Jesus went to Galilee to proclaim the gospel of the kingdom of God. He said: "The time is fulfilled, and the kingdom of God has come near. Repent, and believe in the gospel!"

The four gospels are quite clear that the main message of Jesus was or was related to the "Kingdom of God." The expression "kingdom of God" appears 122 times in the New Testament, of which 99 are found in the three Synoptic Gospels, and 90 are spoken by Jesus. Over the last nearly 20 centuries of the existence of the Christian Church, there have been about four different viewpoints on what this Kingdom of God could have indicated or been in Jesus' message. Before touching on these different viewpoints, the book "Theology of the New Testament," by G. Ladd, tells us that this kingdom in Jesus' teaching was and is the gift of God, which could be a good that admits being desired, granted, possessed, or accepted. In Jesus' words as the good shepherd, the kingdom of God represents the fold, into which his flock enters following his call or word (gospel) and has the hope of being safe and saved with their shepherd. Along with this Kingdom exists what we know as the message or announcement of the Kingdom, which we know as "The gospel of God or of Jesus Christ." The word Gospel means "Good news of salvation," but although it sounds good, etymologically it is far below what it actually means. This term was first used by Roman emperors, before and after they had been introduced in wars where their security as a nation was under threat of being taken captive or destroyed by other empires, the emperors had to prepare some kind of message of hope or saving security so that the Romans would not lose their hopes and feel the saving security of the emperors. This message from the emperors was known as their gospel. The problem is that all the gospels of the different emperors were temporary gospels and only offered a fleeting hope, since none could actually offer what only Jesus of Nazareth offered, eternal life. In all the different viewpoints we will show for this Kingdom of God, it is clear that to participate in this Kingdom in all its different aspects, men are asked for a decisive personal response, to repentance, conversion, and faith. In Jesus' message, we see the four different forms that represent this Kingdom of God. We will make a division in each form that it is expressed.

Jesus is the Kingdom of God Himself:

According to the Christian mystical perspective of some of the church fathers, the word kingdom was directly associated with Jesus himself. According to this thought, Jesus himself is the kingdom of God that has come or has drawn near to humanity. For Origen of Alexandria, one of the most outstanding mystical fathers, the word auto-basilea, as a scholar, pointed out that the term basilea in the Gospels does not necessarily mean a "kingdom" in the sense of territorial dominion like the earthly government of a king, rather, it refers to "royalty" in the sense of the power, authority, and sovereignty itself of a king. To designate a space, territory, or place for the kingdom of God would be to limit God himself, therefore this kind of thinking did not focus much on showing the kingdom as a projectively earthly place. It is true that in this thought, Jesus as a human being would be limited to his flesh, and it could also be said that the kingdom of God would be limited in Jesus. This perspective did not tend to limit the kingdom solely in Jesus; it identified more with his message and the Word itself within Him. Jesus made the call for everyone to enter the kingdom which was entered by accepting being part of the community that Jesus established as Master, Messiah, King, and the highest authority. The fathers were clear that the only limit that existed as a kingdom in the person of Jesus himself had been his flesh (although among many still his flesh revived and continues to revive in the Eucharist, or sacrament known as "transubstantiation," which is believed that the bread becomes the very body of Jesus that was once given), but not the Word that sustained him, which is the very incarnate thought of the eternal God and Father, which would represent in and as Jesus the kingdom of God itself. This kingdom in the representation of Jesus himself in his resurrection, we would see ascend to a completely spiritual body dimension, which would remain forever. According to this perspective, Jesus himself would lead men to God through Himself, God Himself would be present among men if Jesus is present, as He represents the very presence of God manifested on earth. Some verses that support this kind of idea are the following.

Synoptic:

Matthew:

Matthew 3:2; and said: "Repent, for the kingdom of heaven has come near."

Matthew 10:7; Go and proclaim: "The kingdom of heaven has come near."

Matthew 12:28; But if I cast out demons by the Spirit of God, then the kingdom of God has come upon you.

Matthew 13:24; Jesus told them another parable: "The kingdom of heaven is like a man who sowed good seed in his field;

Mark:

Mark 1:15; He said: "The time is fulfilled, and the kingdom of God has come near. Repent, and believe in the gospel!"

Mark 4:30-32: *He also said: "What shall we compare the kingdom of God to? What parable shall we use for comparison? It is like a mustard seed (Jesus), which, when sown (death) on the ground, is the smallest of all seeds on earth. Yet when it is sown, it grows (resurrection) and becomes the largest of all garden plants, with such big branches (kingdom) that the birds can perch in its shade."*

Luke:

Luke 10:9; Heal the sick who are there and tell them, "The kingdom of God has come near to you."

Luke 11:20; But if I drive out demons by the finger of God, then the *kingdom of God has come upon you.*

We have seen that according to these verses, the kingdom of God is closely correlated with the person of Jesus himself, as seen by many of the church fathers.

The Kingdom Among Us:

A second spiritual perspective of the kingdom of God is the belief that this kingdom would reside within the heart of man. This line of thought was also introduced by Origen himself. According to the prayer model that Jesus taught his disciples, they were to pray saying, "Thy kingdom come," indicating that God's will would be done over the heart and personal will of men, which dwells within their hearts. God reigns among holy people and can be said to reign over all the earth as the Creator or absolute God, although this is believed by theological sovereignty, because on earth, visibly, we see the evil one having more advancement on this polluted earth. The dominion or sphere of the evil one present on earth cannot be doubted, where evil is applauded much more than good. Bad things are called good, and good things are called bad. But this sphere of the evil one also finds its limit among the holy people, known as the Church of God, over which the dominion or sphere of the evil one cannot govern because it has no power over that kingdom; only God governs over the heart of the church. This kingdom in the heart of men grants them the benefits of their citizenship that only their King offers. In this kingdom, the benefits are known as love, peace, joy, power, authority, etc., over which the kingdom or sphere of the evil one has no control, dominion, or power. Sin (internal) and the presence of the evil one (sphere) are present in the world (cosmos), especially among the hearts (souls) of men, but once this kingdom of God penetrates and enters the heart of men, man is freed from all the power and bondage of sin that once lorded over him. In this way, the true power of the kingdom of God in the lives of human beings is understood and seen. The idea is clear: the kingdom of God is not found in a specific place, like Eden or an imaginative Greek paradise; it is not a place like this world. It is within man, there it grows, and from there it manifests for all men.

The Kingdom as the Church Institution:

In the 19th and early 20th centuries, the prevailing thought among Christians (Catholics) was that this kingdom of God would represent the very Church of Christ. Not everyone thought this way, but it could be said that it was part of the consensus since the church represented or is the very body of whom Jesus is the head. It was thought that the church together with Jesus would be the same system as the kingdom of God. According to this almost mystical perspective, the kingdom of God would be composed of the indivisible union of God, Christ, and the Church; everything would be an inseparable whole, therefore everything would represent the kingdom of God. This ecclesiastical thought would soon lose its power, although some continued to think this way. Among Protestants, this thought was never part of any consensus. This thought would not last long since it is clear that the kingdom of God is not the church; the kingdom of God is much more than the church. The church would be a part of the kingdom but not the kingdom itself. The church would have a part in the kingdom of God, but in no way would it be the kingdom itself. Viewing the church as the kingdom of God would be a completely erroneous idea since it is visible and does not have absolute power in itself. All power is generated solely by God, the owner of the church.

The Coming Kingdom:

This coming kingdom of God is categorized eschatologically or apocalyptically. Jesus was considered an apocalyptic prophet since we see him speak prophetically based on future events that would fulfill the concept of the end of the world. We see him announce this kingdom of God or the kingdom of heaven as a government that will be implanted with power and majesty in a sense of judgment for the unjust and a time of peace and joy for the just. In several prophecies in the book of the prophet Isaiah, we see this coming kingdom as one full of peace, joy, and tranquility for the people of the Lord, where: "The wolf and the lamb will feed together, and the lion will eat straw like the ox, and dust will be the serpent's food. They will neither harm nor destroy on all my holy mountain," says the LORD.

And also, as Revelation says, "He will wipe every tear from their eyes. There will be no more death, mourning, crying, or pain, for the old order of things has passed away." It is clear that even the church itself, which is part of the kingdom of God on earth, is not experiencing this kind of life prophesied apocalyptically speaking. Therefore, this kind of thinking is still part of the current thought of the church of Jesus Christ. Currently, all these viewpoints are accepted by the church as what we interpret the kingdom of God to mean. At least among evangelicals, the kingdom of God is not just one thing or one viewpoint. The kingdom of God is a combination of all these different thoughts, excluding the idea of the church as the absolute kingdom, but rather the church being only a part of the larger and more extensive eternal kingdom of God. On several occasions, Jesus shows and speaks about this coming kingdom; some verses will help us see and understand it a little better.

<u>Matthew:</u>

<u>Matthew 5:3;</u> *Blessed are the poor in spirit, for theirs is the kingdom of heaven.*

<u>Matthew 5:10;</u> *Blessed are those who are persecuted because of righteousness, for theirs is the kingdom of heaven.*

<u>Matthew 5:19-20;</u> *Therefore, anyone who sets aside one of the least of these commands and teaches others accordingly will be called least in the kingdom of heaven, but whoever practices and teaches these commands will be called great in the kingdom of heaven. For I tell you that unless your righteousness surpasses that of the Pharisees and the teachers of the law, you will certainly not enter the kingdom of heaven.*

<u>Matthew 7:21;</u> *Not everyone who says to me, 'Lord, Lord,' will enter the kingdom of heaven, but only the one who does the will of my Father who is in heaven.*

<u>Matthew 19:28;</u> *Jesus said to them, "Truly I tell you, at the renewal of all things, when the Son of Man sits on his glorious throne, you who have followed me will also sit on twelve thrones, judging the*

twelve tribes of Israel."

Matthew 25:34; Then the King will say to those on his right, "Come, you who are blessed by my Father; take your inheritance, the kingdom prepared for you since the creation of the world."

Mark:

Mark 9:1; And he said to them, "Truly I tell you, some who are standing here will not taste death before they see that the kingdom of God has come with power."

Luke:

Luke 13:28-29; There will be weeping there, and gnashing of teeth, when you see Abraham, Isaac, and Jacob and all the prophets in the kingdom of God, but you yourselves thrown out. People will come from east and west and north and south, and will take their places at the feast in the kingdom of God.

John:

John 18:36; Jesus said, "My kingdom is not of this world. If it were, my servants would fight to prevent my arrest by the Jewish leaders. But now my kingdom is from another place."

These are just a few of the many verses that show the kingdom of God as coming to earth or being in a place completely outside of the earth. In Revelation, we see the doctrine known in the church as "the millennial kingdom of Christ," where there are three different Christian viewpoints. We will not go into detail because this is neither the time nor the place, but these three different views are known as premillennialism, postmillennialism, and a millennialism. Among these three different viewpoints, some believe they will physically see this kingdom of Christ in two stages. First, the church will be raptured to this heavenly kingdom of Christ in heaven, and then after a period, it will return with Christ in what will be his second coming to earth. For others, this kingdom will also physically come a second time, but not along with the church. Instead, the church will not be raptured before his second coming; it will wait after having endured all kinds of suffering for its King, who will bring justice and reign in this coming millennial kingdom over it. A millennialists do not believe in a physical kingdom or a specific millennial period; this is more symbolic. They do not think of this kingdom as coming visibly. Instead, they believe that the millennial kingdom of Christ, which alludes to or indicates a long period, could be said or used with the same term "forever and ever" to indicate perpetually always. For a millennialist, this invisible kingdom is already present on earth in the hearts of God's people. The evil one is defeated, and death has no dominion and power over those who are part of this kingdom of God, as we have shown previously.

JESUS AND PRAYER
Part 4

Matthew 6:6;

But when you pray, go into your room, close the door and pray to your Father, who is unseen. Then your Father, who sees what is done in secret, will reward you.

The word we know as Prayer, in the great encyclopedic dictionary by Ropero, is the Hebrew word "tejinnah," which means thanks, plea, supplication, prayer, from the root "janan," which implies bowing, imploring, bending before someone superior, seeking the favor of another, and requesting grace and mercy. In the New Testament, prayer is always directed to God. Another similar or quite close Hebrew word is "Tephillah" from the root "palal," which refers to judging, interceding, or seeking justice. The Greek word used in the LXX version for praying or prayer is "Proseukhe" or "Proseukhomai," this is the same in the New Testament for praying to God, but the term most frequently used for praying is "deomai," which means to plead or ask. Also, the word prayer, from the Latin *"orare"* "to orate" or "to supplicate," means to direct words or thoughts towards a deity or another superior metaphysical instance to praise, request mercy or gifts; synonymous words could be, implore, invoke, beg, or ask. Prayer is a phenomenon that has existed very anciently and in all religions. It is believed that the practice of prayer has been in existence for approximately more than 5000 years. We see it frequently throughout almost the entire Bible by men and women. It is a fundamental and very important theme of the Bible. For Jesus, all prayers should be made to God the Father, all his prayer time the text tells us that he directed them to his Father. One of the most exemplary characteristics for the person who wants to learn to pray to God is found in Jesus of Nazareth. For Jesus, part of his great ministerial success is believed to be due to the practice of prayer in his life. In ancient times, the Hebrews/Israelites, through their tribal patriarchs, priests, and prophets, were taught how to approach God in prayer and supplication. Jesus was no exception among the many rabbis who taught prayer of supplication before God to their students or disciples, but we have to show the difference between the prayer of the religious rabbis or Pharisees and scribes of the time of Jesus and the prayer that Jesus himself lived. Jesus did not see prayer as an established time of definite hour, although as a Jew he kept Jewish customs, but he did not see prayer personally as the Jews were accustomed to seeing it. Generally, Jews prayed three times a day, this custom is very ancient in the Old Testament, it is said that Daniel prayed three times a day. Jesus knew and understood this, even to the disciples he says when you enter your room to pray, pray this way, the famous "Our Father," the model prayer that Jesus taught his disciples in Matthew 6:9-13. It is also very important to know and understand that this style of prayer or the prayer called "The Lord's Prayer" is a fairly old prayer, although the Christian tradition originates it in Jesus, in reality a large number of theologians and learned scholars tell us that Jesus was not completely the originator or founder of this prayer, the form that Jesus shows you is an idea or style of His own as a reform or restructuring, but the liturgy of prayer already existed from ancient times, most likely since the return of Juda in her Babylonian captivity. He was known as *"Avinu Malkenu"*, (Father, our King) were the first words that were recited in traditional Jewish prayer and liturgy on each of the X days beginning Rosh Hashanah, the New Year. This prayer came from the book of the prophet Isaiah 63:16, 64:8, and other quotes. Our Father, translating the abbreviated prayer in my own words, said the following: *"Avinu Malkenu, our Father, King, listen to our voices and prayer, we have sinned in Your presence, have compassion on us and our children, help us bring an end our pestilence, and diseases, let all our hatred and oppression disappear from the earth, write our names in the book of life, and allow a good new year for us.* This prayer, which was longer, together with others, had the same style and meaning as that of Jesus, it was the way that the Jews prayed. Jesus as a rabbi wanted to give his own form or original version to his diciples, a much more intimate prayer towards the Father and also leave them a continuous custom rather than a tradition practiced on specific dates such as Rosh Hashanah, Yom Kippur, holidays or days of fasting such as they used to be done. But later a brief form was instituted among the Jews by Rabbi Akiva Ben Josef during the 1st and 2nd AD centuries. Jesus knew that among them prayer was done in a period of time as we will later see in Acts when the customary hours for prayer in the temple are mentioned, Jesus' prayer model is much more than a time custom, or that of a dedicated posture with a view towards the temple as the Jews customarily did since monarchy times, beginning with king Salomon in his temple dedication prayer. For Jesus prayer is not about the place, the time, and even less the festivity or holiday, for Jesus prayer is an intimate relationship with God, a continuous uninterrupted communion with the Father, this was part of the mystery that he came to bring us and give us. Prayer is more than a time or a separate moment, it is more than a corner or a built altar, prayer is practiced both while walking and also when resting, and above all without the need to look towards Jerusalem as they already did. The time had come for the Father to seek true worshipers not only in Jerusalem or in Samaria but everywhere around the world, prayer now would be without earthly sight, but rather in the spirit. Jesus' example is that prayer has no space or limit, it could and can be practiced at all times. Jesus lived prayer, he lived all the time talking to his Father everywhere without the need to look towards Jerusalem, he spent entire nights in communion with his Father, something that none of his disciples did, for Jesus is was like prayer had no definite set time, something that would literally disturbed or shattered their custom culture point of view of prayer. One thing for sure is that Jesus way or style of prayer was very different, His prayer devotion was being looked at and compared to that of the pharisees and the scribes, but they all saw something different, first His authority, and above all the immediate response from His Father after His prayers, I mean at times Jesus would only say *"Father I thank you that You have heard me, I know you always hear me"*... and His prayers would be answered publicly, something never seen in religious leaders of His time. Is exactly what Paul later would consider *"Prayer without ceasing."* Jesus was always in a motive of prayer, he taught us to pray in secret alone as we see in (Mt 14:23)(Mk 1:35)(Lk 9:18)(Lk 22:39-41), in public in front of many (Jn 11:41-42)(Jn 12:27-30), before eating food we see him praying (Mt 26.26)(Mk 8:6)(Lk 24:30)(Jn 6:11), before making some important decisions in his life like the choice of his disciples (Lk 6:12-13), before doing some healings looking up to heaven to show dependence on his Father (Mk 7:34-35), after some other healings (Lk 5:16), to fulfill and do the will of the Father (Mt 26:34-44), among many other things he taught the importance of prayer (Mt 21:22)(Mk11:24-26)(Mk 7:7-11)(Lk 11:9-13)(Jn 14:13-14)(Jn 15:13,16)(Jn 16:23-24)(Mt 5:44)(Lk 6:27-28)(Mt 6:5-16): Including the Our Father in (Lk 11:2-4)(Mt 18:19-20). Jesus was so zealous about prayer to God that entering the temple on one occasion, very upset, he overturned the tables of the money changers telling everyone, "My house will be called a house of prayer" but you have made it a den of thieves, Jesus saw that the sacrifices and all the money in the temple had taken away the true interest of prayer and the very purpose for which it had been built, when Solomon said in 1 Kings 8:12-66 "Hear the prayer that your servant makes here. Hear my pleas and those of your people Israel when we pray toward this place. Hear them in heaven, where you live, and forgive us," etc. If we take all these examples about Jesus and prayer, we will soon realize how important prayer really was to Jesus. From the beginning to his last prayer before the cross, he prayed for all his disciples to the Father in John 17. These are just a few verses where we see the example of Jesus in relation to prayer. There are almost 40 more verses that we can list throughout the New Testament about Jesus and prayer, not including his current state which the writer of Romans 8:34 tells us; *"Who then is the one who condemns? No one. Christ Jesus who died—more than that, who was raised to life—is at the right hand of God and is also interceding for us."* We see that the current state of Christ is one of continuous prayer for us. This is the reason why early on his disciples asked him to teach them to pray. The prayers of Jesus always seemed to have been answered by his Father, unlike the Pharisees and the scribes, who always prayed without receiving an answer from God in public to be seen by men.

These Pharisees were lacking in authority, and their prayers were made for themselves thinking they were directing them to God, in reality, they never prayed to God, they prayed for themselves. Instead, Jesus prayed to the Father, in favor of all others, and when he spoke, he did so to such an extent that everyone who listened to him was amazed, saying, where does he get this authority, which the most respected Pharisees and scribes did not have. This authority and power that Jesus had, which he received from his Father throughout his ministry, he obtained through the inseparable communion he had with his Father through prayer. This example that Jesus gives us, he also left it for us so that like him, we have the same communion with our heavenly Father. We must see prayer as Jesus saw it, not merely as a time or a specific hour, but rather as a fervent spirit, at all times, continuously, without ceasing.

Alexander Frias

JESUS HIS MIRACLES AND WONDERS
Part 5

Luke 7:22;

And He answered them, "Go and tell John what you have seen and heard: the blind receive sight, the lame walk, those with leprosy are cleansed, the deaf hear, the dead are raised, and the good news is proclaimed to the poor."

In Israel, with the rise of the messianic hope by the prophet Isaiah, it was expected that the coming Messiah would somehow surpass all the previous prophets from Moses to Malachi in all the signs that they performed. The Jews loved miracles and signs; from the beginnings of the formation of the people of Israel, they came to know God through the wonders that Moses performed with the staff he carried. The parting of the sea and the plagues on Egypt were traditionally among the most well-known miracles in the entire nation of Israel. With the arrival of other prophets, such as Samuel, Elijah, and Elisha, throughout the northern area, all the traditions of the miracles and the mighty signs that these prophets performed to show the authentic authority in their messages from God to the people became known.

We also see many prophets who did not perform as many miracles or signs, but the level of authority in their divinely prophesied words was greatly respected throughout the nation of Israel. We see prophets like Jeremiah, Ezekiel, and Daniel himself, who were men and priests with respect completely accepted by the Jewish nation. With the prophet Isaiah, in his prophecies about the rise of a new messianic era with a new Messiah to come, we see in his prophecies the kind of image this anointed one of God would bring upon his arrival. In Isaiah 35:4-6, the prophet says the following: *"Say to those with fearful hearts, 'Be strong, do not fear; your God will come, he will come with vengeance; with divine retribution he will come to save you.' Then will the eyes of the blind be opened and the ears of the deaf unstopped. Then will the lame leap like a deer, and the mute tongue shout for joy. Water will gush forth in the wilderness and streams in the desert."*

This declaration by the prophet Isaiah had never been seen in Israel; no prophet had ever given or restored sight to the blind. Some raised the dead to life, others by their word healed lepers, purified contaminated waters, multiplied oil and flour, and also called down fire from heaven. It was normal in Israel for signs and miracles to follow the prophets, and with Jesus, this would be no exception. Jesus multiplied all the miracles that all the prophets did, surpassed them, and did them much better than all. Above all, John tells us, *"Jesus did many other things as well. If every one of them were written down, I suppose that even the whole world would not have room for the books that would be written."* He also shares the purpose of the ones that did reach us: *"But these are written that you may believe that Jesus is the Messiah, the Son of God, and that by believing you may have life in his name."*

It is believed that in all the information found in the Gospels, the writers only composed a minimal part of Jesus' ministerial life. Here we can see a breakdown of the amount written dedicated by each Gospel to Jesus' last week:

- One-third of Matthew 21-28
- One-third of Mark 11-16
- One-fourth of Luke 19-24
- Almost half of John 12-20

With this information, we can see that all the writers actually recorded very little compared to all the things Jesus did during His three years dedicated to ministry. Among all the Gospels combined, we have a total of 89 chapters, of which 29 are dedicated to the last week of Jesus. This has led many scholars to categorize the Gospels as a Passion narrative. This also shows how Jesus lived His life dedicated to service and sacrifice for others. These 29 chapters dedicated to Jesus' last seven days reflect the mindset He had during the remaining 1,088 days of His ministry, not counting all the years we are sure He lived in some way as a human helping and dedicated to others. This is a call for a personal examination or evaluation. If we were to ask ourselves, or ask God to examine us, to see how much of our lives and our Christian walk are centered on Jesus' suffering and His work for us on the cross at Calvary, where He left and gave everything for us, what would we find?

When was the last time you evaluated how great Jesus' sacrifice was, placed on a cross, and not just His death but all the suffering He endured long before the day of His death? This same passion that Jesus suffered out of love for us is what should also remain in us as children of God for those who are still lost in the world. Let us ask God every day for the opportunity to share the message of Christ with those who are lost and need to reach this wonderful grace. Here is a brief list of all the direct and prophesied miracles and wonders by Jesus present in the Gospels.

- Jesus turns water into wine (John 2:1-11)
- The healing of the man with an unclean spirit (Mark 1:23-28; Luke 4:33-37)
- Jesus heals Peter's mother-in-law (Matthew 8:14-17; Mark 1:29-31; Luke 4:38-39)
- Many healed in the evening (Matthew 8:16-17; Mark 1:32-34; Luke 4:40-41)
- The miracle of the fish (Luke 5:1-11)
- The healing of a leper (Matthew 8:1-4; Mark 1:40-45; Luke 5:12-16)
- The healing of a paralytic (Matthew 9:1-8; Mark 2:1-12; Luke 5:17-26)
- The healings by the sea (1) (Matthew 4:24-25, 12:15-16; Mark 3:7-12; Luke 6:17-19)
- Jesus heals the centurion's servant (Matthew 8:5-13; Luke 7:1-10)
- Healing of the son of a royal official (John 4:46-53)
- Jesus raises the widow's son at Nain (Luke 7:11-17)
- Jesus calms the storm (Matthew 8:23-27; Mark 4:35-41; Luke 8:22-25)

Jesus of Nazareth

- The demoniacs of Gadara (Matthew 8:28-34; Mark 5:1-20; Luke 8:26-39)
- The healing of a woman with a hemorrhage (Matthew 9:20-22; Mark 5:25-34; Luke 8:43-48)
- Jesus raises Jairus' daughter (Matthew 9:18, 23-26; Mark 5:21-24, 35-43; Luke 8:40-42, 49-56)
- Healing of a paralytic at the pool of Bethesda (John 5:1-15)
- The healing of two blind men (Matthew 9:27-31)
- The healing of a mute demon-possessed man (Matthew 9:32-34; Luke 11:14-15)
- Jesus heals the man with a withered hand (Matthew 12:9-14; Mark 3:1-6; Luke 6:6-11)
- Few healings in Nazareth (Mark 6:5-6)
- Feeding of the five thousand (Matthew 14:13-21; Mark 6:32-44; Luke 9:10-17; John 6:1-15)
- Jesus walks on the sea (Matthew 14:22-33; Mark 6:45-52; John 6:16-21)
- The healings in Gennesaret (Matthew 14:34-36; Mark 6:53-56; John 6:22-25)
- The healings by the sea (2) (Matthew 15:29-31)
- The healing of a deaf-mute man (Mark 7:31-37)
- Feeding of the four thousand (Matthew 15:32-39; Mark 8:1-10)
- The healing of the blind man at Bethsaida (Mark 8:22-26)
- Jesus heals a demon-possessed/epileptic boy (Matthew 17:14-21; Mark 9:14-29; Luke 9:37-43)
- The woman healed on a Sabbath (Luke 13:10-17)
- Jesus heals a man with dropsy (Luke 14:1-6)
- The healing of the ten lepers (Luke 17:11-19)
- The healing of the man born blind (John 9:1-41)
- Jesus raises Lazarus (John 11:1-44)
- The healing of two blind men in Jericho (Matthew 20:29-34; Mark 10:46-52; Luke 18:35-43)
- The withering of the fig tree (Matthew 21:19-22; Mark 11:20-26)

- Jesus heals the servant's ear (Malchus) (Luke 22:50-51)
- The resurrection (John 2:19-21, John 10:17-18, 1 Corinthians 15:1-8)
- The miraculous catch of fish (John 21:4-11)

Among all the prophets who performed miracles in the Bible, the prophet Elijah was among those who performed the most miracles. Jesus of Nazareth far surpassed the prophet Elijah in his miracles and wonders, not counting all the miracles he performed that were not written in the biblical text. But here we leave you a list so that you feel free to refer to the biblical text.

JESUS AND FORGIVENESS
Part 6

Matthew 18:21-22;

Then Peter came to Jesus and asked, "Lord, how many times shall I forgive my brother or sister who sins against me? Up to seven times?" Jesus answered, "I tell you, not seven times, but seventy-seven times."

Forgiveness is the second most important theme or action in the entire Kingdom of God and the Bible. The first is love, the second is forgiveness. For Jesus, forgiveness and the experience of it were very important and critical for life. There were two kinds of thoughts among the Jews, one was the one Peter showed of forgiving up to seven times, but among the doctors of the law and the religious Jewish rabbis, the thought and teaching about forgiveness had limits. Generally, the Jews had measures for forgiveness; the rabbinic schools taught that when an offender offended someone, they should acknowledge their mistake since the offense was not part of the seed of Israel. A second offense, if the offender repented and asked for forgiveness, should be forgiven by their brother. After a third offense against their brother, it would also be forgiven, but at the fourth offense, there would be no forgiveness for the offender. Jesus is a rabbi and teacher completely different from the Jews of his time; for Jesus, forgiveness had no measures or limits either. Jesus' perspective on forgiveness was seen in another way: if your brother offended you, it was not the offender who should ask for forgiveness; rather, the offended one should approach their brother, apologize, and reconcile with them. For many, this kind of attitude and life was too difficult to accept; for this reason, Jesus himself said that not everyone could truly drink from his cup or truly call him Lord, Lord, since they did not do what He told them to do. For Jesus, there was no room or freedom for anger against others; reconciliation was vital and prompt, to prevent any root from sprouting in the hearts of men. This kind of forgiveness was not part of the law of Moses; it was part of the life of the new kingdom of God that Jesus presented to humanity. In this biblical portion, the number 7 is a very symbolic and significant number for the people of Israel throughout the scripture. The first communities that gathered and read the scrolls knew almost by heart much of the texts of the Old Testament. When Jesus or a scholarly rabbi quoted a passage from the Torah, they quickly identified it and knew where it was. The number 7 was the most sacred number that reminded them of the seventh day, the Sabbath; this was the day when all the Jews rested and dedicated it to the Lord as Moses had charged the children of Israel. On the seventh day, according to the text of Genesis, God rested after creation in the company of human beings. Additionally, they were very aware that every 7 years they should forgive all debts and release slaves. Jesus, responding based on forgiveness, does so with reference to a text taken from Genesis, in its chapter 4, Lamech seems to have known the judgment and punishment of Cain, and referring to himself, he says that if he is harmed, he will be avenged. "For Cain will be avenged seven times, but Lamech alters this, and Cain's revenge even more, Lamech says that his revenge will be seventy times seven." This passage is taken from the Greek translation known as the LXX or Septuagint, which was well known to the early Christian communities. In the Gospels, Peter appears firstly as Simon, and in his beginnings, he is a very impetuous, rough, quick man, and just as his name identifies him, "stone or rock," with a character very difficult to mold by Jesus. Peter is the one who brings the question to Jesus about how many times he would have to forgive his brother who sins against him; to this question, Peter answers himself if it would be seven times. Jesus knows that Peter, being a good Jew, knows the Torah and takes advantage of the moment to show or make a parabolic comparison about what forgiveness represents in this new kingdom of God present, and later what it will represent for them in the New Covenant. Jesus tells Peter that forgiveness will no longer be just seven times, but rather 70 times seven. With this answer, Jesus was not commanding him to multiply as many tend to reason, for a total of 490 times; Jesus, with this, was teaching not to have in their hearts the vengeance that was in Lamech's heart and all those who thought like him. Jesus wanted there to be no obstacle or tolerance and resistance to forgiveness. The kingdom of God consists first of all in love, and secondly in absolute forgiveness. Jesus himself would be the greatest example among them, dying to forgive and rescue the world from its own condemnation. The last words we see from Jesus on the cross were a prayer to the Father, asking Him to forgive all those who had done him such wrong without knowing what they were really doing, and then we see Stephen, the first martyr, imitating this grand gesture learned from Jesus himself, repeating in front of all his oppressors and facing his own death receiving the stones thrown against him the same prayer of *Jesus "Father forgive them, and do not hold their sin against them because they do not know what they are doing."* God is the God of many opportunities, and the God who forgives. He not only forgives 7 times, and not even 490 times; He forgives all our sins and all our offenses towards Him, so as God forgives us, Jesus tells them that we must also forgive all those who offend us always. Jesus was showing them how from the beginning, when the justice of God was supposed to reign over the human, the kingdom of death due to sin was the one that ruled, as Paul says in Romans 12, from Adam to Moses, because of humanity's sin. Revenge from the beginning was one of the most serious sins in humanity, so much so that there was no longer unity among nations; in Deuteronomy 32:35, God had to tell his people "Vengeance is mine" because of so much indifference and problem that existed between Israel and the other peoples. In Matthew 5, in his sermon, Jesus used a quote from the O.T. that his Jewish listeners already knew very well; he reminded them: "You have heard that it was said, 'Eye for eye, and tooth for tooth.'" The punishment of "eye for eye" was only administered once the offender had been judged by the priests and judges, who weighed the circumstances and the degree of premeditation of the offense; only if the accused arrived at one of the cities of refuge could he be free of his guilt while he was there. Over time, the Jews had changed the application of this law, creating a tradition of man; the Jews took advantage of this law to justify their private resentments of hatred and bitterness and all the excesses they committed driven by a spirit of revenge. Sometimes they took it to such an extreme that the evil they committed was greater and superior to the small evil received; revenge and injustice had taken over the nation. It was under these conditions that Jesus taught them the true purpose of turning "the other cheek." Jesus with these words was not teaching what we sometimes think in a 21st-century context; Jesus was reflecting the authentic spirit of the Law given by God to Israel. With this, Jesus was not saying that if someone receives a slap from someone else, they should offer the other cheek to receive another slap; this thought is what we use to support the humility and meekness that a Christian should maintain. In reality, what Jesus wanted to show was that in biblical times, as it often happens today, by slapping someone, the intention was not to physically harm them, since it was done with an open hand and not closed like a fist. Rather, this slap was intended to insult to provoke a reaction of revenge or confrontation. Obviously, therefore, Jesus sought that if one person tried to provoke another by slapping them on the face or committing a shameful act against them, the one being attacked should not seek any revenge. For Jesus, it was very important to try as much as possible to avoid all revenge and to overcome evil with good, at all costs even if forgiveness were necessary. Jesus had come to restore all things to their original state and to reconcile the Father with his creation, and this would have to do with forgiving all things. We see Jesus elevate the value of forgiveness on many occasions. Sometimes as human beings, we do not understand the power and value of forgiveness; we sometimes understand these words of Jesus as something we have to do towards others, but in reality, this is not only about something we must do towards others, it is about the freedom and peace that our souls need, which are only received through the healing power of forgiveness. Sometimes we must also learn to forgive ourselves; forgiveness must bring true freedom and true peace. The peace that Jesus wants us to have and feel should not only be for God, it should also be among our neighbors, brothers, friends, and as much as possible even with our enemies. In the last chapter of the Gospel of John, we see the most glorious ending that can be found in all the books of the Bible; we see Jesus appearing on the shore to his disciples, he prepares fish and some bread on a fire, and while they are eating, he shows total forgiveness to his best friend Peter, who just days before had betrayed him by denying him three times before the very cross where Jesus was hanging. This undeserved forgiveness towards Peter not only freed him from the bitterness in his heart, but it also restored him and gave him back all the courage he had lost. The world today more than ever needs to experience the love and peace of forgiveness. Jesus commands us to pray to the Father asking Him to forgive us all our offenses and also to help us forgive those who offend us. Now we know that forgiveness is an act of courage, and often quite difficult to accept and manifest; sometimes there are so many different reasons or situations that over time created many roots of anger, hatred, resentment, and bitterness towards people in life, and these conditions sometimes need a lot of time to heal. In any case, Jesus will always be there to forgive and heal the lives of all people who want to receive the forgiveness of the Father and heal their hearts.

The specific words correlated with forgiveness like forgive, forgiveness, forgiven appear more than 130 times in the Bible. Forgive 83 times, Forgiveness 28 times, and Forgiven 26 times. There are many other words to refer to forgiveness, such as cancel, release, absolve, erase, remove, reconcile, wash, cleanse, cover, hide, bear, and more. The theme of forgiveness, like prayer, is also a very broad topic. In this work, we have limited ourselves only to forgiveness related to Jesus, but this is a word and a theme that is found throughout the Bible from Genesis to Revelation. Some verses related to forgiveness are as follows:

Matthew 6:14-15; *For if you forgive men their trespasses, your heavenly Father will also forgive you. But if you do not forgive men their trespasses, neither will your Father forgive your trespasses.*

Luke 6:37; *Judge not, and you shall not be judged. Condemn not, and you shall not be condemned. Forgive, and you will be forgiven.*

Matthew 6:12; *And forgive us our debts, as we forgive our debtors.*

Luke 17:3-4; *Take heed to yourselves. If your brother sins against you, rebuke him; and if he repents, forgive him. And if he sins against you seven times in a day, and seven times in a day returns to you, saying, 'I repent,' you shall forgive him."*

Luke 23:33-34; *And when they had come to the place called Calvary, there they crucified Him, and the criminals, one on the right hand and the other on the left. Then Jesus said, "Father, forgive them, for they do not know what they do." And they divided His garments and cast lots.*

Matthew 5:38-44; *You have heard that it was said, 'An eye for an eye and a tooth for a tooth.' But I tell you not to resist an evil person. But whoever slaps you on your right cheek, turn the other to him also. If anyone wants to sue you and take away your tunic, let him have your cloak also. And whoever compels you to go one mile, go with him two. Give to him who asks you, and from him who wants to borrow from you do not turn away. You have heard that it was said, 'You shall love your neighbor and hate your enemy.' But I say to you, love your enemies, bless those who curse you, do good to those who hate you, and pray for those who spitefully use you and persecute you.*

JESUS AND HIS PROMISES
Part 1

John 6:37;

All that the Father gives me will come to me, and whoever comes to me I will never cast out.

The Bible contains countless promises that God gave and has given to His people. Many have been fulfilled, others continue to be fulfilled, and many are still awaited. Of the many promises that God has given us, in this part, we want to specifically focus on some of the promises that Jesus gave only to His followers (the Church). Just as Jesus used His title "I Am" to show His power and authentic authority, He also gave us, as few others did, around 30 promises using powerfully the statement "I will," establishing that He will fulfill and do everything He has promised. Let's now share some of the promises made only by Jesus to all who believe in Him;

Salvation:

John 10:28; And I give them eternal life, and they shall never perish; neither shall anyone snatch them out of My hand.

Jesus as a teacher, the Good Shepherd, and the King of kings showed His people, and all who believe in Him, that only He can offer and give eternal life to whom He chooses. This eternal life, since ancient times, in the Mesopotamian epics and Sumerian stories, nearly six millennia ago, men and kings have always sought ways to attain immortality. Some faced monsters and crossed legendary seas searching for eternal life, yet all died without achieving or receiving immortality after death. Among all the great leaders venerated in the many different religions, there is not a single man who died and attained eternal life after his death. The only one we have who not only rose from the dead but also conquered the empire of death was Jesus Christ. He had said He would die, before He died, and just as He said, He gave His life and took it back on the third day. The amount of verses and biblical texts we have to support His resurrection are too many. The stories we see and read in the Gospels, the Acts, and the letters of Paul contain so many details that it would be almost impossible to say that it was all a simple invention by the Christian sect that was growing the most in the first century of our era. For those who have doubted the true historicity of the resurrection of Jesus Christ, there is a list of events that we would have to evaluate carefully. We would have to ask ourselves, how is it possible that a group of more than 10 disciples, being locked up, hidden, filled with fear because of the death of their teacher, knowing the possibility of them being crucified soon afterward, all showed up in Jerusalem, declaring with boldness, courage, and power without fear about the appearance of their teacher alive and resurrected? We would have to wonder how it was possible that they all had such a strong conviction in just a few days if they had not really seen their teacher resurrected. They not only had courage and power, but they all died as martyrs without denying the resurrection of Jesus. We see Mary Magdalene, the other women mentioned who saw Jesus resurrected, then more than 500 raised by the resurrection of Jesus, who were alive at the same time testifying, among many other questions we would have to answer if we really can doubt the resurrection of Jesus, then we would have to question all the experiences of the thousands of testimonies in the lives of those who have known Jesus, above all and most importantly the testimony of the great apostle Paul, who for more than 30 years preached the same personal testimony of how Jesus appeared to him on the road to Damascus. A large number of academic scholars have come to think that this could have been an ecstasy or a vision, but it is very difficult to call this a vision or an ecstasy since the Bible is clear when it comes to a vision, visions or dreams in the Bible are called for what they are, and not for what they are not. Just as Jesus rose from the dead, He Himself said that He is the life and the resurrection, and He Himself gives life to all those He desires. Jesus brought His friend Lazarus back to life by awakening him from the dead, raised others, and promised to give life to all who believe in Him. This eternal life begins to be experienced as soon as one knows

God and Jesus Christ. There is no better experience in life than truly having an encounter with Christ and receiving the ineffable, inexplicable joy that is produced in the feeling of life when a person receives and feels the conviction of salvation that only the presence of the Spirit of Christ gives to life. For many centuries, the nation of Israel lived perishing at the hands of many empires. Every time an empire conquered and took control of the land, Israel would be turned into a vassal and slave of the other empires. It was so with Assyria, Babylon, the Greeks, and also with the Romans. For thousands of years, they lived perishing, living solely by the promises made by God to the patriarchs that one day they would be established and have peace in their land. Jesus promised that no one, including a nation or empire, could snatch Israel (the church) from His hand. No one in the Old Testament and neither in the New Testament outside of Jesus promised to give eternal life in abundance to human beings, only Jesus, and He showed evidence by becoming the firstfruits of those who sleep and rise in resurrection to eternal life. We have received life in Christ, and we also await the eternal life manifested in the resurrection of all those who sleep in Christ Jesus because whether we sleep or whether we are alive, we know that very soon we will see Him again. Jesus is the only one who can give eternal life to humanity, and He says that whoever comes to Him, He will never cast out.

Rest and Strength:

Matthew 11:28; Come to me, all you who labor and are heavy laden, and I will give you rest.

Everyone desires in life a time of rest and renewal. People in the world are burdened with worries and concerns; stress in life is abundant, and there are people so tired and burdened with a kind of load that is much more than mere exhaustion—the weight of sin and slavery increasingly dominating life. It's as if, no matter how much we try to find that rest and renewal in the many important earthly activities in which we invest, they are not sufficient for the true rest we need. The answer is that the true rest needed by the soul of the world cannot be found in the earthly activities of this world. The rest of the soul and the strength of life that this world cannot offer, because it does not possess them, the world cannot give and produce what it does not have. This world can offer occasional temporary rest, and momentarily earthly rest, but it cannot give the internal rest in the soul and the inner being of man that can only be found in Jesus. Jesus knows how tired man is, to the point that he cannot find where to deposit the heavy burden he carries inside. He Himself makes the call, "Come to Me, all you who labor and are heavy laden, and I will give you rest." Jesus knows perfectly the rest we need, and only He can give it because He is the repose and renewal in the life of man. Coming to Jesus, handing over our burdens, is receiving the true rest that the inner man needs. Once this inner rest is received, the physical man completely renews all his strength. Jesus promises to give rest and strength to all who come to Him.

The Promise of the Holy Spirit:

John 14:16; And I will pray the Father, and He will give you another Helper, that He may abide with you forever:

The promise of the Holy Spirit in the life of the believer is the most powerful gift and gift that a human being can have in life. The Holy Spirit, as Comforter, the Paraclete, and the helper of man, is the one who will direct, guide, and lead to the fulfillment of God's purpose in man's life. If we wonder how Jesus could become the best example for humanity, it was all thanks to the Holy Spirit who was upon Him. The Holy Spirit has the task of forming and giving the necessary life to man according to his true purpose. There are men who have lived in life, in some way died without having achieved their true purpose, for one reason or another their lives ended tragically prematurely because they did not have a guide to trust or who gave them comfort. Thousands and thousands end their own lives because they do not have a comforter, someone to help and encourage them; they seek refuge in many other places and vain ways to feel good or as if they are fulfilling the real purpose for which they exist in the world. But the truth is that there is no other comforter that can compare to the Holy Spirit of God, which is the completely free gift that God offers to the world solely and exclusively through the merits of Jesus of Nazareth. The Holy Spirit Omni presently covers the whole cosmos with His presence, but does not dwell within all humanity; this gift from God is only and exclusively for those who believe and live in Jesus the Son of God. The secret to knowing the true purpose and goal of man's life is found in his creator, and the gift that this creator has given to man who believes and serves His Son is the Holy Spirit. This unparalleled help will fulfill, form, vivify, and guide man to his perfect destiny as God designed for his life. "What father among you, if his son asks for a fish, will instead of a fish give him a serpent; or if he asks for an egg, will give him a scorpion? If you then, who are evil, know how to give good gifts to your children, how much more will the heavenly Father give the Holy Spirit to those who ask him!" Let us take advantage of the Holy Spirit while we can and have inseparable communion with Him.

The Return of Jesus for Us:

John 14:3; And if I go and prepare a place for you, I will come again and receive you to Myself; that where I am, there you may be also.

One of the most beautiful and hopeful promises that Jesus gave to His disciples and all who believe in Him is found in His return to earth. The vast majority of people in the world walk and live daily expecting their end; they simply live waiting for their death. For the world, death is the ultimate test, but for those of us in Jesus, the hope in the life we live is not found in waiting for death as the world lives. Rather, our hope is found in the promise that Jesus gave us before He left, in which He said He was going to prepare a place and dwellings for His own, just as God promised the land of Canaan to Abraham, Isaac, and Jacob, and fulfilled it truly and historically by delivering it to His people Israel. As they walked in the desert, God in personified attitude went three days ahead of them looking for a place for their rest while they walked in the desert toward the promise. When the time came, God introduced them into the land, just as He had promised. Likewise, Jesus promised us that as they saw Him go, they would also see Him return once more and forever. Jesus went to prepare a better place for His people (the Church) but would return again; the promise would not only be to return, but also to include taking us with Him, to be with Him forever. This is the purpose and greatest hope that is lived in the few years we receive on earth. What would be the purpose and end of living barely 70 to 80 years in life if in the end everything is spoiled, or if there is nothing more after this? I believe that the eternal God would not waste time creating something so earthly without a heavenly end. If this life only ends in a moment and nothing more, then the creation would have been in vain. The purpose would be more complete with an eternal life as God's gift after this earthly one, which Jesus has promised us along with Him. Life without spiritual hope would be worth nothing, as everything earthly perishes and will perish; everything has an expiration date on this earth. But if even for this earth there is hope of being restored and liberated, how much more for those who believe in Jesus Christ, the Living One. We see a great many more promises made by Jesus which time and the pages of this work will not allow us to continue explaining one by one, but here are a few more.

Matthew 6:25-25; Therefore, I say to you, do not worry about your life, what you will eat or what you will drink; nor about your body, what you will put on. Is not life more than food and the body more than clothing? Look at the birds of the air, for they neither sow nor reap nor gather into barns; yet your heavenly Father feeds them. Are you not of more value than they?

Matthew 6:31-33; Therefore, do not worry, saying, 'What shall we eat?' or 'What shall we drink?' or 'What shall we wear?' For after all these things the Gentiles seek. For your heavenly Father knows that you need all these things. But seek first the kingdom of God and His righteousness, and all these things shall be added to you.

Matthew 18:20; For where two or three are gathered together in My name, I am there in the midst of them.

Matthew 28:20; teaching them to observe all things that I have commanded you; and lo, I am with you always, even to the end of the age. Amen.

Jesus of Nazareth

John 11:25-26; Jesus said to her, "I am the resurrection and the life. He who believes in Me, though he may die, he shall live. And whoever lives and believes in Me shall never die. Do you believe this?"

John 14:21; He who has My commandments and keeps them, it is he who loves Me. And he who loves Me will be loved by My Father, and I will love him and manifest Myself to him.

For a more in-depth analysis of many of the promises found in the Bible, I recommend the book "Bible Promises" by Whitaker House, a book that will help you see and know many of the biblical promises.

Alexander Frias

JESUS AND SALVATION
Part 2

Luke 19:9

And Jesus said to him, "Today salvation has come to this house, since he also is a son of Abraham."

Ancient Thought (Intertestamental) on Salvation:

In this section about Jesus and salvation, we can divide the structure of thought or doctrine of salvation in two ways. Our general intention is the Jewish cultural focus that Jesus presented before the futuristic focus on salvation that would dominate Christianity and continue in Pauline theological thought. We will explain salvation historically/culturally seen, but also the Pauline cosmic (futuristic) theology. To do this, allow me to clarify some etymological points to better understand where different thoughts on salvation come from, both within and outside of Israel. There is no doubt that salvation as a theological soteriological doctrine took a more complete form with the thoughts of the Apostle Paul and the writers of the rest of the New Testament. This kind of Pauline doctrine, such as Christian salvation only through the sacrifice of Jesus of Nazareth and faith in Him, is one of the reasons—though not the complete theme—why many scholars attribute the paternity of Christianity to the Apostle Paul. But with this said, since it is relevant to the topic, we ask ourselves how Jesus forgave sins and saved a few before His death. The only way to receive forgiveness and salvation according to Paul would be through the sacrifice; so then, unless Jesus was talking about another kind of salvation, and this is the purpose of this part of the chapter: how did Jesus view salvation? It is worth saying that for many, Paul is neither the father nor the inventor of Christianity; this is also questioned and doubted by many conservative scholars.

Now, we know that the thought of salvation in the culture and people of Israel from ancient times was not seen as a cosmic salvation, or a form that had to do with the afterlife, or even with any existing paradise. In Israel, at first, it was believed that everyone who died met their end; after death, there was nothing more. The word Sheol was used, meaning the place below or the depths of the earth where all the dead went. It was not thought that people went to heaven after their death. Over time, the Israelite tribes began to adopt the thought of other nations, most likely from the Egyptians themselves, who mummified and buried their pharaohs with all their belongings, even with food, so that they could have everything in their next life. Each nation had a way of seeing and believing in a type of salvation in another life. In the Torah of Moses, the primary interest is not a spiritual or cosmic salvation from another world; salvation is earthly, from one way of life to another, or from complete freedom from slavery. Later, with the passage of time in Canaan, the children of Israel began to bury their relatives and family members with the thought that someday in another life they would live together again in tribes or families. This is the reason why Joseph asked his brothers not to leave his bones in Egypt, as he wanted to be buried with his people in Canaan.

In any case, with the arrival of the early intertestamental period in Israel, with the advancement and evolution of knowledge among scholarly Jews, Greek Jews, and the influence itself by the Greeks with their different philosophical schools, we see the beginning of the tripartite thought of man, composed of Soul, Spirit, and Matter. The early Hebrews, Israelites, and Jews did not know this Greek thought regarding the tripartite form of man. For them, life consisted only of matter (flesh) or (body) and the spirit, or breath of life. The term soul had not yet been adopted by the Jews. For them, the term soul had not been used, as it is a Greek word. The Soul ("pneuma" in Greek) was for them the ("Nefesh" in Hebrew). Both words are known as breath, but for the Hebrews/Jews this breath was more literal, as if we were using literal organ words to refer to it, like lungs or the throat through which breath literally comes out. For the Greeks, this soul was not the lung or the throat. The soul came to be like the primary person and the greatest substance in the life of the body. It was neither matter nor literal; it was more centralized in thought, feeling, consciousness, etc., all completely spiritual elements of the soul. For the early Jews, this thought of the Nefesh was more literal, although over time they adopted Greek philosophical thought to give the soul the same spiritual thought that the Greeks did, and also as the seat of emotions and thought. Finally, the increasingly implemented knowledge led them to see life consisting of matter (flesh) or (body), the spirit, or divine breath of life, and the soul (feelings, emotions, etc.).

With this knowledge of the soul within man, the Greeks saw the soul as the pure and true person of man. They saw the flesh as the prison of that soul, and also believed that the soul did not die, because it is spiritual. They believed in a place divided into four parts: Tartarus, Asphodel, Elysium, and the temple of Styx. In the New Testament, we see two of these places used to interpret the destiny of man. This Tartarus is seen as the place of suffering within Hades, another word they used in two ways: Hades as the god of the underworld, and Hades as the place where he kept souls imprisoned. Hence the thought of a patron over the dead. This was the place for the unjust and the evil. To this place, the Jews gave a parallel to the known "Gehenna" within the valley of Hinnom in Israel. During the times of the kings after Solomon, the Jews began a pagan practice of passing through the fire or offering their children in sacrifice to a god called "Moloch." God had rejected this practice and punished the people for these evil acts. Much later, during the first century, this place was used as the dump where all the waste, dry branches, dry sticks, and the town's trash were thrown. They burned everything there, and the fire burned continuously. It is also believed that they threw the dead who could not be buried there for various reasons during the many wars inside and outside Jerusalem. This idea is not a consensus, but it is very plausible among scholars.

In the same way that Jesus, parabolically, making a midrash, uses this Greek thought with the Jewish Gehenna—the place where the fire does not go out—and implements his teachings about perpetual punishment if man does not repent and change his consciousness. During the intertestamental period, Jewish priests, Pharisees, and Hellenized Jews already knew the difference between the different places destined for man's end. For the common Hellenized Jew, there was already a belief in a place of suffering for the unjust and a place of peace or blessing for the just. For the Jews, the thought developed that the children of Abraham would return to his bosom. This was a kind of thought in which they believed that one day the children of Abraham would be resurrected to live with all the patriarchs in the end, especially with Abraham and also with Jacob. But Jesus came to show a completely different and much better salvation.

To conclude this first part, salvation as a futuristic, cosmic place or space, the place that for the Greeks is "Elysium," is the place where the just are taken by the gods to dwell with them in a type of paradise with splendor and glory, ruled by the gods. Of the two ways that Jesus identifies salvation, the latter is quite similar though not the same. The Greek mythologies have passed and died, but the words of Jesus have remained and will remain, because it is written, *"Heaven and earth will pass away, but My words will not pass away."* The salvation of Jesus Christ is real and true; it is felt, and e Doctrinal Salvation: "The Blessed Hope" Theological in Jesus and Paul:

As the Messiah and son of David, Jesus had come to rescue and save what was lost. There were a number of different messiahs in Israel; it came to be that there were about seven different types of messiahs in Israel. At times, there were even two messiahs at the same time in Israel. One could be the governor while the other the priest, as seen in **(Zechariah 4:11-14):** *"Then I said to him, 'What are these two olive trees on the right and the left of the lampstand?' And a second time I answered and said to him, 'What are these two branches of the olive trees, which are beside the two golden pipes from which the golden oil is poured out?' He said to me, 'Do you not know what these are?' I said, 'No, my lord.' Then he said, 'These are the two anointed ones who stand by the Lord of the whole earth.'"* But it is clear that the messianism of Jesus is completely different from the others. It was and is a spiritual messianic kingdom that apocalyptically, at the end of times, will re-enter human history to save His Church and bring judgment to men, governments, and earthly empires that rebelled against Him. We see Jesus and Paul, among others, apocalyptically prophesying this salvation for those who believe in Him, and condemnation for the wicked, for example:

1 Thessalonians 1:10: *"and to wait for His Son from heaven, whom He raised from the dead, Jesus who delivers us from the wrath to come."*

Romans 5:9: *"Much more then, having now been justified by His blood, we shall be saved from wrath through Him."*

1 Thessalonians 5:9-10: *"For God has not destined us for wrath, but for obtaining salvation through our Lord Jesus Christ, who died for us, so that whether we are awake or asleep, we will live together with Him."*

Romans 8:17-25: *"and if children, heirs also, heirs of God and fellow heirs with Christ, if indeed we suffer with Him so that we may also be glorified with Him. For I consider that the sufferings of this present time are not worthy to be compared with the glory that is to be revealed to us. For the anxious longing of the creation waits eagerly for the revealing of the sons of God. For the creation was subjected to futility, not willingly, but because of Him who subjected it, in hope that the creation itself also will be set free from its slavery to corruption into the freedom of the glory of the children of God. For we know that the whole creation groans and suffers the pains of childbirth together until now. And not only this, but also we ourselves, having the first fruits of the Spirit, even we ourselves groan within ourselves, waiting eagerly for our adoption as sons, the redemption of our body. For in hope we have been saved, but hope that is seen is not hope; for who hopes for what he already sees? But if we hope for what we do not see, with perseverance we wait eagerly for it."*

Revelation 1:8: *"'I am the Alpha and the Omega,' says the Lord God, 'who is and who was and who is to come, the Almighty.'"*

Revelation 7:16-17: *"'They will hunger no longer, nor thirst* *anymore; nor will the sun beat down on them, nor any heat; for the Lamb in the center of the throne will be their shepherd, and will guide them to springs of the water of life; and God will wipe every tear from their eyes.'"*

Hebrews 7:25: *"Therefore He is able also to save forever those who draw near to God through Him, since He always lives to make intercession for them."*

Revelation 12:10: *"Then I heard a loud voice in heaven, saying, 'Now the salvation, and the power, and the kingdom of our God and the authority of His Christ have come, for the accuser of our brethren has been thrown down, he who accuses them before our God day and night.'"*

Revelation 19:1: *"After these things I heard something like a loud voice of a great multitude in heaven, saying, 'Hallelujah! Salvation and glory and power belong to our God.'"*

Revelation 22:12: *"'Behold, I am coming quickly, and My reward is with Me, to render to every man according to what he has done.'"*

Luke 12:43-44: *"'Blessed is that slave whom his master finds so doing when he comes. Truly I say to you that he will put him in charge of all his possessions.'"*

Luke 21:27: *"'Then they will see the Son of Man coming in a cloud with power and great glory.'"*

Matthew 25:13: *"'Be on the alert then, for you do not know the day nor the hour.'"*

Matthew 24:42-44: *"'Therefore be on the alert, for you do not know which day your Lord is coming. But be sure of this, that if the head of the house had known at what time of the night the thief was coming, he would have been on the alert and would not have allowed his house to be broken into. For this reason, you also must be ready; for the Son of Man is coming at an hour when you do not think He will.'"*

In these few verses, among many, we see the aspect of a coming salvation, a salvation that will manifest futuristically in what is to come. According to these verses, theologically and doctrinally, the Christian community or Christianity is called to see salvation as a later event, an event like the hope that God through Jesus will return to earth to save His people from the system of this world, to a heavenly spiritual kingdom where none of the suffering we see on this earth will have dominion over the children of God. This salvation is the salvation that the Church from the mid-first century after the death of Jesus has maintained as its coming hope. We call this doctrine "The Blessed Hope." Christians in the first century, following the words of Jesus such as, "I go, but I will come back to take you, so that where I am, you may also be," or "In my Father's house are many mansions, I go to prepare a place for you," or "Behold, I am coming quickly," manifested an urgent longing for Him in the heart of their community. The salvation they expected and wanted was the return of Jesus for them. Finally, this kind of salvation by Jesus in Pauline theology and the other apostles is seen related to and manifested through the death and resurrection of Jesus Christ.

Mark 1:15; *saying, "The time is fulfilled, and the kingdom of God is at hand. Repent, and believe in the gospel."*

Mark 10:42-45; *But Jesus called them to Himself and said to them, "You know that those who are considered rulers over the Gentiles lord it over them, and their great ones exercise authority over them. Yet it shall not be so among you; but whoever desires to become great among you shall be your servant. And whoever of you desires to be first shall be slave of all. For even the Son of Man did not come to be served, but to serve, and to give His life as a ransom for many."*

Matthew 5-7... *The entire Sermon on the Mount.*

Matthew 5:5; *Blessed are the meek, for they shall inherit the earth.*

Matthew 5:44; *But I say to you, love your enemies, bless those who curse you, do good to those who hate you, and pray for those who spitefully use you and persecute you.*

Jesus of Nazareth

Matthew 20:16; *So the last will be first, and the first last. For many are called, but few chosen.*

Luke 1:52-53; *He has put down the mighty from their thrones, and exalted the lowly. He has filled the hungry with good things, and the rich He has sent away empty.*

Luke 4:18-19; *The Spirit of the Lord is upon Me, because He has anointed Me to preach the gospel to the poor; He has sent Me to heal the brokenhearted; to proclaim liberty to the captives and recovery of sight to the blind; to set at liberty those who are oppressed; to proclaim the acceptable year of the Lord.*

Luke 19:9-10; *And Jesus said to him, "Today salvation has come to this house, because he also is a son of Abraham. For the Son of Man has come to seek and to save that which was lost."*

Luke 10:25-37; *And behold, a certain lawyer stood up and tested Him, saying, "Teacher, what shall I do to inherit eternal life?" He said to him, "What is written in the law? What is your reading of it?" So he answered and said, "'You shall love the Lord your God with all your heart, with all your soul, with all your strength, and with all your mind,' and 'your neighbor as yourself.'"* And He said to him, *"You have answered rightly; do this and you will live."* But he, wanting to justify himself, said to Jesus, *"And who is my neighbor?"* Then Jesus answered and said, *"A certain man went down from Jerusalem to Jericho and fell among thieves, who stripped him of his clothing, wounded him, and departed, leaving him half dead. Now by chance a certain priest came down that road. And when he saw him, he passed by on the other side. Likewise, a Levite, when he arrived at the place, came and looked, and passed by on the other side. But a certain Samaritan, as he journeyed, came where he was. And when he saw him, he had compassion. So he went to him and bandaged his wounds, pouring on oil and wine; and he set him on his own animal, brought him to an inn, and took care of him. On the next day, when he departed, he took out two denarii, gave them to the innkeeper, and said to him, 'Take care of him; and whatever more you spend, when I come again, I will repay you.' So* *which of these three do you think was neighbor to him who fell among the thieves?"* And he said, *"He who showed mercy on him." Then Jesus said to him, "Go and do likewise."*

John 3:14; *And as Moses lifted up the serpent in the wilderness, even so must the Son of Man be lifted up.*

John 17:3; *And this is eternal life, that they may know You, the only true God, and Jesus Christ whom You have sent.*

In all these biblical quotes, we see an immediate, instantaneous salvation, not a hope for the future. Jesus gave all who believed in Him a new life, a new consciousness, new from the moment they received Him. When the Pharisee came to see Jesus, Jesus told him that to see the kingdom, it was necessary to be born again. Jesus was not talking about a kingdom that would come; Jesus was talking about a kingdom that had already come and was present in front of Nicodemus. Jesus, as the kingdom of God among His people, had come to turn the heart of man back to God and for them to truly know Him. This is true salvation. According to this perspective, salvation is received immediately upon knowing and confessing Jesus. It is not a salvation that is only hoped for to enter eternal life; eternal life begins the very moment we have an encounter with Jesus, as each one had in the synoptic Gospels.

For the woman with the issue of blood, her salvation was her complete healing. She knew that if she touched Jesus, she would receive salvation from Him. Some say there was a mistake in writing the term *"I will be saved"* instead of *"I will be healed."* There was no mistake. This woman's perception after having spent everything on doctors and not being saved placed her in a short time of waiting for her death. The blood represented life, and only through Jesus could she be "saved." She achieved this salvation by touching Jesus. After this woman touched Jesus, He said to her, "Woman, your faith has saved you; go in peace."

To Zacchaeus, after experiencing a life transformation—he was a tax collector and said that if he had cheated anyone out of anything, he would pay back four times the amount—after these words, Jesus

Jesus of Nazareth

declared in front of everyone in Zacchaeus's house, *"Today salvation has come to this house."*

Receiving the forgiveness of sins through Jesus was another way of receiving salvation from Him. To the paralytic, He said, *"Son, your sins are forgiven."* Why would Jesus forgive someone's sins if not to give them salvation? We also see the same instantaneous salvation given by Jesus to the thief on His right side, even while they were still alive when He said, "Today you will be with me in paradise." It is true that salvation here had to do with paradise, but Jesus was giving it to him from that moment on the cross.

This salvation that Jesus offers us at the moment we receive Him is a gift from God. It is the transformation of life and consciousness. It is the salvation from ourselves. Without God, man destroys himself. Without God, he has no way of overcoming himself and the sin that dominates him. It is only through the salvation given by Jesus, which is received instantly when we receive Him. Now, with this salvation, we live in the love of God. We enjoy life in Christ, live according to His righteousness, and seek first His kingdom.

In the Sermon on the Mount, Jesus shows us the beatitudes of this salvation, and it is reflected in those who show mercy, who forgive, who pray for their neighbor and also for their enemies, who overcome evil with good, who mourn in God, who depend on God, who act meekly, who live with pure hearts, who are peacemakers. All these attributes are granted to those who receive salvation through Jesus. All these characteristics and personalities are not to be lived and kept to practice in heaven when Jesus comes. These are the characteristics that salvation offers to all who receive it, and they are to be manifested now, already. We were saved, we are saved, and we will be saved.

In conclusion, it is important to understand well that salvation is not just an act of hope for Jesus to come for us to receive eternal life as many think. Salvation is the metanoia of life, and the same eternal life begins on earth from the moment we confess Jesus as our King and Savior, accepting His death and also His resurrection.

Alexander Frias

JESUS AND DEATH
Part 3

Revelation 1:18;

"I am the Living One; I was dead, and now look, I am alive for ever and ever! And I hold the keys of death and Hades."

In Judaism, death is an inevitable part of life. Just as we are born, we must also die. The psalmist tells us in (Psalm 89:49), *"What man can live and not see death, or save himself from the power of the grave?"* Selah. Throughout the various reforms of Judaism as a Hebrew culture and practiced religion, the perception and view on death have undergone different changes in thought. In the book of Exodus, we see that death, at the end of the plagues, is seen as the angel of death, who is ordered or directed by Yahweh Himself. For Paul in the New Testament, in his first letter to the Corinthians, he calls death the last enemy. For Paul, death is seen as an enemy of God and of man himself. This thought might have been entirely Greek or the way the Greeks in Corinth viewed death. For the Greeks in their mythology, the personified god of death was known as "Thanatos." We do not know if when Paul describes death as an enemy, he had this Greek god in mind, which would make sense to call him an enemy since the gods were considered pagan and antagonistic enemies of God by Christians. For the Jews, God had no opponent because He was and is the only God that exists. The thought of many gods was more seen and understood by the polytheistic Gentiles. The Jewish people went through different stages, from their henotheism to reaching their monotheism.

As we showed in the previous part about salvation, death was also seen somewhat differently among all the nations present during the time and before the children of Israel entered Canaan. One thing they all had in common was what the Hebrews call "Sheol." This was another word for the lower, subterranean part of the earth. From there, the afterlife began, depending on the different thoughts in all the nations. Other nations such as the Sumerians, Egyptians, Babylonians, Assyrians, and Persians had much parallelism, though few differences concerning death. Now, I believe that for those who are in Christ, death is not seen as an enemy but rather as a vehicle or transition to reach the very presence of life in Christ. But if we are outside of Christ, then I believe that death acts as an enemy of God because it keeps us away from Jesus Christ. In any case, we cannot ignore death, as the writer of (Hebrews 9:27) says, *"Just as people are destined to die once, and after that to face judgment."*

For Jesus, death was not a character, a god, nor an angel. It might have been seen as an enemy of men, which ruled over them from Adam to Moses. What we are sure of is that after Jesus resurrected, we see that in His words in Revelation are quite clear when He says, *"I am the Living One; I was dead, and now look, I am alive for ever and ever! And I hold the keys of death and Hades."* Men knew that there was no empire or emperor who could control or dominate death; it took whoever it wanted whenever it wanted. Jesus had decided to enter into it, being the life of men, He died, but with the purpose of rescuing and redeeming man so that he would not remain in it. Since all who were overcome by it remained under its power and control. Death separated man from his Creator, but once Jesus died, on the third day, He resurrected and rose after having died. No one had defeated death, or at least appeared alive before so many people after having died. Jesus had risen from the dead as He had said previously, defeating it and taking away its power over men. Now death has no dominion over those who believe in Jesus, as it is appointed for them to die once. The purpose of death was not to become what it is today for the children of God, a gateway to the entrance of heavenly dwellings. The power of death consisted in holding men so that they would remain in condemnation and complete eternal separation from God. This is what the Bible calls *"The second death."*

Death in the Bible also contains three different forms or conditions of manifestation in men. There is what is known as the first death, the second death, and the third death. The Bible does not call it the first or third, but the second does appear. We have categorized the first as the spiritual death or the dryness that man feels when he transgresses God's law in his life, like a tree that dries up, and while silent, his bones grow old. The third is the physical death which every man has to pass through. The second, as we have said, is the eternal separation between the soul of man and his Creator, known as perpetual condemnation and suffering. Jesus saw this death as the guilty one that separated God from man and His creation and had resolved to confront it at all costs, putting His life in atonement for humanity.

Death today still exists only on earth and with some power over men who are not in Christ. For those who are in Christ, dying in Christ is gain because the hope is to be absent from this body to be present in a spiritual body before Christ. But for those who are not in Christ, death still dominates them and keeps them separated from God.

In conclusion for this part, one thing we declare against death and its power over the world is what it says in **(Revelation 20:13-14),** *"The sea gave up the dead that were in it, and death and Hades gave up the dead that were in them, and each person was judged according to what they had done. Then death and Hades were thrown into the lake of fire. The lake of fire is the second death."* Death will end and cease to exist. It will have to release and return all its dead in resurrection, both evil and good. All will appear before the throne of God for judgment, and then death and Hades themselves will be thrown into the lake of fire. This is the second death.

This terminology represents two things. First, death and Hades will both be consumed by God, the Creator of all things, and will also cease to exist outside of God's presence and separation. The writer refers not so much to God's presence because neither death nor Hades is near God, nor do they have power over Him. What the writer is telling us is that as God's children and people, concerning men, death and Hades as a temporary place for the dead will no longer exist because both will be destroyed and disappear once and for all. Jesus has already conquered death, and today He lives to give

Jesus of Nazareth

life and life abundantly to all who come to Him and believe in Him. Death has no and will not have dominion over the children of God.

Alexander Frias

JESUS AND HELL
Part 4

Matthew 8:12:

"But the subjects of the kingdom will be thrown outside, into the darkness, where there will be weeping and gnashing of teeth."

It has come to be believed that Jesus spoke about hell (Gehenna or Hades) as a place of punishment or condemnation more than any other figure in the Bible. The Great Encyclopedia Dictionary of the Bible by Alfonso Ropero tells us that the word Hell "from below" in Hebrew is the same term as Sheol, and in Greek, the same word as Hades. At one time, before the introduction of Hellenistic Greek influence, it was believed that all the dead went to hell or Sheol. Very little was known or understood about the afterlife or a place of condemnation. However, for the Egyptians, they believed in a kind or class of hell or the afterlife after death. It was not exactly the same as what we see in Christianity, but there was a belief in a place where all human beings go after this life.

Jesus, as a wise rabbi, but also in His deity as the Son of God, divinely with a completely unique style, revealed many of the mysteries that were hidden from man and that no one had ever shown or revealed. For this reason, when people saw Him casting out demons or unclean spirits from individuals, they marveled, saying, *"What is this? A new teaching—and with authority! He even gives orders to impure spirits and they obey him."* This kind of authority was unmatched by anyone in the entire Bible and the history of Israel. The authority that King Solomon traditionally is thought to have had could not compare to the level of authority that Jesus displayed. Truly, we have to say as Nicodemus did, "We know that you have come from God because no one could perform the signs you are doing if God were not with him." To this, we will add, who else can reveal the hidden things of God and the afterlife if not the One who came from God, the divine Word incarnate among men, Jesus of Nazareth. Jesus came to reveal the greatest mysteries of life and man in all humanity.

"The Duat" was the underworld in Egyptian mythology, the place where the judgment of Osiris took place. There, the dead wandered, navigating among evil beings and dangers, as described in the Egyptian Book of the Dead. Each human's heart was placed on a scale, and if it was found out of balance in justice, the person was taken to the Duat (hell). To learn more, you can read the traditional Egyptian book "The Book of the Dead," which provides a broader idea of the kind of hell for the Egyptians. In any case, this thought is quite ancient. The other Mesopotamian nations had the term "Kigallu" or "Arallu," which means the great land or the kingdom of the dead, as Ropero tells us in his dictionary.

With the arrival of the Greeks, their mythology and philosophy learned in ancient Greece and Egypt, they knew this underground world as Hades. For them, it was a place of darkness and hidden where the humans who went there had consciousness but lived in sadness and suffering. This would become the reformed idea from Sheol to Hades and then to Gehenna (Hell), which the Jews, during the entire period of Hellenization, adopted and used throughout the intertestamental period until the New Testament was translated into Latin when we see the word hell. Some scholars tell us that it is very likely that before or with the exodus of the Jews from Babylon and the Persians, they may have had a limited belief or adopted the belief that after death, all were united as a family to live together. The Jews had the hope of reuniting with their fathers and especially with their patriarchs. It is believed that for this reason, whenever a patriarch or a king died, they buried them alongside their children. In the case of Joseph, he requested that his bones be taken to the land of Canaan, where he would be with all his people. Another example is seen with Naboth in the Old Testament; he had received a vineyard where his parents' remains were, and it was customary for the family and nearby graves to remain together so that when they awoke, they could be united in the bosom of Abraham. This thought originated and emerged during the Second Temple era in Jerusalem by the Jew

Simon I the Just and remained as the cultural religious hope in Judaism, believing that all would be sharing and eating together.

We see Jesus in the Gospel of Matthew use a similar expression when He says, *"I say to you that many will come from the east and the west and will take their places at the feast with Abraham, Isaac, and Jacob in the kingdom of heaven."* It is true that Jesus' thought about heaven, paradise, or the place of glory for the children of God might have been entirely Jewish. But in the Gospels, being written in Greek during a time when Greek thought dominated, the general purpose was to arise from Greek thought and ideas. With the arrival of the Greeks, they would have a broader concept of the underworld (hell). The term Sheol would then have a change in thought, but as we said previously, nothing or almost nothing was known about the afterlife.

Among all the other rabbis and teachers, before and after, Jesus far surpassed them all in revealing what hell was. We do not find an earlier rabbi or teacher who can compare in teaching like Jesus. The most respected Jewish teachers have contributed nothing as much as Jesus of Nazareth did about condemnation after human death. The only theologian poets who wrote during the medieval era wrote poetically added imaginary visions of hell but still inspired by the foundation laid by Jesus Himself.

Jesus not only revealed the operation or order of the spheres (kingdom) of darkness, Jesus revealed many things among which are the kingdom of God, salvation, condemnation, but most importantly of all things He came to reveal the only eternal God and Father of lights, and He did so better and more superior than all His contemporaries, before and after. No one had revealed God like Jesus; this mystery is unique to Jesus of Nazareth. While men had different ancient concepts for the spiritual place of condemnation "Hell" as seen in the Gospels by Jesus, Jesus indeed was among the teachers and prophets who spoke the most about the place of condemnation where the unjust and those who do not seize God's salvation for mankind will end up. This place is described in the Gospels as a place of suffering, separation, weeping, and gnashing of teeth. The fire as a consuming heat is present, representing the continual ardor that increasingly consumes a person inwardly towards evil. This perspective of fire present in places of condemnation is seen in early Greek mythological thought. In Jewish intertestamental thought, we already see in some deuterocanonical books the belief in a hell as a place with unquenchable fire and flames; in others, it is described as a volcano, intensely hot, but also with a freezing kind of cold that burns the skin when exposed to ice. This idea is seen in the Book of Enoch, a book widely used and created by Jews during the intertestamental era. Therefore, the idea of a place of punishment or condemnation represented by fire is not an idea or creation of Jesus as a teacher. Jesus, although quite original in all His teachings and parables, never taught by changing the thought or worldview of the time. Jesus knew He had not come to change the words, cultures, or the way many things were seen or believed; His greatest purpose and interest were for people to repent and receive a new and clean conscience towards God, to turn back to God, to make a complete turn towards the Creator. For this reason, we see Jesus regarding hell or a place of condemnation using earthly elements such as fire, which was used by many Jewish writers to compare the consummation of the unjust and the wicked. Before Jesus, we see John the Baptist himself using fire as the place where trees that do not bear good fruit will be thrown; trees are a representation of humans or human beings who are called to bear fruits of righteousness in life before others. John, as a prophet of the old covenant, uses fire as a representation of the consummation and the burning of sin in the life of a person who lives separated from God by attitude and a constant life given over to sin. Just as the prophet Elijah asked God to send down fire so that the sacrifice's water would be consumed, and also on several occasions asked for fire to consume some defiant men who were servants of the evil king Ahab, in the same style, John with his authority as a prophet is showing both earthly and eschatologically the punishment of God's wrath to all men who do not take advantage of repenting their sins and receive forgiveness through the sacrifice of the Lamb of God, Jesus of Nazareth. To Jesus, hell or condemnation is that place where man is in complete darkness, separated from God, a place where darkness is multiplied for man; there man feels lost, has no dominion, peace, joy, hope, and is also taken, influenced, and even controlled by another, in this case, unclean spirits or the devil himself, the adversary. In this hellish state in which man finds himself, for Jesus, man is completely bound, enslaved by the power of sin and also by the devil. For this reason, He said, I have come to undo all the works of the devil, but He also said to men, I have come that they may have life and have it abundantly. Some have assumed that this work of the devil to which He referred was the world system of Rome; personally, I believe that Jesus was referring to something completely spiritual, stronger, and greater than the Roman Empire. Jesus was referring exactly to the spiritual enemy of humanity, to Satan, the evil one, a spiritual being in whom no righteousness dwells. Also, for Jesus, the man who finds himself in hell or in the same state is one who is in complete misery without hope. According to Jesus, hell is the place for all who break God's law and justice, but it is also the place that is prepared and reserved for the devil and his fallen angels. In Mark, Jesus continually mentions hell as the place where the fire is not quenched, and then makes a comparison with man as the sacrifice upon which salt is thrown before being sacrificed and cooked; in this way, suffering is clearly shown as the consummation that convicts man in his evil, his guilt, his shame, his anger, his hatred, anger, and all the feelings that corrupt and destroy man. There is a high probability, and it is most likely that Jesus never used the exact word "Hell" since it comes from Latin; we know that Jesus knew all things as Peter says at the end of John's gospel, but the truth is that apart from theology we do not know if Jesus historically spoke Latin since this was the language mostly used by the Romans, this is still in discussion among scholars, because if it is true, we see Jesus in the Gospels speaking with a centurion, then with a Syrophoenician woman, with some Greeks who come to consult Him, and in His last days with Pilate, All these people generally had their own dialect or language, we do not know if each of these people spoke Aramaic so that they could understand each other since Aramaic was Jesus' primary language, the Gospels do not tell us if on occasion Jesus had interpreters for these conversations, the Gospels show Jesus directly speaking with each of them, for this reason it has been thought that Jesus could have known and spoken at least a little of each of these languages, we have no evidence data to show that Jesus knew how to speak in all these languages, but we do not have evidence that shows otherwise, we know that Jesus was quite intelligent, and wise, this is the reason why a great sum of scholars believe that Jesus instead of "Hell" could have better used the word "*Gehenna.*"

Aramean was the official language of the Jews, but there were many Jews in all parts of the land of Israel and other cities outside Israel where Jesus also visited at some point in His ministry. Whether Jesus used the word "inferno" (Hell) or not, two things are clear: first, that the word did not change the perception and real concession of a place of condemnation for transgressors and rebels against God's law, and even the word Gehenna, if it referred to a terrestrial place present in the valley of Hinnom, Jesus did not literally refer to this place where the body is only burned and consumed for a moment until it disappears and turns to dust. He used it as a parabolic springboard to show the truth of His message and how the kingdom of God operates for the righteous and also for the disobedient. Whether it was the word "Hell" or "Gehenna," Jesus used it with reference to the reality of the perdition, separation, and eternal condemnation of wicked wrongdoers.

To conclude this part, I cannot close without adding the following: among the more than twenty centuries of Christianity's existence, this place of condemnation known as Hell religiously underwent changes in thought, especially during the late medieval era between the 13th and 14th centuries before the Protestant Reformation. With Western philosophy and poetic literature, Hell began to be narrated and written about to such a mythological and imaginary extent that it convinced Christianity of its time that a whole world was known about what happened there and who was in Hell, as seen in theaters and movies where it was thought that Satan has a throne in Hell and is the leader of the place, and the demons or fallen angels are the leaders there. It has even been thought that all those who have died in their sin are burning alive in fire there, from Korah's family to Judas Iscariot. Medievally, it was believed that the unjust would also be there alive, burning in flames as seen in movies; this idea and image are completely erroneous and anti-biblical. The Bible clearly shows that no one can enter that place without first getting a body in resurrection, because there will be a resurrection for both the good and the bad, and there they will be thrown into eternal punishment, but so far everyone rests until their due moment.

This thought was taken by some based on the parable of the "rich man (*Epulon*) and the poor beggar Lazarus" by Jesus in Luke 16:19-31, "It happened that the beggar died, and was carried by the angels into Abraham's bosom; and the rich man also died, and was buried. And in Hades he lifted up his eyes, being in torment, and saw Abraham far away and Lazarus in his bosom. And he cried out and said, 'Father Abraham, have mercy on me, and send Lazarus so that he may dip the tip of his finger in water and cool off my tongue, for I am in agony in this flame, and so on." This parable unfortunately was taken literally by many who thought that Jesus was speaking about a current historical event, which we know was not Jesus' primary intention. According to scholars, historians, and biblical students, the story of the rich man and Lazarus was considered a re-elaboration of a very ancient tale of Egyptian origin. The details of this story can be read in F. L. Griffith, Stories of the High Priest of Memphis [Oxford: Clarendon, 1900] 42–43, Gressmann held that the Egyptian legend or story was introduced into Judaism by means of Alexandrian Jews crystallizing into the tale of the rich publican "Bar Ma'yan" (j Ḥagiga 77d [2:2]). In the text of the Talmud, the story appears not exactly the same but similar; it is not known if it was grafted there as a tradition before Christ, or if it was reworked by the Talmudic Jews. In any case, if we see the Egyptian influence of the story, which is believed to have been reinterpreted by the Babylonians and subsequently until it was crystallized as part of thought in Judaism, and then among the rabbis as Jesus himself. Jesus as a teacher took it to bring a teaching to his people of how the

Jesus of Nazareth

life of those who have their eyes set only on all the wealth of the earth will end up, and in those who live unjustly ignoring the poor and the needy. Jesus never preached this parable as a historical fact, although he did teach it as an absolute truth; personally, I believe that he preached it for the purpose of listeners avoiding an end like that of the condemned rich man. The percentage of rich people in Israel Jews was a minority, and the vast majority of the rich people in the New Testament were tax collectors, Sadducees, and Roman leaders, but very few Jews could be rich, especially with the large taxes imposed on them by the Romans. Bruce Chilton shares with us in his book "*Rabbi Jesus*" an important fact: in Galilee, the Jews did not even use coins or money much among themselves; this was kept for when they went to the temple or to roman arch shops; the galileans in Galilee used to exchange needs, for example if someone needed wheat or grain they would exchange it for another's wine or salt and so on among the poorest to sustain themselves. Jews in general were poor, and almost all of them were indebted to the romans, which is why Jesus dedicated a significant part of His life to preaching about the future hope for the poor and indebted. Jesus wanted the poor to maintain their hope in God even with little, knowing that their end would be much better, as we also see later in the words of Paul. I believe that any Jew familiar with the parabolic style of the rabbis would clearly understand the parable of the rich man (Epulon) and Lazarus. For those who have used this parable to believe in a current state of condemnation where those who die without Christ burn alive in Hell, it's because they have not understood the context and its cultural and historical purpose. I would dare to say that it is a poor and fatally distorted theology to use this parable to describe the current state of those who are still asleep awaiting resurrection, as mentioned from Daniel to Jesus, when they will be judged by God to receive their punishment and condemnation.

Both Jesus and Daniel clearly understood that no one can go to Hell or a place of condemnation without first being resurrected. We see this in the following verses: Daniel 12:2, *"Many of those who sleep in the dust of the earth shall awake, some to everlasting life, and some to shame and everlasting contempt." And John 5:29, "And come out, those who have done good to the resurrection of life, and those who have done evil to the resurrection of judgment."* It is true that Hell will be the punishment and place for transgressors and the unjust, but all in due order and time, as the author of life, Jesus, said.

Part of the great misunderstanding of these images of Hell adopted by many modern Christians can be traced to Dante Alighieri's famous work, "*The Divine Comedy*," one of the ornamental works of transition from medieval to Renaissance thought and a pinnacle of world literature. Dante, an Italian Christian, interpreted a wide range of Hell, so much so that to this day much of Dante's thinking has influenced the thoughts and sermons of many Christians and preachers. For serious readers and scholars, listening to many modern Christian sermons about Hell quickly reveals the similarity to Dante's thoughts that have permeated Christian tradition over time. Unfortunately, much of the thought on Hell in Christianity has become mixed with medieval poetic thinking. However, it is worth noting that Dante's imaginative and poetic Hell is not what we read and see in the New Testament, and even less so in the words of Jesus of Nazareth. Therefore, the call and task are to carefully study the Scriptures again to teach and preach properly using the word of God as it is written, without adding or subtracting from it. Jesus taught and spoke about Hell more than anyone else, but He did so with the purpose that no one should have to live in that state and none should spend eternity there. He came so that we may have life and have it abundantly.

JESUS AND THE CHURCH
Part 1

Matthew 16:18

"And I tell you that you are Peter, and on this rock I will build 'my church', and the gates of Hades will not overcome it."

The word "Church" from the Greek "Ekklesia" and Latin "Ecclesia" generally refers to the assembly of people gathered. In current usage, the word can also denote the place, sanctuary, or temple where the congregation gathers for worship of God. Etymologically, if we were to go back to the original and etymological sense of the Greek word Ekklesia in Hebrew, it would be "Qahal." This word is used in reference to a community, congregation, assembly, people, or body of united persons. Some examples are as follows:

Genesis 28:3;

Genesis 49:6.

Etymologically, the word qahal was used to refer to the people of the sons of Israel gathered in the wilderness. The translation of the Hebrew word qahal to Ekklesia by the Septuagint or LXX, as well known, translated the Hebrew word qahal to Ekklesia using it some 100 times to refer to the "Church of God", from where the Latin takes the same word Ecclesia which today in Spanish is called "Church." Some scholars think that Jesus never had the idea and neither did he refer to the size or how big His church would be today, each community had its own rabbi or teacher, some had few students and others had more, in the case of Jesus it is completely different, what we see in Jesus some call a hyperbole, others say that the evangelists wrote to show an innumerable amount, and it is that from the beginning of Jesus' public ministry, we see that from early on thousands of people followed him, this idea for many scholars and historians is not very credible, since it is thought to be like this it would awaken the wrath of the Roman empire too quickly. From the days of the Jewish empire with Judas the Maccabee who had a number of followers openly in rebellion against the Seleucids, later succeeding a few making him pass for chosen (Messiah) of God as Gamaliel tells us in the N.T by saying; "Some time ago, Theudas appeared, claiming to be somebody, and about four hundred men rallied to him. He was killed, all his followers were dispersed, and it all came to nothing. After him, Judas the Galilean appeared in the days of the census and led a band of people in revolt. He too was killed, and all his followers were scattered."

Matthew 26:13;

Jesus said, "Truly I tell you, wherever this gospel is preached throughout the world, what she has done will also be told, in memory of her."

Matthew 28:19;

Therefore, go and make disciples of all nations, baptizing them in the name of the Father and of the Son and of the Holy Spirit,

Luke 10:1;

After this the Lord appointed seventy-two others and sent them two by two ahead of him to every town and place where he was about to go.

In these and many other verses, we see Jesus with a strong desire for his community and the kingdom of God with his gospel to reach the entire world. Some may say that the whole world was not known, but it is quite clear that by the 4th century BC, Alexander the Great and the Greeks knew from Portugal to India, and the Romans knew all of Asia. Therefore, Jesus must have had considerable knowledge of the world like everyone else in the first century of our era. Sometimes we confuse Christianity with the Church of Jesus Christ. I emphasize briefly on this matter because it is not the same to talk about the Church or community of Jesus Christ and to talk about Christianity. One thing is Christianity, and another thing is the Church of Jesus Christ. The Church of Jesus Christ has no denomination and is not a religion either. Christianity is the religion or the well-known concept of the formal system composed and created by the early apostolic fathers to separate true orthodox followers of Jesus in the traditions of the apostles against traditionalist Judaizing Jews and against all other sects or groups of heterodox Christianism that were formed from the 2nd century onwards. The fathers used the name given to the early followers of Jesus in Antioch, "Christians," to call the system or formation of the universal unity "Christianity." Currently, globally, Christianity is the largest religion with the most believing followers. This term is used for every believer who believes in Jesus as the Savior who died as a sacrifice to forgive their sins, then rose again, but who will return a second time to save his people. These are among many other beliefs of the general Christian, but to speak of the Church of Jesus Christ is much broader than speaking of the Christian or Christianity. The Church of Jesus Christ is incalculable, and there is no statistic or earthly measure that can measure it because only the same Head and Foundation, which is Christ, is the only one who knows and knows how far it extends. With that said, we conclude this part by mentioning the following: Jesus, before leaving after having risen and appearing to the disciples while they were all terrified and filled with fear, said to them, "Peace I leave with you; my peace I give you... And surely I am with you always, to the very end of the age." Jesus is the owner of the Church. By the way, He knew He would raise a powerful Church all over the world and would be with her and in her forever, as He has remained to this day for more than 2000 years.

Alexander Frias

JESUS AND THE RESURRECTION
Part 2

Luke 24:6-7

He is not here, but has risen. Remember how he told you, while he was still in Galilee, that the Son of Man must be delivered into the hands of sinful men and be crucified and on the third day rise.

A small written work would not be sufficient to discuss the resurrection of the Lord Jesus Christ; therefore, in this part, we will focus on two distinct purposes regarding Jesus and the resurrection. The first purpose or theme about Jesus and the resurrection that we will address is to try to interpret how the thought or doctrine of the resurrection came to Jesus, how Jesus knew that he was the resurrection, and what the resurrection meant for Jesus himself. The second point we want to touch on is what the resurrection meant or how important it was for Jesus, his apostles, and his followers; what did the resurrection of Jesus of Nazareth achieve for the history of humanity before and after.

The Origins of Resurrection in Israel:

To begin with, the word "resurrection" is the same term used in Latin as "resurrectio," which comes from the Greek "Anastasis" and the Hebrew "TejiatHaMetim," meaning to rise, stand up, revive, be born again, ascend from below, and refers to the action of coming back to life or acquiring a new being or new life after death. Etymologically, among the Hebrew people who later became the nation or people of the Jews, the idea of resurrection is somewhat confusing and progressed over time. What we mean by this is that initially, in the theological origin of the Hebrew people, there was no belief or thought of a resurrection or a kind of life after death in paradise or heaven. Orthodox Jews know that in the Torah, traditionally attributed to Moses as its author, there is no promise of resurrection or life after death. It is not so important to go back 400 years before Moses to Abraham and the patriarchs, trying to find a resurrection when not even in Moses and the Torah is such a thing found. The revelation of the doctrine of resurrection was completely progressive among the children of Israel in the Old Testament. As previously shown, the idea of life after death is quite obscure and very limited in the thought of the Israelites or the children of Israel. For them, death was not an enemy or something bad; on the contrary, in old age, death was seen as the fulfillment of the joy of the long life that God had given them on earth. They saw death as part of life itself. The idea of a kind of salvation was entirely earthly, and life, pleasure, and enjoyment in peace that the nation could have from all its enemies on earth. We see in Genesis a number of graves with the expectation of reuniting with their fathers and the people as a family, as we have said.

One clarification I want to make for a better understanding of the progressive evolution of thought regarding resurrection among the Jews is as follows. Academically and historically, it is believed that King David lived during the 10th century BC onwards. We have a series of psalms that express in one sense life after death dedicated to David, which traditionally are believed and attributed to him as the author and writer. This thought is highly debated and not widely accepted by historians and academic scholars; they suggest that many of these psalms were attributed to David but were actually composed by scribes or priests in Babylon to serve as examples for the Jewish people. In any case, if we maintain the theological thought and view David as the author of the psalms where he frequently mentions "Sheol," he calls on his God using an anachronistic word that his soul not remain in Sheol forever, recognizing Sheol as the place where the dead go and cannot return. In the Psalmist's thought, the dead are completely separated from the living. In Job, we also see the term Sheol used to refer to the dead who have descended below and cannot rise. It is also very important to understand that in ancient Hebrew anthropology, there was no concept of the soul in human beings; they saw living humans as carnal through the spirit of Yahweh breathed into life. For them, human life consisted only of body and spirit. For this reason, when a person stopped breathing, they thought the spirit or breath within the person had left the dead body and returned to God. The tripartite thought of body, soul, and spirit emerged with the arrival of the Greeks, and what they believed was adopted by the Jews throughout the Greek Hellenistic period. In ancient Hebrew thought regarding Sheol, this was not a place of complete suffering as later seen in the New Testament; Sheol was simply where the dead were like shadows of what they once were, fulfilling the final destiny of the end of life in the flesh. This was more or less the thought during ancient Hebrew times and during the era of the monarchy of Israel and the Judeans. With the arrival of the prophets, a more expansive vision of the doctrine of resurrection also gradually emerged. The earliest events of the dead being raised are seen during the reign of the first king of Israel, Saul, who lived in the 10th century BC, and later with the northern prophets Elijah and Elisha, who lived in the 9th century BC. It is worth mentioning that these events of raising the dead do not actually categorize as resurrection; a better term for these miracles would be revival or resuscitation, as they were awakened by another and not by themselves. These miracles do not fall under resurrection since those revived were merely brought back once more to Sheol, the place of the dead. In the case of Saul, Samuel's appearance is more an illusion or magical aspect than a resurrection, as the image of the prophet Samuel only appears momentarily and then disappears. In any case, these miracles teach us a very important point: despite not knowing the place from where they were raised or where they came from, it is evident that there was a belief in the possibility of God's power to bring the dead back to earthly life. Therefore, it can be said that in Israel, the thought of the dead returning to life is very ancient. It is true that we do not have exact dates for the compositions of these books, and many argue that they were composed from ancient traditions long after adopting the idea from other nations. This thought has not been fully substantiated; therefore, personally, I believe that not all the idea or thought of the raising of the dead to life in Israel was adopted from another culture or nation. I believe that the idea of revival or return to life by the prophets in ancient Israel, as seen in the books of Samuel and the Kings, could have existed.

The oldest apocalyptic testimony we have for the doctrine of progressive resurrection is found with the prophet Isaiah in 26:19, where he says, "Your dead shall live; their bodies shall rise. You who dwell in the dust, awake and sing for joy! For your dew is a dew of light, and the earth will give birth to the dead." This verse speaks of resurrection, and we see that God, through the prophet, calls the dead from the dust of the earth. In this sense, the belief in the soul likely did not circulate in Israel yet, as it predates Greek hellenization. However, what's interesting is that in this verse, we see a collective resurrection for many and not just for an individual, as seen in the cases of the mentioned prophets. This would ultimately be the idea of resurrection not only among Jews but also in christianity—a collective resurrection for an entire people, with the exception of the first fruits of resurrection being the Lord Jesus Christ, through whom others will rise.

Here we see the prophet's thought on resurrection: for the prophet, the dead remain as dust in the earth, they do not go to a different place, and there is also no notion of a soul; the earth will return the dead who are buried within it. It is believed that the later chapters of Isaiah (specifically chapters 24-26), for speaking of this kind of resurrection, were inserted during the intertestamental era when the doctrine of resurrection was more developed among the Jews. Not all scholars, especially conservative theologians, agree with this view and believe that Isaiah could indeed have prophetically foreseen the Messianic resurrection doctrine that would occur at the end of times with the coming of the Messiah. Academically, the book of Isaiah is believed to be divided into several sections, with at least three or four different authors contributing to the book. Traditionally and theologically, the composition is attributed solely to the known prophet Isaiah. This book contains pre-exilic portions, portions from the captivity, and also post-exilic portions; this among other reasons is why it is thought that other writers contributed to Isaiah, as the proto (first) Isaiah did not live during the era of the Babylonian captivity.

During the Babylonian captivity, we continue to see the progression of resurrection with the prophet Ezekiel. Not only do we see the restoration of Jerusalem, but in chapter 37, we encounter the apex of Jewish thought regarding a collective resurrection of the people of Israel. For many, this is the beginning or the start of the thought for the doctrine of resurrection among orthodox and traditional Jews, although for many who only believe in the Torah and not in the Tanakh, there is no such thing as resurrection. In a vision, the prophet Ezekiel finds himself in a valley full of extremely dry bones, a multitude enough to form a people. These bones represent the house of Israel, who, after being driven out of Israel and Jerusalem by the Assyrians and Babylonians, dried up spiritually until they died as a people or nation in Babylon. They mourned because they had lost their sacred texts, land, and temple, and now they found themselves far away in a foreign pagan land. It is here that the prophet Ezekiel sees the condition of the people in his vision amidst a conversation with God. God asks him if these dry bones (dead bodies) can live again; the prophet responds to God that he has no idea if they can come back to life. It is then that God commands him to speak to the spirit of the four winds and prophesy to the bones to come to life once more. The biblical text tells us that each bone came together with its bone, and the dead were incorporated into a vast and extreme army. After the prophet had prophesied, God told him to tell the people that He would open their graves, bring them up from their graves, and bring them back to their land, the land of Israel. God said they would know that He is their God when He brings them out of their graves and puts His spirit in them, and they will live and rest in their own land.

It is true that in this textual portion, we can see an apocalyptic foreshadowing of the final resurrection doctrine, but we cannot overlook or narrow the historical purpose of the vision for the revival of the people of Israel in the words of the prophet Ezekiel.

This vision is not entirely the apocalyptic resurrection of the end times or the coming kingdom; rather, it is the resurgence of the people of Israel, especially Judah, who would once again become a nation with land, law, and a temple. The part that theologians use to apply it to the doctrine of the latter times or the fulfillment of the promise in Christ for Israel is when Ezekiel announces that God will put His Spirit in them. Earlier in chapter 36, we see Ezekiel himself proclaim that God would sprinkle clean water on His people to cleanse them from their impurities, give them a new spirit, remove their heart of stone and give them a heart of flesh, and put His Spirit within them, etc. This promise can be applied in various ways, although traditionally, Jewish traditionalists will never accept Acts 2 as its fulfillment. For Christ's apostles, Messianic Jews, and Christians, this promise fulfills all that the prophets, beginning with Isaiah, spoke about regarding Yahweh's Spirit upon His people and the inhabitants of the earth.

In any case, we are advancing, historically seeing the progression of the doctrine of resurrection. First, we saw in the ancient prophets a singular resurrection (reanimation); from Isaiah and now Ezekiel, we see a collective, earthly, and temporary resurrection for an entire people. We have reached the most important point of transition for the doctrine of resurrection; it is here that we will see the thought of resurrection being reformed once again among the Jews, to the thought that we currently hold for this doctrine. The book of the prophet Daniel is the key book for such a transition and reform of the doctrine of resurrection.

Now, this cannot be explained without first clarifying for our readers. Allow me for a moment to untangle the thought regarding Daniel. Firstly, for Jews, Daniel is not a prophet; Daniel is a historian, a figure who existed during the Babylonian captivity and wrote only some chapters of history in Babylon. Jewish tradition believes that Daniel may have written at least the first six chapters of the book, with the rest being added later, most likely by apocalyptic students of Daniel's schools in Babylon. Some think he wrote less, and others believe he wrote nothing, being a figure borrowed from a wise babylonian Danel involved in mesopotamian god stories that the returning Jews adopted, adopting the idea to write a narrative of some of their own stories of the Jewish people in Babylon. Currently, the crucial point for scholars and academic historians is not so much the historical existence of Daniel or whether he was a prophet; the important thing is the historical date of the writing and composition of the book itself. The Jewish and Christian tradition holds that this book dates to the 6th century BC, but this idea has been largely refuted by scholars who date at least from chapter 6 onwards to the 2nd century BC, nearly 400 years later.

I think we have previously clarified the ideas of scholars as to why they think Daniel was written for the 2nd century BC. In any case, the key chapter of the book of Daniel for the doctrine of eternal resurrection is chapter 12; it is here that we see a complete reform from an earthly to an eternal, spiritual, and entirely apocalyptic resurrection. Daniel 12:2 tells us, "And many of those who sleep in the dust of the earth shall awake, some to everlasting life, and some to shame and everlasting contempt." For Daniel in this case, people are not dead but sleeping; it is the same term that Jesus later used in John for His friend Lazarus, whom, although dead to all, Jesus said was only sleeping.

Up to this point, no one had prophesied a resurrection to eternal life, showing us a progression in intertestamental Jewish doctrinal thought. With this reform in doctrinal thought about resurrection, we will later see a large number of Jewish texts such as 2 Maccabees, the Book of Enoch, and others, all expressing the same idea of a spiritual and eternal resurrection for the righteous. Historically, the beginning of the thought of resurrection to eternal life among the jewish people is attributed to all the jews who died and slept under persecution by Antiochus Epiphanes IV during 167-164 BC. This reward, or what Daniel calls the righteous, would be all those Jews who did not bow down or accept the pagan and impure idolatrous life of Antiochus, preferring instead to suffer death rather than apostatize like many Jews corrupted by pagan Hellenistic idolatry to the god Zeus.

From this intertestamental period onward, with the existence of the sect of the pharisees (Perushim), doctors of the Torah in Israel, the hopeful faith of the Jewish people imposed the belief in resurrection to eternal life as a perpetual belief in mainstream Judaism of the time. The Sadducee priests continued to deny such doctrine, but the hope of resurrection was much more believed and accepted by Jews than the percentage who did not believe. This is why throughout the 1st century AD we see significant confrontations between the Pharisees, Sadducees, and Jesus of Nazareth himself. The sadducees denied eternal resurrection, the Pharisees believed in it but did not fully understand it, yet Jesus of Nazareth understood it fully and had come to manifest it truly, for He is the resurrection and the life. Everyone from Adam onward who slept and sleeps will be raised in resurrection through Him who raised Himself from the dead and now lives at the right hand of the Father, the unique Jesus of Nazareth, the first and the only one to die and rise forever for all eternity.

In the New Testament texts, we find countless individuals who saw Him alive after He had died: first the women who went to His tomb, the two disciples on the road to Emmaus, the gathered apostles, the more than 500 who were still alive during that time, John in his apocalyptic vision, and the apostle of the gentiles, Paul, who until his last day, facing death by the Roman sword, testified of the living and resurrected Christ whom he saw on the road to Damascus. Jesus is the author and fulfillment of the doctrine of resurrection to eternal life; what the prophets prophesied was fulfilled in Jesus. And since it was fulfilled first in Jesus, this indicates that the hope of resurrection for those who sleep in Jesus is not in vain and is not perishable. The dead in Christ, as Paul announces by revelation from Christ Himself, will rise to eternal life.

In this part, we have shared an overview from its beginning to the current thought in christianity regarding the doctrine of resurrection. Now, let's continue in the second part where we will briefly explain the importance that the resurrection of our Lord Jesus Christ manifested and what it meant.

The fulfillments manifested by the resurrection of Jesus:

We had said that the resurrection of Jesus not only remained in the earthly sphere, but rather crossed into the dimension of the spiritual world or sphere. Paul tells us that on the cross of Calvary, through the death and resurrection of Jesus Christ, both death, the devil, and the powers of darkness or the evil one were overcome and destroyed by Jesus himself. What Paul is saying with these words is that the power that death held and also the figure of the devil or Satan in the thinking that both Jews and Greco-Romans feared greatly had been completely nullified by this Messiah Jesus. Now neither death nor Satan and his demons, who were thought to be subject to their master, had their own will or decision-making power; all would be under the dominion and authority of Christ, as originally believed and thought where God absolutely had control over all things, good or bad. With this hope and absolute power that Jesus would give to his followers, Paul would persuade all believers in Jesus to truly understand the power of the resurrection and of the Holy Spirit that would now operate in the children of God over sin, death, and Satan himself. The fear that once existed about the power of death, the slavery of the power of sin, and the power of Satan himself had been rendered powerless over the followers of Christ Jesus since they had now received greater power than all their spiritual adversaries. Death was no longer seen as the end of life; now it was seen as the gateway that would lead them to their Christ. The power of sin now seemed inferior due to the conviction received from the power of the blood shed by Jesus of Nazareth on the cross for them; now they had someone to go to for forgiveness of their sins, and now they saw Satan and his demons as objects of testing on the path to show their God true faithfulness through faith in the only Son of God and almighty Jesus Christ. To conclude this part, I will share a small list of many things fulfilled and manifested by the resurrection of Jesus.

THE RESURRECTION OF JESUS FULFILLED AND MANIFESTED:

- Eternal life (John 11:25-27)
- Power over death (Acts 2:24)
- Healing (Acts 4:10)
- Promises made to David (Acts 13:34)
- Forgiveness of sins (Acts 13:37-38)

Jesus of Nazareth

- His complete authority (Romans 1:4)
- Justification (Romans 4:23-25)
- New life (Romans 6:4, 8-11)
- Union with Him (Romans 6:5-8)
- Bearing fruit in Him (Romans 7:4)
- Giving us life (Romans 8:11)
- Ending the power of the flesh (Romans 8:12-13)
- For a future of glory (Romans 8:18)
- Freeing creation (Romans 8:21-22)
- Adopting us as His children (Romans 8:23)
- Interceding for us (Romans 8:34)
- Fulfilling the Scriptures (1 Corinthians 15:4)
- Fulfilling our faith and preaching (1 Corinthians 15:24-27)
- For our resurrection (1 Corinthians 15:20-23)
- To destroy all powers that have been (1 Corinthians 15:24-27) and much more...
- To save us from ourselves (1 Corinthians 15:32)
- To give us incorruptible bodies (1 Corinthians 15:42-48)
- To clothe us with the new man according to the one who created him (1 Corinthians 15:49)
- To give us a better purpose in life (2 Corinthians 15:15)
- To make us complete in Him (Colossians 2:9-12)

(Partial list borrowed from "Risen" by Steven D. Mathewson)

This is only a small list of many of the things that the resurrection of Jesus of Nazareth manifested. As I mentioned at the beginning of this section, there is no book that can contain all that the power of the resurrection of Jesus of Nazareth fulfilled and manifested. This small list was borrowed from one of the books that I have most cherished in my studies and preachings about the resurrection of Jesus, a highly recommended book for all who are interested in reading about the many things that were changed by the resurrection of Jesus Christ, the book is called "*Risen*" by Steven D. Mathewson.

Alexander Frias

JESUS AND THE HOLY SPIRIT
Part 3

John 14:25-28:

"All this I have spoken while still with you. But the Advocate, the Holy Spirit, whom the Father will send in my name, will teach you all things and will remind you of everything I have said to you. Peace I leave with you; my peace I give you. I do not give to you as the world gives. Do not let your hearts be troubled and do not be afraid."

In this final part, we will focus on Jesus' thoughts about the Holy Spirit as the promise sent by the Father to his followers in the name of Jesus. In the Old Testament, the references and terminologies used to refer to the Holy Spirit, or the Spirit of Yahweh, may have different nuances compared to the New Testament. The title or name given to the Holy Spirit of God is not really a name but rather denotes his essence or completely holy characteristic, which signifies his purity, without contamination, integrity, and supreme holiness above all other created spirits. The title for the Holy Spirit in Hebrew is "RuachHaKo'desh," while in Greek it is "PneumaHagion." This title, which we will use as His name, is more frequently and commonly used in the New Testament than in the Old Testament.

To discuss the personhood of the Holy Spirit would be a topic so vast that time or pages would not suffice to explain. Therefore, we will provide a brief and concise explanation of how the Holy Spirit was viewed in the Old Testament, in order to focus more on Jesus' thoughts about the Holy Spirit in the New Testament.

The Holy Spirit in the Old Testament:

According to the Old Testament, we will show at least in an explanatory list 6 different ways how the Spirit of Yahweh was known and seen. We will share this list so as not to confuse ourselves so much and simplify the different forms in which the

Spirit of Yahweh was manifested.

1. THE WIND OF YAHWEH:

According to the first book of the Pentateuch or the Torah known as the book of creation called Genesis in Greek, from the beginning we see the writer telling us that the Spirit of God was moving over the face of the waters. In the ancient Hebrew-Jewish thought, the Spirit of Elohim was always in union with Elohim Himself, the creator. Although in the Old Testament and New Testament the Holy Spirit is the same Spirit of God, it is given a distinct character or mentioned always as the essence or manifested presence of God in some visible form on earth, but never a separate work from God Himself. Jesus in the book of John tells us that the Father is Spirit, although it sounds like a double Spirit or as if there were two different Spirits, one the Father as a spiritual being and the other the Holy Spirit of the Father; in Christian doctrine or Jewish thought it has never been so, the Father is the invisible glory and the Creator of all things, while His Spirit (person) is the manifested force that operates on earth and men. It is important to understand that in ancient Jewish thought the Father always dwelt on high, or in heaven, while His Spirit was not only in heaven, but He descended continually. Generally, the focus of the writers on the spiritual part of the Father is directed more to the Holy Spirit than to the Father Himself as spirit. This kind of view of the Holy Spirit as the wind of God, or sometimes as the very presence of God manifested through earthly elements like wind, clouds, fire, or in representation of water and even oil, we see in the desert in the form of a column of cloud or fire to guide or direct His people, all representing the same essence of the Father and the Holy Spirit of God. When we read the Torah and the Tanakh, we realize that the writers show God the Father as the one who initially speaks but His Spirit as the one who manifests among them. Many have seen the Holy Spirit as a force or energy that comes from God, but through history and biblical theology we will later realize that for Jesus and the apostles, the Holy Spirit of God is more than an energy or a simple active force of God. Therefore, in this part we see the Holy Spirit as the wind of God that walked upon the face of the waters at the beginning, working in creation, and it was believed that this same wind was what God breathed into man. I do not entirely believe that this breath, as some suppose, for the Jews was the same or a spark of the essence of His own Spirit; I believe that the breath of the Father in the human being is the spirit created in each human being which gives him life and the opportunity to have communion with the same Spirit of God in spiritual life but not the same Holy Spirit which is neither divided nor received in measures as we will see in the New Testament. The Holy Spirit as the wind of God is united with the Father in the entire creative process.

2. **THE SPIRIT OF GOD UPON MEN:**

In Genesis 41:38 and also in Exodus 31:2-3, we see two special cases. In the first, we find the Egyptian pharaoh in need of a man on whom the Spirit of God rests or is present. This man was Joseph, the son of the patriarch Jacob, who had a special gift of interpreting dreams and understanding upcoming events. It appears that the Egyptians believed that divine spirits could visit or dwell upon men. This pharaoh was fully aware of Joseph's God, seemingly believing in and acknowledging the God of his fathers. When the Bible uses the term "know," it can indicate serving or worshiping the same God. For this reason, when Joseph dies, the Genesis writer tells us that a new pharaoh arose over Egypt who did not know Joseph. According to Jewish tradition, this doesn't mean he didn't know who Joseph was, as everyone did; rather, he refused to acknowledge Joseph's God, making it difficult for the people to continue in Joseph's faith from then on. This special grace that flowed upon Joseph's life was known as the Spirit of God upon a man.

In the second case, we see God telling Moses that He has called by name a man named Bezalel from the tribe of Judah. God tells Moses that He Himself has filled him with the Spirit of God, in wisdom, understanding, knowledge, and in all craftsmanship, to devise artistic designs for work in gold, silver, and bronze, and in the cutting of stones for settings, and in the carving of wood, so as to perform in every inventive work. In these two instances, we see the

Holy Spirit upon men in the form of wisdom to know how to do and build for the good of the people: one for their sustenance during a famine and the other for the worship and construction of the tabernacle. This idea is somewhat similar to what we will see in the New Testament, but not entirely.

3. THE HOLY SPIRIT AS A DIVINE POWER:

In the book of Judges, we see the Holy Spirit manifesting as a divine and active power upon men. The personhood of the Holy Spirit remains, as the concept is not merely that of a simple energy; rather, it is God Himself being with the judge whom He uses to accomplish His purpose of salvation or liberation for the people. Noticeably, when men like Samson feel that God has departed from them, in their state of captivity or despair, the text tells us they cry out to their God for vengeance. This cry of Samson is not directed towards a mere energy or force but precisely to the God who was with him when he defeated all his enemies. This kind of power that came upon Samson wasn't purely spiritual; rather, it was a physical strength he received to defeat Israel's oppressors, notably the Philistines, Israel's foremost enemies. This strength enabled Samson to tear apart chains, lions, and even the gates of enemy cities in favor of the people of Israel.

4. THE HOLY SPIRIT UPON THE INSPIRED PROPHETS:

The reason we believe in the inspiration of the scriptures of the prophets is precisely because, as 2 Peter 1:20-21 tells us, "knowing this first, that no prophecy of Scripture is of private interpretation, for prophecy never came by the will of man, but holy men of God spoke as they were moved by the Holy Spirit." Since the appearance of the prophets beginning with Moses, especially with the first of the prophets and Judge Samuel onwards, they wrote down the prophecies, ordinances, and divine instructions for all generations of the people of Israel and all foreigners who would serve Him as their God. The prophets received the divine message through the Spirit of Yahweh (Holy) to transmit it to the people and the kings of their time. Not all prophets were inspired to write, but the Spirit of God rested upon all of them to guide and direct them in their prophetic work among the people. In the Old Testament, we see that the Spirit of God rested upon kings, priests, and prophets. We see some of the prophets using terminologies like Nehemiah himself saying that the hand of God was with him to help him, which is also a way to refer to the Spirit of God being with him. This kind of acknowledgment of God's grace as His Spirit upon the individual is frequently seen in the Old Testament. Concluding this part but not without first mentioning the prophet who makes the most allusion and mention of the Holy Spirit of God among all the prophets, which is the prophet Ezekiel. He mentions the Holy Spirit of God over 50 times in his book and is known as the prophet of the Holy Spirit. In Ezekiel, we clearly see an application and foreshadowing of how the coming of the Holy Spirit in the promise of the Father in the New Testament will be. We will explain this idea further on.

5. **THE HOLY SPIRIT AS THE AGENT OF HOLINESS:**

Throughout the time from the exodus from Egypt onwards, we continually see the call to the people of Israel for repentance, for a path of steadfastness, for the will of their God, and to walk in righteousness and humility towards all others. They are called to walk in holiness, away from what is profane, and to live separated for their God. This call is directed by the Holy Spirit of God to the people of Israel. After being anointed, King David, with the Spirit of God being with him on numerous occasions in the Psalms, shows us that a life in sin and outside the will of God is the worst feeling or state that someone can experience. So much so that in Psalm 51 he said, "Create in me a clean heart, O God, and renew a steadfast spirit within me. Do not cast me away from Your presence, and do not take Your Holy Spirit from me." The joy that David had and felt in his life belonged and came through the Holy Spirit of God, which continually prompted them all to live an integral and holy life. We see the Holy Spirit in this way also in the Old Testament.

6. THE HOLY SPIRIT AS FULLNESS UPON THE MESSIAH:

Finally, to conclude this part with the Holy Spirit in the Old Testament, the messianic prophet Isaiah prophesies about the coming Messiah that from the stem of Jesse, father of David, a Branch will sprout forth, and upon him will rest the Spirit of Jehovah—Spirit of Wisdom and Understanding, Spirit of Counsel and Might, Spirit of Knowledge and the Fear of Jehovah. The prophet tells us that the Spirit of God will be in fullness with all these capacities upon the Messiah or the coming Anointed One by the Lord. The Messiah who was to come and experience all the previously seen and explained forms of the Spirit of God upon His life. There is no doubt or confusion in knowing and understanding that the only one upon whom all these abilities were clearly and most fully seen fulfilled was upon the Son of David, our Lord Jesus Christ.

The Holy Spirit in the New Testament:

We will begin by stating that the person of the Holy Spirit in the New Testament is primarily and generally closely linked to the person of Jesus Christ of Nazareth. All the work that the Holy Spirit would undertake from this point onward would be involved with or related to the Son of God. The first to be filled with the Holy Spirit in the New Testament, although he still belongs and is the last of the prophets under the covenant of the law of Moses, was John the Baptist. We have previously discussed John quite extensively; for more information on him, you can refer back to the section dedicated to John. For now, we will only mention him to introduce the Holy Spirit in the New Testament.

This demonstrates a representation that with every plan of initiation by God when He was about to do or create something new, the Holy Spirit was always present. Just as in the beginning God's Spirit hovered or moved over the face of the waters, in the same way the Spirit would descend to fill John, who would be the voice in the wilderness to open the way and welcome Jesus of Nazareth, the Son of God.

In the New Testament, we see a variety of names or titles for the Holy Spirit. Therefore, it is important that whenever we hear these titles mentioned by the apostles or the New Testament writers, we understand that they are referring to the same essence. Some examples that we find are: the Spirit, Eternal Spirit, the Holy Spirit, Spirit of promise, the Holy, Spirit of God, Spirit of the living God, Spirit of our God, Spirit of glory, Spirit of your Father, Spirit of the Lord, Spirit of Christ, Spirit of adoption, Spirit of truth, Spirit of grace, and many more.

The person of the Holy Spirit in the New Testament is seen not just as an energy, force, or wind, but completely as a person with feelings, voice, and personality.

The Holy Spirit in Jesus:

With the elderly Simeon, briefly mentioned in Luke and directed by the Holy Spirit, and later John filled by the same Spirit, but both will soon disappear from history, one due to old age, and the other through martyrdom, only Jesus remains as the man of the Spirit. From his baptism, we see the text telling us that the Holy Spirit descended upon Him. After spending 40 days in the desert, the text tells us that Jesus descended wrapped in the power of the Holy Spirit. This descent of Jesus was quite important; from then on, we see the Holy Spirit working in a different way with Jesus than with all previous prophets.

While the Holy Spirit worked among the prophets in the Old Testament to deliver a message to the people or to warn the king and the nation of Israel in some way, some performing miracles, none resembled the way the Spirit worked in Jesus' ministry. The work of the Holy Spirit in Jesus' ministry was entirely on a more spiritual dimension than in all other ministries. Jesus did not come to fight against a Goliath; Jesus did not come to ask Pharaoh to release his people, nor did He invite false prophets to Mount Carmel. Jesus came to destroy and undo all the works of the devil.

Jesus of Nazareth

While the prophets and kings worked earthly matters with limited direction from the Spirit, Jesus came to address and fix everything lost in the world and the spiritual sphere between God and humanity. Jesus came to confront the realms of evil, Satan's kingdom, the empire of death, and to destroy the power of sin and its enslavement. While the prophets came and went, died and others rose up, fulfilling their purpose limitedly and partially, Jesus audibly in His own city of Nazareth entered the synagogue and read from the scroll of Isaiah, then closed the scroll and publicly announced, saying, "The Spirit of the Lord is upon me, because he has anointed me to proclaim good news to the poor. He has sent me to proclaim liberty to the captives and recovering of sight to the blind, to set at liberty those who are oppressed, to proclaim the year of the Lord's favor." Then He began to say to them, "Today this Scripture has been fulfilled in your hearing." Throughout Jesus' work, we always see it linked to the Holy Spirit. We see Him countless times healing the sick, freeing the demon-possessed, giving sight to the blind, raising the dead, healing lepers, and doing many other things. We also see Him with an authority and power unmatched to the point that His disciples and the people said to themselves, "Who is this, that even the demons obey Him?"

Jesus was anointed by the Spirit, empowered to perform miracles, wonders, and signs among His people and everywhere He went. In Jesus, we see the Holy Spirit helping Him through all His temptations and against evil; we see Him helping Him in all His evangelistic work until the end. Jesus, at least in the texts of the Gospels, never seen giving His disciples or apostles so much information about the Holy Spirit. We clearly see that this issue was too difficult for the disciples or the apostles to understand. Jesus Himself once in the Gospel of John says to them, "I still have many things to say to you, but you cannot bear them now. When the Spirit of truth comes, he will guide you into all the truth, for he will not speak on his own authority, but whatever he hears he will speak, and he will declare to you the things that are to come. He will glorify me, for he will take what is mine and declare it to you. All that the Father has is mine; therefore, I said that he will take what is mine and declare it to you." There were many things that Jesus wanted to tell and show His followers, but they were so spiritual that at the moment they would not understand them, for this reason we do not see Jesus expand well with luxuries and details or talk about the whole work of the Holy Spirit. But later when the apostles are invested by the Spirit as Jesus had told them, then everyone said we now better understand what the teacher told us. Now, if something was clear to Jesus although they could not understand Him either, it was the following, from the moment Jesus began to announce that He would be delivered into the hands of His oppressors to die, then He would rise to His Father, they not understanding very well, He repeated to them saying that the time would come when He would return to His Father but He would not leave them alone or alone, He would send them the Holy Spirit, another comforter, the "paraclete" helper, who would remain with them every day until His return for them. Without the Holy Spirit in the lives of the apostles, they would never understand the words that Jesus had previously given them, everything made sense to them after having been invested by the power of the Supreme. Finally, we see Jesus as the only means to receive the promise of the Father, which is the Holy Spirit as He told His disciples when He said that only the Holy Spirit had heard from Him. In the Old Testament, God through His prophets had announced the promise and the coming of the Holy Spirit upon His people on numerous occasions, we see it in the books of the prophet Joel, Isaiah, Ezekiel, and others, the question is that nobody knew the time, the form and how God would bring this promise to fulfillment. The only one who could finally reveal when and how the promise of the Holy Spirit would be fulfilled was Jesus of Nazareth through the gospel doctor Lucas, in his gospel chapter 24: 44-49 where he tells us; "And he said to them, 'These are the words that I spoke to you, while I was still with you, that everything written about me in the Law of Moses and the Prophets and the Psalms must be fulfilled.' Then he opened their minds to understand the Scriptures, and said to them, 'Thus it is written, that the Christ should suffer and on the third day rise from the dead, and that repentance for the forgiveness of sins should be proclaimed in his name to all nations, beginning from Jerusalem. You are witnesses of these things. And behold, I am sending the promise of my Father upon you. But stay in the city until you are clothed with power from on high.'" Jesus ordering them to stay in Jerusalem was an indication that the time had been fulfilled and that the long-awaited promise would now be fulfilled. Then we see in Acts that Luke gives us a little more details, in the first chapter he tells us that after all the commandments that Jesus had given to the apostles had been for the Holy Spirit, and one of the most important data is the following, in verse 4 of the same chapter says *"And being together, he commanded them not to leave Jerusalem, but to wait for the promise of the Father, which, he said, you heard from me. For John baptized with water, but you will be baptized with the Holy Spirit within not many days."* Jesus had said that the promise was only a few days away from receiving it, this indicates that the communion that Jesus had with the Father and the Holy Spirit was completely inseparable and quite intimate.

The Holy Spirit and the Church:

Finally, I would like to conclude this work, but not without adding this last part which, although it no longer deals directly with Jesus and the Holy Spirit, rather with the Holy Spirit and the Church of the Lord Jesus Christ. The Holy Spirit will always take from Jesus to speak or make Him known to the church or His people, as Jesus previously said. From that day of Pentecost described in Acts, where the Holy Spirit descended like a mighty wind upon the upper room and rested like fire upon the apostles and all the Lord's disciples who were there, they were filled and empowered by the Holy Spirit. There were about 120 people, and upon them the Holy Spirit had descended like fire, manifesting in them by speaking in other tongues. A large number of Jews from all parts of the world were present in Jerusalem for the festivities held there at that time. Interestingly, all those who heard them speak understood them in their own language. These speakers were Galileans, in other words, common people without education, and certainly without any knowledge of the other languages spoken by Jews from all other nations or parts of the world. Evidently, there is no doubt that this was the unique manifestation of the promise of the Holy Spirit by the Father, foretold by the prophets, fulfilled, and delivered by Jesus Christ.

From this first day onward, with the arrival of the Holy Spirit upon those invested with power after Peter's public preaching, 3,000 Jews were added to the number who received and confessed Jesus. From that day on, we see each of these men in the church being used by the Spirit with power, performing many miracles and wonders. We also see them freeing the demon-possessed and occasionally raising the dead to life. This was the indication of a new creation, a new approach of God to the earth, and the fulfillment of what John the Baptist said when he proclaimed, "I baptize you with water for repentance, but he who is coming after me is mightier than I, whose sandals I am not worthy to carry. He will baptize you with the Holy Spirit and fire." Christ's mission and His Holy Spirit would now be carried out through His church. While Jesus intercedes as Judge at the right hand of His Father for the church, the Holy Spirit is responsible for empowering and guiding the church to fulfill the Father's purpose.

From then on, the apostles and disciples, empowered by the Holy Spirit, dedicated themselves to preaching and spreading the gospel of Christ everywhere, even to dying as martyrs for the testimony and word of Jesus. Meanwhile, we also see Jesus reaching out to what would be called the last of the apostles, the apostle Paul, who would dedicate himself to carrying the gospel to all of Asia Minor (modern-day Turkey) and almost all of Europe. With the death of the apostles, we see the rise of the apostolic fathers among many others who also dedicated themselves, with the doctrines of the apostles, to better form the church with due order and to spread the gospel and bring good news everywhere until the last day of their lives, as seen in many of their writings and books. With their deaths, we see a succession of different fathers and bishops, apologists, philosophers, and theologians, all in one way or another expanding and continuing the word and testimony of Jesus until they laid down their lives as martyrs.

We see with the edict of Serdica (Edict of Toleration) by Galerius and then the edict of Milan by Constantine during the 4th century the cease of christian persecution, in which we see the Roman Empire converted to Christianity. Then, on February 27th, 380, Emperor Theodosius I promulgated the Edict of Thessalonica, by which Christianity became the official religion of the state and the empire. Christianity would become not only the religion of the state but the largest religion in the world. We also see the rise of new Christian theological schools in Syria, Alexandria, and other places. Christianity, with all its weaknesses and imperfections among men, continued to grow through the work of the Holy Spirit.

As mentioned earlier, the Church of the Lord is much more than Christianity. Universally, to have a statistical idea or count of the number of adherents or believers in each religion, Christianity is generally categorized as the Church of Jesus Christ. But once again, I remind you that we must take into account that truly Christianity or Christianity's are only part of the true Church of the Lord. Today, the Holy Spirit continues to work in the Church of Christ, still saving and convincing those who are lost. Today, God calls all who are interested in joining the army of Christ and continuing with the call and great commission that Jesus gave, entrusted to the apostles and to all who believe in Him. There is still much work to be done and many souls to reach; the harvest is plentiful, but the laborers are few. The Holy Spirit of God waits for you and says to you, this is the time that God has for your life, rise up, do the work of an evangelist, and fulfill your calling in the Lord and the power of the Holy Spirit of God.

Mark 16:15-18

"And he said to them, 'Go into all the world and proclaim the gospel to the whole creation. Whoever believes and is baptized will be saved, but whoever does not believe will be condemned. And these signs will accompany those who believe: in my name they will cast out demons; they will speak in new tongues; they will pick up

serpents with their hands; and if they drink any deadly poison, it will not hurt them; they will lay their hands on the sick, and they will recover.' So then the Lord Jesus, after he had spoken to them, was taken up into heaven and sat down at the right hand of God. And they went out and preached everywhere, while the Lord worked with them and confirmed the message by accompanying signs. Amen."

Bibliography

- Holy Bible, Reina Valera 1960
- La Biblia de Jerusalén
- The New Oxford Annotated Bible
- The Very First Bible 144 A.D., Marcionite Christian Church
- Holy Bible, NIV
- Josh McDowell, Evidence for Christianity, Historical Evidence for the Christian Faith
- Alfonzo Ropero Berzoza, Gran Diccionario Enciclopédico de la Biblia, porClie
- Diccionario Bíblico Ilustrado Holman, por B&H Español
- Eusebius of Caesarea, Church History
- Steven D. Mathewson, Risen, 50 Reasons Why the Resurrection Changed Everything
- Jimmy Akin, The Fathers Know Best, Your Essential Guide to the Teachings of the Early Church
- Alfonzo Ropero, Obras Escogidas de Tertuliano, por Clie
- Raúl Zaldívar, Las Fuentes Que Dieron Origen al Nuevo Testamento, por Clie
- John MacArthur, Doce Hombres Comunes y Corrientes, por Grupo Nelson
- Juan Bautista Bergua, Los Evangelios Apócrifos Tomo 1, 2, 3, por La Crítica Literaria
- Reza Aslan, Zealot, The Life and Times of Jesus of Nazareth
- César Vidal Manzanares, Más Que un Rabino, po B&H Español
- Flavius Josephus, Antiquities of the Jews
- Flavius Josephus, The Wars of the Jews
- Herodotus, The Histories
- Greg Haugh, Fully Human, Why the Humanity of Jesus Changed Everything
- E.W. Bullinger, Number in Scripture
- St. Athanasius, On the Incarnation
- Phillip Keller, Psalm 23
- Kevin J. Conner, The Tabernacle of Moses

Alexander Frias

- Robert Ellsberg, All Saints
- Antonio Piñero, Los Libros del Nuevo Testamento, por Editorial Trotta
- James D.G. Dunn, Baptism in the Holy Spirit
- Scott Shauf, The Divine in Acts and in Ancient Historiography
- John DeSalvo, Dead Sea Scrolls
- Tim LaHaye, Jesus, Who He Is?
- Robert Chaney, The Essenes
- Samuel Pagan, Jesucristoes el Señor, por Clie
- St. Irenaeus of Lyon, Against Heresies
- Alfonzo Ropero, Selected Works of Justin Martyr and Clement of Alexandria, por Clie
- G. Ladd, Teología del Nuevo Testamento
- Joseph Ratzinger (Pope Benedict XVI), Jesus of Nazareth
- Writings of the Apostolic Fathers
- Tim LaHaye, The Merciful God of Prophecy
- Matthew Henry, Commentary on the Bible, por Clie
- George Robinson, Essential Judaisms
- Juan Marcos Bejarano Gutiérrez, The Judaisms of Jesus' Followers
- Michael D. Coogan/Mark S. Smith, Stories from Ancient Canaan
- Joseph Telushkin, Hillel, If Not Now, When?
- Bruce Chilton, Rabbi Jesus
- Dante Alighieri, The Divine Comedy of Dante
- Bart D. Ehrman, The Triumph of Christianity
- John Foxe, Foxe's Book of Martyrs
- George G.M. James, Stolen Legacy
- Bart D. Ehrman, After the New Testament
- Bart D. Ehrman, Lost Christianities
- Thomas P. Rausch, The College Student's Introduction to Theology
- H.L. Strack, Introduction to the Talmud and Midrash

Made in the USA
Columbia, SC
05 November 2024

9b69a44e-2a10-4e92-8ee1-f04913357b63R01